PENGUIN BOOKS

ARCHAEOLOGY AND LANGUAGE

Colin Renfrew was born in 1937 and studied natural sciences and archaeology at Cambridge, graduating with first-class honours. While at Cambridge, he was President of the Union. He travelled in Eastern Europe and in Spain and then undertook fieldwork in the Cycladic Islands of Greece. In collaboration with Professor J. D. Evans, he led an expedition to excavate the first stone age settlement to be discovered on the Cyclades. In 1969 and 1970 he was field director of the Anglo-American excavations at the important prehistoric settlement mound at Sitagroi in North Greece, and from 1974 until 1976 he directed the excavations at the bronze age town of Phylakopi on the Cycladic island of Melos.

He was a research fellow at St John's College, Cambridge, from 1965 to 1968, has lectured in European prehistory at the University of Sheffield and at the University of California at Los Angeles and was Professor of Archaeology at the University of Southampton. He was a member of the Royal Commission on Historical Monuments (England) for ten years until 1987 and is a member of the Ancient Monuments Advisory Committee. Professor Renfrew was made a Fellow of the British Academy in 1980. He has been Master of Jesus College, Cambridge, since 1986 and is Disney Professor of Archaeology at the university.

As well as contributing scientific papers to *Nature*, *Scientific American* and archaeological journals, he has written and edited many publications on archaeology. His own books include *The Emergence of Civilization* (1972), *Before Civilization* (1973, Penguin 1976), *Problems in European Prehistory* (1979), *Approaches to Social Archaeology* (1984), *The Prehistory of Orkney* (1985), *The Archaeology of Cult* (1985), *Archaeology and Language* (with G. Daniel (1987)) and *The Idea of Prehistory* (1988), and he has edited *The Explanation of Culture Change* (1973), *British Prehistory, a New Outline* (1974) and *Theory and Explanation in Archaeology* (1982). He has also co-authored several works.

ARCHAEOLOGY
AND
LANGUAGE

The Puzzle of Indo-European Origins

———————

COLIN RENFREW

Penguin Books

To the memory of my father,
ARCHIBALD RENFREW

PENGUIN BOOKS
Published by the Penguin Group
27 Wrights Lane, London w8 5TZ, England
Viking Penguin Inc., 40 West 23rd Street, New York, New York 10010, USA
Penguin Books Australia Ltd, Ringwood, Victoria, Australia
Penguin Books Canada Ltd, 2801 John Street, Markham, Ontario, Canada L3R 1B4
Penguin Books (NZ) Ltd, 182–190 Wairau Road, Auckland 10, New Zealand

Penguin Books Ltd, Registered Offices: Harmondsworth, Middlesex, England

First published by Jonathan Cape 1987
Published in Penguin Books 1989
3 5 7 9 10 8 6 4 2

Copyright © Colin Renfrew, 1987
All rights reserved

Filmset in Bembo (Linotron 202) by
Rowland Phototypesetting Ltd, Bury St Edmunds, Suffolk
Made and printed in Great Britain by
Richard Clay Ltd, Bungay, Suffolk

Contents

Acknowledgments   xiii

Preface: What Song the Sirens Sang   1

1   The Indo-European Problem in Outline   9

2   Archaeology and the Indo-Europeans   20

3   Lost Languages and Forgotten Scripts:
    The Indo-European Languages, Old and New   42

4   Homelands in Question   75

5   Language and Language Change   99

6   Language, Population and Social Organization:
    A Processual Approach   120

7   Early Language Dispersals in Europe   145

8   The Early Indo-Iranian Languages and their Origins   178

9   Ethnogenesis: Who were the Celts?   211

10 Indo-European Mythologies   250

11 Archaeology and Indo-European Origins:
    An Assessment   263

Notes   291

Bibliography   307

Index   337

Illustrations

		page
2.1	Geometric vase from Thera *c.* 750 BC (*after Finley*)	25
2.2	Sword scabbard from La Tène *c.* 300 BC	26
2.3	Corded ware from northern and eastern Europe	31
2.4	Beaker assemblages	32
2.5	Linear-decorated pottery	36
2.6	The homeland area of the Kurgan culture (*after Gimbutas*)	40
3.1	Cuneiform script at Persepolis	44
3.2	Copy of a hieroglyphic Hittite inscription	48
3.3	Map of the principal Indo-European language groups of Europe and Asia	52
3.4	Map of Anatolia in the second millennium BC	54
3.5	Map of the Aegean, with Minoan and Mycenaean sites	58
3.6	Minoan Linear B script	60
3.7	Map of the Old Silk Road	63
4.1	The evidence of linguistic palaeontology for the homeland of the Indo-Europeans	79
4.2	The distribution of Bell Beakers in Europe	87
5.1	The family tree model for the Indo-European languages	101
5.2	Distribution of the Indo-European languages seen in terms of the wave theory	105
5.3	The use of lexicostatistical data to infer history of linguistic descent	113
5.4	Relationships between different Indo-European languages based on glottochronological correlations	116
6.1	Population growth curves	127
6.2	The wave of advance model	127
6.3	Computer simulation of the wave of advance	128
6.4	Diagram (a) to show system collapse	134
6.5	Diagram (b) to show system collapse	135
7.1	Emmer wheat, einkorn and six-row barley	146

7.2   Modern distribution in the Near East of the wild
      prototype of domesticated einkorn   147
7.3   Modern distribution in the Near East of the wild
      prototype of domesticated barley   148
7.4   Radiocarbon dates for the spread of farming
      economy to Europe   149
7.5   The impact of farming on the existing mesolithic
      communities of north-west Europe along the
      'Atlantic façade'   151
7.6   The early spread of farming in Europe   155
7.7   Hypothetical sequence of cultural and linguistic
      transformations during the early spread of farming in
      Europe   160
7.8   Stamp seals from Anatolia and Europe   169
7.9   The original area of the Anatolian early farming culture 176
8.1   The Indus script on copper tablets from Mohenjodaro   184
8.2   Map of India indicating sites of the Indus Valley
      civilization   186
8.3   Decorated antler cheek-pieces for horse-bits
      c. 2000–1800 BC   199
8.4   Map of proposed alternative origins for the
      Indo-Aryan languages   206
9.1   Map indicating notional Celtic lands   213
9.2   The Botorrita tablet   230
9.3   The early linguistic population of Iberia   231
9.4   The evidence of Celtic place names   237
11.1 Map of the Pacific showing the major
      Austronesian linguistic divisions   278
11.2 Family tree diagram for the Fijian and Polynesian
      languages   279
11.3 Diagram indicating the chronology of Pacific
      island discovery by founding populations   280
11.4 Map showing the dispersal of the Bantu languages
      of Africa   282

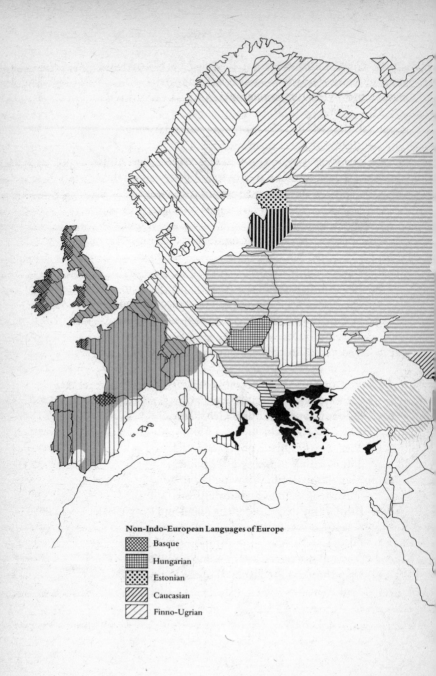

Non-Indo-European Languages of Europe

- Basque
- Hungarian
- Estonian
- Caucasian
- Finno-Ugrian

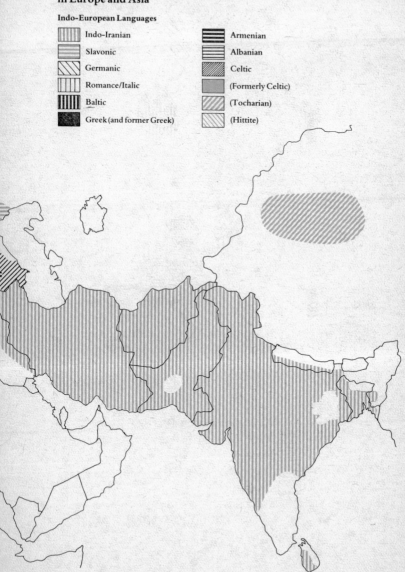

The Indo-European languages in Europe and Asia

Indo-European Languages

- Indo-Iranian
- Slavonic
- Germanic
- Romance/Italic
- Baltic
- Greek (and former Greek)
- Armenian
- Albanian
- Celtic
- (Formerly Celtic)
- (Tocharian)
- (Hittite)

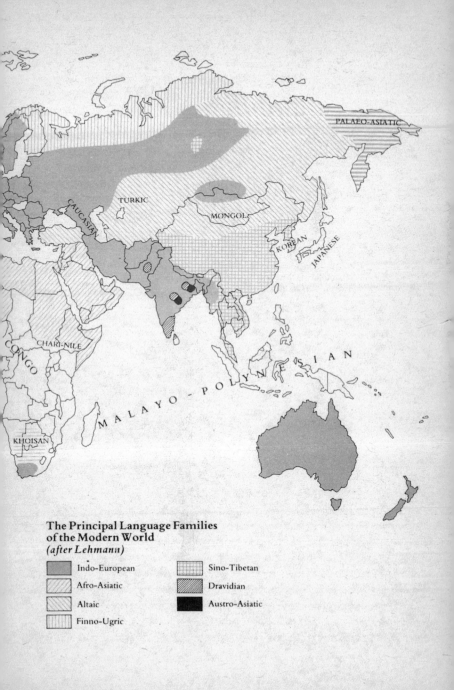

The Principal Language Families
of the Modern World
(after Lehmann)

Indo-European	Sino-Tibetan
Afro-Asiatic	Dravidian
Altaic	Austro-Asiatic
Finno-Ugric	

PALAEO-ASIATIC

TURKIC

CAUCASIAN

MONGOL

KOREAN

JAPANESE

CHARI-NILE

CONGO

MALAYO-POLYNESIAN

KHOISAN

Acknowledgments

Many people have contributed to this volume, and I have benefited from discussions over the years with a great number of friends and colleagues, since the first two articles published in 1973 and 1978 when my ideas began to take shape. Amongst them I should like to express my gratitude for stimulating discussions to: Dr John Alexander, Dr Raymond Allchin, Dr Paul Bahn, Professor Lewis Binford, Professor L. L. Cavalli-Sforza, Dr John Chadwick, Dr Sara Champion and Dr Timothy Champion, Dr David Collett, Professor R. A. Crossland, M. Jean-Paul Demoule, Professor Sir Kenneth Dover, Dr David French, Professor Ernest Gellner, Professor V. I. Georgiev, Dr I. Gershevitch, Professor Christopher Hawkes, Mr Sinclair Hood, Dr Teresa Judice Gamito, Sir John Lyons, Professor Peter Matthews, Mr N. J. Merriman, Dr Roger Moorey, Dr K. R. Norman, Mr Sebastian Payne, Mr John Ray, Dr Robert C. Reed, Dr Jane M. Renfrew, Dr Anne Ross, Dr M. J. Rowlands, Dr Stephen Shennan, Dr Andrew Sherratt, Mrs Elizabeth Warren, Professor Peter Warren and Dr Patrick Sims Williams. Sir John Lyons, Mr John Ray, Dr Roger Moorey, Dr Jane Renfrew, Dr Chris Scarre and Dr Stephen Shennan have all kindly read the text and have offered valuable corrections and comments. Needless to say, not all of them agree with the views expressed here.

Mrs Jose John kindly typed much of the final text, and Mr Malcolm Payne redrew several of the figures. Dr Chris Scarre has greatly assisted in assembling the plates, and I am particularly grateful for the patience and skill with which Mrs Jenny Cottom has edited the work and seen it through the press.

I should like to acknowledge the great stimulus offered by the work of Professor Marija Gimbutas, who has, in recent years, been the foremost and most consistent archaeologist to consider the origins of the Indo-European languages. I am much aware that my view of Indo-European origins is very different from her own, but I am grateful for her friendship and for the intellectual excitement which her ideas have provoked.

My father was a keen student of language. I have on my shelf his copy of Bodmer and Hogben's *The Loom of Language* which, as the annotations indicate, he read four times. He would greatly have enjoyed, and would no doubt have been keenly critical of, the discussions undertaken here, and this book is dedicated to his memory in affectionate gratitude.

Grateful acknowledgment is made to the following for permission to reproduce figures. Figs 2.3 and 4.2: Institute of Archaeology, London; Fig. 2.4: Dr Stephen Shennan; Fig. 2.6: Professor Marija Gimbutas; Figs 3.4 and 7.9: Mr James Mellaart; Fig. 3.6: Dr J. T. Hooker; Fig. 3.7: Mr Peter Hopkirk (from his book *Foreign Devils on the Silk Road*, published by John Murray); Fig. 5.3: Dr D. R. Clark; Figs 7.2 and 7.3: Professor D. Zohary; Figs 7.4 and 8.2: Professor J. G. D. Clark; Fig. 7.5: Dr Ian Kinnes; Figs 7.6 and 8.3: Professor Stuart Piggott; Fig. 9.1: Professor Paul-Marie Duval; Figs 11.1 and 11.3: Professor J. D. Jennings.

Note: Wherever possible the original map or diagram has been reproduced for the sake of verisimilitude.

Preface: What Song the Sirens Sang

Language is the most remarkable and the most characteristic of all human creations. It may be that our species did not become fully human until the abilities of reasoning, as well as speaking, which accompany the use of language were fully developed. Certainly there are many archaeologists today who would argue that this moment must have been associated with the emergence of fully-modern man, *Homo sapiens sapiens*.

Yet it is notable that archaeologists of late have, in general, had very little to say about the origins of the languages which are used in the world today, or of the others, now extinct, of which we have written records. During the early days of archaeology this was a major topic of interest, and there were many who endeavoured to trace the origins of the Celts, or the Greeks, or some of the tribes of North America, by examining the archaeological record for indications of their supposed migrations. Often their conclusions took a very simplistic form, with a particular kind of pottery, or perhaps a specific form of burial, regarded as the clear indicator of a recognizable early tribe whose members were hailed as the original speakers of this or that language. The prehistoric map of the area in question was soon filled with bold arrows marking the supposed paths of these peoples, often identified there only by the name of the language in question, so that to the casual eye it looked as if the languages themselves had paraded from place to place across the map.

Now it must be admitted – and this is an inescapable limitation of the present book just as much as it is of those which it seeks to criticize – that we can, by definition, never speak with certainty about a 'prehistoric' language. We have direct experience of living languages, and of those earlier ones which were either set down in writing by their speakers or recorded in some written form by others who came in touch with them. For prehistoric languages the evidence is generally very much less direct. But this does not mean that we have absolutely no ways of approaching such matters. In the words of Sir Thomas Browne:[1]

> What Song the Syrens sang, or what name Achilles assumed
> when he hid himself among women, although puzzling
> Questions, are not beyond all conjecture.

The term 'prehistoric' means 'prior to the use of writing' (for
whichever region is in question) and it implies that there are
stringent limitations upon what it is possible for us to know today.
But that does not mean that we have to assume complete ignorance.
It is well attested that certain languages are closely related – such as
French and Spanish, or several of the languages of Polynesia. In
some cases these relationships have historical causes which can be
documented – for instance the role of the Romans in carrying the
Latin language across the wide extent of their empire. In others an
explanation for the relationships can be put forward, and supported
by other classes of evidence in a perfectly convincing way. Thus the
archaeology of Polynesia now indicates the approximate date at
which some of the islands were first occupied by humans. In many
cases the archaeological evidence and the linguistic evidence
harmonizes well to indicate clear patterns of colonization which
satisfactorily account for the linguistic relationships observed. No
one can now prove precisely which languages were spoken in
different parts of the Pacific in, say, AD 1500 since direct evidence
for them does not exist, but some outline, supported by different
lines of evidence, can be offered.

You may ask, who cares? What on earth does it matter what
language was spoken by long-dead people? As Hamlet asked of the
player:[2] 'What's Hecuba to him, or he to Hecuba, that he should
weep for her?' So at first one might think. But language and identity
are closely linked and there are few things more personal than the
language one speaks. Indeed language and national identity are
today very widely equated. One's 'ethnic' affinity is often determined much more by language than by any identifiable physical
characteristics, and elections are won or lost by Flemish and
Walloons, bombs detonated by Welsh nationalists and Basque
separatists, and massacres perpetrated in many parts of the world –
most recently in Sri Lanka – on the basis of distinctions which are
linguistic and cultural more than anything else. Often the differences are religious too, since religion as well as language is fre-

quently a fundamental component of national or ethnic identity. So if we are interested in the origins of the modern world, we must understand the nature of past societies; this includes the social organization of these ancient peoples and their sense of self-identity, which brings us to the questions of ethnicity and language.

Over the past two decades, archaeology has looked with considerable disfavour on the work of those earlier generations of scholars who sought to explain the changes observed to have taken place in the archaeological record in terms mainly of migrations. We see now that the particular kinds of pottery so meticulously studied in the past are not necessarily secure indicators of particular groups of people – the pots themselves may have been traded, or a fashion in pot-making adopted, without any change in population. We see more clearly that social groups are not necessarily precisely the same thing as linguistic groups, and we are much more willing to accept changes in the archaeological record as the result of locally-occurring developments within the societies concerned rather than as the result of outside influences, or immigration.

All this has made unfashionable the kind of work prevalent fifty years ago, when the leading scholars of the day would write books with such titles as *The Coming of the Greeks*, or *Prehistoric Migrations in Europe*.[3] We are now aware that major developments in human history, such as the emergence of early urban society in the East Mediterranean, were the products of the interplay of social and economic factors, and are not usually explained adequately simply by documenting the migrations of groups of people.

But have we thrown the baby out with the bathwater? For while we are surely right in looking to social and economic causes for most of the major developments, are not questions of national or ethnic identity (and hence of linguistic identity) often an important element in the social reality?

This book sets out to argue that this is indeed the case, and that archaeologists have, with a few notable exceptions, failed in recent years to take adequate account of the linguistic evidence in building up our picture of the past. Of course there are sound reasons for that. Along with the enlightened interest in early Europe which led the great Australian archaeologist, V. Gordon Childe, to publish his book[4] *The Aryans* in 1926, arose a much more tendentious inclination to use (and sometimes to distort) the historical evidence for partisan political ends. Hitler and the National Socialist movement in Germany exploited to the full, in their unwarranted claim for a Germanic 'master race', the rather simplistic account of prehistoric linguistic origins in Europe which scholars such as Gustav Kossinna[5] had set out. Most archaeologists of the time were appalled to see what were no more than plausible theories about prehistoric languages and cultures converted into military propaganda about racial superiority and brought to a nightmarish *reductio ad absurdum* in the destruction of millions of people, supposedly belonging to other 'races', in the holocaust. Small wonder, then, that archaeologists have avoided so emotive a topic. Childe subsequently avoided all mention of his book *The Aryans*, although in fact it offered no evidence in favour of the delusion of racial superiority and was very careful to distinguish between language and culture and supposed racial classifications.

Racial explanations have, however, receded in archaeology, since most of the earlier work on supposed racial types, based largely on the measurement of skulls, has been shown to be inaccurate and lacking in statistical validity. Craniometry, the study and measurement of human skulls, has in recent years enjoyed about as much prestige in scientific circles as phrenology. There are still a few physical anthropologists who feel able to make comments about the racial affinities of prehistoric individuals on the basis of their skeletal remains, but such work is now being superseded by much more complicated, computer-aided taxonomic studies, where whole populations are compared, using an entire series of different measurements on each individual. I personally remain to be convinced that any clear historical conclusions can be drawn from such work, although it is theoretically possible that they might. In the same way, the study of the blood groups of ancient populations may prove informative, since in some cases they can be determined using the preserved skeletal remains. These are research programmes for the future. At the moment it is safe to look on any supposed claims about 'racial' groups or 'racial affinities', based on a study of skeletal materials over the past 10,000 years, with the gravest suspicion. Racial anthropology – *Rassenkunde* to use the

German term – has been convincingly discredited. This does not mean that modern biological anthropology will not develop methods by which the physical relationships and affinities of past populations may be studied. It implies only that the groundwork for such studies is now being laid, and that there are at present few conclusions that can be relied upon.

Linguistic archaeology earned itself a bad name, then, from some of the writings of the 1920s and 1930s. In many ways that was unfortunate, for while many of the approaches and conclusions of that time are not now convincing, the questions asked were legitimate and some of the insights entirely sound. Re-reading today Gordon Childe's *The Aryans*, one can see that some of the questions which he posed remain entirely valid, and in most cases unanswered. So it is time, I feel, to return to some of those old questions, as well as to several new ones, without incurring the opprobium which such discussions understandably, and perhaps rightly, earned at the end of the Second World War.

Archaeology has moved on from its preoccupation with races, ethnic groups and prehistoric migrations. It has learnt to speak with greater authority and accuracy about the ecology of past societies, their technology, their economic basis and their social organization. Now it is beginning to interest itself in the ideology of early communities: their religions, the way they expressed rank, status and group identity. The question of language is important here, and we can approach it anew, abandoning some of the old preconceptions. Because we have rejected as inadequate the evidence which was often put forward in the past to document the movement of a group of people, we can ask afresh just what indications we expect to find when a group of people did in fact move. The arguments of the processual school in archaeology (as we should now term the successors of the New Archaeologists of the 1960s and 1970s, now that the latter are no longer new) have sometimes been misunderstood. No one is asserting that migrations do not occur or have not occurred. The point is rather that the evidence which was formerly put forward to document supposed migrations was in many cases inappropriate to the task. It is not so much the reality as the methodology which is under criticism. I think this is the right time for a reconsideration of these issues, taking into account the lessons of the New Archaeology, and trying to work in harmony with the processual school.

I shall try here to develop some of the principles which seem relevant if we are to understand the archaeological evidence relating to the question of language change. My area of special interest will be the languages of Europe and parts of Western Asia, but I hope that the general issues will be relevant to those studying the early development of languages in other areas – for instance the Bantu languages of Africa.

The solution which I propose for the languages of Europe is in many ways a surprising one, and it has its implications for the modern world. Today, for instance, many people believe that the first Celtic inhabitants of Britain and Ireland arrived in these areas somewhere around 2000 BC from a homeland elsewhere in Europe. Others would prefer a date fifteen hundred years later. I shall argue that there is no evidence whatever for that, and the Celtic languages may have much longer antecedents in the areas where they are now spoken. Such an argument has the effect of removing the hiatus between the British and Irish neolithic periods – the time of the megalith builders and of the art of the Irish passage graves – and the succeeding phases of prehistory. It means, if we accept it, that our origins – and in general this is claimed here for other parts of Europe too – go very much deeper. These lands have been our lands, and those of our forefathers, for thousands of years longer than is widely thought. Many of the features, then, which define the Irishness of the Irish, or the Spanishness of the Spanish, or the Britishness of the British, go back very much deeper. Sir John Myres, many years ago, answered the question posed in the title of his book *Who were the Greeks?* with the very wise answer that they 'were ever in process of becoming'.[6] We can begin to see that something of this is true for many of the lands in Europe. This, I think, is a fundamental change in perspective, and one which carries many interesting implications with it.

In the introductory chapter which follows I shall outline the early development of the discipline dealing with the formation and evolution of languages – historical linguistics (or comparative philology, which is much the same thing) – by looking at the first European languages. We see that the first answers offered were essentially linguistic, based on the evidence derived from the languages themselves. Around the beginning of this century, the archaeological evidence was energetically studied, and the information which it might offer for migrations of peoples was seriously assessed. Basically these are the two approaches still widely practised today: the traditional linguistic (based on studies of vocabulary, grammar and sound changes) and the traditional archaeological (based on the equation of particular artefact forms and other classes of finds with supposed ethnic groups).

In the following chapters it will be argued that modern linguistics and current processual archaeology offer the opportunity for a new synthesis. The development of linguistic studies over the past two decades allows a much less simplistic view of linguistic origins, which is applicable to the Indo-European languages as much as to others. And contemporary archaeology is no longer content to equate specific groups of artefacts (or 'cultures' in traditional parlance) with particular groups of people supposedly speaking different languages. We can now consider the conditions in which demographic change and linguistic change may be associated, and the other reasons why the language spoken within a given region may change. Archaeology today is better equipped to consider such questions as population density and the dynamics of culture change than it was a couple of decades ago. Although it is too early yet to offer a convincing synthesis between the new linguistic and archaeological approaches, some of the directions which they may follow can certainly be indicated. The examples chosen for discussion here nearly all come from the field of Indo-European studies, but the principles governing the relationship between language and archaeology ought to be universal. In Chapters 5 and 6 I discuss these principles in fairly general terms, before settling down to suggest their application to a proposed new solution of the Indo-European problem in Chapter 7.

Since that solution proposes a much earlier common origin (and subsequent separation) for most of the Indo-European languages than is generally accepted, it has some significant implications for the now-fashionable concept of 'Proto-Indo-European society', which has been further developed recently by the distinguished French scholar, Georges Dumézil, and his followers. It can be shown archaeologically that many of the features of the different societies in question, features hailed by Dumézil as essentially Indo-European, only emerged in those societies *after* the date which I would suggest for the early movement of people speaking early Indo-European languages into the relevant lands. I shall argue that today many of the supposed equivalences in social structure often claimed as fundamentally Indo-European are, in fact, the product of parallel evolution. The same social forms can indeed be seen in other societies of the time whose languages did not belong to the Indo-European family. So the implication must be that a good part of the claimed 'Indo-European' basis for the structure and organiz-ation of the societies in question is a modern myth. This conclusion, if accepted, would be of great significance for our understanding of the early literatures and religions of the different regions of Europe as well as for the comprehension of their languages and archaeology.

These are immense questions, to which it is certainly not yet possible to supply wholly satisfactory answers. What I believe one can do is to show that most of the answers currently on offer are seriously deficient. However in order to suggest a new approach, a different methodology will be needed before significant progress can be made. I have attempted here to begin this task.

1. The Indo-European Problem in Outline

In the year 1786, an English judge, serving in India at the High Court in Calcutta, made a quite extraordinary discovery. He was Sir William Jones, who had trained as an oriental scholar before reading law. On arrival in Calcutta, three years earlier, he had taken up the study of Sanskrit, the language in which the earliest literary and religious texts of India are written, many of them from the fourth to the sixth centuries AD, by which time Sanskrit was no longer spoken but served as the language of scholarship and literature; much as Latin was used in the west in Renaissance times. In his 'Third Anniversary Discourse' to the Asiatic Society of Bengal he briefly mentioned an observation he had made which can be taken as a starting point for the whole study of historical linguistics, and certainly for the field of Indo-European studies:[1]

> The Sanskrit language, whatever may be its antiquity, is of a wonderful structure; more perfect than the Greek, more copious than the Latin, and more exquisitely refined than either, yet bearing to both of them a stronger affinity, both in the roots of verbs and in the forms of grammar, than could possibly have been produced by accident; so strong indeed that no philologer could examine them all three, without believing them to have sprung from some common source, which, perhaps no longer exists; there is a similar reason, though not quite so forcible, for supposing that both the Gothic and the Celtic, though blended with a very different idiom, had the same origin with the Sanskrit; and the old Persian might be added to the same family, if this were the place for discussing any question concerning the antiquities of Persia.

This brilliant observation has been further developed and analysed by generations of scholars in many major works, and there is little doubt that Sir William Jones was right. He saw that in comparing two languages, points of resemblance in the grammatical structure are as important as similarity between the words of the vocabularies. He appropriately compared Sanskrit, Latin and Ancient Greek, all by then dead languages, which had flourished at about the same time, and he drew into the discussion two of the languages of northern Europe – Gothic (the ancestor of German) and Celtic – and rightly compared these with the Old Iranian (Persian) language in which the hymns of the *Avesta*, the ancient Iranian scriptures,[2] are written.

Sir William Jones saw that these resemblances were so striking as to be more than fortuitous. These different languages are all related in some way to one another. The most obvious explanation (although, as we shall see, not the only possible one) is that they are all descended from some common source.

The idea of languages being related to one another was not a new one. It had long been realized that many of the languages of contemporary Europe – for instance Italian, French, Spanish and Portuguese – were related, both in vocabulary and in grammatical structure. Indeed in this case the explanation was not far to seek. The 'common source' in this case was Latin, which of course exists today in written form, and at the time of Sir William Jones was still actively used in some scholarly writings as well as in the litany of the Roman Catholic Church. Resemblances between Latin and Sanskrit had already been recognized by a few scholars, but to link these various languages together in this way was a bold stroke. Gothic was readily seen to be the 'common source' of several languages, such as German and Dutch, which today we would call 'Germanic'. And Sanskrit was already understood to be the ancestor of Hindi (with Urdu) and many of the other languages of India, including Sindi, Nepali, Bengali and Sinhalese.

English	Sanskrit	Greek (Doric)	Latin	Old High German	Old Slavonic
I bear	bharami	phero	fero	biru	bera
(thou bearest)	bharasi	phereis	fers	biris	berasi
he bears	bharati	pherei	fert	birit	beretu
we bear	bharamas	pheromes	ferimus	berames	beremu
you bear	bharata	pherete	fertis	beret	berete
they bear	bharanti	pheronti	ferunt	berant	beratu

Table 1   Comparisons of the verb 'to bear'

The sort of comparison which Jones had been making might be set out by more recent scholars in Table 1,[3] using the present tense of the verb 'to bear' or 'to carry'. This table indicates the remarkable close forms in the conjugation of the verb, as well as in the word form itself. It also reflects one of the fundamental principles of linguistics, that of sound shift, where the consonants (and vowels) of one language differ in a consistent way from those of another. Thus the *f* sound in many Latin words corresponds to the *b* in Germanic languages – for instance in the Latin *frater* and the English *brother*.

This really is an extraordinary state of affairs. That several languages of Europe should be derived from Latin is not very surprising. We can fairly readily accept that other European languages (what we would today call the Slav languages) might be related to these and to the Germanic languages also, as well as to Ancient Greek, but that these should be all closely related to many of the languages of India and Iran is something which our knowledge of the history of Europe and Western Asia would simply not lead us to predict. For between Europe and Iran and India lies a great tract of land where very different languages are spoken. So how and why should these five languages, and indeed many others, be related? In 1813 the English scholar Thomas Young[4] coined the term 'Indo-European' for this widely spread group of related languages, and 'Indo-Germanic' is occasionally used in the same sense. But what is the historical reality underlying this relationship? Where did these languages come from? Did they derive from a single group of people who migrated? Or is there an entirely different explanation? This is the Indo-European problem, and the enigma which has still not found a satisfactory answer. It is the central question of this book, and it is also, of course, a central question for European and Asian prehistory. If there were indeed major movements of early populations, which might have been responsible for this language distribution, then they should be reflected in the archaeological record, and they should be part of the story which the archaeologist tells. If, on the other hand, folk movements are not the explanation, and the resemblances between the languages are the result of contacts between the various areas – perhaps through trade, and exchange of marriage partners – then the archaeological record, properly interpreted, should also reflect this. There is very little in the early histories or literature of the languages concerned to explain the links between them. Here, then, is one of the most notable and enduring problems in the prehistory of the Old World.

The question is not just limited in its interest to the inhabitants of Europe and India. Today most of the inhabitants of North America speak English, and much of South America speaks Spanish or Portuguese. Indo-European languages are spoken wherever the empires of the European colonial powers held sway. We can, of course, give a satisfactory description of the mechanisms for the dispersal of these languages around the globe in colonial times; to account for their original distribution in Europe and other parts of the Old World is much more difficult.

There is just one possible exception to the lack of historical information. It comes from a remarkable source, once again in India – the *Hymns of the Rigveda*.[5] These religious texts were apparently first set in writing as late as the fourteenth century AD, but they are written in what is agreed to be a much earlier form of language, generally termed Vedic Sanskrit or simply Vedic, than the classical Sanskrit literature of the sixth century AD. They may have been collected and arranged before 1000 BC and were preserved orally, with remarkable accuracy, by being passed on from Brahmin teacher to pupil, until they were set in writing at a time when Vedic was no longer well understood, and indeed when even Sanskrit was no longer spoken. The topographical references in the *Rigveda* are generally taken to relate to the Punjab, and several of the hymns invoke the support of the gods in supporting the warlike *Arya* in defeating their enemy the *Dasya*. There is much talk of horses and of chariots, and many commentators have concluded that some of these passages refer to the initial conquest of the land by heroic, nomadic tribesmen, the *Arya*. But this interpretation assumes that the *Arya*, to whom the hymns refer, were intrusive to north India or Pakistan, and there is nothing in the Vedic hymns themselves which makes such a conclusion necessary.

The early observations of Sir William Jones were soon followed by the much more systematic linguistic researches of scholars such as Friedrich von Schlegel[6] and Franz Bopp,[7] so that within fifty years the foundations of comparative linguistics were securely laid.

The same certainly cannot be said of the historical interpretation. When Sir William Jones was writing, it was still widely assumed that the account (and the chronology) of the Creation, given in the Bible, should be literally followed. On the interpretation of Archbishop Ussher, the world was created in the year 4004 BC. This did not, of course, allow very much time for the development of human language or culture. An evolutionary view, with a chronology for human development extending over millions of years only became possible in the year 1859 with the publication of Charles Darwin's *The Origin of Species*.[8]

Until that time, some of the explanations on offer for the origin of the languages of Western Asia were based on little more than biblical myth. Thus the story[9] in the book of Genesis of the three sons of Noah, Ham, Shem and Japheth was taken as a perfectly acceptable explanation for the divergence of early languages. The languages of Africa were thus termed Hamitic, those of the Levant Semitic, and those of the lands to the north Japhetic. This absurd and simplistic terminology to some extent survives today in the usual designation for the 'Semitic' group of languages. Arabic is, of course, the principal language of the Near East today, and it can be shown to be related to earlier languages of the area including Aramaic (the language there at the time of Christ), Hebrew and Akkadian (the language of the Assyrian empire), forming together the Semitic languages.

In the early days of the study, in the aftermath of Sir William Jones's great discovery, the energies of linguistic scholars were devoted primarily to studying the comparative grammar and the vocabulary of the different Indo-European languages then known. The explanations offered for the distribution of the languages remained at a much more superficial level.

That this should have been so was perhaps inevitable, since archaeology, especially prehistoric archaeology, did not develop as a discipline until about the middle of the nineteenth century. Most Near Eastern archaeologists were quite naturally preoccupied by the remains of the great civilizations then beginning to come to light. They devoted little time to the more scanty prehistoric remains until well into the present century – although there were notable exceptions, such as the highly original work of Sir Flinders Petrie in Egypt. In Europe in the nineteenth century, much of the best work was very properly devoted to the development of local cultural sequences, and so hypothetical a matter as the supposed relationship between prehistoric archaeology and linguistic reconstruction was not pursued at any very detailed level.

Around the middle of the nineteenth century the whole study of the subject entered a new phase, which was again linguistic rather than archaeological, but linguistic in a different way. It was by now generally assumed that the similarities in the different Indo-European languages were to be explained by their derivation from a single ancestral language, older than Greek or Latin or Sanskrit, older even than the *Rigveda*. This *Ursprache* as German scholars termed it (i.e. early or original language), which we might term Proto-Indo-European, could (they believed) be reconstructed by studying what was common to specific cognate (i.e. related) words in the different languages. For instance a comparison of the English word *birch*, the German *birke*, the Lithuanian *berzas*, the Old Slavonic *breža* and the Sanskrit *bhurja* would seem to indicate that there was a parent word for birch in Proto-Indo-European. Through the understanding of the rules governing sound changes, this might be reconstructed as *bhergh* – the asterisk being used by convention to indicate reconstructed parent words which were not directly attested in any actual language known.

What the linguists now suggested was that by building up the vocabulary of Proto-Indo-European in this way – the protolexicon, as it has sometimes been called – it should be possible to construct some sort of picture of the world of these people and of their environment before their supposed dispersal from their hypothetical homeland, the *Urheimat*, as German scholars termed it.

This method was lucidly set out in 1859 by Adolphe Pictet.[10] Using an analogy with the branch of natural history where early and now-extinct life forms are studied, he called this approach 'linguistic palaeontology'. Soon scholars were building up a picture of the supposed *Urheimat*, noting for instance the common Indo-European words for various trees. The common terms for various animals (e.g. sheep, goat, ox, cow and horse) were listed, from which it was sometimes inferred that the economy in the homeland had been one based on pastoralism rather than agriculture. By arguments such as these a whole series of possible homelands was suggested, amongst which Central Asia and Northern Europe were among the favourites. In 1890 Otto Schrader[11] put forward the influential suggestion that the appropriate homeland for the Proto-Indo-Europeans might be the South Russian steppe, from the Carpathians to Central Asia, where nomad pastoralism was known to have been practised, at least from the time of the Scythians onward. But he was not yet able to refer to any body of archaeological evidence. Up to this time essentially all the arguments put forward depended on the linguistic evidence alone.

It was in the later nineteenth century also that the idea of the racial superiority of the Indo-Europeans began. It was generally associated with the notion of blue-eyed, blond Aryans, whose homeland was invariably located somewhere in northern Europe – whether in Germany, in Scandinavia or in Lithuania. This theory grew in popularity in some quarters until after the Second World War, and has been argued in some quarters even subsequently.

Until the turn of the century, then, the question of the origins of the Indo-European languages had been treated as one to be resolved primarily on linguistic evidence, although of course the Proto-Indo-European language itself must have been spoken in prehistoric times. With the development of prehistoric archaeology it was, however, inevitable that the material evidence surviving from the prehistoric period should be scrutinized for any light it might shed on the question. The first scholar to do this systematically was Gustav Kossinna,[12] whose article 'Die indoeuropäische Frage archäologisch beantwortet' ('The Indo-European question answered archaeologically') was published in 1902. He considered the available prehistoric material, and concluded that the expansion of a group of people, supposedly indicated by the characteristic pottery termed Corded Ware, and by other associated artefacts, indicated the wide dispersal of Indo-Europeans in Germany. He thus proposed a north German homeland for the Indo-European languages. Kossinna was effectively the first to equate prehistoric peoples (and hence languages) with pottery types, and he founded thereby a school of thought which survives to this day.

The most influential exponent of this approach was V. Gordon

Childe, whose first paper,[13] 'On the date and origin of Minyan Ware', was published in 1915. He argued that this characteristic pottery of the Greek middle bronze age (c. 1900 BC) might be recognized as the indicator of the arrival for the first time of Greek-speaking people in Greece. Childe was a philologist by training, although he later turned to archaeology, and in 1925 produced his great synthesis of European prehistory,[14] *The Dawn of European Civilization*. He combined the two approaches the following year with his book *The Aryans*,[15] where he surveyed each of the four major contestants for the status of the original homeland. He reviewed in turn the archaeological arguments for Asia, Central Europe, North Europe and South Russia, opting firmly for the last of these. In fact Childe's treatment of the archaeological evidence is much slighter in *The Aryans* than in *The Dawn*, and I suspect that *The Aryans* was in essence the text of the dissertation[16] which he wrote in Oxford in 1916 for the degree of Bachelor of Letters.

As mentioned earlier, the excesses of racialist thought which later defiled European scholarship did not emerge in their most virulent form until rather later, and Childe should not be judged too harshly for the quite limited reliance which in that book he placed on the physical anthropology of the time. Later he regretted expressing the views which he had set out in the very last paragraph of the book:[17]

> At the same time the fact that the first Aryans were Nordics was not without importance. The physical qualities of that stock did enable them by the bare fact of superior strength to conquer even more advanced peoples and so to impose their language on areas from which their bodily type has almost completely vanished. This is the truth underlying the panegyrics of the Germanists: the Nordics' superiority in physique fitted them to be the vehicles of a superior language.

Although Childe later repudiated the approach which he took in *The Aryans*, he remained deeply preoccupied with the question of Indo-European origins. In a work written just after the war,[18] *Prehistoric Migrations in Europe*, he returned again to the problem, and deployed in doing so all his remarkable command of the archaeological evidence. This time he no longer advocated a homeland in the steppes of South Russia. And although now entirely rejecting any inferences drawn from measurements of skulls, he continued to accept that the approach of linguistic palaeontology, with its reliance on the terms found in Proto-Indo-European, could give useful indications about the homeland. He now favoured an Anatolian origin, seeing the Indo-European languages reaching central and north Europe as late as the late bronze age.

In the years that followed there were several more important syntheses[19] based largely on the archaeological evidence, among them those of Pedro Bosch-Gimpera, Giacomo Devoto and Hugh Hencken. The most influential recent archaeological treatment has undoubtedly been that of Marija Gimbutas, of the University of California at Los Angeles, who since 1970 has published a series of papers[20] in which she locates the Indo-European homeland in the steppes of South Russia, very much as Childe did earlier. She, of course, has much more archaeological material with which to work. She uses the term Kurgan culture (i.e. the Barrow culture, referring to the prehistoric burial mounds used in the area) to designate the material assemblage of these Proto-Indo-European speakers. As she wrote in 1970:[21]

> Constantly accumulating archaeological discoveries have effectively eliminated the earlier theories of Indo-European homelands in central or northern Europe and in the Balkans. The Kurgan culture seems the only remaining candidate for being Proto-Indo-European: there was no other culture in the Neolithic and Chalcolithic periods which would correspond with the hypothetical mother culture of the Indo-Europeans as reconstructed with the help of common words, and there were no other great expansions and conquests affecting whole territories where earliest historic sources and a cultural continuum prove the existence of Indo-European speakers.

Gimbutas, building on the work of Childe and before him of Schrader, thus lays considerable stress upon the arguments from linguistic palaeontology – the 'common words' to which she refers. In the further development of her theory, great weight is placed on especially significant features – for instance the kurgans (burial mounds) themselves, and the Corded Ware which, since the early paper by Kossinna, had attracted the attention of archaeologists.

Her work displays full control of the recent archaeological material and of the literature of several east European languages and she may be acknowledged as the leading exponent of the direct archaeological approach today.

In my view, however, there should be a fundamental re-examination of the foundations of this theory. One important question is the extent to which it is legitimate to reconstruct a Proto-Indo-European language, drawing upon the cognate forms of the words in the various Indo-European languages that are known. Certainly it is questionable whether the nouns (for linguistic palaeontologists make little use of verbs or adjectives) can legitimately be used in the way advocated by Pictet and by Schrader to create an inventory, as it were, of the *Urheimat*, the original homeland of these Proto-Indo-Europeans. Nor does modern archaeology so readily accept that the appearance of a new pottery style over a wide area necessarily betokens the migration of a whole people or conquest by warrior nomads. The whole assumption that in speaking of early Indo-Europeans we are necessarily dealing with nomads certainly merits re-examination. These issues lead on to more general and fundamental questions. How are we to explain, in linguistic terms, the emergence of languages which are clearly related to each other, and which we can classify into language groups? And in what historical circumstances do we expect to find one language replaced by another in a particular area? Until we have clarified these points, we can hardly go on to consider what trace these processes may leave upon the archaeological record.

There is a very real risk that in searching for the homeland of the Indo-Europeans, we are founding our arguments upon a circularity. In the passage quoted above, Professor Gimbutas spoke of the 'hypothetical mother culture of the Indo-Europeans as reconstructed with the help of common words', and Childe in *Prehistoric Migrations* used a similar starting point, but we should not overlook the extent to which the linguistic palaeontologists rely upon the archaeologists in reaching their own conclusions. Thus Paul Friedrich, in a consideration of 'Proto-Indo-European trees' which is certainly one of the most thorough treatments to date in the field of linguistic palaeontology, actually begins his discussion as follows:[22]

This short study treats one small portion of the language and culture system of the speakers of Proto-Indo-European dialects, who are assumed to have been scattered in a broad band over the steppe, forests and foot-hills between the western Caspian and the Carpathians, during roughly the fourth millennium and the first centuries of the third millennium BC.

His assumption is highly questionable. So complete an adoption of one specific solution to the question of Indo-European origins is bound to have a considerable impact upon his analysis of the origins of the tree-names, and the historical conclusions he reaches. It is scarcely surprising if this theory harmonizes with the historical reconstruction upon which it is based. It is perhaps reasonable that the historical linguistics should be based upon the archaeology, but that the archaeological interpretation should simultaneously be based upon the linguistic analysis gives serious cause for concern. Each discipline assumes that the other can offer conclusions based upon sound independent evidence, but in reality one begins where the other ends. They are both relying on each other to prop up their mutual thesis.

2. Archaeology and the Indo-Europeans

Anyone setting out to investigate the early origins of a language, or of a group of languages, in whatever part of the world they are working, is faced with an obvious and very substantial problem. It is almost inevitable that no adequate records will survive of the very early forms of the language or languages. We can only have direct knowledge of a language used in the past if it was, at times, employed in the composition of written documents. The existence of writing is indispensable to the adequate study of any past language. But the practice of writing, and the development of a coherent system of signs, a script, is something which is seen only in complex societies, which are also usually urban societies with a centralized government characteristic of the state. Writing, in other words, is a feature of civilizations. In nearly every case these very early written documents were set down by the scribes (or sometimes the priests) working within societies with, what the anthropologist would call, a state level of organization – indeed an urban civilization.

There are, however, several ways in which it is possible for us to obtain glimpses of fragments of early languages, even when these were not in fact set down in writing by their speakers at the time. For instance the historians and geographers in literate lands did sometimes record something of the customs and vocabulary of their illiterate neighbours. In this way we know a little of the languages of the unlettered communities on the fringe of the Greek and Roman worlds – the people the Greeks called 'barbarians'. The natural starting point for the Celtic languages is the picture offered by Greek and Roman writers, although it turns out that their view of the Celts was sometimes rather an imaginative one. Those early accounts do contain the authentic names of people and of places in Celtic lands as well as a few words of their vocabulary (see Chapter 9). Our slight knowledge of the language of the Scythians, the nomadic inhabitants of the south Russian steppes in classical times, has come to us in a similar way.

It is also the case that place names, including river names, do continue to be used in a given area long after their original meaning has been forgotten, so that words belonging to a much earlier and pre-literate form of a language can be preserved by spoken tradition, and first set down in writing long after the original language form has otherwise disappeared.

On occasion, very much larger nuggets of an earlier language form can be kept through oral traditions. To the modern reader, used to employing written notes as an *aide-mémoire*, it is almost inconceivable that earlier generations relied exclusively upon their memories to preserve large tracts of literature. But it is now generally agreed that this is precisely how the epics of Homer were preserved, for some centuries after their composition, before they were written down, and the Irish epics were preserved in much the same way. Recent studies of the oral transmission of literature – which generally took the form of songs sung by specialist bards or priests – have shown, in Yugoslavia, Africa and elsewhere, how effectively both the spoken texts and the language in which they were composed can be passed on in this way.[1] The Vedic Hymns of India are the most remarkable example of this. They were sung and handed down over the centuries, until the meanings of individual words which had passed out of use, and even of entire passages, became obscure. Only centuries later were they written down for the first time, thus recording a whole literature, and an entire early language form, which would otherwise have been lost completely.

Oral tradition, however, strengthened in this case by the sanctity of the texts which made accurate transmission a serious obligation, can only occasionally preserve important evidence of an otherwise lost language. It cannot conceal from us that central dilemma facing the study of the early origins of any language: that there is little direct linguistic evidence to go by until the language was first set down in writing. That, almost by definition, will not have happened until the society, after a long period of development, reached the point of formulating a system of writing.

Early scholars faced this problem, just as we do today. But it was not until the middle of the nineteenth century that an alternative emerged to the sheer fanciful and unbridled speculation which reigned until that time. When the antiquity of man was established,[2] it became clear that humankind has a very long prehistory, running back many thousands of years before that nominal date of 4004 BC which some biblical scholars had established for the Creation, and with the development by the Danish antiquaries of the Three Age system, by which the prehistoric past of Europe and the Near East was divided into periods of stone-using, bronze working and then iron production, it became possible to make meaningful statements about that remote past, and the discipline of prehistory was born. Prehistory sets out, of course, to inform us about past human societies dating from a time when writing was not available – and deals mainly with illiterate or (more politely) non-literate societies. By studying their material remains, using the techniques of this newly developing discipline, it was hoped it would be possible to find out about the peoples who first occupied Europe and other lands, to study their origins, and understand how their societies developed into those later societies about which we are better informed, through the availability of written records. As early monuments were recognized, studied and dated, early tombs and cemeteries discovered, and prehistoric settlements unearthed, the realization dawned that it might be possible to know about the subsistence and the settlement and the trade, and perhaps also too the social organization and religion of prehistoric communities.

If this rich archaeological record, which during the last century was being increasingly well understood, could be interpreted also to yield information about prehistoric peoples, and perhaps also their movements and interactions, should this not make possible certain inferences about the languages which they spoke? That is the central question of this book, and the answer which we shall reach, although critical of much earlier work, is not an entirely negative one.

There is, of course, nothing much to be learnt of linguistic significance from an assemblage of artefacts belonging to a pre-historic community, when these are taken in isolation. There is no possible way that we can make the 'rude stones speak' unless they carry with them some written information. When dealing with an unwritten language it is essential to move back from what is known and understood, towards the unknown. To what extent we can do this, and by precisely which methods, constitutes the nub of the question. First, however, it may be useful to cast an eye over the raw archaeological material and to review the way in which it has been used by succeeding generations of scholars.

Patterns of the Past

The whole subject of prehistoric archaeology depends upon the observation that there is patterning in the archaeological record of the past. To say this, of course, is to make the very simple observation that human communities at a specific time and place have their own way of life, which is related to the technological abilities available then. This way of life is reflected in the artefacts, the house remains, the monuments and all the other aspects of material culture which the archaeologist finds. In the early days of prehistoric archaeology the focus of study was upon the chronological aspects of this patterning: that in the Old Stone Age chipped stone tools were used, that with the development of farming a new range of equipment including pottery was developed, and so forth.

In the early years of this century,[3] however, it was realized that there was significant spatial patterning as well as temporal patterning. It was noted that at a given time different assemblages of equipment, for instance different kinds of pottery, were consistently found in adjacent areas. Sometimes these reflected different ways of life in the economic sense: one assemblage of equipment could be ascribed to settled farmers, another perhaps to mobile nomadic groups. But it was also realized that some assemblages in adjacent areas did not reflect the same adaptation to the environment: for instance two very different material assemblages, both belonging to early settled farmers, might be found in the same area. Geographers and anthropologists, especially those belonging to the German 'Kulturkreis' school, pointed out the modern parallel with tribal groups in the non-urban areas of Africa, America and the Pacific, and indeed elsewhere, where different tribal groups, with notably different ranges of artefacts, live in close proximity.

It was natural, therefore, to make a comparable equation for the assemblages of finds on archaeological sites, and to see these as the material possessions of different peoples. This line of inference was developed by such scholars as Gustav Kossinna from around the

turn of the century, and it was set upon a much clearer methodological base in 1929 by Gordon Childe.[4] He applied the term
'culture' to a recurrently occurring assemblage of artefacts from
archaeological sites in a region and went on to identify these
different archaeological cultures with different 'peoples' in the
ethnographic sense. At first sight, it looks like an excellent idea, and
for Childe it opened up the way to discussing the origins and
movements of these 'peoples',[5] and hence perhaps also of the
languages which they spoke, even though there could be no direct
evidence for these.

This rather obvious-looking first step in fact hides quite a
complex and problematical process of reasoning. We shall see that
the concept of 'people' is far from a simple one in many cases,
linking as it does with the whole question of ethnicity. The equation
of different languages with different 'peoples' as reconstructed in
this way is even more hazardous. Later we shall come to reject the
solutions which Childe and others have proposed for the Indo-
European problem and do so largely out of dissatisfaction with the
methods of reasoning used about these issues.

The Raw Material: Europe in the First Millennium BC

The first literate communities in Europe were the Greeks and
Romans. It thus makes excellent sense for any investigation into
European language origins to start with the Greek and Latin
languages and with their European contemporaries. For here at
least we can study, in conjunction, the languages on the one hand
and the archaeological remains on the other. This was the starting
point for most scholars in this field. It was only in the present
century that still earlier Indo-European languages became known
from Europe and Western Asia.

The material works of the Greeks and Romans had, of course,
been well known and well studied since the Renaissance. These
researches were at first limited mainly to the standing monuments,
to major works of sculpture and to the handsome, red and black
painted vases of which so many were found in the tombs of Etruria
in Italy that they were initially called 'Etruscan'. Only later was it
realized that the finest of these were in fact of Greek manufacture,

exported to Italy, and buried by the Etruscans in their tombs.

The German excavations at Olympia in the later part of the nineteenth century effectively initiated the study of the early, pre-classical Greeks.[6] With the development of Greek archaeology, however, it soon became clear that before the heyday of Greek civilization in the fifth and fourth centuries BC there was an earlier Archaic period contemporary with the earliest known Greek inscriptions, and that before this again was a formative period, characterized by pottery largely lacking in figured decoration, yet profusely ornamented in rectilinear style. For this reason it was termed Geometric pottery. This, and its predecessor, Protogeometric pottery, is the dominant ceramic find for the tenth to eighth centuries BC in Greece, and with it, from cemeteries and settlements, comes a wealth of other finds illustrative of the formative phase of Greek civilization.[7]

FIG. 2.1 Geometric vase from Thera *c.*750 BC. Height 77 cm (*after Finley*).

Before the Protogeometric period, in the eleventh century BC came what was for long regarded as the 'Dark Age' of Greek civilization, which archaeological research is only now beginning to clarify. Before that was the Mycenaean civilization, whose scribes, as we now know, wrote an early form of Greek.

The Romans were, of course, the other great early literate civilization of Europe. The characteristic pottery and other finds of the Roman empire had been familiar for centuries, but again it was only during the last century that archaeology began to reveal something of early Rome itself.[8] Archaeologically its origins go back to the early iron age of Latium, just as those of its rival civilization the Etruscans to the north, soon to be eclipsed by Rome, go back to the iron age of Etruria. The processes by which these complex societies of the Italian iron age emerged from the background of the Apennine bronze age are currently the focus of active research.[9]

To the north and west of the Alps at the time of early Greece and Rome were those tribal groups which the classical authors call Gauls or Celts. The task of the archaeologist thus seemed a relatively straightforward one in identifying the material culture used by the inhabitants of the time, and hence the artefacts of these Celts.

It was in 1872 that the Swedish archaeologist Hildebrand used the

FIG. 2.2 Sword scabbard from La Tène, with incised decoration (*c.* 300 BC). The finds from La Tène gave their name both to a culture and an art style generally associated with the Celts (*after Vouga*).

archaeological finds from the north Alpine area to divide the pre-Roman iron age there into two phases, which he named Hallstatt and La Tène, after sites of important archaeological discoveries in Austria and Switzerland. Together these phases cover most of the first millennium BC. The finds from La Tène included iron swords, some of them with splendidly decorated scabbards, whose art style could be compared with finds from chieftains' graves in France and Germany. It was the British scholar Sir Augustus Franks[10] who was the first to realize the geographical extent of the La Tène culture, and to identify it with the Celts, described by classical writers such as Caesar and the geographer Strabo. Then in 1871, the French scholar Gabriel de Mortillet indicated the resemblance between swords, spear-heads and brooches found in north Italy and those from the Marne area of France. He suggested that the north Italian finds were the equipment of the Celtic invaders of Italy, about whom a number of classical writers including Livy had written. The Celts as they appear in the classical writers had thus been identified archaeologically, and a distinctive art style, generally designated after the site of La Tène, had been recognized as special to the Celts. The languages spoken by the Celts and Gauls described by the classical writers also came to be classified as 'Celtic'. This was perfectly reasonable, but we should note that the term 'Celtic' was by now being used in four different ways: to refer to the people so called by the Greeks and Romans, to designate a group of languages, to name an archaeological culture, and to indicate an art style. (The substantial problems caused by the equation of these overlapping, but in reality rather different, concepts are discussed in Chapter 9.)

The origin of these 'Celts' was naturally sought, and the assumption was rarely explicitly questioned, that the origin for the ethnic group, the language group, for the culture and for the art style would be one and the same. The prevailing model for culture change at the time was essentially a migrationist one. So it was almost inevitable that archaeologists should speak of 'waves' of migrating Celts. It was generally agreed that the Hallstatt culture which preceded La Tène also represented Celtic-speaking peoples. The question then arose as to whether its late bronze age predecessor, generally termed the Urnfield culture, was an immigrant one, bringing the first Celtic speakers to western Europe, or whether much earlier archaeological cultures should instead be regarded in this way.

The other name used by the classical authors to designate tribal groups of central and northern Europe, and specifically those in lands to the east of the Celts and Gauls, was 'German'. The finds from these areas, broadly occupying modern Germany and parts of Scandinavia, are in many ways similar to those from their contemporaries to the west, but the striking 'Celtic' La Tène art style is less common and there are not such splendidly rich, princely graves as are found further to the south and west, where contacts with the classical world were stronger. Further east on the other hand, the Thracians (in what is today Bulgaria) and the Scythians north of the Black Sea buried their princes under richly furnished mounds. The golden objects within them were often decorated in a lively animal style which is related to, and may indeed originally have influenced, the La Tène style of the Celtic areas.

These then are some of the elements of the archaeology of the first millennium BC, the European iron age,[11] which scholars were able to discuss and sometimes to associate with the earliest securely documented Indo-European speaking groups in these areas.

It should be noticed that throughout much of Europe, iron age society was a warlike society. Princes and chiefs were buried with richly decorated swords and other weapons and chariots were widely used in battle in the later iron age. It is easy then to see in these remains, especially in the richer burials, the sort of heroic society which we encounter in the epics of Homer, or in the early Celtic literature of Ireland, or indeed in Caesar's narrative of his conquest of Gaul.

Where did these people come from, and what was the source of the underlying community of language which these various Indo-European speakers shared? To answer this, scholars naturally turned to earlier periods.

The Raw Material: The Earlier Prehistory of Europe

Before the first millennium BC, the time of the Greeks, Romans and Etruscans, the Celts and the Germans, stretch the long, non-literate ages of European prehistory. It is from the interpretation of the material remains of that time, as recovered by archaeology, that some solution to the Indo-European problem must come, if any is to be found. Earlier archaeologists saw that prehistory in terms of migrating tribes of people, whose movements would explain the changes in the material culture which may be observed in different areas. Today we are less inclined to think in migrationist or diffusionist terms; but there are certainly changes in the material record, reflecting major transformations in the way of life, which remain to be accounted for. It is scarcely possible here to give a systematic account of European prehistory,[12] but it is appropriate to mention some of those changes which, either because they do indeed seem to have been of profound significance, or because they have been seized upon by scholars in this field, are of possible relevance. At the same time it is pertinent to indicate some of the problems prehistorians are now studying.

To go deep into the past, the earliest hominids for which we have evidence in Europe came into the area around 850,000 years ago. The earliest of them made simple chopper tools, for instance those from Vertesszöllös in Hungary. They resemble tools of some of the early hominids found in the Olduvai Gorge in Tanzania, where hominid origins have a much longer prehistory. Later in Europe those handsome implements known as 'handaxes' came to be used. The fossil remains of their makers were formerly classified as *Pithecanthropus erectus* ('the upright ape man'), now termed *Homo erectus*. Around 85,000 years ago a rather different tool kit, or series of tool kits, was made, with less emphasis on handaxes and more upon flakes: it is termed Mousterian, and its maker was Neanderthal man, now classified as *Homo sapiens neanderthalensis*. It is not until around 33000 BC that fully modern man, *Homo sapiens sapiens*, makes his appearance in western Europe along with a different industry of stone tools, laying more emphasis upon blades than on flakes.

Quite how this fundamental change took place – the establishment of modern man upon European soil – is not yet clear. It may be that our species arrived here by a simple process of migration, whether from Africa or the Near East, with the resultant gradual displacement of the pre-existing Neanderthal population. Or it may be that *Homo sapiens sapiens* emerged as a consequence of a process taking place over a much wider area, so that Europe may have been part of that initial area of emergence. This is one of the most interesting questions under investigation at the present time. Certainly during the warmer spells in the latter part of the last glaciation, much of Europe, including south Britain, came to be occupied by such hunter-gatherer groups, physically indistinguishable from modern man.

With the end of the last glaciation around 8000 BC and the retreat of the ice sheets northwards, north Europe presented a very different landscape, which necessitated a different mode of exploitation by the various human groups. Collectively these are sometimes termed 'mesolithic', with an economy based on the exploitation of marine and riverine resources as well as hunting and gathering. Characteristically the tool kits of these hunter-gatherers included numerous small bladelets termed 'microliths'. The material assemblage differs quite clearly in its details from area to area, so that it is quite possible to speak of different 'cultures' in Europe at that time in the sense employed by Gordon Childe. One of the most interesting questions in current research is precisely when in the course of human development such culturally distinct groups with different assemblages of artefacts emerged, and precisely how they should be interpreted. At present it seems that such differentiation may have made its appearance during the Upper Palaeolithic, that is to say shortly after the appearance of anatomically modern man.

In all of these areas a profoundly important transition took place, rather earlier in the south than the north: the development of farming, based largely upon cereal agriculture and the raising of livestock.

The development of farming in Europe is a matter for discussion. The earliest farming settlements in Europe are seen by 6500 BC in Greece, and very soon after in the western Mediterranean. By 3000 BC nearly all of Europe except the extreme north was occupied by a great diversity of communities, all of them relying on farming to a significant extent. (Whether the new economy, which was partly based on domestic plants and animals not native to Europe, was the result of an influx of new human population, or was rather the consequence of a process of adaptation by the existing populations of the area is further considered in Chapter 7.) These communities did differ considerably from each other in their farming practice, social organization, monuments (if any), pottery and equipment. Moreover in south-east Europe copper metallurgy had developed by this time, and it was beginning in Iberia too. Quite how copper metallurgy began in Europe has been a matter for debate. I have argued that this was a local and independent development, which took place before 4000 BC. It was not until after 2500 BC that tin was used as an alloying agent to make bronze. This specific technical advance does seem significant, since major trading networks then emerged across Europe, in which copper, bronze and by inference tin played a major role.

In a brief synopsis of European prehistory it is possible only to refer to some of the more obvious and widespread developments. One of these, especially notable in parts of western and north-western Europe onwards, was the practice of constructing impressive collective burial monuments of large stones, the megalithic tombs. These are bound to have a place in our discussions because their distribution was initially explained in terms of a migration or influx of people, the 'megalith builders'. Later their development was ascribed instead to a process of the diffusion of culture – that is to say to influences from more civilized lands in the Near East – but the calibration of radiocarbon dating has made this explanation

FIG. 2.3 Corded ware from northern and eastern Europe (*after Childe*).

untenable, since the earliest examples of such tombs up to now investigated have been found in Brittany. A local European origin for them is now generally preferred. However, this does not really explain why these burial monuments are found along the Atlantic coasts from Iberia to Britain and Denmark, yet not in central or eastern Europe. Although the hypothesis of independent origin seems well established, there are still puzzling features to this process, and much to explain.

Towards the end of the neolithic period in Europe, which is simply to say around the time that bronze was beginning to come into use shortly after 3000 BC, new ceramic forms associated with new burial customs are widely seen. In northern and eastern Europe, single burials (in contrast to the earlier collective burials) are found under low earth mounds or tumuli, accompanied by new kinds of pottery and often by a handsome stone axe provided with a shaft hole, and often termed a battle axe. The pottery is often decorated by means of impressions of fibre cord, and so is termed 'corded ware'. In central and western Europe, from around 2600 BC, a rather different burial assemblage is found, also with single inhumations covered by a round tumulus. The characteristic grave

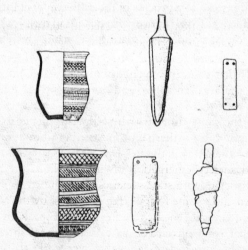

FIG. 2.4 Beaker assemblages from Britain and Hungary showing Beaker pottery, copper dagger with tang and archer's wristguard (*after Shennan*).

goods are a deep, handleless pottery drinking cup or 'beaker', a copper dagger, generally of a type with a hafting tang, and other characteristic forms.

This beaker assemblage was in the past, and is still today, often regarded as the indication of immigrant groups of people. A more recent and alternative view is that the distribution of these burials, with their prestigious gravegoods, is due to the establishment of networks of social contacts, sometimes serving also as trading networks, where prominent individuals displayed their high status through the ownership and use of such objects. Certainly in the succeeding early bronze age, still richer burials are commonly found, and it is clear that a new social principle of ranking has emerged, displayed in the ostentatious use of costly objects. This process of the emergence of ranking is currently one of the most actively discussed in the field of European prehistory, and different approaches are taken by those with different theoretical standpoints. To my mind the most persuasive arguments suggest an explanation in terms of the internal workings of the societies themselves, but even within these terms very different scenarios have been offered.

These developments in burial and artefact use are indicated here because they have often been discussed in considerations of the Indo-European language problem, and it was natural to look in the archaeological record for some correspondingly widespread phenomenon. If that could be equated with a possible influx of new people into the area, then the ready ingredients of some sort of explanation were there.

At about the same time that these developments were taking place in central and northern Europe, striking but very different changes were underway in the Aegean. In Crete, around 2000 BC, a palace-based society emerged, showing the literate bureaucracy which we associate with state societies: the Minoan civilization. It was followed, after some four or five centuries, by the Mycenaean civilization of Greece. These were the first European civilizations, and from that time onwards, apart from a brief interlude, the Aegean was the home of societies that were at least in part both literate and urban.

These days, the development of the full European bronze age is generally seen as representing a continuity with the preceding beaker phase and its contemporaries, but in the later bronze age a new burial custom is seen over much of central Europe and indeed beyond. This is the practice of cremation, with the burial of the ashes and some gravegoods in a large pot or urn. Communities displaying this burial form have often been collectively designated as Urnfield Cultures, just as the predecessor was sometimes termed the Tumulus Culture. Certainly an outside source has at times been sought for the bearers of the Urnfield Culture; but many observers agree that to say this puts too much emphasis upon the burial custom, and that the continuities with preceding periods should not be overlooked. Once again it is the task of the prehistorian to seek to understand and in a sense to explain these changes. It is often easier to see what was wrong with earlier explanatory frameworks, with their emphasis on migration and diffusion, than it is to develop consistent and compelling alternative explanations.

Around 1000 BC iron working is first seen on a significant scale in Greece and in south-east Europe, and shortly thereafter in much of the rest of Europe, and this was the time of the emergence of chiefdom societies in south France and Germany during the Hallstatt iron age, with prominent individuals being given a princely burial. By about 600 BC the first Greek colony was founded on the south French coast at Massalia (Marseilles) and from then on greater quantities of imported goods are found in these rich burials. Indeed it may well be that the early Celtic chieftains and their precursors achieved wealth and prominence by controlling the flow of imported goods to their own territories. Be that as it may, this contact represents the sort of interaction between the literate Mediterranean world and the chiefdom societies of the 'barbarians' to the north, referred to by the various classical writers. It was this interaction and these records which brought them within the light of history, and which therefore is responsible for the direct knowledge which we have of their languages.

From this time onwards literacy spread in Europe and, despite some recession at the fall of the Roman empire, it survived to the extent that we have at least some knowledge of nearly all the European languages spoken since that time down to the present day.

Archaeology and the Indo-Europeans: Earlier Syntheses

Nearly all scholars who have considered the Indo-European problem have felt able to propose a specific place of origin, a homeland, for those early speakers of a Proto-Indo-European language, postulated as ancestral to these languages which were later recorded and therefore known to us. One exception was the Russian scholar, N. S. Trubetskoy, who questioned the whole notion of an ancestral Indo-European language. A similar position has been taken up much more recently by Jean-Paul Demoule. Such critical examination of our assumptions is necessary if a solution to the problem is ever to be found. With these notable exceptions, however, the various theories currently available differ primarily in the location of the *Urheimat*, the area where the Proto-Indo-Europeans supposedly lived before splitting and setting off in their different ways. They differ also about the date, or dates, at which this supposed split occurred.

The case for a homeland in the eastern part of the area of the modern distribution of the languages had not been argued recently with any conviction until the paper by the Soviet scholars, Gamkrelidze and Ivanov, was published in 1983.[13] In 1927, A. H. Sayce, who was the first to recognize the extent of the Hittite empire in Anatolia (see Chapter 3) suggested that[14] 'it was in Asia Minor that the Indo-European languages developed'. However this was not backed up by the detailed archaeological evidence found in Europe, and was a simple but rather shaky exercise in linguistic geography. The same may be said of the arguments of Lachmi Dhar in 1930 for an Indian origin.[15] Probably the most interesting arguments for an Asian source were those of Wilhelm Koppers[16] in favour of an origin in west Turkestan, in view of the supposed similarities of the Indo-European languages to those of the Altaic peoples. But again this was not followed up with any detailed analysis as to how and when the supposed dispersal occurred. Such arguments, with an emphasis on the importance of the horse, were followed up by Wilhelm Schmidt in 1949.[17] He envisaged two 'waves' of colonization reaching Europe from the east. Despite the interest of his ideas, he was not very precise about when these movements occurred, nor indeed where they began. No detailed case, with a consideration of the archaeological evidence, has ever been set out for an Asian homeland.

Western Europe has never been considered as a homeland, nor has southern Europe often seriously been put forward until the very interesting, recent paper by Diakonov.[18] Indeed it is fair to say that most subsequent arguments have followed either the lines first set out by Kossinna for north-central Europe, or by Schrader, followed by Childe, for east Europe and the margins of the steppe lands. Just one or two scholars have in fact opted for northern Europe (e.g. Lithuania), but the arguments are close to those for north-central Europe, and they can be taken together.

Before considering these two main contenders, however, it is worth mentioning the interesting suggestion of Herbert Kühn,[19] made in 1932, and followed up by Gustav Schwantes[20] in 1958, that it was necessary to go right back to the palaeolithic period, and specifically to the Magdelenian culture, well before 10000 BC, in order to find the necessary cultural unity for a suitable homeland. He suggested that the original roots of the Proto-Indo-European cultures should be sought right back in the Aurignacian culture, which can today be set around 30000 BC. Kühn did not, however, offer any explanation for the existence of the eastern group of Indo-European languages, and restricted his consideration to Europe.

The north central European option, as proposed by Kossinna in 1902[21] and subsequently elaborated by him, was the first to take specific bodies of archaeological material and to treat them in detail,

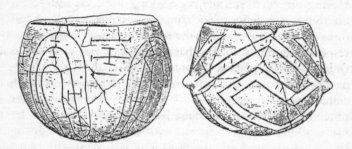

FIG. 2.5 Linear-decorated pottery (*after Kilian and Kahlke*).

using the supposed spread of particular pottery forms as indicators of the movements of groups of people. He drew attention to the Linear Pottery (decorated with curved lines incised into the surface before firing) which is today regarded as the earliest pottery from the first farmers of Germany and Holland. This, in his more elaborate theories, he saw as having a northern origin, and as being displaced southwards under Indo-European pressure from the north, and as ultimately moving east so that the Linear Pottery people would also be ancestral to those speaking the eastern Indo-European languages, such as Persian and Indian. Among the groups whose expansion from northern Europe supposedly formed the impetus for the further process of dispersion were the people making the cord-decorated pottery known as Corded Ware.

Kossinna's approach in many ways seems a very unsatisfactory one today, but no one could deny that he had a very thorough grasp of the prehistoric material. He was the first to treat a particular artefact type – a pottery form, or even a style of decoration – to trace what he thought were the migrations of groups of people and the displacement of languages. This general approach was closely followed by Gordon Childe, and it is still widely found today.

The main alternative theory, and the one now favoured among many linguists, is that of the south Russian homeland. The case for it was first made on linguistic grounds by Schrader,[22] and in 1926 by Gordon Childe in *The Aryans*. Childe had no hesitation in defining the south Russian steppes as the homeland of the early Indo-Europeans:[23]

Having surveyed all other regions of Europe we turn to the South Russian steppes. The climate and physiographical features thereof, as Otto Schrader so convincingly argued, correspond admirably to the characters of the Aryan cradle as deduced by linguistic palaeontology. And the earliest connected remains of post-glacial man there likewise reveal a culture which harmonizes to a remarkable degree with the proto-Aryan culture described by the philologists. The remains in question are derived almost exclusively from graves containing contracted skeletons covered with red ochre (ochre-graves) and surmounted by a mound or *kurgan*. The people here interred were generally tall, dolichocephalic, orthognathic and leptorhine, in a word Nordics. There was however, at least a small minority of brachycephals present in the population.

The material from the poorest *kurgans* is poor and rude, yet is relatively uniform over the whole area from the Caspian to the Dniepr . . . In the first place these Nordics of the steppe were pastoralists, since the bones of animals are found in the *kurgans*. The remains include not only sheep and cattle but also the bones of that peculiarly Aryan quadruped the horse . . . The ochre grave folk further possessed wheeled vehicles like the Aryans, since a clay model of a wagon has been found in one such grave . . .

We have seen in the preceding chapters that the characteristic attribute and symbol of the Nordic cultures which we now recognize as Aryan was the perforated battle-axe. Now the genesis of this very peculiar weapon can be explained in South Russia better than anywhere else.

He went on to discuss 'The Migrations of the Aryans':[24]

One such expansion will be admitted even by the Germanists. It led the battle-axe folk to Troy and the east Balkans . . . But the most compact and ruthless body of invaders would have been those who used cord-ornamented pottery. Their starting point would be near the Donetz valley where such pottery is found in the oldest class of barrows and whence their kinsmen would have set out for Transylvania . . . Thus Kossinna's migrations would be reversed.

With that last, telling phrase, Childe described very accurately what he had done – for much of Kossinna's reasoning was taken over by Childe. The further process of the spread of the Indo-European languages westward and southward from central and northern Europe could follow some of the outlines which Kossinna had proposed. The essential difference was that Childe had Single Grave/Corded Ware/Battle-Axe peoples moving westward from the steppes of south Russia rather than eastward, as Kossinna had done. In this way, also, Childe's early Indo-Europeans had more easy access, so to speak, to Anatolia, Iran and India. Kossinna's notions on this point were very hazy and were seen as weak right at the outset. Moreover Childe could emphasize the role of the horse in some of the migrations, and could link the economy of pastoralism with the early Indo-European dispersal.

Childe's theory has been developed and elaborated by various other workers. In 1933 the Polish scholar Tadeusz Sulimirski supported the idea of a steppe homeland for the Corded Ware culture.[25] Childe returned to the question in 1949 in his *Prehistoric Migrations in Europe*,[26] and there inclined more towards an arrival of Indo-Europeans during the late bronze age of Europe, aided by the horse-drawn chariot and the war horse. He identified the 'Urnfield' groups of the late bronze age as the principal agents of the migration process. He was by now much less definite about the location of the original homeland.

By far the most influential recent exponent of the steppe home-land theory has been Marija Gimbutas. Her 'Kurgan' theory, like Childe's, rests on the view that the Proto-Indo-European culture predicted by linguistic palaeontology and by other arguments may be equated with the rather homogenous Kurgan culture found in the Pontic and Volga steppes. She argues that distinct features of this Kurgan culture were widespread in east Europe at the end of the copper age there. She first set out her views in 1956, and in successive papers in 1968, 1970, 1973 and 1979 filled in the details, using a very full knowledge of the Russian material as well as that of eastern Europe.[27] In the 1970 paper she illustrated the Kurgan expansion with the map reproduced in Fig. 2.6. A succession of Kurgan 'waves' of expansion was set out, the fourth influencing the Vučedol culture of Yugoslavia. This was significant for the further 'Kurganization' of Europe by the Bell Beaker people:[28]

> The Bell Beaker complex, an offshoot of the Vučedol bloc, continued Kurgan characteristics. The Bell Beaker people of the second half of the third millennium BC were vagabondic horse riders and archers in much the same way as their uncles and cousins, the Corded people of northern Europe and Catacomb-grave people of the North Pontic region. Their spread over central and western Europe to the British Islands

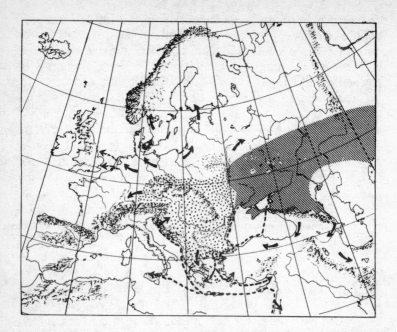

FIG. 2.6 The homeland area of the Kurgan culture (shaded), identified by Gimbutas as the earliest Indo-European speakers. The dotted area represents 'the area infiltrated not later than 4000–3500 BC'; arrows show tentative movements after *c.*2500 BC (*after Gimbutas*).

and Spain as well as the Mediterranean islands terminates the period of expansion and destruction.

In her 1973 paper she goes further, to link the development of the European bronze age with the Kurgan peoples:[29]

> The rapid spread of bronze metallurgy over the European continent was due to the mobility of the Indo-Europeans. The appearance of bronze weapons – daggers and halberds together with thin and sharp axes of bronze and maceheads and battle-axes of semi-precious stone and flint arrowheads, coincides with the routes of dispersal of the Kurgan people. The name 'Kurgan' is a blanket name for a cultural complex that caused a dramatic change in Europe as is assumed by this author to

represent the Indo-European culture of the 5th, 4th and 3rd millennia BC.

This view of the problem has been followed by a number of further scholars such as Stuart Piggott in his *Ancient Europe*.[30]

Although the central-north Europe position of Kossinna, and especially the south Russian view of Childe and Gimbutas, represent the two most influential positions today, there are certainly others of note. P. Bosch-Gimpera in 1960[31] argued for a central European area of formation of the Indo-European peoples, back in the early neolithic period, so that the differentiation of the various Danubian cultures in the later neolithic would correspond to the dispersal of the Indo-European peoples. The other major study of recent years is that of Giacomo Devoto, published in 1962,[32] although he reaches no such clear-cut conclusions about an original homeland.

Most of these studies, while based on a very thorough knowledge of the archaeological material from Europe, like the review undertaken by Hencken,[33] (for few could claim to equal the encyclopaedic grasp of a Gordon Childe or a Marija Gimbutas) rest almost without exception on a series of assumptions going back to the time of Otto Schrader and Gustav Kossinna. It is now necessary to question these. If they are rejected, it soon follows that the conclusions that have been drawn from them are to a large extent erroneous. This in turn has a number of serious consequences for our understanding of European prehistory and of the origins of the peoples of Europe. Before undertaking this critical re-examination, however, it is appropriate to take a closer look at the evidence now available for the earliest documented Indo-European languages.

3. Lost Languages and Forgotten Scripts: The Indo-European Languages, Old and New

The Indo-European (or Indo-Germanic) languages, spoken in countries as far removed as Ireland or Brittany in the west and India and Pakistan in the east, are generally supposed to owe their affinity to some common descent. This conclusion derives from the idea of a family tree, although it does not deny that languages can converge, as the 'wave' idea predicts, with the acquisition of loan-words and other features from one language to another. Few scholars today would go so far as Trubetskoy in suggesting that there is no genetic or family-tree relationship at all among the Indo-European languages, and that they just came to resemble each other through the effects of prolonged contact. And very few indeed would agree with the French archaeologist, Jean-Paul Demoule,[1] that there really is no Indo-European language group at all, or that the similarities observed are unimportant, insignificant and fortuitous.

If we are to criticize recent attempts to explain the origins of these languages, and then to offer some alternative, and hopefully better-based, explanation in their place, we need to look more closely at the similarities between them, in particular the languages which are documented from early times.

Here we are aided by some remarkable discoveries which, along with the study of the early religious hymns of India (the *Rigveda*) and their counterpart in early Iran (the *Avesta*) have transformed our perception of the problem.[2] Each was in its way highly romantic, and they show how the discoveries of archaeology can advance our knowledge in altogether unexpected ways. Nothing is more mysterious or more intriguing than the discovery of a hitherto unknown language in an unreadable script, and few advances in scholarship are more dramatic than the decipherment of such a script and the subsequent translation of the language in which it was written.

1 The Language of the Persian Kings

When the early European travellers first systematically explored Iran in the seventeenth century, the great Persian Empire which Alexander the Great had conquered was known only through the writings of the Classical writers, principally of Herodotus.[3] He had reported in detail the Persian Wars, some 260 years before Alexander's conquest, when Darius the Great King, and then his successor, Xerxes, had twice come close to destroying the growing power of Athens and of Greece.

The history of the Persian empire was well documented through these Greek sources, but on the ground nothing was known or understood. It was not until 1621 that the Spanish ambassador to Persia correctly identified the site of Persepolis, the great Persian palatial centre. He commented on the relief sculptures, which offer such a vivid picture of life and clothing as they were in the early fifth century BC, and he went on to describe an inscription in the language of the Persian Empire – an Indo-European language then unknown to scholarship:[4]

> There is a remarkable inscription carved on black jasper. Its characters are still clear and sparkling, astonishingly free from damage or deterioration despite their very great age. The letters themselves are neither Chaldean nor Hebrew nor Greek or Arabic nor of any people that can be discovered now or to have ever existed. They are triangular, in the shape of a pyramid or miniature obelisk and are all identical except in position and arrangement. But the resulting composite characters are extraordinarily decisive and distinct.

This is the script which later scholars have come to call 'cuneiform' – meaning literally 'wedge-shaped'. It was a system of writing which we now know was invented by the Sumerians, the people of the first civilization of the Near East, shortly after 3000 BC. In modified forms it was used in many of the Near Eastern languages, several of which belonged to the Semitic language group. It was first illustrated by the Italian, Pietro della Valle, after his own visit to Persepolis in a letter published in 1658. Splendid inscriptions from the royal palaces at Persepolis and from other sites were

FIG. 3.1 Old Persian inscription in cuneiform script as recorded in the eighteenth century at Persepolis (*after Niebuhr*).

published by later scholars. It was an enterprising officer of the British East India Company, Henry Rawlinson, who completed the task of its decipherment. Already in 1835–7, while on posting to Persia, he accomplished the considerable feat of copying the great rock inscription of King Darius on the cliff at Behistun. Then, relying on the start with the decipherment which earlier scholars had made, and on his knowledge of the languages of the *Avesta*, the sacred books of the Zoroastrian religion (which were set down in writing many centuries after the Old Persian inscriptions were carved) he was able, by 1839, to unlock the system. Later workers have improved on his decipherment, but by 1846 Persian cuneiform had effectively been deciphered and translated. This was in its way almost as great an achievement as the decipherment by the Frenchman, Jean-François Champollion, some twenty-four years earlier of the famous Rosetta Stone, by which the hieroglyphic script of the Ancient Egyptians was first read by modern scholars. As Champollion's decipherment opened the way to the literature of Ancient Egypt and made possible the discipline of Egyptology, so Rawlinson's decipherment was the first major step in Cuneiform studies, and led to the reading of the earliest texts of the Near East.[5]

Rawlinson was working with inscriptions carved on rock in a form of cuneiform script which was used to record the Old Persian language, the language of the court of King Darius. However his decipherment held a far greater significance than this, for at this time, great quantities of clay tablets were being found in the course of excavations in the Near East. These were the archives of the palaces and temples of the early cities of the first civilizations of Mesopotamia. They were written in a variety of languages, but most of them were set in writing in some form of cuneiform script. Moreover, some of the great rock-cut inscriptions which Rawlinson had studied reproduced the same text in three languages. At Behistun in 520 BC Darius the Great recorded the official version of the controversial events surrounding his accession to the throne, in three different types of cuneiform script. A relief, showing the king triumphant over rebels, is flanked on the viewer's right by the text in Elamite; on the left is the version in Babylonian (i.e. Akkadian); below is the text in the Old Persian language written in a new type of cuneiform script, of which Darius writes: 'I have made the writing of a different sort in Aryan, which did not exist before.' When an extension to the relief in 518 BC damaged the Elamite text, a second identical Elamite version was added. This was the language of Susa in south-west Iran. It is a language which, like Basque in modern Europe, is unrelated to its neighbours, and is unlike any other language known. Babylonian, on the other hand, belongs to the well-known Semitic group of languages, and with the aid of the understanding offered by other Semitic languages (including Hebrew) and the great trilingual inscriptions, the Babylonian cuneiform script could soon be read and its language translated.

Rawlinson's decipherment of Old Persian cuneiform thus opened the way to the reading of Babylonian, and the related Assyrian languages, so that much of the literature of the early Near East was unlocked. Two further languages of interest to us were also written in cuneiform scripts: Hittite and Hurrian. The development of the various cuneiform scripts has been set out by Maurice Pope (see Table II).[6]

It should be noted here that the family tree shows how the different *scripts* are related to each other: it does not indicate relationships between the languages themselves. Similar tables have been made to indicate the descent of the alphabetic scripts which we ourselves use, following the Greeks and Romans. The Greeks developed the alphabet from the Phoenicians, who spoke a language which does not belong to the Indo-European group, but

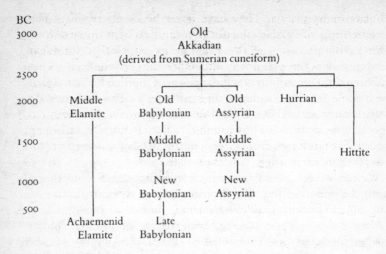

Table II   The descent of the cuneiform scripts

rather to the Semitic group, along with Hebrew, Babylonian and Assyrian.

From the point of view of the Indo-European languages, Rawlinson's achievement was to bring to light the Old Persian language. This was the ancestor of modern Persian, in much the same way that Latin was the ancestor of French and Italian. And somewhere between the two, between Old Persian and modern Persian, come the languages of Middle Persian, including those of the Parthian and Sassanian kings who ruled Persia at the time of the Romans. The language of the books of the *Avesta* is a sister language of Old Persian, and these sacred hymns may go back as far as the time of the Persian kings, including Darius, although they were not set down in writing until very much later. As with the sacred hymns of India, the *Rigveda*, they were preserved orally for many centuries first.

Several of the known Indo-European languages, like Ancient Greek and Latin, the Old Celtic tongue of the epics, the Vedic Sanskrit of the *Rigveda* and the Old Persian of the *Avesta*, had all become dead languages – that is to say they were no longer spoken actively as a first language by any living group of people. But they were nonetheless all remembered, in their different ways, by scholars or by priests. They have never been entirely lost. The decipherment of Persian cuneiform brought to light the first 'lost' Indo-European language. Yet, despite its importance for Near Eastern studies this was not an altogether unexpected result. What had been brought to light was the ancestor of modern Persian and of the Middle Persian languages, and the sister language of the Old Persian language of the *Avesta*. Moreover, before the decipherment a good deal was already known about the Persian Empire, including the names of its kings, from Greek sources. The next decipherment was far more extraordinary in its revelations.

We can use this discussion of the Iranian languages to introduce again the notion of the Indo-Iranian group of the Indo-European languages. The term Old Iranian includes both the language of the hymns of the *Avesta* and of the cuneiform inscriptions. The other side of the family is represented by the Vedic language of the *Rigveda* from which Sanskrit developed, and through it the modern Indic languages.[7]

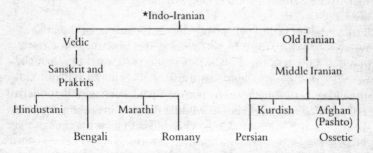

Table III   Hypothetical development of the Indo-Iranian languages

2 The Discovery of Hittite and the Anatolian Languages

The next step in the story of the Indo-European languages takes us to an unexpected area, Anatolia, now Turkey, and to a whole vanished civilization, that of the Hittites. The Hittites had long been known as a rather obscure tribe, mentioned in several places in the Bible, living in north Syria, while the Assyrians flourished in northern Mesopotamia, around the eighth century BC. In the later

FIG. 3.2 Copy of a hieroglyphic Hittite inscription from the site of Carchemish (*after Akurgal*).

years of the nineteenth century AD, a number of carved reliefs and inscriptions in a hitherto unknown hieroglyphic script began to turn up not only in North Syria but in Anatolia. And in 1880 the young British scholar, Archibald Henry Sayce, gave a lecture[8] before the Society for Biblical Archaeology in London in which he made the remarkably bold claim that these remains, including the inscriptions, belonged to a now-forgotten empire in Anatolia, that of the Hittites. It was pointed out that the hieroglyphic inscriptions of the Ancient Egyptians referred quite often to battles with the 'Heta', which is how the Biblical 'land of Hatti' would read in Egyptian. The pharaoh Thutmosis III had in the fifteenth century BC been forced to pay tribute to the Hittite people and Rameses II claimed to have won a great battle against the Hittites at Kadesh, in what is now Syria. At first the claims by Sayce for a Hittite empire did not seem altogether convincing, and these supposed links did not win universal assent; but again archaeology intervened with some striking new discoveries.

In the year 1891 the British archaeologist, Sir Flinders Petrie, began his excavations at the capital city of the oddest and most individual of the rulers of Ancient Egypt, the pharaoh Amenophis IV, the heretic king, better known by the name which he adopted:

Akhnaten. The pharaoh set aside the traditional gods of Ancient Egypt, and worshipped instead the Sun God. As part of his pro-gramme of innovation, he built himself a new capital at Amarna. Petrie was led there by the chance discovery in 1887 by local villagers of the royal archive, a great collection of clay tablets. They dated mainly between 1370 and 1350 BC, during the short period when Amarna was occupied (for the city was abandoned when Akhnaton's successor returned to the religion of his forefathers).

The archive contained the pharaoh's diplomatic correspondence, and the tablets were written in the cuneiform script. The language was Babylonian (Akkadian) – one of the three languages on the great Persian inscription at Behistun, which Rawlinson had de-ciphered – for this was the language of diplomacy in the Ancient Near East. Amongst them were many accounts of raids by Hittite warriors across the northern borders of the very extensive Egyptian empire, into what is now Syria. One tablet had been sent to Akhnaton to congratulate him on ascending to the throne by a 'King of Hatti', Suppiluliumas. The various tablets in the archive showed clearly that Sayce had been right, and that the Hittites had indeed been a great force in Anatolia as well as in Syria. Indeed it later emerged that they became influential in Syria long after they had established power in Anatolia.

Two letters amongst the Amarna tablets were particularly intrig-uing since they were written in an unknown and altogether unintel-ligible language. The script was cuneiform, and so it was readable, but it could not yet be interpreted. These letters were addressed to a king in the unknown land of Arzawa. In 1893, a French archaeolog-ist discovered fragments of clay tablets clearly written in the same unknown 'Arzawa' language at the impressive site of Boghazköy located on the Halys river in north-central Anatolia. The German archaeologist, Hugo Winckler, began excavations at Boghazköy in 1906, and he was soon rewarded with the discovery of a great archive of some 10,000 clay tablets.[9] Some of these were written in Akkadian (Babylonian) and could be read at once. They made it clear that at Boghazköy Winckler had discovered the capital city of the empire which Sayce had so perceptively suggested, and the seat of the kings who had corresponded with the Egyptian pharaohs. The archive, and with it the destruction of Boghazköy, was later dated to around 1200 BC, and the occupation of the site had spanned some 400 years. Akkadian was only one of the languages of the archive, there were several others. One of them, in which many of the tablets were written, was the incomprehensible 'Arzawa language', which the scholars soon renamed Hittite.

In 1915 a volume of the *Communications of the German Orient Society* contained a remarkable paper entitled 'The solution of the Hittite problem' by the Czech scholar, Dr Bedřich Hrozný.[10] It was odd that, during the First World War, he was able to work upon such problems at all, since he was a serving officer in the army of the Austrian empire. It was only through the genial attitude of his commanding officer, who exempted him from military duties, that Hrozný was able to bring about one of the most remarkable feats in the history of philology. His decipherment of this hitherto unknown language was published in book form in 1917, and the first sentence of the preface stated:[11]

> The present work undertakes to establish the nature and structure of the hitherto mysterious language of the Hittites and to decipher this language . . . It will be shown that Hittite is in the main an Indo-European language.

This claim was at first met with astonishment and incredulity in the scholarly world. But Hrozný's work was well-founded, and his decipherment and interpretation of the language, although it has naturally been improved by later scholars, has won universal recognition.

Some words in Hittite are very readily recognized as Indo-European: *watar* is the Hittite for 'water', *genu* for 'knee' (like the Latin *genu*), and *kwis* for 'who' (like the Latin *quis*). But in fact the greater part of the Hittite vocabulary is non-Indo-European. The relationship is clearer in aspects of the grammatical structure, for instance in the inflexion of the noun: the case endings relate very closely to those of Greek and Latin, and the conjugation of some verbs is very close to that of Greek.

It was soon noticed that Hittite does not share the most obvious features of the so-called 'satem' group of Indo-European languages (which included Persian and Indian), and so the conclusion was proposed that it belonged to the 'centum' group, along with Latin, Greek, Celtic and the German languages. However, this classification is over-simplified, and Hittite is now generally recognized as representing a distinct branch of the Indo-European family. With the discovery of the archive, and then the decipherment of the cuneiform Hittite language, it was possible to elucidate much of the history of the Hittite empire, and one of the major civilizations of the Ancient World was brought into the light of history.

The Boghazköy archive contained texts utilizing eight[12] different languages altogether. We have already spoken of (1) Akkadian and (2) of cuneiform Hittite. There were also texts in (3) Sumerian, the very ancient language of the Sumerian civilization and the first to develop the cuneiform script, which although by this time (i.e. 1200 BC) a dead language, was still studied. Another language represented was (4) Hurrian, which is not an Indo-European language, nor a Semitic one. It was the language of the Land of Mitanni, to the east of the Hittite empire, in what is today north Syria and north Iraq.

The hieroglyphic Hittite language seen on the stone monuments which Sayce had identified as Hittite was not represented in the archive at Boghazköy, although it occurs there on seals and seal impressions. The hieroglyphs were distinctive symbols in their own right, and comparison with Egyptian hieroglyphic writing offered no real help. Indeed it was not until the year 1947 that a good bilingual inscription was found at the site of Karatepe, written in Phoenician (a well-known Semitic language) as well as in hieroglyphic Hittite, so that real progress could be made with it. Hieroglyphic Hittite was a script occurring mainly on rock-carvings and on stone monuments, as well as on seals and on seven letters found on strips of lead during excavations at Assur. The decipherment has shown that the language in question is a dialect of language (5) which is seen on the Boghazköy tablets: Luwian. This is closely related to Hittite, and was probably spoken in western Anatolia. Indeed it seems to be ancestral to one of the languages spoken there during the classical period, and known as Lycian. Language (6) of which traces occur in the tablets is known as Palaic. Again, like Hittite and Luwian, it belongs to the Indo-European language family. The three languages, Hittite, Palaic and Luwian

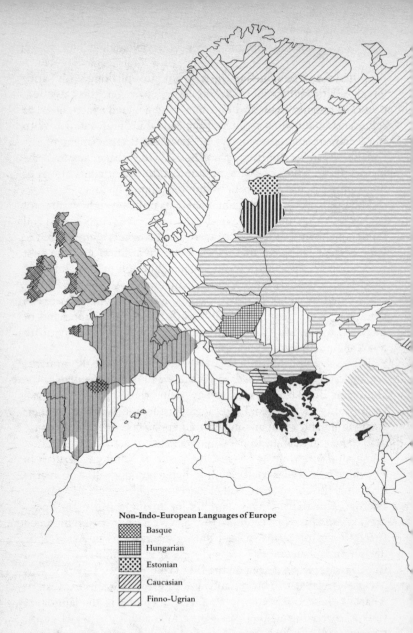

Non-Indo-European Languages of Europe

- Basque
- Hungarian
- Estonian
- Caucasian
- Finno-Ugrian

FIG. 3.3 The principal Indo-European language groups of Europe and Asia indicated by shading. Some extinct Indo-European languages (Hittite, Tocharian) are also marked.

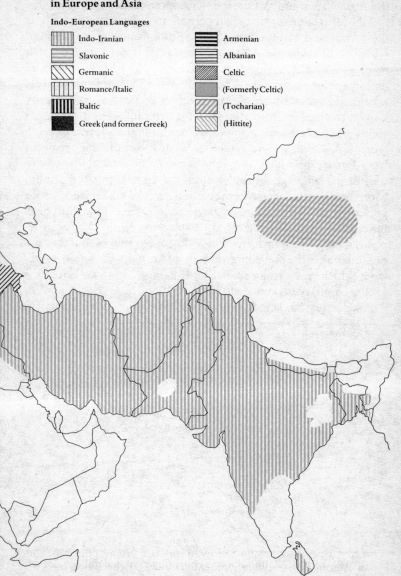

The Indo-European languages in Europe and Asia

Indo-European Languages

- Indo-Iranian
- Slavonic
- Germanic
- Romance/Italic
- Baltic
- Greek (and former Greek)
- Armenian
- Albanian
- Celtic
- (Formerly Celtic)
- (Tocharian)
- (Hittite)

(along with hieroglyphic Hittite) are generally classed together as the Anatolian group[13] of the Indo-European family.

All of this seems at first sight complicated, but it simply reflects the power and importance of the Hittite capital at Boghazköy, which went under the name of Hattusas. It is not surprising that there were tablets in Akkadian, which as noted earlier was the main diplomatic language of the Ancient Near East, just as Sumerian was a language of scholarship. And Hurrian was a language already known to scholars from an important letter found in the Armana archive, written by the King of Mitanni to the Egyptian pharaoh Amenophis III in around 1400 BC. What was really important for Indo-European studies was the discovery of a whole new, un-dreamt-of language group within the Indo-European family. Moreover Hittite represents the earliest instance which we have of a preserved Indo-European language: our earliest Indo-European inscription. The discoveries at Boghazköy, with Hrozný's de-cipherment, have transformed Indo-European studies, but they did not much alter the prevailing view about the Indo-European home-land, which was already set out by Kossinna[14] in 1902, before the Hittite language was understood.

For this reason, language (7) of the Hattusas archive is particu-

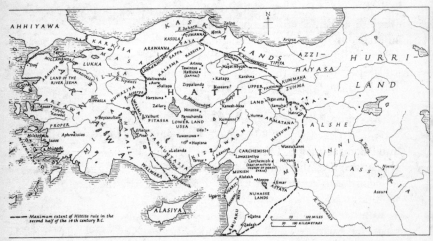

FIG. 3.4 Map of Anatolia and adjoining areas in the second millennium BC (after Mellaart).

larly interesting. This language, termed today Hattic, or Hattian, or Proto-Hittite, raises several interesting historical problems. It is not an Indo-European language. It occurs mainly in ritual texts, and the Hittite text sometimes states that the reciter will now speak *hattili*: 'in the language of Hatti', and sentences in the language now called Hattic then follow. This is the same procedure followed for the other languages of the tablets. The language which we today call Luwian is preceded in the same way by the adverb *luwili*, and Hurrian by the adverb *hurlili*. But, significantly, the language which we today call Hittite is preceded, when clarification is necessary, by the adverb *nesili* or *nasili*.

There is a real modern confusion here: the Hittites (as we term them) called their capital Hattusas, and their kingdom is referred to in correspondence with the Egyptian pharaoh as 'the Land of Hatti'. Moreover the successors of the Hittite empire, who carved their 'hieroglyphic Hittite' inscriptions in what is now north Syria in the tenth to the eighth centuries BC, were termed 'Hittites' in the Bible. Of course 'Hittite' and 'Hattic' are essentially the same term, although we may choose today to use these two minor variants of it to refer to two entirely different languages.

The explanation generally offered for all of this is that the Hittites (as we term them) were an Indo-European-speaking people and therefore immigrants into Anatolia from some Indo-European homeland to the north. There are alternative sets of theories as to whether they reached Anatolia from the north-west, across the Bosporus, or from the north-east, across the Caucasus. On this theory, the people with the non-Indo-European language which we call Hattic would have been the original inhabitants of the area. Then supposedly came the Indo-European immigration, which would also have brought with it (so it is argued) the Hittite, Luwian and Palaic languages. I think that much of this argument is based on the *assumption* that the (Indo-European) Hittite language was *introduced* into Anatolia just a few centuries before the date of the Boghazköy/Hattusas archive (see Chapter 8).

Another relevant point which is often made is that the Hittite rulers have names which are not Indo-European, and that many of the deities in their pantheon have names which cannot be recognized as Indo-European either. But when a new language is introduced into an area by the process of élite dominance (see Chapter 5) it is normally the language of the new élite which is the introduced language, and that of the greater mass of the people which is indigenous. Then, depending upon circumstances, one or other language will probably survive. There is nothing in the tablets themselves which tells us whether terms in Hittite (i.e. *nesili*) or those in Hattic (i.e. *hattili*) are the earlier, nor indeed is it necessary to give chronological priority to either, except at Hattusas itself, where the language of Nesa (i.e. Hittite, in our terms) does apparently displace the language of Hatti (i.e. Hattic). These could equally be local movements, the result of minor conquests by neighbouring principalities, and they do not in themselves necessitate any theory of long-distance language displacements or migrations.

We should note also the interesting suggestion that the location, Nesa, where the language in question would be considered by its speakers originally to belong, has been equated by some scholars[15] with the site of Kanesh, the modern Kültepe near Kayseri, the classical Caesarea, in Cappadocia. At this site a major archive of the records of a trading station set up from Assur in north Mesopotamia has been found, dating mainly to the nineteenth century BC. The records are in the cuneiform script, and in the Assyrian language (a Semitic language). Various scholars have claimed to recognize several names occurring in the tablets which may be regarded as of Hittite origin. It is not yet clear how much weight to put on this observation, but it suggests that the Indo-European Hittite language was already spoken in Anatolia at least as early as 1900 BC.

All this seems rather complicated precisely because it *is* indeed rather complicated! But the broad outlines are clear, and we can indicate the Anatolian language group as follows:[16]

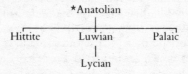

Table IV   The Anatolian language group

3 Before the Greeks

'Who were the Greeks?' has for many years been one of the burning questions[17] of classical scholarship. The epics of Homer, being the earliest surviving writings in any European language, were the obvious place to begin to look for an answer. They, and other early Greek writings, gave a clear picture of a heroic age, the time of Agamemnon, Lord of Mycenae and of the War of Troy. After this brilliant period, there seemed to be a Dark Age around 1000 BC of which little was known, from which the iron age civilization of Classical Greece gradually emerged. There were stories in the classical authors of the movements of tribes during the early years of this period of emergence, and it was possible to equate the different dialects of the Greek language, and the different areas where these were spoken, with these supposed movements. The Dorian invasion was the first, bringing the Dorians into southern Greece, and later came the Ionian Greek dispersal, with the peopling of the islands of the Aegean, especially the eastern ones, by Greeks speaking a different dialect. These at any rate were some of the ideas current, and it was widely supposed that the Greeks, who were of course recognized as one branch of the Indo-European family, entered Greece shortly before 1000 BC.

Archaeology took a hand in the story with the exciting discoveries of Heinrich Schliemann at Mycenae, the legendary home of Agamemnon. There, in 1874, following indications given by the classical geographer and travel writer Pausanias, he dug inside the Lion Gate, and discovered the now famous Grave Circle. Inside were six shaft graves, containing the remains of nineteen individuals, and with them a wealth of equipment; swords and other weapons, drinking vessels, gold jewellery and fine, gold, face masks. These may well have been death masks: certainly it could be reasonably inferred that they represented the rulers of Mycenae. He named the finest of them the Mask of Agamemnon.

Schliemann's findings created a stir. There was great controversy about the date of all these things. He himself claimed that they were prehistoric, before the Greeks, and he named the civilization which he had discovered 'Mycenaean'. Although there were doubters – some thought they belonged to the post-classical, Byzantine

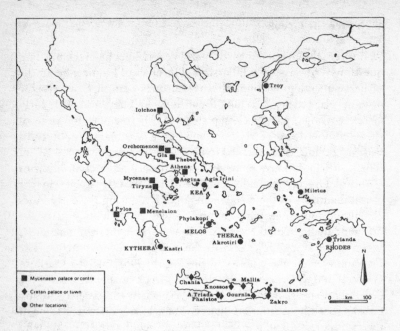

FIG. 3.5 Map of the Aegean, with Minoan and Mycenaean sites.

period, others that they were fakes – Schliemann's view prevailed in the end, and the shaft graves which he discovered, whose treasures can be seen today in the National Museum of Athens, are now dated to around 1600 BC. But what were the origins of this civilization? And how did it relate to that of the Greeks which followed it after the Dark Ages? Many writers assumed that it was pre-Greek, probably pre-Indo-European. Others were not so sure.

The next stage in the story takes place in the Aegean island of Crete. It was there that the English archaeologist, Sir Arthur Evans, decided to dig. He had for several years been studying the intriguing indications that in the prehistoric Aegean there had been a writing system which antedated the alphabet of the classical Greeks. So far the indications came mainly from signs and short inscriptions found on the sealstones (engraved stones which could be impressed on moist clay to give a personal seal) of Crete and the mainland. In 1895 he published his paper 'Cretan pictographs and the prae-

Phoenician script', and in 1901 he began his excavations at the site of Knossos in north Crete.

Evans was at once rewarded with remarkable success. In the first weeks of his excavation he found an archive of clay tablets which clearly recorded the administration of a palace organization, in the same way as many of the archives of clay tablets of the Near East, but these tablets were in a script differing entirely from those of the Near East, although related to what he had been studying in his earlier paper. In fact there was not one script but three, or perhaps more.[18] It soon became clear that some time shortly after 2000 BC there had evolved a script composed of signs, or pictographs. This is usually termed the Cretan hieroglyphic script. Then, from around 1600 BC this was gradually replaced by a different script which probably evolved from it. Evans called this Linear A. This in turn was replaced by a different, although quite similar, script after about 1450 BC. Evans called this Linear B. The important archive which he discovered in the very early days of his dig was written in Linear B. Evans, remembering the early Greek legends of King Minos, the ruler of Crete and his palace at Knossos, called the prehistoric Cretan civilization which he had discovered 'Minoan', and the script of the late Knossos archive is generally termed Minoan Linear B.

To decipher these scripts was not going to be an easy task, and progress was hampered by Evans's failure to publish promptly the necessary transcriptions of the tablets which he had discovered. More tablets in the Minoan Linear A script were discovered in other Minoan palaces of Crete, but for a long time nothing more was found in Minoan Linear B.

Then fragments of tablets in Minoan Linear B began to turn up in excavations at sites on the Greek mainland, notably at Mycenae. In 1939, the American archaeologist, Carl Blegen, beginning his excavations at the supposed palace of Agamemnon's fellow prince Nestor at the site of the legendary Pylos in west Greece had the good fortune to find another archive of Linear B tablets, dating from around 1200 BC. These were published after the Second World War, and a number of scholars began to make good progress with their analysis; seeing that they were palace accounts, working out the system of numerals, and studying the way word endings varied (as they do in inflected languages), even before they had any idea of how the script should be read, let alone the nature of the language itself. It was clear because of the number of signs, some eighty-seven in all, that this was certainly not an alphabetic script like that of the classical Greeks. Nor was it a script where each word can have a different sign and thus made up of very many signs, like the Chinese pictographic script, and indeed like most hieroglyphic scripts. Instead it would have to be a 'syllabic' script, like most of the more developed scripts of the world (including cuneiform) where each sign represents a sound.

It was the brilliant achievement of the English architect and amateur classical scholar, Michael Ventris, to decipher the Linear B script. His friend and collaborator John Chadwick[19] has told the story well in his book *The Decipherment of Linear B*. Ventris employed some of the techniques of analysis which code breakers use in their own attempted decipherments of signal traffic. Having made some progress, as so often in decipherments starting with proper names, in this case the name for Knossos itself, he tried out his emerging words on Etruscan and then on the Greek language. To his astonishment, the words which he was beginning to obtain from his decipherment made good sense if they were regarded as being in Greek. Progress was rapid, and by 1952 Ventris soon accomplished the decipherment of the whole syllabary of signs and, with the collaboration of John Chadwick, was able to make sense of many of the Pylos and Knossos tablets.

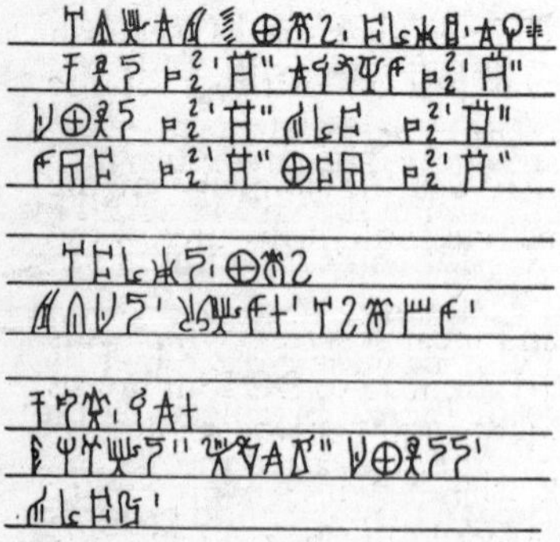

a-pi-no-e-wi[-jo]	ka-ke-we	ta-ra-si-ja	e-ko-te
to-ri-jo BRONZE M1 N2	e-do-mo-ne-u BRONZE M1 N2
mi-ka-ri-jo BRONZE M1 N2	pu-ra-ta BRONZE M1 N2
u-wa-ta BRONZE M1 N2	ka-ta-wa BRONZE M1 N2

. a-ta-ra-si-jo   ka-ke-we
wi-ti-mi-jo 1 ma-no-u-ro 1 a-we-ke-se-u 1

to-so-de   do-e-ro
pe-re-qo-no-jo 2 ai-ki-e-wo 2 mi-ka-ri-jo-jo 1
pu-ra-ta-o 1

FIG. 3.6 Mycenaean Greek: text of a clay tablet from Pylos in the Minoan Linear B script, with transcription following the decipherment by Michael Ventris (*after Hooker*).

As so often happens, the decipherment was followed by controversy, and some scholars declined to accept that the language of the Linear B tablets was an early form of Greek, as Ventris had claimed. More and more studies were made in which the Greek interpretation seemed to make good sense, and this has now been widely accepted. Many of the entries of the tablets do indeed make excellent sense as an early form of Greek. One of the earliest to be transliterated read as follows:[20]

PU-RO i-je-re-ja do-e-ra e-ne-ka ku-ru-so-jo i-je-ro-jo
WOMEN 14

which could be transliterated as follows (the WOMEN 14 entry is given by a pictograph, interpreted as meaning 'women' and the numeral 14):

PYLO(S) *iereias doulae eneka chrusoio ieroio* ('women' 14)

At Pylos: slaves of the priestess on account of sacred gold: 14 women

Other readings followed, and soon it was possible not only to study the grammar and syntax of Mycenaean Greek, but to proceed further with the analysis of the social organization of Knossos and Pylos on the basis of the readings.

It was altogether surprising that the language written at Knossos during the time of the late use of the palace was an early form of Greek. It would have come as a great shock to Sir Arthur Evans (who died in 1940). He had always claimed that the Mycenaean civilization of the Greek mainland was just an offshoot of the Minoan civilization of Crete. How could it be then that the Minoans were writing in Greek, which was the language of the successors of the Mycenaeans, and thus one could now infer of the Mycenaeans themselves?

The answer must lie with the Minoan Linear A script, which was used in the earlier palace of Crete, up to about 1450 BC, but not to any significant extent on the mainland, although there are indications that it was used on the Greek islands which were under Minoan influence at the time. Linear A could not be read successfully as Greek, and so far it has not been read at all, although the signs of the syllabary are sufficiently close to those of Linear B that one may guess what sounds they represent. But the inscriptions thus revealed do not make sense in any known language. Some writers, notably Cyrus Gordon,[21] have tried to advance the claim that the Minoan language – i.e. the language of Linear A – belongs to the Semitic group, but these claims so far carry little conviction.

At present it seems likely that the Minoans did indeed develop their own writing systems for their own language: first the hiero-glyphic script, then Linear A. And it also seems likely that Crete may have been conquered by groups from the mainland sometime around 1450 BC, and the island administered from the palace at Knossos. On this view, the new élite of Mycenaeans would have adapted the existing Linear A script to their own Mycenaean Greek language, producing the new Linear B script. The system of writing, and the new script with it, would then have been adopted on the mainland too, for archives such as that found at Pylos.

All of this has important implications for Indo-European studies. It is now clear that the Mycenaeans were indeed speaking Greek, which was already well-differentiated as a language, within the Indo-European family, by 1400 BC. The search for the origins of the Indo-European speech of Greece is thus linked with the understanding of the origins of the Mycenaean civilization and its antecedents.

In constructing the hypothetical family tree for the Indo-Europeans, the Hellenic branch will thus simply be the direct descent:

Mycenaean Greek
|
Classical Greek
|
Modern Greek

Table V   The Hellenic languages

The Greek language of the classical period continued in use during the Middle Ages, and survived as a court language at the Byzantine capital of Constantinople, and as a language of cult in the Greek Orthodox church. The modern Greek language is the direct descendent of these. Although it has dialects, some of them spoken in parts of Anatolia until the exchange of population between

Greece and Turkey in 1922, it has never subdivided into a separate family of languages in the way that Latin did. It began to do so in the aftermath of the empire of Alexander the Great, but in most areas Greek was ultimately replaced by other local tongues. A version of Greek is, however, still spoken in parts of southern Italy – a last remnant there of the colonies of the classical period.

4 In the Great Desert of Chinese Asia

The discovery of the fourth lost Indo-European language was even more unexpected than the revelation of Hittite. It was certainly much odder than the decipherment of Old Persian or of Mycenaean Greek, since both of these were languages with well-known and living successors, which they do to some extent resemble, and in the light of which they could be interpreted. That was certainly not the case with 'Tocharian'.

It was not until the later years of the nineteenth century that travellers and explorers began to investigate what was then, and still

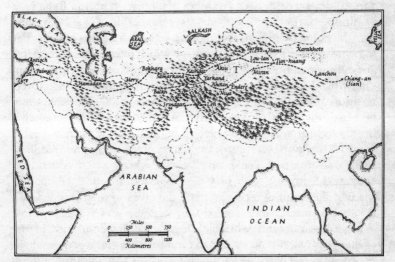

FIG. 3.7 Map of the Old Silk Road, indicating the Taklamakan desert (marked T) in Chinese Turkestan, with sites (notably Kucha, Khotan and Tun-huang) where inscriptions in Tocharian have been found (*after Hopkirk*).

remains, one of the least-investigated areas of the earth.[22] This is the
region way to the east of Iran and Turkmenia, east of the Kara Kum
desert and the river Oxus, east of Samarkand and Soviet Turkestan,
east of the Altai Mountains and the Pamirs, and on to the last
stations of the Silk Road before China itself, into Chinese
Turkestan, the modern province of Sinkiang. There, to the north of
Tibet, and to the south of Mongolia and the Gobi desert, lie a series
of oases which for a while were able to support a remarkable urban
civilization, while to the north and indeed all round were the arid
steppe lands peopled only by nomads.

In and near these oases lie forgotten cities, half obscured by sand,
where wood and other organic materials are remarkably well
preserved in the arid conditions of the desert. This is one of the very
few areas of the world where paper and wood and textiles, centuries
old, have been preserved in great quantities – only on the borders of
other large deserts, especially in Egypt, have comparable archives
on perishable materials been preserved.

It was into this region, notably into the Tarim depression and
various nearby oases, that a number of scholars ventured at the very
beginning of this century. The most remarkable of these travellers
was the Hungarian-born Aurel Stein, although he was not the first
to come upon the script and language which interests us here. After
an education in Budapest and a number of universities he worked in
the British Museum for a while, and was then posted in 1886 to the
position of Principal of the Oriental College at Lahore. From there
he began the series of Asian explorations for which he is remembered, and for which he was later knighted. His most remarkable
triumph was at the location of the 'Caves of the Thousand Buddhas'
at the oasis town of Tun-huang, which, when he first visited it in
1907, was a thriving town on China's western frontier.[23] Although
the Buddhist community was small, the caves were still tended by a
number of priests and monks. One of these was a Taoist priest,
Wang Tao-shih, who, when cleaning the painted decoration of one
of the walls of a cave in 1900, had found a crack in the plaster which
revealed a secret chamber, walled up, containing a whole library full
of ancient documents. Concerned at the magnitude of this discovery he had walled it up again, but Aurel Stein persuaded him to
open it and to sell him a number of the documents. These included

Buddhist religious texts dating back to the fifth century, written in Chinese and other languages, Tibetan manuscripts, and other works in a whole variety of scripts and languages, mainly from the seventh and eighth centuries AD. The site was later visited by the French scholar, Paul Pelliot, who was a distinguished orientalist well able to judge rapidly the likely significance of any document, and he was also able to obtain a large quantity of manuscripts.

From these sources, and from discoveries on a smaller scale made a few years earlier in towns lying a few miles to the west, it became clear that, amongst all the mass of written material in a variety of known scripts and languages, there were documents in two related languages of which no trace had previously been recognized.

It is one of the unfortunate conventions of archaeology that each culture and each language must have a name, and it often turns out that the name first given to important new discoveries is not at all appropriate. It is particularly unfortunate when languages are given names before they are fully understood, for decipherment can produce embarrassing evidence to show that the name was not well chosen. We have already seen this was the case with 'Hittite' – the Hittites themselves applied the name 'Hittite' to a different language which we are now forced to term 'Hattic'. In much the same way, scholars at first identified the writers of the newly discovered languages of Chinese Turkestan with a tribe which the classical writer, Strabo,[24] mentioned as defeating one of the local Greek rulers of Bactria (eastern Iran) in the second century BC. These were the Tocharoi, and with their arbitrarily chosen, and probably quite inappropriate name, the languages of the Tarim depression are now known as 'Tocharian'.

The great mass of written material from the Turfan expeditions of Grünwedel and von le Coq,[25] as well as that recovered by Aurel Stein, was quickly understood. The Tocharian manuscripts[26] were largely written in a north Indian alphabet of the Brahmi type, and it was soon realized that much of the material consisted of translations of Sanskrit originals. Some of it was actually bilingual. The records are from the seventh and eighth centuries AD, and they include monastery correspondence and accounts. The texts are written on palm leaves, occasionally on Chinese paper, and there are also caravan permits written in ink on wooden tablets.

Of the two Tocharian languages,[27] the first, often termed Tocharian A, was also known from finds of texts at the towns of Karashahr and Turfan: it is sometimes termed Turfanian. The other, Tocharian B, is known largely from texts found at Koucha: it is thus generally termed Kouchean. Some of the records which Stein recovered from Tun-huang were in this language.

These languages have several grammatical features which link them with the Indo-European group.[28] As a language so geo-graphically remote from its congeners, the vocabulary does not show many links with other branches of the family, but some links are there. They are seen in the numbers, which (in Turfanian and Kouchean respectively) are as follows:

1: *sas, se*; 2: *wu, wi*; 3: *tre, trai*;
4: *stwar, stwer*; 5: *pan, pis*; 6: *sak, skas*;
7: *spat, sukt*; 8: *okat, okt*; 9: *nu, nu*;
10: *sak, sak*; 100: *kant, kante*.

The word for 100 reminds us that these languages do not fall within the *satem* language group, as the eastern Indo-European languages were supposed to do, but rather within the *centum* group, along with most of the European languages. This has undermined confidence in the satem/centum distinction, which like most very simple typological distinctions is now felt to be too simplistic to carry much weight.

The people who spoke these languages were certainly in contact with the Chinese, and the records in question were written at the time of the Tang dynasty of China. Chinese records, already from the fourth century BC, mention a troublesome group of nomads on their western frontier, called the Hsiung-nu, and these are identified by many scholars with the groups which later in the west are termed the Huns. These Hsiung-nu in the second century BC displaced, according to the Chinese, another group, the Yü-chi, who moved westwards. These are equated by some scholars[29] with the people who were speaking the Indo-European Tocharian languages. That remains hypothetical, but it reminds us that there is still the hope that the Chinese historical records may one day be used to cast more light on the people who spoke these two languages. Most scholars dealing with Indo-European languages tend to place little weight on the evidence of Tocharian, regarding these languages as lying on the extreme eastern fringe of the distribution of the Indo-European languages. This in a sense is true. It is only because there were oasis cities in this vast area of steppe land which had an urban and literate culture that we have any knowledge whatever of this long-forgotten language. It is very possible, indeed likely, that there were other groups in the intervening territories speaking Indo-European languages which have less evident traces.

The Tocharian languages are generally regarded as constituting a further sub-group of the Indo-European language family.

5 The Languages of Europe

Family tree diagrams for the main European language groups are given below.

(a) The Italic languages[30]

The early languages of Italy have been particularly well studied by a series of distinguished scholars.[31] In addition to Latin, there is the Umbrian language with its fascinating and extensive text inscribed on the bronze Tablets of Gubbio.[32] The Etruscan[33] language is also a topic of particular fascination, since it appears to be non-Indo-European and hence, on the theory developed here, probably of longer standing in Italy than its Indo-European neighbours. Then there is a whole series of further languages, including those of Sicily, known at present only from shorter inscriptions.

The Romance languages are all descended from Latin. There are also several other languages descended from Latin, including Swiss Romansch, Catalan and Sardinian. The relationship of Oscan and Umbrian to Latin is a matter for discussion, as indeed is that of the Venetic language of north-east Italy. All of these succumbed to Latin by the first or second century AD.

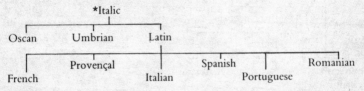

Table VI   The Italic languages

(b) *The Celtic languages*

The main Celtic languages can be set out in the following series of relationships, some of which are open to debate.

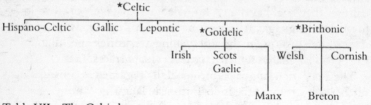

Table VII   The Celtic languages

(c) *The Germanic languages*

The Germanic languages form a complex group.[34] The earliest known Germanic language is a translation into Gothic of the Bible, made in the fourth century AD, parts of which still survive.

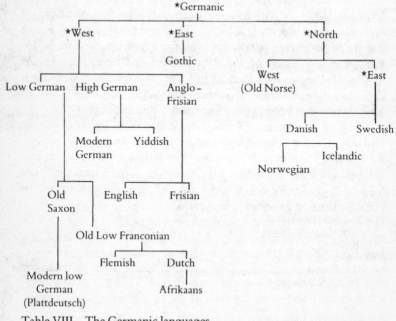

Table VIII   The Germanic languages

(d) *The Slavonic languages*

The division may be set out schematically as follows.[35] Church
Slavonic was first written in the ninth century AD.

Table IX   The Slavonic languages

(e) *The Baltic languages*

The earliest known document in Lithuanian is dated to about 1515,
and the origins of the Baltic languages are poorly documented.
(Estonian belongs to the quite different Finno-Ugrian language
group, see g. below).

Table X   The Baltic languages

(f) *Illyrian*

The principal remaining Indo-European languages of Europe can
be classed under this heading (although Thracian and Dacian are
dealt with below). There are no texts surviving from the Illyrian
language in classical times, although Greek references do mention
the Illyrians in what is now Yugoslavia and Albania. Modern
Albanian may be descended from the ancient Illyrian language, or
possibly from Thracian.

(g) *The Non-Indo-European languages of Europe*

It may well be that the key to the understanding of the origins of the Indo-European languages of Europe is to be found in the early non-Indo-European languages with which they came into contact. Two ancient and well-known languages fall into this category, although there are several others, less well-known, which some scholars would also place here.

Etruscan is an ancient language of central Italy, which flourished there as an early contemporary of Latin. Latin was the language of Latium, and Etruscan that of Etruria, although Latin became dominant by the first century BC. Etruscan has always seemed a mysterious language because it is apparently unrelated to the other languages of Europe. The script presents no problems: it is just a version of the same alphabet, derived originally from the Phoenicians, which was used by the Greeks and the Romans. The language is still only partly understood, since there are few texts preserved (and very few bilingual texts) to allow a full decipherment. There are of course many theories[36] about the origins of the Etruscan language. The two most popular are either that it is indigenous (as many modern scholars think), or that, as the Greek historian Herodotus suggested, it was carried to Italy by emigrants from Lydia in west Anatolia early in the first millennium BC, which would imply an Indo-European origin for it.

Basque is the language of northern Spain, and it is still a living, indeed flourishing, tongue. It appears to be a language without close affinities,[37] and as such it has given rise to much speculation.

Iberian is another non-Indo-European language of Spain, although (like Etruscan in Italy) it did not survive the classical period.

The *Estonian* language is closely related to *Finnish*, and both are related to *Hungarian*, forming the Finno-Ugrian branch of the Uralic family of languages. The arrival of the Magyars, speaking Hungarian, into the Hungarian Plain at the end of the ninth century AD is historically documented (see Chapter 8). Etruscan, Basque and Iberian have antecedents in their own areas going back into prehistoric times, but Hungarian is a language which has displaced its predecessor, and for that reason it is in many ways less relevant to a discussion of the early languages of Europe.

6 Between Europe and Asia

The one remaining major Indo-European language which constitutes a branch of the family in itself (in the same manner as does
Greek) is Armenian. This is sometimes classed as a Thraco-
Phrygian language,[38] but this very term is an unsatisfactory one for
it purports to form a link with the language of Thrace, in the
south-east corner of Europe and with the western part of Anatolia.
The Thrace of classical times is today divided between the eastern
nomos (province) of Greece in the north Aegean area, and Bulgaria,
to which must be added that small part of the modern Turkey
which lies within Europe. The surviving records of the Thracian
language, which cover a period from the time of Homer to the
Middle Ages amount to little more than about twenty-five words
altogether. It is no doubt related to the language which was spoken
in what is today Romania before that area was occupied by the
Romans. The area became the Roman province of Dacia, and its
early language is therefore Dacian.

The Phrygian language[39] – the language which survived in the
Anatolian province of Phrygia in Greek times – is known from
some twenty-five inscriptions from about the sixth century BC,
and another hundred or so from the first three centuries AD. They
are written in the Greek alphabet. Philologically the status of
Phrygian is obscure, and it is far from clear that it should be classed
together with Thracian and Dacian: recent work suggests that it is
closer to Greek.

Armenian, of course, is spoken in the Armenian Soviet Socialist
Republic of the Soviet Union as well as in the neighbouring
Georgia, in north-west Iran, and in the north-eastern *vilayets* (provinces) of Turkey. It is thus at the eastern end of Anatolia, and there
is no clear reason to link it with Phrygian, let alone Dacian or
Thracian. However, works on the Indo-European languages, with
their propensity to talk in terms of migrations, make statements like
the following:[40]

> The Armenians made their way from south eastern Europe
> across the Hellespont and into Asia Minor in company with the
> Phrygians (Homer's Trojans) to reach their present homeland

at the eastern end of the Black Sea, between the eighth and the sixth centuries BC.

In reality there is no very clear reason to link the Armenian language with western Anatolia or Thrace. One point plausibly suggested by several writers is that some features of Armenian may descend from the non-Indo-European language spoken in the area in the first millennium BC, the language of the civilization of Urartu, centred upon the Lake Van area of eastern Anatolia, and sometimes called Urartian. This in turn is thought to be the descendent of one of the non-Indo-European languages which is used in some of the Boghazköy tablets nearly a millennium earlier: Hurrian. Just as the tablets preface some texts by the term *hattili*, 'in Hattic', so some are prefaced by *hurlili*, 'in Hurrian'.

While referring to the Hurrian language, which at the time of its maximal expansion, during the second millennium BC, was spoken deep into central Anatolia, Syria, Palestine and Mesopotamia, and perhaps also into western Iran, it is very interesting to note that there is some evidence that it contained some Indo-European words. Indeed several scholars have pointed out that some of the names of the leaders of the Land of Mitanni, where the Hurrian language was spoken, appear to have had Indo-European names – that is to say that the names have coherent meaning when interpreted in terms of the early Indo-Iranian languages. For some of the rulers of Mitanni in the fifteenth and fourteenth centuries BC, with Indo-European names, are known from letters from the rulers of Mitanni to Amenophis III and his son Akhnaten, found in their foreign office archives at Tell el-Amarna. But the most tantalizing piece of evidence occurs on a tablet found at Boghazköy and gives indications of the eighth language to be found in the archive there. The tablet is written in the Indo-European language which we call Hittite. It is a splendid text, dating from the fourteenth century BC, and deals with the training of chariot horses.[41] It is described as being written by a man called Kikkuli, a Hurrian from the state of Mitanni. The text contains several technical terms which scholars infer to have been borrowed from the Hurrian language. Some of these are clearly derived from a language related to Indo-Iranian. For example the term *nawartanni wasannasya* meaning 'for nine turns of the course' may be compared with the reconstructed Sanskrit form *navartane vasanasya*. The numerals *aika-* ('one'), *tera-* ('three'), *panza-* ('five'), *satta-* ('seven') and *na-* ('nine') occur in this way.

It does seem plausible to assume that these terms were indeed used in the Hurrian language, (although I believe that it could be argued, since they are from a Hittite text found at Boghazköy, that they were in fact in use in the land of the Hittites, and were therefore not derived from Hurrian terminology at all). If we accept the evidence of the half-dozen or so special words in this treatise on horsemanship together with the Indo-European names for the Mitanni kings[42] in the Amarna letters, significant historical inferences may be drawn.[43] For scholars agree that linguistically the resemblances of these words are with the Indo-Iranian languages rather than with Hittite itself – that is to say with the Vedic Sanskrit of the *Rigveda* of north India, and with the Old Persian of the *Avesta* of western Iran – but the Boghazköy tablets are many centuries earlier than any direct evidence which we have for these. If we follow the case that has been widely made by scholars, the Hurrians of the land of Mitanni must already have been in close contact with groups speaking the language from which these various terms were drawn.[44] Indeed some writers go so far as to suggest that the Hurrians had indeed been subjugated by a group of people speaking that language. This would supposedly account for the names of the rulers. And if the hypothesis is followed that this new élite achieved its conquest with the use of the war chariot, which was then a very new innovation, it is not surprising that some of their terms for horse-training should occur on a tablet written for the Hittite rulers by a Hurrian from the land of Mitanni. Perhaps that suggestion is just too easy, and it is certainly based on a very restricted group of words, but any hint that we may have evidence of another very early Indo-European language, actually as early as 1400 BC, is an important one.

7 The Indo-European 'Family'

It is now possible to put together the evidence which we have reviewed in this chapter and to produce a diagram[45] (Table XI) of

possible relationships, on the family tree model. The existence of
the various 'branches' of sub-groups is in most cases quite plausibly
argued by the rather close similarities, both in grammar and in
vocabulary, among the languages within them. Between the branches it is much more difficult to say anything of significance,
although their general affinity, justifying their linkage together as
'Indo-European' has, as we saw earlier, been widely accepted. As
usual an asterisk implies that the particular language in question is
inferred or reconstructed, rather than being documented by actual
texts. The supposed language of the rulers of Mitanni has not been
shown since its existence is an inference based only on a few
personal names and on a handful of further words.

It should be noted, however, that this diagram is only one
interpretative summary of the available evidence. It is open
to criticism on several counts, but it does remind us of some of
the main headings under which more detailed evidence can be
discussed.

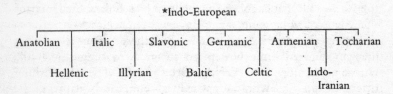

Table XI   The Indo-European family

4. Homelands in Question

The time has now come to question more seriously whether the various attempts hitherto undertaken to locate some original 'homeland' for the Proto-Indo-Europeans have had any very sound basis. I have already indicated that in my view they have not. Although there are many good ideas and many relevant comments in what has been written on this subject, I believe that no coherent and plausible theory has yet been advanced. I shall argue in this chapter that most writers have fallen into what can now be recognized as dangerous traps. They have placed too much faith in the idea of some reconstructed Proto-Indo-European vocabulary, from which some kind of word-picture of the original homeland might be put together. They have too readily assumed that a given pottery form, or an assemblage of items of material equipment, can be equated directly with a group of people and hence supposedly with a particular language or language group. And they have not adequately explained *why* all these languages, or the speakers of all these languages, should be wandering around Europe and western Asia so tirelessly, in a series of migrations, thus setting up the pattern of different languages which we see today. Later I shall make some suggestions which I believe overcome these particular difficulties: they will be found controversial by most authorities on the subject for the very good reason that in several respects they disagree with most existing views on it.

First it is worth re-stating some general and important points. In the first place, as the great linguist, Max Müller, said in 1888,[1] the term 'Indo-European' refers to language, not to people or groups of people. Of course the languages were spoken by people, but that does not justify our speaking of 'Indo-Europeans' or 'Aryans' in any other sense than of those persons who spoke the languages in question. That implies that if I am brought up speaking only one language, for example a Semitic language, and then I learn an Indo-European language, in a very real sense I have *become* an Indo-European. And my children, especially if this language which

I have learnt becomes their first language, will be Indo-Europeans too, even if both their parents originally spoke a Semitic language and came from a different cultural background.

In this sense, then, it is not correct to speak of an Indo-European culture. Nor, if the terms Celtic and Germanic and Italic are similarly defined in terms of language, is it correct to speak of a Celtic or a Germanic or an Italic culture. Tremendous confusion about linguistic and cultural origins has come about because language and culture have not been properly distinguished. Of course language and culture often go together. In a modern European nation-state, very often as you cross the frontier, the language changes, and sometimes so does the whole way of life, and with it the system of beliefs and religion. But this is not necessarily so. Groups of people with very different cultures can speak the same language, and, conversely, within an area where the way of life is essentially the same, different languages may be spoken.

Above all it is a serious mistake to equate race and language. The term 'race' has of course been seriously abused in the past, and very often it is not clear at all exactly what it means. Of course if one asks a Chinaman, a Frenchman and a Nigerian to stand in line, they may look decidedly different from each other (even there one has to be careful over definitions: there are plenty of black Frenchmen, and there are white Nigerians). But when we consider Europe and western Asia, it is not at all clear in terms of physical anthropology that there are different races at all. Yet it is true that there can be physical features which correlate at a statistically significant level with country of origin or with descent: a higher proportion of Swedes have fair hair and blue eyes than Italians. Today blood groups can be studied as well as external physical characteristics, but the notion of 'race' is extremely difficult to define with precision.[2]

The difficulties become overwhelming when one is dealing only with skeletal material, as is the archaeologist's usual lot in life. There is at the moment no scientifically acceptable way of taking a set of skeletal measurements and saying that a body or a skull which shows them must be assigned to a particular 'race'. The metric characteristics of different populations can be compared, and it may be possible to make inferences on that basis, but they will probably not be racial ones in any meaningful sense. If there were significant, recurrent patterns in the skeletal material which allowed us to distinguish between different groups of people in a meaningful and valid way, then we would have to develop a study of prehistoric races. The reason for discounting this approach is not so much that we dislike the consequences of 'racism', but that it does not accord with the data.

If we agree to try to separate language, race and culture in a clear way, the starting point for a consideration of Indo-European problems must always be the study of language. Indo-European studies represent a very considerable field of scholarship, and the techniques of comparative linguistics are sophisticated and well developed. There is not much point in an archaeologist who is not properly trained in the linguistic field setting out to make new or challenging statements of a linguistic nature; but when we begin to speak about the groups of people who spoke these languages, and about the historical circumstances which brought about their distribution, then we are fairly and squarely within the field of archaeology. These are the issues which I propose to follow up here.

1 The Lure of the Protolexicon

Much of the confusion which surrounds the question of the origins of the Indo-European languages comes from the notion that the languages themselves contain all the evidence that is necessary to permit an accurate historical reconstruction and an identification of the location of an original homeland. Early enthusiasm for the 'comparative method' of linguistic reconstruction (as noted in Chapter 1) led to the application of the view that when related (cognate) words were discovered in two different Indo-European languages, the original word in the proto-language notionally parental to both of them could be found. In this way, Proto-Indo-European was reconstructed, the original language (*Ursprache*) of the original people (*Urvolk*) in their homeland (*Urheimat*). This was the method of linguistic palaeontology, as it was grandiosely termed, and with its aid the actual vocabulary of words, the protolexicon, of the *Urvolk* could be established.

There remains much of value in the comparative method, and the approach is indeed one of the most useful ways to study the relationship between the Indo-European languages, but as we shall see in the next chapter the 'family tree' model of language change, on which the initial ideas of linguistic palaeontology depended, is now thought to be too simple an idea. Loan-words (words borrowed from a neighbouring language) are acquired by languages and they are not always easy to recognize. Yet obviously, when several common loan-words were acquired by two languages in, say, the first century AD, they can give no insight into the vocabulary of the notional parental language spoken centuries or millennia earlier. The wave model for linguistic change leads to a different picture.

If the languages with related words are geographically far apart, the linguistic palaeontologist can argue that borrowing from one by the other is unlikely. So he will argue that because the Irish *ri*, 'king', and the Latin *rex* along with the Sanskrit *raja* are cognate and geographically remote, then a word for 'king' formed part of the protolexicon.

The basic principle of linguistic palaeontology is that if the Indo-Europeans can be shown by linguistic analysis to have had the name of a specific thing within their protolexicon, then they can be assumed to have been acquainted with the thing itself.

Thus the best modern survey of historical linguistics, by Winfred Lehmann, can say:[3]

> Proceeding to the everyday life of the Indo-European community we find terms for 'herd, cow, sheep, goat, pig, dog, horse, wolf, bear, goose, duck, bee, oak, beech, willow, grain'. The lack of specific terms for grains or vegetables indicates a heavy reliance on animals for food.

This argument, and really very little else, has led to the notion that the Proto-Indo-Europeans were nomads. The method can even be used to make chronological inferences. To quote Lehmann again:[4]

> The time during which the Indo-European community flourished has been subject to less dispute. When we attempt to

reconstruct words for metals, we can ascribe to the Indo-Europeans vocabulary no words even for 'silver' or 'gold', let alone 'iron' and scarcely even a general term for 'metal, bronze, copper', Latin *aes* 'copper, bronze', Old English *ar* 'brass, copper' leads to New English *ore*, Sanskrit *ayas* 'bronze', later 'copper'. On the basis of such vocabulary we characterize the Indo-European community as late neolithic. Fortunately archaeological discoveries have led to the identification of this community with a culture located north of the Black Sea from the fifth millennium BC . . .

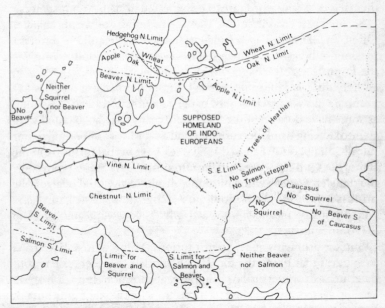

FIG. 4.1 The limits of the distribution of various plant and animal species in Europe: the evidence of linguistic palaeontology for the homeland of the Indo-Europeans (*after Mann and Kilian*).

The method is applied to the localization of the homeland by focusing on features of the natural environment. The protolexicon contains the names of certain animals and trees. It follows from the application of the general principle that the Indo-Europeans must have been acquainted with these things. If, then, we can point to

some region in Europe or Asia where it can be demonstrated that
these species were living a few thousand years ago, and if that is the
only area where they could all be found, then that must be the
homeland, so it is argued, and the problem is solved.

Alas, matters are not so easy, and the method has many objec-
tions. In the first place, any innovation, any discovery which results
in a new product, will often carry the name of that product with it.
So to find a word for 'wheel' or 'cart' or 'copper' or 'bronze' in
several languages does not necessarily tell us very much about the
origins of those languages, although it is of interest for the words
themselves. Loan-words are to be expected in such circumstances.

Secondly, it is well known that the meanings of words change.
Often an old word is retained and used with quite a different
meaning when some innovation has occurred. A good example is
the English 'car' (carriage) which a couple of centuries ago had an
entirely different meaning. Or as J. Fraser pointed out nearly sixty
years ago in a very well-argued paper,[5] it is not necessary to assume,
as some have done, that the Indo-Europeans were acquainted with
an intoxicating drink because they had a word corresponding to our
'mead', and because Sanskrit and Greek have verbal forms from the
same root with the sense of 'to be intoxicated'. As Fraser points out,
the transference of a name meaning 'drink' to any kind of alcoholic
drink is common. The Slavonic *pivo* is cognate with the Latin *bibere*
and originally meant simply a drink, but now means 'beer' in
Slavonic languages.

Similar problems apply to institutions. Some writers have tried
to suggest that the terms for 'father, mother, brother, sister, son,
daughter, daughter-in-law' indicate a common Indo-European
kinship system, with a close relationship with the son's wife but not
between a man and his in-laws. But the British social anthropologist, Jack Goody, has cogently argued that such inferences are
not warranted.[6]

Again, some writers have taken the presence in several Indo-
European languages of a cognate term for 'king' as an indication of
the institution of kingship in the 'homeland'. But the opposite
conclusion is also advanced. To quote Lehmann again:[7]

But the absence of general terms for leaders of larger social
groups requires us to conclude that social organizations in the

Indo-European community were restricted in size. A word for 'ruler', related to the Latin *regere* 'guide' is found in Latin *rex*, Irish *ri*, Sanskrit *raj* – but other dialects have different terms, such as Greek *basileus* and Old English *cyning*. Accordingly we may posit for the Indo-European community a well-developed family system but not higher social or political organization.

This, however, looks like very dangerous special pleading, for there are very few words indeed which are represented by cognate forms in *all* Indo-European languages. As Stuart Piggott has very pertinently remarked, quoting A. B. Keith:[8] 'taking the linguistic evidence too literally, one could conclude that the original Indo-European speakers knew butter but not milk, snow and feet but not rain and hands'.

The argument about the distribution of living species is put most vigorously, but it too has its pitfalls. Simply to draw on a map the boundary of the occurrence of the various species of trees which have cognate names in the Indo-European languages does not establish for us the boundaries of Proto-Indo-European, as some have argued.[9] For the existence of cognate, or even identical words in various dialects and regions does not indicate that they all refer to the same things. It has often been pointed out that a robin in England is not the same bird at all as a robin in America. So that when we find words related to 'birch' and 'beech' in several Indo-European languages it does not follow that the common word in Proto-Indo-European from which they were descended had the same specific meaning.

Indeed if we look at the modern boundaries for a particular species of tree on a vegetation map, it will not surprise us that the various languages within the boundary have terms designating that tree, and presumably the languages which lie entirely outside the boundary will not have a name for a tree they do not know exists. If the Proto-Indo-Europeans did indeed originate within the area, they may well have had in their protolexicon terms ancestral to the modern ones, as the linguistic palaeontologists would suggest. But if we imagine that there was an original homeland *outside* the boundary, and that the territories within it came to speak Indo-European languages through the processes of linguistic displacement, then they would need to develop an appropriate vocabulary after their arrival. They might well then draw upon pre-existing terms in their own vocabulary which had previously held a rather different meaning (like the immigrants to the New World with their 'robin'). Or entirely new words might be developed and be adopted, following the wave model for language change, throughout the territory to which they were appropriate. Either way, the territory through which the term for the species in question is found will not extend far beyond the natural habitat of the species, and there may be a good deal of uniformity in the terms used within that boundary.

These points were well stated by Fraser in his article, which it is worth quoting at length:[10]

I have already pointed out that the significance attached to the fact that the Indogermans were acquainted with the horse and the cow may have been exaggerated. We do not really know the precise meaning of the Indo-Germanic words in question; we do not know whether they mean the domesticated or the wild animals; and for that reason it is difficult to see how these names can safely be used for the purpose of determining the original home of the Indogermans. The same difficulty arises in the case of other etymological data used by the Linguistic Palaeontologist. We are constantly told that the Indogermans knew the beech and the birch trees, and this has counted for a great deal in the attempts that have been made to fix their home. But strictly speaking, we do not know that they were acquainted with those trees; all we know is that their vocabulary contained two words the later form of which in the historical Indogermanic languages are, generally, the name of the beech and the birch respectively. But it must be noticed that in Greek the word cognate with the English 'beech' is the name of the oak; and we must assume that this is not the only case in which either word has undergone a change of meaning. And if the speakers of a language when they change their homes and move into new surroundings, give the names of things familiar in their old homes to things in the new that resemble them or take their place, it may appear that in arguing from the beech and birch to the original home of the Indogermans we are arguing in a vicious circle.

It is the case that the words which are repeatedly used in trying to establish a homeland are rather few. The names for trees have indeed been argued with comprehensive scholarship by Paul Friedrich in his book *Proto-Indo-European Trees*.[11] The animal species were briefly quoted above. Childe, in *The Aryans*, gave a considerable list, derived from the work of Otto Schrader. To avoid seeming selective, I quote below the words which Childe listed:[12] he went on to give their equivalent form (where it exists) in Sanskrit, Greek, Latin, Celtic, Teutonic, Lithuanian, Tocharian and Armenian.

god, father, mother, son, daughter, brother, sister, father's brother, grandson or nephew, son-in-law, daughter-in-law, father-in-law, mother-in-law, husband's brother, husband's brother's wives, husband, woman, widow, house-father, clan, village headman, ? sib, ? tribe or clan, king, dog, ox, sheep, goat, horse, pig, steer, cow, gelding, cattle, cheese, fat, butter, grain, bread, furrow, plough, mead, copper, gold, silver, razor, awl, sling-stone, bow-string, javelin, spear, sword, axe, carpenter, chariot or wheel, axle, nave, yoke, ship, oar, house, door-frame, door, pillar, earth-walls.

The argument most frequently put forward from this list of words is that it includes more names of animal species than of plants, and that the subsistence of the Proto-Indo-Europeans was therefore that of a pastoralist economy. But this view is, unfortunately, based upon a very simplistic view of pastoralism. It is now well-established that a pastoral economy, with emphasis upon domestic animal species, can only arise following the emergence of agriculture. The old idea that pastoralism could represent some intermediate stage between the hunting and gathering of the palaeolithic and mesolithic periods and the agriculture of the neolithic, has now been thoroughly discredited. Everywhere pastoralists are dependent upon their co-existence with farmers (see

Chapter 6), and much of their diet is formed by agricultural produce. Writing of the Basseri in his *Nomads of South Persia*, the social anthropologist, Frederik Barth, points out:[13]

> The normal diet of the Basseri includes a great bulk of agricultural produce, of which some tribesmen produce at least a part themselves. Cereal crops, particularly wheat, are planted on first arrival in the summer camp areas and yield their produce before the time of departure; or locally resident villagers are paid to plant a crop before the nomads arrive, to be harvested by the latter . . . A great number of the necessities of life are thus obtained by trade and flour is the most important foodstuff, consumed as unleavened bread with every meal; and sugar, tea, dates, and fruits and vegetables are also important. In the case of most Basseri, such products are entirely or predominantly obtained by trade . . .

Of course it is not to be argued that all nomad groups have a subsistence economy like that of the Basseri. Some may place more emphasis on milk products than they do, others also drink the blood of their cattle. But the underlying point remains, that all pastoral nomads are also dependent on the domesticated plants produced by agriculture.

It thus seems entirely naïve to use the argument that because several animal species have cognate names in the Indo-European languages, animals were originally more important in the economy than plants. If the Proto-Indo-Europeans were familiar with domesticated sheep, goats or cattle, then they must certainly also have been acquainted with wheat, barley and peas and also a range of other animal species. If there are no common words today among the Indo-European languages for these species, then other explanations must be found. Once this point is accepted, the preponderance of animals amongst the cognate names must be seen as the result of essentially linguistic factors, rather than as a feature of the presence and absence of the relevant species in the natural environment of the original *Urvolk*. The whole argument collapses, and the myth of the pastoralist Indo-Europeans loses all substance.

Many of the arguments bearing upon the natural environment are equally weak. Much is made of the absence of words for

Mediterranean species, such as the vine and the olive, from the supposed protolexicon. But if these words were present in some protolexicon, they could scarcely be expected to have continued in use in areas where these species are no longer encountered. We know that the domesticated vine is a relatively recent species in central and northern Europe: the absence of a relevant term in the early languages of those areas need thus occasion no surprise.

In all of these discussions, it may further be argued, there has been a tendency to forget that we are not dealing with a single time period, but over a vast time depth. To reconstruct, from the existing languages, a proto-language at a particular point in time is thus an over-ambitious task. The linguist, Ernst Pulgram, caricatured this tendency, and following Fraser, offered a splendid *reductio ad absurdum*:[14]

> If we reconstructed Latin on the evidence of the Romanic languages alone, ignoring and neglecting the existence of Greek, Keltic, Germanic and the other ancient Indo-European dialects, and if thereupon we derived from the state of the common Romanic vocabulary conclusions on the culture of the speakers of Latin (whom then we should call Latins, I suppose, and ascribe to one race or another, depending on our patriotic or political leanings), we might well arrive at the following results: Proto-Romanic *regem* and *imperatorem* show us that the Latins lived in a monarchy under kings or emperors (but what shall we make of *rem publicam* which could presuppose a Latin republic?); since all Romanic languages contain words cognate with French *prêtre* and *évêque*, 'priest' and 'bishop', the Latins were Christians; also words cognate with French *bière*, *tabac*, *café* are common Romanic, evoking a picture of Caesar's soldiers guzzling beer and smoking cigars in sidewalk cafés; and since all Romanic languages name a certain animal *cheval*, *caballo*, *cal*, etc., and have words for '*war*' like *guerre*, *guerra*, the Latins called the horse *caballum* and the war *guerram* and were no doubt warlike people with a strong cavalry.

In reality, of course, the Roman words for 'horse' and 'war' are *equus* and *bellum*, and this marvellous piece of nonsense reconstruction brilliantly exemplifies the dangers of linguistic palaeontology.

Now these arguments are not intended as an attack upon the comparative method, as used by competent linguists to examine the histories of particular words, and to study by this means the relationships between specific languages. I hope that I am aware of the very considerable erudition which underlies many of the linguistic arguments which are put forward. My criticism is of the simplistic use of such data to reach supposedly historical conclusions. Certainly the circumstance that the Sanskrit word for 'chariot', *ratha*, is agreed by competent linguists to be cognate with the Latin for 'wheel', *rota*, is interesting, and merits historical explanation. But that is a far cry from saying that the two cognate words tell us that some hypothetical Proto-Indo-Europeans used chariots with wheels (or indeed carts with wheels) in their original homeland.

There may be good arguments for placing the Indo-Europeans in an original homeland in south Russia, but in my view the findings of linguistic palaeontology are not among their number. They could probably be accommodated to almost any homeland theory, just as they have already been made to fit a good many very different ones. The present distribution of the Indo-European languages has to be seen not as simply the dispersal of an *Urvolk* from an *Urheimat*, speaking an *Ursprache*, but rather as the end product of a whole series of *processes*. The methods of comparative linguistics have much to offer in the study of these processes, but the construction of a protolexicon may not be their most useful contribution.

2 The Formation of New Groupings: Corded Ware and Bell Beakers

If the first error of the champions of an Indo-European 'homeland' was to base their thinking upon the shifting sands of linguistic palaeontology, their second was archaeological. It is one which has bedevilled much of European prehistory, indeed world prehistory in general: to conclude that the emergence of a new pottery style or a new complex of finds in an area indicated the development – or even the arrival – of a new group of people. Modern archaeology is shifting completely away from that kind of 'migrationist' thinking. Probably the most graphic examples are offered by the interesting cases of the Corded Ware People and of the Beaker Folk. Both form an essential link in the chain of argument of those claiming a south Russian homeland and of those pressing for central or northern Europe.

There is absolutely no disagreement about the reality and the widespread nature of the Beaker phenomenon. As we saw in Chapter 2, a Beaker is a drinking vessel, with incised decoration, falling into one of a number of characteristic forms, of which the most famous is the Bell Beaker, so-called after its shape, which the French call 'campaniforme'. Towards the end of the late neolithic period, around 2300 BC following calibrated radiocarbon dates, burials are found in many parts of western Europe containing the

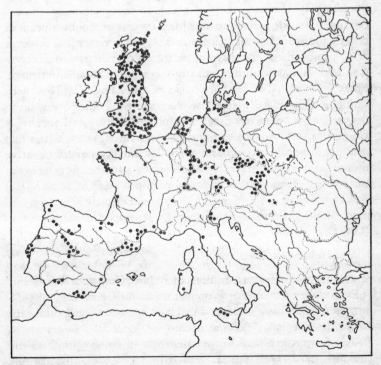

FIG. 4.2 The distribution of Bell Beakers in Europe (*after Childe*).

skeleton of a single individual accompanied by the characteristic drinking vessel and by other items which form a recognizable 'kit'. These do indeed often include stone arrowheads and sometimes a perforated stone object often interpreted as an archer's wristguard, so that the proposal that these people were archers seems well-substantiated. Sometimes there is a copper dagger and on occasions other objects of metal, such as gold earrings. These are among the earliest finds of metal objects in the areas in question. There is, however, no convincing evidence that they rode horses, but there are at least some indications that in western Europe the first appearance of horses' bones is associated with Bell Beakers.[15] Many archaeological studies contain maps of the finds of Beaker burials: Gordon Childe's map of 1949 is shown in FIG. 4.2.[16]

There have been many theories about the origin of the Beaker assemblages. Although there is a fashion today among archaeo-logical theorists for seeing independent origins of innovations, it is difficult to avoid the conclusion that there was a connection of some kind amongst these various finds. In the 1920s, when most changes were accepted as resulting from movements of people, all these things were hailed as the work of a 'Beaker Folk', who, it was claimed, were racially distinct, that is to say that their skull measurements showed them to be distinctly brachycephalic (round-headed). Argument has raged ever since as to whether the origin of this 'folk' was in the west, in Iberia, or in the east, perhaps in Hungary or Yugoslavia, or again in the north, in Scandinavia. Indeed very elaborate theories have been produced to account for the variations in the evidence in even greater detail. The German archaeologist, Edward Sangmeister, developed a theory of a 'Reflux', a *Rückstrom*, whereby Beakers and their accompanying assemblages were developed first in Spain and moved gradually across Europe, to be followed by the Reflux[16] which carried various central-European features back to Iberia.

Even so harsh a critic as Professor Grahame Clark, who in 1966 published an influential paper entitled 'The invasion hypothesis in British prehistory', could not escape the notion of a migration to Britain from continental Europe of people bringing with them the customs of Beaker burial.[17] In 1977, however, the British archaeologist, Stephen Shennan, in his doctoral dissertation entitled

'Bell beakers and their context in central Europe: a new approach',[18] came up with a new set of ideas. He suggested that we should view the Beaker assemblages as 'status kits' – collections of objects possessed by individuals of rather high status in the community, which were used by those persons to assert and display that status, and hence to enhance it. The importance of material goods in the assertion and maintenance of the ranking of prominent individuals within their communities has been increasingly recognized by archaeologists over the past fifteen years. Indeed the basic idea goes back to the very earliest days of archaeology, when excavators recognized the skeletons they were uncovering as 'chiefs' or 'princes' if these were accompanied by rich gravegoods such as gold and amber objects. The gravegoods accompanying Beaker burials are never as rich and impressive as those of the succeeding early bronze age, but they do represent, in most areas where they are found, a new tendency to emphasize the individual during burial by means of accompanying gravegoods of special value.

This approach by Shennan emphasizes an increasing tendency among archaeologists to think in social terms. In Britain the Beaker burials follow a period where there was already much ritual activity documented by the large 'henge' monuments of the late neolithic period. Stonehenge is the most famous of these (although the great stone circle was erected later), but there are other, larger ones, such as Avebury. I suggested in 1974 that one might think of these late neolithic societies as 'group-oriented chiefdoms',[19] where the central power within the societies of the time was expressed in these massive communal works. These could be contrasted with the 'individualizing chiefdoms' of the succeeding early bronze age where rich gravegoods accompanied specially favoured individuals. Shennan suggested that the emergence of Beaker burials, with their accompanying prestige goods, could be seen as part of this process, and as part of the transformation in British society between the neolithic and the early bronze age. He also suggested that the idea of Beakers and the accompanying 'kit' spread rapidly through north and central Europe (and so to Britain) as local leaders copied their neighbours, vying with each other in the display of these fashionable goods:[20]

We have, then, in the Bell Beaker phase, at the very beginning of the Bronze Age a highly significant pattern of contact linking virtually the whole of central and western Europe in what is essentially a time of innovation, diffusion and adoption in various spheres, including ritual and ideology, in a number of very different local situations.

Instead of the old explanation in terms of migration and diffusion it is possible in many cases to recognize a process of what has been termed 'peer polity interaction', where a number of local communities, none more prominent than the next, interact together. In this way a new 'nuclear area', a new 'style zone' comes about, and new things are created and diffused. This is what seems to have happened in the case of the Bell Beakers.[21] What we see emerging in north-central Europe, and soon after in Britain, is a new system. As the British archaeologist, Alasdair Whittle, writes (with particular reference to Britain):[22]

1. There were important changes in environment and resource by the mid-third millennium b.c. which are likely to have affected subsequent economy, settlement and society, providing a situation in which competition for basic resources is plausible particularly in southern England.

2. The Beaker phenomenon was not ethnic, nor was it in essence novel. Attention must be paid to its details, particularly the settlement evidence, to provide an empirical demonstration of this view but the main aim should then be to interpret the phenomenon in other ways.

3. Here it was seen as part of wider and longer-lasting processes of social change in which communal needs for cohesion were increasingly replaced by more individual acquisition of status in response to competition for scarce resources. Many other features of the period may illustrate these processes too. In this sense the specific content of the Beaker phenomenon is of no concern, only its wider function.

These ideas are now at the centre of a whole phase of new research in Britain, where economy, social organization and ideology are taken into account together with their interactions. Of course it soon becomes very detailed. The Swiss archaeologist, Alain Gallay,[23] has given a most plausible review. The overall result of these studies is to admit the significance of the Beaker phenomenon, and to see it as a symptom of very significant changes taking place in European society at that time. These changes were, in part, related to the impact of the new technology of metallurgy, and also to developments in subsistence practice.

All of this means that there were indeed new exchange networks being built up in Europe, and new ideas (and new kinds of competition and emulation) developing because of them. It is perfectly correct to talk of processes of diffusion, but there is no longer a unique centre of diffusion. The interactions are taking place between equals, between peer polities. The old ideas of ethnic influence are thus rejected, and there is no suggestion that there were necessarily significant movements of peoples at that time. Nor is it argued that the élite individuals which we see in the Beaker burials, often under burial mounds or barrows, were incomers. There is no need to argue any widespread occurrence of élite displacement. These were probably local élites, coming into greater prominence partly through their manipulation of the exchange networks, and adopting the paraphernalia of élite display that their neighbours were in some cases already using. In adopting them they sometimes added to them, and these ideas may have been taken up by *their* neighbours. There was a whole network of interactions, and no single point of innovation can be identified.[24]

In these circumstances (in terms of the discussion to be developed in Chapter 6) there is no special argument here in favour of language displacement. The demographic composition in each area was largely unchanged, and in most cases the local élite had local origins. There was plenty of opportunity for the adoption of loan-words: the acquisition of new objects and new techniques offers plenty of scope for that. And the more intensive networks of communication which arose at that time would certainly make easier the spread of linguistic innovations. In these circumstances we can see that this would not have been a time when a new language, even an Indo-European language, would have been dispersed from its 'homeland'. There was nothing particularly 'vagabondic' about the populations involved, and no argument for seeing the Beaker élite as footloose wanderers.

These arguments seem to me totally destructive of the suggestion that there were Kurgan invasions at this time, or that a new Kurgan language spread throughout the regions in question. It is certainly true that the Beaker élite were sometimes buried under a mound, a barrow, which in Russian might very properly be referred to by the term 'kurgan'. But so what? Even if this particular feature had indeed been learnt from south Russia, it scarcely carries with it linguistic implications, other than the possibility of an interesting loan-word. In fact collective burial under burial mounds had been carried out for two thousand years in the west, and the Beaker burials are not the first in these areas to employ single burial.

Very comparable arguments can be applied to the Corded Ware culture of north Europe. Again it is not in doubt that there is a large area in which burials occur, usually single burials, under burial mounds, with the deceased accompanied by cord-decorated pottery, sometimes with a 'battle-axe' (i.e. perforated stone axe). In 1969 the Czech archaeologist, Evžen Neustupny, wrote an influential and persuasive article on 'The Economy of the Corded Ware Culture'[25] in which he showed that there was no good argument for the widely-held notion that these were nomad pastoralists with an economy different from that of other farming communities of neolithic Europe. And in 1981 the East German specialist, Alexander Haüsler, examined in detail the arguments for an eastern origin of the Corded Ware cultures, and argued firmly for a local origin, dealing also with the implications for the Indo-European problem.[26]

The socio-ideological approach has recently been applied by the British archaeologist, Christopher Tilley, to the origin of the Corded Ware/Battle Axe cultures of Scandinavia. There the transition is between the middle neolithic TRB (i.e. Trichterbecher = Funnel Beaker) culture and the succeeding BAC (Battle Axe/ Corded Ware) groups. As Tilley emphasizes:[27]

Both the TRB and BAC appear to have been characterized by cereal-based economies, supplemented by hunting, fishing, gathering and livestock . . . In phase IV of the TRB all aspects of ceramic design are simplified and at some stage the tombs ceased to be centres of ritual activity and the change to BAC occurred. The individual is asserted for the first time in burial practices and there is little evidence of elaborate ritual surrounding the funerary activities. A small range of grave goods accompany the dead, but no hierarchical distinctions are apparent.

Tilley's approach to the Corded Ware is in some ways very different from Shennan's view of the Beakers, but they see no fundamental change in farming practice, and no incursion by incoming groups: in both cases the explanation is framed primarily in social terms.

It should be noted that none of these studies excludes the possibility that local groups might well be biologically distinctive. The Swiss physical anthropologist, R. Menk, has indeed suggested that the Beaker-using population of Switzerland was different physically from contemporaries of other cultures. But he points out that:[28]

> The Corded Ware complex is biologically heterogeneous. The local groups of the core area (Central Germany, Czechoslovakia, Poland) form a very homogeneous bloc . . . This bloc shows no biological affinities to the Ukrainian Kurgan populations.

It would in my view be wrong to place much weight upon conclusions drawn from physical anthropology until the methodology is better developed. At any time the existence of local populations who are to some extent biologically distinguishable should cause little surprise.

The overall implications of these conclusions about the Beaker and Corded Ware cultures are considerable. We have seen how major culture complexes may emerge through the operation of local factors. Through networks of interaction they can be influential over wide areas, leading to the widespread adoption of new ideologies and new ways of expressing them. Nothing in what we have seen suggests that this was a period when language replacement was a particularly active process. These conclusions are also important for the later bronze age and iron age, when other very wide-ranging culture complexes are seen (the so-called Urnfields). They are also relevant to our understanding of the Celts and Germans (see Chapter 9).

3 The Dynamics of Population Change

The existing homeland theories, as we have seen, make the fundamental mistake of equating the emergence of a new culture complex with the intrusion of a new linguistic group, and they rely unwisely upon the resources of linguistic palaeontology for a physical description of the homeland. Unfortunately they also suffer from a third, equally damaging deficiency: they give absolutely no clear and adequate indication as to *why* there should have been a spread at all.

In the old days of Kossinna it might be possible to suggest that the innate racial superiority of the Proto-Indo-Europeans allowed them to expand their territories at a certain point in time and conquer most of Europe and northern India. That was always naïve as well as arrogant, and such ideas of racial superiority are happily less prevalent today. But even accepting that unpersuasive premise, the theories had internal inadequacies. They rarely explained why the Indo-Europeans should choose that particular moment to break out, as it were. Or to put the matter another way, they did not explain why these Indo-Europeans had hidden their light under a bushel, for so long upon the steppes of south Russia, before setting out to fulfil their fateful destiny.

No post-war writer has adopted such arguments, and there seems no need to take them seriously today. Why then should there have been a dispersal from the supposed homeland at all?

Two possible mechanisms for language displacement can be proposed. The first is the demographic one: that there were massive transfers of population or significant technical advances allowing a significant increase of population. That view was adopted rather unthinkingly by earlier writers, who liked to use the metaphor of a swarm of bees: the Indo-Europeans *swarmed* from their northern *hive*. But it is not at all clear why the population density should be greater in the 'homeland' than in neighbouring areas. That explanation simply does not apply.

The other main theory is élite dominance. In some cases an incoming minority can indeed take control of an existing system, and the takeover can sometimes result in language replacement. However, for a really effective takeover, there needs to be some pre-existing hierarchical structure to be taken over. And while in Britain it could be argued that the late neolithic monuments imply the existence of chiefdoms, the evidence from continental Europe does not always lead to the same conclusion. Even more essential is the existence of some hierarchical social structure within the invading group who will form the new élite. It is difficult to see the necessary conquest, and the new élite administration, being brought about by immigrant groups whose social structure is essentially egalitarian. Yet the case for an effective ranked society, for the existence of chiefdoms, amongst the 'Kurgan' groups in their south Russian homeland has never been effectively argued. Professor Gimbutas has given the best account,[29] and she lists several village settlements within what is sometimes termed the Srednij Stog II culture, at Dereivka in the lower Dnieper region, for instance. There are also various hill-fort sites, including Mikhajlovka. She looks primarily to the Maikop tomb away to the east in the Kuban region of the north Caucasus for rich graves in the 'homeland'. In the Balkans, where she lists several Ochre Graves as documenting the Kurgan immigrants, it is not clear that they are of particularly high status.

Nor is it entirely clear what made the Kurgan people efficient as warriors. The appeals of older generations to the 'warlike spirit' of the Proto-Indo-Europeans are entirely unsubstantiated: the suggestion that they were mounted warriors does not carry conviction. There is indeed the strong likelihood that the horse was intensively exploited in the steppes of south Russia at about this time and there is some evidence that it was used for riding. The story of the use of the horse is indeed a crucial one for the steppelands, but there is little evidence for westward incursions by mounted warriors at this time: that case cannot really be made before the late bronze age.

The central idea underlying much that is written is that the people of the homeland were pastoral nomads, and that this somehow gave them some adaptive advantage in their move westwards. This idea, however, quite wrongly implies that a pastoralist society is particularly suited to the economic exploitation of central and western Europe, as indeed it is for the steppe lands of eastern Europe and of central Asia. We have already seen that recent work on the Beaker and Corded Ware peoples suggests that they were as much settled farmers as their predecessors.

Around this time, late in the European neolithic, there was a move towards a more intensive subsistence economy in many areas, involving the increasing use of milk and cheese, of animal traction for the plough, and perhaps of wool and hides. This 'secondary products revolution', as Andrew Sherratt[30] has termed it, probably did allow the more intensive exploitation of areas that were not used before, and may well have led to more widespread grazing of livestock, perhaps in uplands which were not previously used. Transhumance, with the moving of cattle away from the village and up to summer pastures, may have developed at this time. But central and western Europe is not really suited to *nomad* pastoralism, with the implication that the whole community leaves its winter base during the summer months and moves over great distances. Of course the reason that Europe is not effectively used in this way is that it gets by very well, with a higher density of exploitation, with mixed farming. Nomad pastoralist economies generally operate either where farming economies are not very successful, or (more often) on the margins of such economies. The development of a greater degree of pastoralism during the later neolithic, in the regions where it did occur, may have filled an ecological niche that was not previously well used. It no doubt supplemented the existing pattern: it did not replace it.

There is, moreover, no reason to think that any move towards the greater use of domestic animal resources was prompted from outside each individual area. The domestic animals were already available in each. Such developments as did take place may be seen as part of a locally-occurring process of intensification: they need not indicate the arrival of new groups of people. Thus while it is perfectly possible that a nomad pastoralist society did develop in the south Russian steppes at about the time suggested, this development in itself is not likely to have influenced central or western Europe very much, either directly or indirectly.

It is interesting, also, to enquire more closely into the origins of this nomadic way of life in the steppes. How did the steppe pastoralist economy originate? As indicated earlier, nomad pastoralism is always dependent in part on the existence of agriculturists. It is clear that nomad pastoralism normally develops out of mixed farming and herding, where a pattern of transhumance can be adapted to one of true nomadism appropriate to the more difficult steppe environment. If the problem is put in these terms, it is clear that the Kurgan pastoralists must in some senses be a secondary growth following upon a primary mixed farming economy. And where were these primary mixed farmers? The most obvious candidates are those on the western fringes of the south Russia steppe lands: the Cucuteni culture of Romania and the Tripolye culture of the Ukraine.

Ward Goodenough, of the University of Pennsylvania, has persuasively argued this case:[31]

> Once the steppe was conquered it inevitably became a source of out migration. Until it was conquered it was a waste, waiting for people on its periphery to evolve a technology that would allow them to begin to move in and exploit it . . .
>
> What I have been saying obviously leads to a conclusion that the Battle Axe or Kurgan cultures originated about 3500 BC in an area bordering on the region occupied by Cucuteni and Tripolye peoples, who themselves practised a mixed farming and herding economy.

Goodenough rightly sees here the 'evolutionary background of pastoral nomadism as an adaptation of an older European transhumance to the more difficult steppe environment'. This view has, of course, revolutionary consequences for the 'homeland' theory. For it means that the initial colonization of the western part of the steppes took place from the west. The first language of the western steppes must, on this basis, have been the language spoken by the farmers of the neighbouring lands to the west.

4 Conclusion

Three lines of argument thus lead us to reject the notion of a south Russian homeland for the Proto-Indo-Europeans. The main reason for the failure to locate such a homeland arises, I think, first from an unwise reliance on linguistic palaeontology in a rather uncritical way. Secondly it is a migrationist view. And thirdly it springs from a tendency not to consider with sufficient care the *processes* at work. It is all too easy to equate a pottery style with a linguistic group and to proceed upon that rather simplistic basis.

These critical comments do not imply that the works under review have not come up with many relevant observations, and with points which need explanation. Professor Gimbutas, for instance, and archaeologist colleagues in Romania and the Ukraine, have rightly shown that after the early Cucuteni and Tripolye cultures in those areas, there follow pottery styles which have much more in common with those of the steppes. It is possible that once the new pastoralist economy of the steppes was established, the arable/steppe boundary may have shifted some way westward. What may have been in reality an evolution from mixed farming to pastoralism in that area could thus appear in the archaeological record as a westward movement. Nor need one doubt that several of the characteristics of steppe culture which did then develop were indeed taken up in neighbouring lands to the west. These 'Kurgan' influences may in some cases have involved some movement of people. In others they may simply reflect the adoption of some practices derived from the steppes by the populations on their western margins. At a detailed level there is much work to be done in following up these ideas, but from the standpoint of Europe as a whole, it is difficult to believe that there was any significant and sustained movement of population from eastern to central Europe at this time, around 3500 to 3000 BC. This is not the solution to the Indo-European problem, although it may well be relevant to it.

5. Language and Language Change

The study of language has developed remarkably in the past twenty years, and even the more limited field of historical linguistics, focusing upon the origins and development of languages, encompasses a vast literature. To attempt a comprehensive survey in a concise space would be difficult, and for an archaeologist to do so foolhardy, but at least I can try and indicate some of the ideas and concepts which seem particularly useful to our present theme. Things have moved a long way since the days of a century ago, when immensely erudite scholars, mostly German, were comparing the vocabulary and the grammar of all the Indo-European languages then known, with great thoroughness. We can see today that on drawing inferences they made a number of limiting assumptions, which inevitably restricted the historical conclusions to which they came. However, when one appreciates that they needed to understand each of the languages which they were comparing, one can only contemplate their achievements with considerable admiration.

Until the more recent development of sociolinguistics, many scholars tended to have rather a monolithic view of individual languages. Languages were seen as clearly differentiated one from another, and the territories in which they were spoken possessed distinct boundaries. Languages changed in well defined ways, the sound changes following patterns so regular in their behaviour that they could be said to follow laws. Today the variations *within* a language at a set time are given more prominence – the spatial variations reflecting different dialects, and also the different customs of pronunciation, vocabulary and grammar which accompany social distinctions within a community.

The phonological regularities, the changes in pronunciation which took place over time, so that related words in adjacent languages can have quite different appearances, were the first to be understood. Very early on it was realized that there were uniform phonetic correlations between certain languages, and there were regular rules which allowed the scholar to move from one to the other.[1] For instance the consonant **p** in most Indo-European languages is paralleled in Germanic languages, including English, by **f**: e.g.

Latin **pes**: English **foot**
Latin **piscis**; English **fish**
Latin **pater**; English **father**.

Or the Germanic sound **th** is paralleled in most of the other related languages by **t**:[2] e.g.

Latin **tres**: English **three**
Latin **tenuis**: English **thin**
Latin **tacere** ('to be silent'): Gothic **thahan**.

The Germanic **h** is the equivalent of **k** in the related languages: e.g.

Latin **centum**: English **hundred**
Latin **caput**: English **head**
Latin **cornu**: English **horn**.

The patterns of phonetic difference between most of the languages which are related can today be described by a whole series of generalizations, which bring out the underlying relationships very clearly. The phenomenon of sound change is now one of the best described in the whole of linguistics, yet interestingly enough precisely *why* such changes should occur at all is very little understood.

In addition to the change in the form of individual words occasioned by these transformations, there are changes in their meaning. And of course over time there are significant changes in the grammatical form of certain words, such as verbs, and in the structure of sentences. All of this is the bread and butter of linguistics and it is through the study of these things that the relationships between the various languages come to be understood. So that while we shall not seek here to assimilate the huge body of scholarship which is needed to understand these relationships, we should remember that it is detailed work of this kind which allows one to determine the affinities between languages, and which sustains all the further statements about possible historical reconstructions which one may wish to make.

The general classification of languages is however central to our interests. In the early days it was carried out essentially on the genealogical model: in terms of family relationships. Closely similar languages, like French and Italian, were linked in groups, and the groups in turn were linked as one large language family. Resemblances between the languages were considered entirely in terms of parenthood, and this whole model of change was made explicit in the family tree (*Stammbaum*) model proposed by Augustus Schleicher[3] in 1862 for the Indo-European languages.

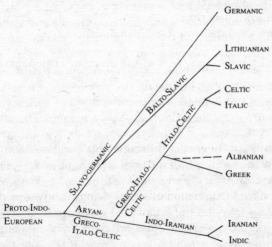

FIG. 5.1 The family tree model for the Indo-European languages (*after Schleicher and Lehmann*).

It was assumed that resemblances between languages arose from their common origin, and languages closely similar to each other were understood to have separated or diverged from each other only comparatively recently. In the tree as shown above, the divergence has gone only so far as to arrive at the principal language groups as they existed nearly two thousand years ago, before further divergence (in most of the groups) produced the contemporary Indo-European languages of today.

In such models it was generally assumed that, until the moment of divergence, a language is relatively uniform throughout the area in which it was spoken. The underlying human reality was thought of in terms of the migrations of peoples. So each split or divergence came about when groups of people occupying a language territory divided, with at least one part of them going off to seek a new home. It was axiomatic to this model, as indeed it is to most others, that once languages, or rather their speakers, become separated and are no longer in contact, they drift apart linguistically.

This whole model was, of course, profoundly influenced by the evolutionary approach of Charles Darwin, and the analogy with the formation of new species is very obvious. The tendency for languages to become less similar after they have separated may be likened to the genetic drift which increasingly separates species isolated from each other. At the time of separation, the pronunciation of words, their meaning and their form and grammatical arrangement would have been identical. As time passes, some words in one of the branches would fall into disuse, while others would no doubt be invented. The pronunciation of words would alter and grammatical convention gradually change. The precise meaning of words could gradually change also, by the process which some linguists refer to as 'semantic drift'.

If we follow such a model for the origins of linguistic diversity, it is possible to reconstruct earlier language forms on the basis of the evidence provided by their modern descendents, using the *comparative method*. This involves the use of the phonological regularities discussed earlier, by which the sound shifts in words can be understood more systematically. For instance, if we consider the words for 'eight' in French, Italian and Portuguese, they might not at first seem to be derived from a common source:[4]

French **huit**; Italian **otto**; Portuguese **oito**

But by assembling other examples it is possible to see how they might be derived from a single common source in their ancestral proto-language. If we take also:

'milk': French **lait**; Italian **latte**; Spanish **leche**; Portuguese **leite**

'fact': French **fait**; Italian **fatto**; Spanish **hecho**; Portuguese **feito** we can suggest earlier forms of these words as ***okto**, ***lakte**, ***faktu**, using the convention where the asterisk indicates a reconstructed form rather than one which has been observed. In this case the procedure can of course be corroborated because the relevant proto-language is in fact known to us, and we can compare these forms with the relevant forms of the Latin nouns: **octo**, **lactem**, and **factum**.

By this means of linguistic palaeontology a vocabulary of reconstructed words, the 'protolexicon' can be built up for the proto-language in question. It depends for its reconstruction on the family tree model of linguistic change, just as the traditional palaeontologists depended on an evolutionary tree model in establishing the relationships between the various species of fossil animals and plants.

The American linguist, Leonard Bloomfield,[5] has however pointed out that:

> The comparative method assumes that each branch or language bears independent witness of the forms of the parent language, and that identities or correspondences among the related languages reveal features of the parent speech. This is the same thing as assuming, firstly that the parent community was completely uniform as to language, and secondly that this parent community split suddenly and sharply into two or more daughter communities, which lost all contact with each other.

These assumptions do indeed work tolerably for the descendents of Latin – and it should be remembered that the derivation of the Romance languages from Latin was the prototype example when the notion of the family tree model was applied to languages, and it remains the most frequently quoted example. However, as Bloomfield concludes:[6]

> The earlier students of Indo-European did not realize that the family-tree diagram was merely a statement of their method: they accepted the uniform parent languages and their sudden and clear-cut splitting, as historical realities.

Although the family tree model is a perfectly coherent one, it certainly does not adequately take into account the variety of ways in which languages change. A language may borrow a word for something from a neighbouring language. Such *loan-words* often describe new products. The word *alcohol*, for instance, was widely adopted when the process of distillation became more widely known. Like many of the words in the European languages beginning with the prefix *al-* it is a loan-word from the Arabic, but a word need not refer to a new commodity to spread in this way. This sort of lexical borrowing is in fact very common. The Germanic languages, for instance, have taken many words from Latin, of which the following are a few examples:[7]

Latin	Old English	Old High German	Modern English	Modern German
altare	altare	altari	altar	Altar
caseus	cese	kasi	cheese	Käse
cuppa	cuppe	chuph	cup	Kopf
milia	mil	mila	mile	Meile
moneta	mynet	munizza	mint	Münze
palma	palma	palma	palm	Palme
planta	plante	pflanza	plant	Pflanze
prunum	plume	pflumo	plum	Pflaume
tegula	tigele	ziagal	tile	Ziegel
vinum	win	win	wine	Wein

Table XII   German borrowing from Latin

It should be noted that not all of these words have retained exactly the same meaning after borrowing, but the relationship is in each case clear. It is well documented that these words were all borrowed from Latin, amongst some five hundred others, during the early period of contact with Latin. This illustrates how the family tree model in its simplest form overlooks the possibility that two languages may have passed through a period of common development, usually when their speakers occupied adjacent territories. They do not need to be 'genetically related', i.e. descended from a common parent language, for this to be so. For instance the languages of north India, which share a common Indo-European origin, nonetheless show signs of common development with languages in that general area which have a different origin and belong to the Dravidian language family. This common development is seen in the loan words from one to another, and in the occurrence of several grammatical forms which they share.

It was in response to this difficulty that the German linguist, Johannes Schmidt,[8] in 1872 introduced his *wave hypothesis*. Different linguistic changes may spread, like waves, over a speech area, and each change may be carried out over part of the area which does not coincide with the part covered by an earlier change. It is necessary here to consider more precisely the areas where a particular word or word form are located. This can be done in practice by drawing lines (isoglosses) on the map to separate places which differ as to any feature of language: an isogloss will thus enclose the area where a particular linguistic form is seen. The result of successive waves will result in a network of isoglosses. The cumulative effect of such changes can be considerable. In particular, to take an extreme case, if one dialect gains a political or commercial predominance of some sort over adjacent dialects, those nearest to this central dialect may give up their own peculiarities and come in time to speak only that central dialect.

Schmidt's wave model can be applied to the Indo-European languages to give the over-simplified diagram seen in Fig. 5.2. Here it would be perfectly possible for all these Indo-European languages or language groups to have differentiated over the years

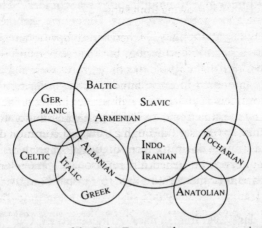

FIG. 5.2 Distribution of the Indo-European languages seen in terms of the wave theory (*after Schmidt and Lehmann*).

in the same location, in the areas in which they are now found. We could imagine the entire area in which they came to be spoken occupied initially by people who spoke a single Proto-Indo-European language. Following various local divergences, the subsequent groupings could then have come about by the operation of the wave model. In this way, the patterns on the linguistic map could have built up without any movements of groups of people at all. But of course we do not have to opt wholeheartedly for the wave model in this way. We could easily prefer a combination of the two models, where there was first some splitting from an original proto-language, involving some displacement of people, followed by the addition of subsequent effects by the wave mechanism.

One important consequence here is that a language should not be thought of as a concrete and well-defined entity. When there are many isoglosses enclosing the same area, we may regard the line which they jointly follow as constituting a language boundary. They need not follow the same line, so the change from one language to another need not be an abrupt one. And two more closely related languages may each have features in common with their own neighbours which they do not share with each other. This feature produces a slightly more complicated diagram which is based on Schmidt's, with modifications by Schrader.[9] The details of the resemblances need not worry us. The point is that the lines are in effect isoglosses, and they show relationships between the languages which are more complicated than any which could be conveyed by means of a family tree.

If we are interested in early languages, the difference between these two models is of crucial significance. This point may be illustrated by a distinction to which historical linguists in the past have attached particular importance, between two large subdivisions in the Indo-European languages. The basis for the distinction is a contrast between the consonant s in one group and ch or h or k in the other. This is seen, for instance, in the word for 'ten':[10]

Sanskrit **dasa**, Old Iranian **dasa**, Armenian **tasn**, Old Church Slavic **deseti**, and Lithuanian **desimt**: *versus* Greek **deka**, Latin **decem**, Old Irish **deich**, and Gothic **taihun**.

This is generally termed the *satem-centum* subdivision, after the word for 'hundred'. The eastern languages are labelled *satem* after the Old Iranian form, and the western languages *centum* after the Latin for a hundred. When this classification was first proposed, scholars assumed that the speakers of Proto-Indo-European had divided into two groups, and that in the eastern group a sound change took place which differentiated the eastern from the western dialects.

Until the early years of this century, the distinction could be set out as follows:[11]

Western Group (*centum*)	Eastern Group (*satem*)
Germanic	Baltic
Venetic	Slavic
Illyrian	Albanian
Celtic	Thracian
Italic	Phrygian
Greek	Armenian
	Iranian
	Indian

Table XIII   The *satem/centum* subdivision

This pleasant geographical consistency was first disrupted by the study of the Hittite language of early Anatolia, which was made possible in 1915 by the decipherment of the inscribed clay tablets found at the Hittite capital of Boghazköy (see Chapter 3). Hittite is a *centum* language, and thus disrupts the convenient distinction between east and west. The distinction received a much more serious setback with the discovery at the beginning of this century in Chinese Turkestan, of Buddhist writings from the sixth to eighth centuries AD, which are clearly Indo-European. The language was given the name Tocharian, and it too is a *centum* language. The notion of a neat, east/west split, which would have been nicely explained on the family tree model, becomes much less plausible in the light of these discoveries, and the *centum/satem* difference is not in itself accorded much significance today.

This change can, however, be accommodated much more readily by the wave model, by thinking in terms of dialect geography. The explanation might now be that the innovation of changing some **ks** to sibilants, as in the word for 'a hundred', spread through the central area, bringing about the sibilant *satem* form in Indo-Iranian, Armenian and Albanian and, imperfectly, in Slavic and Baltic. On this model the original, earlier *centum* form remains untouched in the periphery (Tocharian, Germanic, Celtic) outside the ripples of the wave, with the innovation localized in the middle. The historical reconstruction is thus entirely different from that on the family tree model. Nothing could more clearly illustrate that different reconstructions arise very readily from differences in methodology.

This example also illustrated another important point: that the chronology must also be taken into account wherever possible. Hittite, one of the earliest Indo-European languages recorded, is a *centum* language, yet it is more 'centrally' placed than are the Indo-Iranian languages to the east. The change from *centum* to *satem*, if it took place in this way, must have done so later.

Even on the wave model it is usual to assume a common ancestral origin for the languages within a language group. It would logically be possible to carry further the underlying notion that similarities between languages can develop through time, by a process of convergence (through contact). This indeed was the interesting position adopted by the Russian linguist, N. S. Trubetskoy, in 1939. He argued that the presence of the same word in a number of languages need not suggest that these languages descended from a common parent:[12]

> There is, then, no powerful ground for the assumption of a unitary Indogerman protolanguage, from which the individual Indogerman language groups would derive. It is just as plausible that the ancestors of the Indogerman language groups were originally quite dissimilar, and that through continuing contact, mutual influence and word borrowing became significantly closer to each other, without however going so far as to become identical.

Trubetskoy criticized severely the dangerous assumptions which led to the construction of a supposed Proto-Indo-European language:[13]

> The homeland, the race and the culture of a supposed Proto-

Indo-European population has been discussed, a population which may possibly never have existed.

Instead he set out to define a number of linguistic criteria by which an Indo-European language might be recognized. If a language was found to fulfil these six criteria it was to be seen as Indo-European; if it didn't, it wasn't. He imagined an earlier time when no language would have done so, and he suggested that progressive contact and influence between neighbouring languages had produced changes in many of them which did in fact fulfil the necessary criteria, so that in this way they *became* Indo-European in terms of the definition.

This is a beautifully logical position, and it is illuminating to set it against the family tree model, from which it differs completely. Few linguists would go so far today; and most point to basic structural resemblances between languages which would be much more difficult to transmit or evolve through contact than would mere loan-words. I have already mentioned the principle that adjacent and genetically unrelated languages can influence each other in their grammatical structure as well as in their vocabulary. Trubetskoy's model reminds us that language evolution is a much more complicated process than the early historical linguists imagined. However it is not necessary to go as far as Trubetskoy to see how damaging the idea of convergence, which his theory shares with the wave model, is for the comparative method, and for the construction of a protolexicon.

Loan-words and linguistic innovation must be the enemies of linguistic palaeontology. For when we find the same word, or cognate words, in a number of languages, we cannot assume – even if we accept that those languages did derive from a common ancestor – that the term in question was already present in that proto-language. It might as easily be the product of innovation. Thus, while some of the terms in Latin in Table XII may themselves have been borrowed from elsewhere, others must be regarded as innovations in Latin which were then borrowed by the Germanic languages. We are thus emphatically not justified in suggesting a reconstructed Proto-Indo-European form for each.

It must be admitted, however, that the considerable antiquity of some words, whether or not loan-words, can be correctly judged when they or their derivatives are found in nearby languages, and when they can be shown to have been transformed by regular sound changes. Thus the Germanic 'Karl' (presumably from Charlemagne) gives the Proto-Slavonic *'Karl' and this in turn the Russian 'Korólj' and the Polish 'Král'. The existence in Polish and Russian of these related forms, derivative in a regular way from a Proto-Slavonic prototype, is a good indication that these are not recent loan-words but that the common prototype did indeed exist in Proto-Slavonic.

Even if we should find the same word for something in all Indo-European languages, this would not guarantee it a place in the protolexicon. This is particularly so if it might itself represent a technical innovation, like a previously unknown metal (e.g. tin, or platinum) or a new product, like the wheel or the stirrup. To give a modern example it is totally unsurprising if a new substance, like penicillin, or a new development, like a helicopter, should carry with it the word by which it becomes known in nearly all languages. Sometimes the word will be borrowed directly, or sometimes paraphrased into the language in what is termed a 'calque' (e.g. the German *Fernsprecher* (far-speaker) in place of 'telephone', which is of course itself a synthetic word coined in recent times from ancient Greek components). Thus we can see how the development of linguistics as a discipline has made what once seemed a reliable procedure, the comparative method, something much less secure.

One of the more recent developments in linguistics has been the development of a concept of the linguistic area, and the detailed study of the distribution of linguistic forms in space. Linguistic area refers here not to the distribution in space of a single language, but of related features in a larger group of languages.[14] It implies an approach to classification which is more concerned with spatial variation at a given time than with the historical relationships which may underlie that variation.

In a sense the family tree model and the wave model both reflect different approaches to classification. If we are interested in reaching towards Proto-Indo-European, then spatial factors do have to be taken carefully into account. As Bloomfield remarks:[15]

If Germanic and Balto-Slavic, for instance, have passed through a period of common development, then any agreement between them guarantees nothing about Primitive-Indo-European, but if they have not passed through a period of common development, then such an agreement, on the family-tree principle, is practically certain evidence for a trait of Primitive Indo-European.

This is an important observation, for it does indeed carry with it significant spatial implications. It is, in fact, the resemblances between languages most distant from each other spatially which can least easily arise from the wave-like diffusion of an innovation, and are thus most likely to be the result, rather, of a relationship explicable in family tree terms. Even so, as noted earlier, this will not safeguard us against an almost universal loan-word accompanying some new technical innovation which has spread through the area by some diffusion process. Nor will it prevent our taking as Proto-Indo-European a form which has diffused throughout the entire region under consideration as a result of a wave-spread. Such occurrences are, however, likely to be rare, since, as we shall see, there are intervening areas in Western Asia where non-Indo-European languages are spoken.

Recently linguistic classification has taken a number of new directions. In one of these, languages are classified in terms of characteristics of their syntax. Much attention is now given to word order, which correlates with other significant features. Verb-object (VO) languages (where the verb precedes the object in the order of words) and object-verb (OV) languages may be contrasted informatively. These are seen to be features which can change with time as a language develops. The classification is therefore a synchronic one – it is concerned with present features of the language and does not directly concern itself with earlier forms. Yet the approach can be applied usefully in the historical field. The American linguist, Winfred Lehmann,[16] pointed out that Latin and Old English contain many OV constructions. He suggests that Proto-Indo-European was OV, since this is what we see for the oldest Indo-European texts in Hittite, Vedic Sanskrit and Greek. Today, however, while the Asiatic branches are OV in structure (Indo-

Aryan and Armenian), the southern European languages are consistently VO (Albanian, Greek and Romance, as well as Celtic), while the northern Indo-European languages are inconsistently VO (Persian, Slavic, Baltic, Germanic). These observations suggest new fields of inquiry which may lead to a better understanding of language change, but they do not suggest any obvious conclusions at present.[17]

A further trend in recent years has been the development of sociolinguistics[18] – the study of the relationship between language variation and social difference. This is of crucial relevance for the understanding of language change in general – since new words do not at first spread uniformly through the population, but are adopted by specific social groups and spread from them to others. It is particularly relevant when two languages are spoken in the same area. This generally occurs as a result of the displacement of a number of people and, in the process, some of these people, or more likely their children become bilingual. The distinction is often made by linguists between the upper or dominant language, spoken by a conquering or otherwise more privileged group, and the lower language spoken by the subject people, or by immigrants of low status. Bloomfield makes the important generalization that:[19]

> In all cases, *it is the lower language which borrows* predominantly from the upper.
>
> Accordingly, if the upper language survives, it remains as it was except for a few cultural loans, such as it might take from any neighbour. The Romance languages contain only a few cultural loan-words from the languages that were spoken in their territory before the Roman conquest; English has only a few cultural loan-words from the Celtic languages of Britain . . . In the case of conquest, the cultural loans which remain in the surviving upper language are chiefly place names . . .
>
> On the other hand, if the lower language survives, it bears the marks of the struggle in the shape of copious borrowings. English, with its loan-words from Norman-French and its enormous layer of semi-learned (Latin-French) vocabulary is the classical instance of this.

It is sometimes the case, however, that a (lower) language which does not survive, does have influences both in vocabulary and in pronunciation upon the surviving (upper) language. In such cases the extinct (lower) language is referred to as a substratum, which leaves some traces upon the surviving speech.

It has been emphasized, also, that language is not used only to communicate, but sometimes to exclude. Language is an important component of ethnicity,[20] of group awareness. Linguistic boundaries may be deliberately maintained, and be determined by the territorial boundaries of a particular society. The nature of the social organization can thus play a major role in determining the spatial behaviour of the language.

These generalizations are of considerable interest, and the relationship of linguistic factors with social ones is of real relevance to the archaeologist. For we have no direct evidence whatever (from the time in question) about the language that was spoken in prehistoric times but we do have evidence of the social organization of past societies.

One other recent development in the field of historical linguistics is of great potential relevance to the historical understanding of particular languages and language groups. This is the approach known as glottochronology.[21] The basic idea is a very simple one. It begins with the general observation that the greater the time-depth

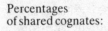

Percentages
of shared cognates:

A-B   40
A-C   20
A-D   20
B-C   20
B-D   20
C-D   65

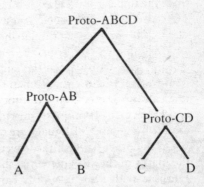

FIG. 5.3 The use of lexicostatistical data to infer history of linguistic descent: a high percentage of cognate words implies closeness of family relationship (*after Clark*).

which separates the members of a language family from the point of separation from their common ancestor, the greater the degree of differentiation between them. In practice they differ, so far as the vocabulary is concerned, because some words drop out of use and are replaced by new words. So two languages which were identical in their vocabulary at the time of separation or splitting become increasingly different as time goes on, through word loss, and through innovation. The exponents of glottochronology, notably Morris Swadesh, claimed that, for the core of essential words in a language, this process took place at a constant rate.

Swadesh set out a basic core vocabulary of two hundred words, later using only a hundred words (see below).[22]

1	I	26	root	51	breasts	76	rain
2	you	27	bark	52	heart	77	stone
3	we	28	skin	53	liver	78	sand
4	this	29	flesh	54	drink	79	earth
5	that	30	blood	55	eat	80	cloud
6	who	31	bone	56	bite	81	smoke
7	what	32	grease	57	see	82	fire
8	not	33	egg	58	hear	83	ash
9	all	34	horn	59	know	84	burn
10	many	35	tail	60	sleep	85	path
11	one	36	feather	61	die	86	mountain
12	two	37	hair	62	kill	87	red
13	big	38	head	63	swim	88	green
14	long	39	ear	64	fly	89	yellow
15	small	40	eye	65	walk	90	white
16	woman	41	nose	66	come	91	black
17	man	42	mouth	67	lie	92	night
18	person	43	tooth	68	sit	93	hot
19	fish	44	tongue	69	stand	94	cold
20	bird	45	claw	70	give	95	full
21	dog	46	foot	71	say	96	new
22	louse	47	knee	72	sun	97	good
23	tree	48	hand	73	moon	98	round
24	seed	49	belly	74	star	99	dry
25	leaf	50	neck	75	water	100	name

Table XIV   Basic core vocabulary

The procedure followed by the glottochronologists, when the time of splitting of two related languages is to be determined, is to list the equivalent words from the languages under consideration, and note the pairs which, on the grounds of their similarity (taking into account the known laws of sound shift) appear to be or are known to be cognates. These are then assumed to be retained from the common ancestor language, while the words which have different forms in the two languages under consideration are assumed to differ because the original word has been lost in one or other (or indeed in both) of the languages. The number of word-pairs which are cognate, out of the original list of a hundred, is thus a measure of the closeness (of the retention of the basic core vocabulary) of the two languages. Conversely the number of pairs that are now different are an indication of the extent to which words have been lost, and hence a measure of the time since the two languages originally separated.

In the original study,[23] various pairs of languages were compared, such as Old English and Middle English, the Latin of Plautus and early modern French, ancient Chinese and modern Mandarin and so on. It was concluded that the average retention rate was 81 per cent per millennium. When the original word list was shortened to the hundred words listed above, the rate was adjusted to 86 per cent per millennium.

Following these arguments, and using this standard retention rate as a guide, the date of splitting of any two related languages could be calculated using the assumption that over a period of a thousand years, each of the languages would have retained 86 per cent of the basic vocabulary of the common protolanguage.[24] It was claimed that these regularities remained valid until the level of merely chance similarity is reached, which is set at about 8 per cent. This would correspond, on the method outlined, to a time depth of 11.7 thousand years.

Various computations have been undertaken on this basis,[25] offering as conclusions that Spanish and Portuguese split at about AD 1586, Italian and French at the same date, Romanian and Italian in 1130 etc. English and Dutch would have split in AD 860 and English and German in 590 and so on.

Some linguists have criticized these calculations on the grounds

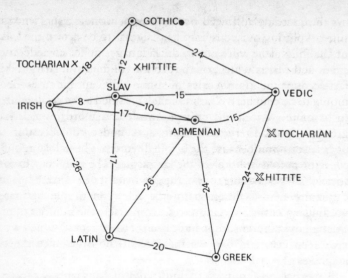

FIG. 5.4 Relationships between different Indo-European languages based on glottochronological correlations. The numbers indicate the notional time in centuries prior to the 13th century BC when divergence between the pairs of languages took place (*based on Escalante and Swadesh*).

that they do not always give precisely the right answers. It is known, for instance, that the Germanic languages became separated at rather earlier dates than those proposed. But to my mind the astonishing thing is that the answers from such calculations are in some cases so close to a date of differentiation which can be established on independent grounds.

There are three principal reasons for criticism here, as I see it.

In the first place, the whole enterprise is predicated upon an absolute family tree model for change. The difference between languages is determined by the date of splitting, and nothing else.

Secondly, and this is a related criticism, the presence of loan-words, which have been adopted by both languages since the period of splitting, is bound to increase the number of apparent cognates, and thus lead to underestimation of the time since splitting. But even if one had some reliable means of spotting all the loan-words – which one does not – the first objection would still be relevant.

The third and main reason for criticism, however, is that there is not the faintest plausible *a priori* reason for assuming that languages suffer word loss at a constant rate.[26] Quite the contrary, the lessons of sociolinguistics teach us that social factors – which differ between times and places – are highly relevant to linguistic change. Such factors as population density, and the extent of interaction commonly occurring between individuals and communities, are bound to be of relevance. The rate of language change among mobile groups might be very different from the rate amongst a sedentary population. Some social groups deliberately use language differences to emphasize their own identity. The extent to which the society uses written records, and written texts within its educational system, will also have a crucial bearing upon the rate of vocabulary change. Even setting these factors aside, a language existing in isolation – for instance on a remote island – is likely to be more conservative, one would think, than one with numerous neighbours.

A further objection to the glottochronology approach can be made in relation to the notion of a 'basic vocabulary', which remains constant from language to language. However, the meanings of the words in the two languages may not be precisely equivalent. If, for instance, in translating a term from the basic vocabulary into the language being compared, one finds there is a choice of two near-synonyms and that one of these is cognate to the term in the original and the other not, which of the alternatives should one choose? If several such choices arose, this could make a considerable difference to the score. The validity of the method is so far undermined by these difficulties as to be seriously in doubt.

However, Swadesh and his colleagues at least offered a generalization which is open to testing, and if necessary rejection. Their proposal is an interesting one because it actually offers a direct and simple procedure for carrying out an analysis, which can be compared with written records of earlier stages in the language development. This implies literacy, and the presence of literacy in a society may itself be a source of conservatism. In short, glottochronology in its simple assumptions is just too good to be true.

Despite this, the method represents in one sense a substantial breakthrough in historical linguistics. It needs only slight modification to be a highly valuable research tool, for it is in fact a pioneering investigation in the much broader field of lexico-statistics; the statistical study of vocabulary.

Many scholars understandably find it difficult to accept a precise and constant rate for word loss from all languages. A high percentage of surviving cognate words in the basic vocabularies of two languages is an indicator of what one might term linguistic proximity, while a low number is an indicator of linguistic distance. The modern discipline of numerical taxonomy is very familiar with concepts such as these. We can use the number of surviving cognate word pairs as a measure of similarity, and proceed to classify the various languages (for we need not restrict ourselves to two at a time) in terms of what the taxonomists call 'taxonomic distance'.[27] That is simply an exercise based on the number of cognate pairs. In itself it assumes nothing about the nature of language change, or the presence or absence of loan-words. In fact, as I have suggested, we should expect geographically adjacent languages to display less taxonomic distance than geographically remote ones which had split off at the same time. And this approach in itself assumes nothing about splitting: it could be applied as readily following Trubetskoy's model for change, although the interpretive conclusions there would of course be different ones. It is worth noting that the languages in the sub-families and sub-groups of a larger family like Indo-European will normally be classed close together in any lexicostatistical approach since they *are* in general very similar to each other. The circumstance that the languages of the Romance group scored much more recent dates of separation than did those of the Germanic group, when the techniques of glottochronology were applied, may not tell us much about actual dates of splitting. However, it does show, objectively, on the basis of the vocabularies, that the Romance group is a more tightly knit one than the Germanic. We should note the further overwhelming limitation of this approach to the study and comparison of languages: that so far it is restricted to the comparison of individual words, and has no regard whatever to grammatical structure.

I have been able to touch only on a few aspects of the modern discipline of historical linguistics here, and no doubt I have overlooked much of the important work which is now going on. Recent developments in structural linguistics will also have their implications for historical reconstruction, although these have not yet been fully worked out. But at least we can begin to see how far modern linguistics differs from the simple family tree approach of a century ago. Any study of the archaeology of language has to bear this in mind.

6. Language, Population and Social Organization: A Processual Approach

How does a specific language come to be spoken in a particular area? That is the underlying question which we have to ask, if we seek to understand the distribution of languages in the different countries of Europe and beyond. In general, archaeologists have rushed forward to equate this particular language with that specific pottery group, and to draw up a whole complicated scenario of movements and prehistoric migrations to account for the distribution seen today, or in documented historical times. The more basic question, as to how the languages spoken in a particular area change, has not been asked. I believe that it is possible to make some valid general statements, which lead the way to a more coherent use of the archaeological record, and so allow us to form some idea about the prehistory of language.

To make general statements of such a kind in the form of explicit models does have a certain usefulness if it focuses our attention on the underlying historical processes which are at the root of change. They involve the lives of real people whose life experiences together shape the history and development of the language. This is not just a question of the movement of people, whether in groups over long distance (i.e. migrations), or piecemeal and over shorter distances (which may amount to what has traditionally been referred to as the 'diffusion' of population). Different social groups or classes have their own varieties of language, each of which may change independently of the others. Moreover the spatial varieties within a language area, and the dialects within it, serve to complicate the picture, as already indicated.

In the light of these factors, any models which we may set up are likely to be over simplified, but I believe the effort is worthwhile.[1] For it then allows us, when considering any specific case of change, to refer it back to the general models which we have, and to see if they are of help in explaining what has been observed. In many cases I believe that they are. This undertaking of attempting some sort of explanation through generalization is what is termed in contemporary archaeology the processual approach. It has the merit of making our explanations explicit, which is a very effective way of bringing their weaknesses to light, and hence also of investigating their strengths.

Three Processes of Linguistic Change within a Given Area

It is useful first to distinguish three very basic, primary processes by which languages come to be spoken in a particular region. I shall call these processes: initial colonization, replacement and continuous development. The reasoning here may be rather obvious, but it does lead on to some important conclusions.

1 Initial colonization

This is the process where human beings enter a previously uninhabited region, bringing with them their own speech, so that the language is introduced to the area. That must have been the process which operated when the first humans reached northern Europe after the retreat of the glacial ice cover. For instance, we can be sure that Scandinavia was colonized in this way by the first mesolithic (hunter-gatherer) communities around 8000 BC. Or, to take another example, the whole land mass of the Americas seems to have been uninhabited by humans until the first hunters crossed the land bridge at the Bering Strait, perhaps earlier than 10,000 BC. The most recent instance of large-scale human colonization is in Polynesia, where from c. 1300 BC, small groups of humans reached each of the islands in turn. Archaeological research has established that Hawaii was not populated until about AD 500, and New Zealand not until c. AD 1000.

2 Replacement

This is the process whereby the language spoken in a particular region is displaced by another, brought in by people from a different, possibly adjacent, region where it is in use. This is the mechanism of language change with which we are most familiar today, because it has operated so effectively in recent centuries. Over the past five hundred years the languages of Europe have spread over two of the five continents (Australia and the Americas) and much of two others (Africa and south Asia), by a simple process of direct replacement. This is the model which most archaeologists have used in considering the distribution of early languages.

3 *Continuous development*

Within any linguistic area there are conflicting tendencies at work. In the first place, education processes within societies lead towards the effective replication of customs, techniques and speech from one generation to the next, and departures from the accepted norm are viewed with disfavour. Special social mechanisms reinforce this sort of stability; and religion is often the most prominent of these. Religious texts, whether written, like the Bible or some of the early Sanskrit writings, or oral, like the Homeric epics in early Greece or the Vedic hymns in India, were often transmitted unaltered over very long time periods.

The opposing tendency is innovation – whether by borrowing from neighbours, or through the invention of new words and the development of new turns of phrase and ultimately new grammatical forms.

Alongside the opposing tendencies towards stability or innovation, we can contrast divergence and convergence. The former, arising most readily in isolation, is often considered a random process, analogous to the genetic drift of the biologists. It is certainly the case that when groups of people speaking the same language separate and are no longer in contact, marked differences in vocabulary and in forms of expression gradually emerge. A good example is Polynesia, where, since the islands are very remote from each other, and interactions are few, the consequences of divergence are particularly plain (see Chapter 11).

Convergence comes about through interaction, so that the languages of neighbouring areas increasingly have more in common. There is one further factor often at work, however, which we have not yet discussed: the remarkable human ability to speak two (or more) languages. It is when individuals speak another language as well as their own native one that convergence occurs most rapidly. Sometimes it can go so far that two languages can effectively amalgamate to form a new hybrid. This arises most frequently when parents speak different languages. In some cases the children adopt a pidgin language which becomes their own primary language. Such a hybrid language is then termed a 'creole'.[2]

When we are trying to understand the historical background to a distribution of languages, as seen for instance in the Indo-European group, these three processes may all be relevant. The first is beautifully easy to study archaeologically, because the archaeology of initial colonization is nearly always clear enough, once the region in question has been well surveyed. The third is the most difficult, since there is nothing outwardly (or archaeologically) very remarkable about the continuous development of a language within an area. In many cases where we have a continuity of occupation indicated archaeologically, such a situation might well be inferred, but the rate of development would be very hard to assess. Of course the glottochronologists like to claim that the process of word loss, which is one element of language drift and hence of divergence, proceeds at a constant rate. I am reluctant to believe so implausible a claim. When we are assessing convergence, it may be that traded goods and other indications of contact in the material culture may help to document interaction; but that is as far as we can go. It is, on the other hand, possible to generalize about language replacement, and to consider much more carefully and in general terms the circumstances in which one language may come to supersede another in a particular area. That is what the archaeologists have hitherto notably failed to do.

Models for Linguistic Replacement

Archaeologists often speak as if it is a very natural thing for the language spoken in one area to be replaced by another. Sometimes, when reading the earlier literature, you would think that every time the style of pottery in use in a village changed, the transition must have been accompanied by a total change of population, and with it of language. But populations do not change so easily; nor do languages. Indeed one of the most striking shifts in archaeological thought in the past few years has been the realization that there have been far fewer wholesale migrations of people than had once been thought. Professor Grahame Clark, in his paper[3] 'The invasion hypothesis in British prehistory', published in 1966, suggested that following the spread of farming to Britain there had perhaps been no more than one significant invasion of Britain before the Roman conquest, and even the single exception which he cited, associated with the appearance of Beaker pottery in Britain, would today be discounted by most scholars.[4]

However, the discussion should not be a matter simply of asserting whether or not one believes that this or that change of pottery or of other aspects of the material culture represents a change of population. We need some principles to guide us. I think there are in fact only two or three major ways in which language displacement is likely to occur. These can be investigated archaeologically, although the method is undoubtedly more difficult than the old procedure of just recognizing the appearance of a different kind of pottery or other artefacts and hailing this as the arrival of the Beaker Folk, or some other supposed immigrant group.

Model I: Demography/Subsistence

The first model assumes that the new language comes about as the result of the movement into the territory of large numbers of people who speak the new language. They do not have to conquer the existing inhabitants by force of arms. Quite the contrary, for on this model it is not necessary to assume that the newcomers had any highly-structured social organization which would enable them to bring about a military conquest. We certainly have no need to assume that they were inherently 'warlike', for there is no reason to imagine that the speakers of one language were militarily more able than those of another. Of course one group may prevail over another on the basis of a different technology: that is a much more relevant question.

People have to have a reason for moving, and often they go somewhere where the resources they need are more easily available than at home. When we are talking of agricultural populations, that generally means land and, other things being equal, people move from an area of higher population density to one of lower. But other things are not always equal, and the movement is sometimes from an area of low prosperity to one of high prosperity, with the immigrants generally taking a relatively low place on the social scale in relation to the existing population.

In general, if the newcomers are either to displace the existing population, or to outnumber them, they can only do so on the basis of a new exploitative technology. Unless they bring with them some special techniques or skills, in fact generally some new mode of subsistence, there is no reason why they should fare better than the existing population. That population will usually already have reached a population density which is to some extent limited by the available resources. So the newcomers must either use different resources, or utilize the existing ones in a new way, if they are to have much impact.

By far the most obvious instance of this process is the introduction of farming into an area previously inhabited only by hunter-gatherers. In Europe it has been calculated that the density of population during the period of hunter-gathering[5] might usually have been no more than about one person for every 10 square kilometres on average. The subsistence techniques of early farming can support, in Europe and western Asia, a population of about five persons per square kilometre[6] without great difficulty, and without advanced farming techniques. That represents a fiftyfold increase – an increase of 5000 per cent!

This, I would argue, is a powerful factor which outweighs almost all others when we are discussing the large-scale dispersion of a new population. Of course it should at once be stressed that the spread of a new technology certainly need not imply the spread of a new population: the diffusion of an innovation is a familiar process, and the existing population is generally perfectly capable of taking up new techniques and applying them. In such a case the language in the territory in question may acquire a few loan-words, but it will not undergo a complete replacement. In general I suggest that replacement of language will usually only take place, in the absence of highly centralized political organization, when the introduced technology itself allows a far higher density of population to exist than formerly. This has been one general feature of the colonization process of the world in recent centuries, although in fact generally accompanied by force of arms applied through a centralized organization. It is likely to have been the case for the dispersal of the Bantu languages in Africa by what seems to have been a process of replacement[7] (see Chapter 11).

The wave of advance model   It is useful here to consider which specific form of the Demography/Subsistence model is appropriate. Our thinking about the way a new technique, which is associated with population increase, can spread geographically has been greatly clarified by an important piece of work by the Italian geneticist, Luigi Cavalli-Sforza, working in collaboration with the American archaeologist, Albert Ammerman.[8] They first contrasted the two usual alternatives offered for the spread of farming. On the one hand, there is the model of diffusion, where the existing, rather sparse population of hunter-gatherers comes into contact with communities in neighbouring territories which already practise farming. From these they acquire the necessary domesticated plants, and the livestock, as well as a knowledge of farming practices, and so they come to take up farming. On the other hand there is the deliberate colonization model where a well-defined group of people deliberately set off for a distant land, to set up a new community.

The wave of advance model differs significantly from both these. Movements of people are involved but only over very short distances. It notes that a marked increase in population follows the adoption of farming in a new territory. The authors argue that in a particular area the increase follows what is termed the logistic growth pattern, which starts off very rapidly (in fact exponentially), but then slows down as the maximum population density, the saturation point for that particular area with this kind of farming, is reached. See Fig. 6.1.

They assume in addition that the local farmers will sometimes shift the position of their farms by a few kilometres, perhaps as the soil in their fields becomes temporarily exhausted. Or it may be that

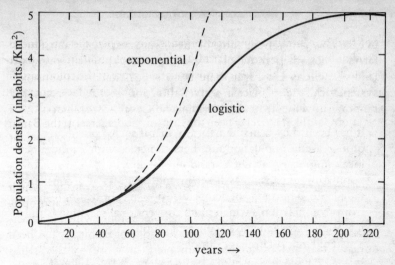

FIG. 6.1 Population growth curves. Under logistic growth, a population starting at a density of 0.1 inhabitants per sq. km. multiplies at an initial rate of about 3.9% per year which determines a doubling in about 18 years. The growth rate slows down continuously until it reaches zero when saturation occurs at 5 inhabitants per sq. km. If growth rate were to continue indefinitely at the initial rate the dotted curve of exponential growth would result (*after Ammerman and Cavalli-Sforza*).

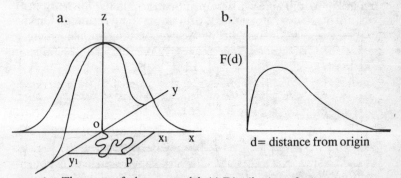

FIG. 6.2 The wave of advance model. (a) Distribution of migration distances assuming that migration is random in direction, in two dimensions x and y. An individual starts his migration at the origin (x=0, y=0) and after following an irregular path arrives at point p at a given time. (b) The distribution surface on the left hand has been transformed into a distribution curve in one dimension (*after Ammerman and Cavalli-Sforza*).

in each new generation, some of the offspring stay on the parental farm, while others move off a few kilometres to seek convenient land elsewhere. However there is no suggestion that this move systematically takes place in a given direction: in that respect it is a random movement. As Ammerman and Cavalli-Sforza put it:[9]

> It has been shown mathematically that if such a phenomenon of increase in population numbers coincides with a model of local migratory activity, random in direction, a wave of population expansion will set in and progress at a constant radial rate. This mode of demic diffusion may be distinguished from 'colonization', which in its conventional meaning is the intentional settlement by a coherent group of people, usually in a distant land. A familiar example of colonization is that which is recorded in classical Greek history. By contrast, the wave of advance model would be one involving slow, continuous expansion with movements usually being over short distances.

The wave of advance, of which they speak, would be a wave of population increase, generally spreading out radially, from any areas where the new technology (in this case farming) has already become well established. The progress of such a wave of advance is seen in Fig. 6.3. There it is assumed that the population density of

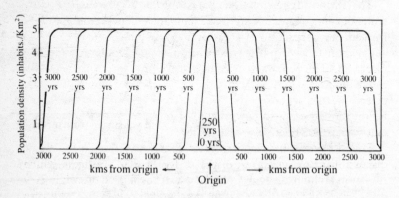

FIG. 6.3 Computer simulation of the wave of advance. The curves give population densities at various times from the beginning and distances from the origin of the simulated spread of early farming in Europe.

farmers goes up to an average of five persons per square kilometre, and that the population grows in the early stages of occupation of an area at such a rate that it doubles every eighteen years. The distance of the local migratory activity – that is the distance of the movement of settlement, which is random in direction – is taken to be eighteen kilometres for each generation of twenty-five years. Under these conditions, the rate of movement of the wave of advance turns out to be one kilometre per year.

It is not necessary to spell out in detail the mathematics on which this model is based. It is sufficient to say that it is an explicit mathematical model, drawn from the statistics of genetics. Given the underlying assumptions, the conclusions follow with mathematical rigour. That does not mean to say that the model has to be right: but if it isn't, there has to be something wrong with the assumptions.

Obviously people do not behave like mathematical automata and any specific region in question will not display the sort of uniform environment which, for simplicity, the model assumes. Nor is it reasonable to assume that the position of the farming settlement of a family will move precisely eighteen kilometres every generation. But we are talking here about average behaviours – some people will move further, some not so far.

There is no suggestion here that people have to be motivated by some burning desire to explore distant lands. The average distance moved per generation is a rather modest one. And there is no suggestion that people have to be moving always in the same direction. The remarkable feature of the model is that they can move randomly with respect to direction, that is to say in whatever direction they choose, and yet the overall outcome will still be the spread of farming outwards from the area already under cultivation, at a relatively steady rate.

This, I believe, has the very greatest potential relevance for our discussion of early language spread: for here is a process which results in an increase of population on an absolutely revolutionary scale, spreading across the lands in question, yet without any suggestion of advance planning, and without any individuals having to move very far. Indeed if the average displacement, of individuals, is random in direction and only about eighteen kilometres, it is hardly appropriate to speak here of a migration at all.

Of course it should be clearly realized that the model itself does not tell us whether this spread results in language displacement or not. It is up to us to determine from the evidence whether the techniques of farming really did spread by this process, rather than by the adoption of farming techniques by the pre-existing local population of hunter-gatherers. That would have different overall effects. Yet in some cases, as we shall see, there is evidence that at the time of the arrival of the first farmers in an area, the hunter-gatherers already there often kept to their own traditional areas, which were not necessarily those which the farmers chose to exploit. It does not follow then that the two groups were competing for the same resources, although this must sometimes have been the case. But we certainly may make the suggestion that when the new farming population outnumbered the hunter-gatherers by fifty to one, and when the two groups spoke different languages, it would generally be the language of the farmers which would prevail.

It should be noted too that it is not an inherent feature of the model that it is restricted to farming. It can apply to any group of people carrying with them a technique of exploitation which results in a very substantial increase in population density. For this reason it applies very appropriately to the spread of cereal farming (with livestock) in North America with the arrival of the Europeans, even though farming based on maize and other local crops was already long known in some regions there, but the European-style farming certainly did permit a substantial increase in population in many areas. The North American example did also, initially, involve colonization of the traditional kind, with the first settlers travelling from their homelands. These were not just a simple peasant population with a new subsistence technique, intermingling peaceably with the original inhabitants; it was of course more complicated than that, with the close-knit social organization of the settlers and their military technology (metal weapons, firearms, horses) playing a significant role not envisaged in the wave of advance model itself.

Although the initial colonization of the New World by Europeans was clearly a case of long distance migration, the subsequent pattern of expansion was very different. A number of studies have shown how the 'frontier'[10] between the European economy and life-style and that of the indigenous population gradually moved to the west. Although there are complicating factors in this case, it is perfectly appropriate to analyse that moving frontier in terms of the wave of advance model.

This model is eminently visible archaeologically. It is a relatively straightforward matter to determine, by excavation, whether a community enjoyed a farming economy or was based on hunting and gathering. The material equipment of the first farmers of a region is generally quite distinctive. Often they used pottery, whereas hunter-gatherers, with a few exceptions (such as those of the Jómon culture of Japan), rarely did.

It is sometimes less easy to decide whether the first farming settlements in an area were occupied by people who were already resident there and who adopted techniques of farming from their neighbours, or whether the first farmers were newcomers. But sometimes the settlement pattern of the hunter-gatherers and of the farmers differs markedly. Moreover, in some cases we see aspects of the material culture of the hunter-gatherers continuing in use alongside the new farming economy. That may be an indication that the original population has survived and has taken up farming. On the other hand, when the tool kits and the artefacts of the two groups are entirely different, that suggests that the farming population may have been immigrants, and that the process can quite properly be described (in some cases) by the wave of advance model.

In Chapter 7 I shall use this model to suggest a possible mechanism for the spread of an early Indo-European language, or languages, throughout Europe.

Model II: Élite Dominance

The wave of advance model, as we have outlined it, is a special case of our first model of language replacement, based on demography and subsistence. It implies the introduction of a new subsistence technology which allows for a significant increase in population density. The second model for language replacement is quite different, depending on none of these things.

It assumes instead the arrival from outside the territory of a relatively small group of highly-organized people, speaking a different language, who because of their military effectiveness are able to dominate the existing population, and bring it into effective subjection. The two languages will then exist side-by-side for some time, with many of the population, probably both the indigenous and the immigrant, becoming bilingual. In some circumstances the territory will continue to speak its original language, and the newcomers will be assimilated and their foreign language forgotten. In others it is the language of the newcomers which prevails, while that of the original population, although they were the more numerous, dies out. That is a case of language replacement.

This model lays stress upon the social organization of the immigrant group. They may not be large in number, but in order to bring the pre-existing population into subjection effectively, they must already display, I would argue, what the anthropologist terms 'ranking': they must already have a ranked or a stratified social organization.[11] Sometimes they will be the agents of a state society – that is to say of a society which displays many of the features which we associate with urban civilization. Such societies have a head or central agency of state, generally supported by an army, based upon the capital city. There is a hierarchy of settlement, with a system of local governors for the subsidiary towns. There are craft specialists as well as priests and warriors, and often the bureaucratic control is administered with the use of writing. Such societies are 'stratified' because they comprise different social classes or strata. The Roman conquest of Europe, for example, was undertaken by a society of that kind. Unlike Model I, it did not necessarily bring about any notable population increase.

In other instances the incoming élite will not be organized on quite so complex a level. They may, rather, show the features of what anthropologists sometimes term a 'chiefdom' society.[12] Here there is still some measure of centralized organization, but there is not the administrative bureaucracy often associated with the state. The society is not now divided into a series of separate social classes, but is organized rather by a system of ranking, based on kinship, where those most closely related to the chief occupy the positions of highest status. From the economic standpoint craft specialisation is a feature of such societies, and there may be other part-time specialists such as priests and warriors.

I would argue that it is only when a small incoming group is organized in such a way that it can expect to dominate a much larger resident population. Of course it helps if the incomers also have some advantage in military technology. For instance, if the incomers know the techniques of horse riding and the locals do not, the former are at a tremendous advantage. That was part of the secret of the success of the Spanish conquistadores in the New World. But organization is more important than military technology alone. Social organization is often visible archaeologically, and there are various indicators by which ranked societies may be recognized on the basis of the finds. The settlement pattern is an important one, since it usually includes centres of power and there is often evidence for persons of high status, whose dwellings are prominent in size and quality of construction.

Above all it must be remembered that a migration is a hazardous business. It has little chance of success unless those moving into a territory can either occupy a new ecological niche, as in the case of Model I, or compete very effectively with the existing population for their own basic resources. It is my argument that most cases of language displacement fall within the scope of this model or the preceding one.

Model III: System Collapse

A third model of change is system collapse.[13] Many early state societies were not very stable organizations; it seems that often they grew rapidly, and in a way which sometimes led to overspecialization. In some cases the population density grew large, and the organization rather top-heavy, so that it could not effectively withstand the sort of adversity which arises when bad weather results in a series of bad harvests, or when the fertility of the land is steadily declining. Instead of diversifying their activities, some early state societies seem instead to have intensified them to the point where the system could no longer stand the strain. The central authority lost control, despite all the prestige its ritual and religion could command. In such circumstances, chaos very frequently set in. The craft specialists were no longer supported by the central administration and had to look elsewhere for their food. Moreover those farmers who had previously produced specialist products for exchange within the redistributive system – the early equivalent of cash-cropping – found that their food supply would be much better assured if they simply produced what they wanted for themselves, rather than specializing in just a few commodities for sale or exchange (such as wine, or olive oil). In these circumstances, while the farmers might be better off by switching to subsistence

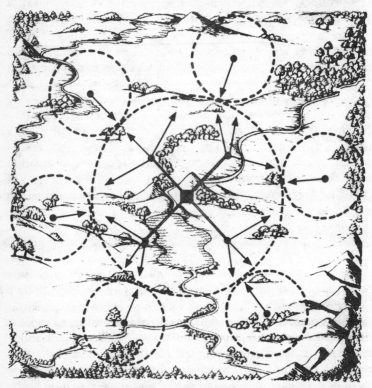

FIG. 6.4 System collapse: (a) the system under pressure. The centralized system has extended its territorial boundaries into the peripheral zone. The central authority is perpetually under pressure from smaller local groups beyond the frontier.

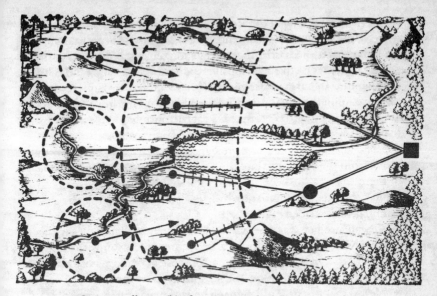

FIG. 6.5 System collapse: (b) after an internal crisis, the central power retreats from the peripheral zone, and the small groups beyond the frontier profit, seizing the opportunity to advance and occupy the peripheral zone.

farming, the overall efficiency of the system, which is often at its highest when geared to specialist production, would decline. That simply exacerbated the crisis.

Such a pattern of events can now be discerned in the case of a number of early civilizations and states, where previously it was often assumed that their demise must have been the consequence of invasion from outside, and of conquest. What I am describing is the phenomenon of the 'Dark Age', such as beset Mycenaean Greece after 1110 BC or the Lowland Maya civilization after AD 890. In these and many other cases it now seems that the organizational system of society simply collapsed. Certainly those archaeologists who have assumed in each case that the Dark Age was brought on by the invasion of a destroying army have found it very difficult to find any trace whatever of these supposed destroyers.

The phenomenon of system collapse can nonetheless result in group movements, some of them with definite consequences for the languages spoken in the area, for when a state society collapses, its systems of boundary maintenance also collapse. The frontiers are no longer patrolled, and there is no longer a standing army to defend the cities or the palaces. There is bound to be a good deal of lawlessness, and armed groups will soon emerge within the territory to exploit the situation. If, on the edge of the territory, there are already well-organized groups, held at bay during the rule of law by the military power of the state, they are bound to take advantage of the new disorder.[14] We can predict, then, that they will tend to move from the periphery into the heart of the state's territory: some of them may be so successful that they will themselves manage to subject the existing population by a process very much like the élite dominance described in Model II.

We can predict, then, when a state system collapses, that the collapse will be followed by local movements of groups from the periphery towards the centre. Some of these may ultimately establish their own organization and language upon the territory as a whole, so that a degree of language replacement will be seen.

In many cases there are few linguistic consequences of note following a system collapse. In the Maya Lowlands, for instance, there does not seem to have been any language shift, but the dominance of the Aztecs in Mexico, and of their language Nahuatl, seems to have followed the collapse of the previous state organization in roughly this way. In Mycenaean Greece, while the Greek language itself was not displaced, there may well have been local movements of groups which resulted in the adoption of Greek dialects in certain areas different from those which preceded them. And the collapse of the Roman empire certainly had a number of striking consequences. Amongst the most significant was the rise to dominance in Britain of groups apparently organized at chiefdom level, who had made their way across the English Channel. There is plenty of evidence of boundary maintenance in the previous (i.e. fourth) century, when the Romans maintained the whole elaborate defensive system which we know as 'the forts of the Saxon shore'. When these could no longer be garrisoned, the sort of local displacements described above occurred: small, tightly organized groups of people moved in from the Low Countries. This was linguistically significant, since the language spoken in the outcome was Anglo-

Saxon. It may be that there were already quite a few people in England before the collapse who spoke a Germanic language. The earlier language, which the Romans in part displaced on their arrival four centuries before the collapse, is generally agreed among scholars to have been a Celtic language, and it is not clear to what extent it was superseded by Latin, throughout the population, during the period of Roman rule. There were Saxon mercenaries already present in England before the power of Rome finally ended, so the subsequent dominance of the Anglo-Saxon language may have been due in part to them, as well as to the small invading groups who profited by the ensuing chaos.

The usefulness of this model is that it serves to explain a number of those cases of language replacement which at first sight do not fall within the scope either of the Wave of Advance model or of the Élite Dominance model, although in a sense they are in fact subsumed within the latter.

The Mobility Factor and Nomad Pastoralism

When we are considering the movement of numbers of people, under the headings of any of these three models, the method by which they moved is a crucial factor.

The technology of seafaring has, of course, been essential for many of the really long-distance colonizations. The European colonization of much of the globe in the fifteenth to nineteenth centuries was naturally due to developments in shipbuilding and in navigation, as well as in the social organization of the parent states. And the Norse colonization of Britain and Ireland, to take another example, was closely related to the development of the famous Viking longship as a seafaring vessel.

On land, the horse was at some periods a crucial resource, but one about which there has been much confusion. It is essential to distinguish between the use of the horse as an animal for traction and as a pack animal, on the one hand; and as an animal for riding on the other. There are indications that the horse may first have been domesticated in what is now western Russia around 3000 BC, but there is no definite evidence that it was ridden as early as this: the first entirely clear evidence which we have of horse riding comes from depictions of horse and rider in the early second millennium, and from finds of horse bits and horse harness from the first millennium BC, although decorated bone 'cheekpieces' from Slovakia and Hungary may indicate horse riding there before 2000 BC. There are indications of horse-drawn chariots in the Near East and in Greece from around 1600 BC, and traces of carts drawn by horses or oxen more than a millennium earlier.

One very important consequence of the domestication of the horse as a pack animal was the opportunity which it opened for the development of a much more mobile, nomad pastoral economy. Such an economy is based largely on the management of livestock (sheep, goats and/or cattle). It is necessary to take the herds long distances between the summer and winter pasturing grounds – distances so great that the entire community moves with the herd. This is an altogether different pattern of subsistence from trans-humance, where the distance between summer and winter pasture is much less (generally a matter of differing altitude in a fairly mountainous environment), so that the main community can live in the same village all the year round. Such very long distance movements, where the community takes with it all its worldly goods, require pack animals, and this must have been one of the main early uses of the horse.

It should be stressed, however, that the nomad pastoral economy always requires the co-existence of agriculture:[15] the pastoral nomads may not cultivate plants themselves (although in practice they quite often do) but they certainly need bread and other plant products, which they exchange for their own animal produce. In the early days of archaeology it used to be thought that the pastoral nomad existence was in some way intermediate in time between that of the hunter-gatherer and the settled farmer. That notion is no longer accepted: pastoral nomadism was only able to emerge as a secondary development following the successful development of agriculture. The economy of the nomad pastoralist is generally one of symbiosis with agricultural communities.

As the Soviet scholar Igor Diakonov[16] has recently written:

> Nomadism supposes riding with cattle: either horse-riding or camel-riding. Chariots are not suitable for tending cattle: they

are no good on broken terrain and require very specialized service. The Near East did not know true nomadism until the last centuries of the second millennium BC . . . Nomadism did not exist in Central Asia and the steppe zone of the European part of the USSR until the second millennium BC either.

The development of the technology of horse riding was significant in different ways. It was obviously a development of great potential military significance which conferred a considerable advantage upon any coherently organized group which could ride. This brings us back to the Élite Dominance model, and we can imagine that in iron age Europe, when some groups had the techniques of horse riding (and the horses) and others did not, the strategies of dominance may have altered significantly.

In the first millennium AD the development of the stirrup, which made fighting on horseback very much easier and more secure, is often said to have had a similar impact. The historian of technology, Lynn White,[17] has argued that it was the stirrup which allowed the military action of heavy cavalry, and he goes so far as to claim that it was precisely this which made possible the rise of the feudal class of the European Middle Ages.

Much the same is true of the kingdoms of West Africa at a rather later period. As the British social anthropologist, Jack Goody,[18] has written:

The horse was the noble animal in every sense, and one reserved for the nobility and its hangers on. It was reserved for the nobility, not because of special sumptuary laws, but because of the large investment in the means of destruction that horses entailed. Chivalry, the horse culture, had a politico-military base . . .

In West Africa, as in medieval Europe and most other parts of the globe, horses were the possessions of a politically dominant estate that was usually of immigrant origin and had established its domination over a land of peasant farmers.

The wheeled vehicle, the cart, plays an important part in mobility. For, while nomad pastoralists have developed a life-style whereby their baggage can be pared down to what may be transported by pack animals, in practice it is difficult for entire groups of farmers to travel very far without wheeled transport. Timothy Champion has stressed the significance of this factor, alongside that of social organization, in his consideration of mass migration in later prehistoric Europe, and has concluded that:[19]

> . . . it is highly unlikely that the population of prehistoric Europe had grown to such an extent, or the agricultural depredation of man progressed so far, that migration should have been the preferred solution to crisis at any time before the first millennium.

These, then, are some of the underlying factors which must have determined the extent to which language displacement would have taken place in prehistoric times. The essential point to reiterate is that modern archaeology no longer regards the displacement of large groups of people as an everyday event. Migrations took place, but they did so only in circumstances which made them necessary, and under conditions which today we can hope to understand. It is these conditions which modern archaeology can set out to investigate: they are often so well-defined that they should certainly leave indications in the archaeological record. These findings will not, however, be so simple and straightforward as specific pottery types, once claimed as the 'visiting card' of individual ethnic groups, but rather take the form of evidence for the social organization of the communities involved, and for their technology and mode of subsistence. Gordon Childe once wrote of the prehistoric archaeology of his day that:[20]

> It aimed at distilling from archaeological remains a preliterate substitute for the conventional politico-military history, with cultures instead of statesmen as actors, and migrations in place of battles.

The discipline of history itself has moved on since that time, with greater attention being paid to the underlying technology of societies and to basic features of their organization. Modern history is no longer concerned exclusively with the deeds and thoughts of great men. Indeed Childe, writing those words in 1957, did himself an injustice. For while his book *The Aryans*, published in 1926, did indeed conform to that view of prehistoric archaeology, Childe was himself a pioneer in the study of the impact of technological change on early societies.[21] He was one of the leading figures in the development of economic prehistory, which, along with social archaeology, offers a more promising approach to the questions we have been discussing, and in particular to this difficult issue of language displacement.

Other Processual Models for Language Change

When we are considering the processes by which changes and displacements in language are effected, it is not difficult to think of other relevant models. These are perhaps less germane to the case in point, since they are not proposed here in relation to the Indo-European problem. However, since this chapter is also intended to serve as a more general introduction towards a processual approach to the problems of language change, it is appropriate at least to mention them.

Constrained Population Displacement

This is the refugee phenomenon, where a substantial body of people moves out of one territory and into another, not directly through the effects of the Demography/Subsistence model, but because constrained to do so by the incursion of a hostile population into their original territory. In certain circumstances the refugees may become the dominant population linguistically in their new territory, and their language survive there.

This was, of course, the model adopted by many scholars in the early days of Indo-European studies, when the initial reason for the supposed westward incursion of Indo-European tribes was sometimes seen as the arrival of other, hostile tribes from the east. This is, however, a model to be viewed with caution, although it may well have operated in some cases. Examples could certainly be claimed, for instance, in the so-called 'migration period' which followed the collapse of the western Roman empire.

However, this is, in a sense, a rather secondary model. For the initial movement, which uprooted the unfortunate refugees in the first place, must itself have been a displacement of people, and it in turn has to be explained in terms of one of the models for language displacement which we have already set out. (In the case of the migration period, the collapse of the Roman Empire was a major causal factor.) The second weakness of the model is that refugees rarely form a dominant group in the territory where they finally settle, and it must be unusual therefore, for the language of refugees to become the dominant language in any society.

Sedentary/Mobile Boundary Shift

It should be noted that, even when the two contrasting (and sometimes symbiotic) economies of mixed agriculture and of nomad pastoralism are well established side-by-side, in a stable relationship, the location of the boundary between the two may change with time. In reality it is not, of course, easy to draw a boundary line, because the areas exploited by the two economies interpenetrate. The nomad may well pass many fields under agriculture on his way from one pasture to another.

However, assuming that one can find some way of defining with a fair approximation the location of the boundary, there is no doubt that it will shift from time to time through the operation of local climatic, economic and social conditions. When it does there may well be a resulting language change in the land lying between the old and the new boundaries.

This point is worth making explicit here, because we shall see that towards the end of the neolithic period in eastern Europe, there are indeed indications that the material culture which is associated further east with a nomadic economy can be found in the area. This has sometimes been taken as the evidence for a widespread migration of nomads into central and western Europe. It could, of course, constitute evidence tending to support such an event, but a good deal of further data would be needed from areas further west before one could feel that a good case had been made out. The other obvious interpretation of the material in eastern Europe would be in terms of the models defined here.

The location of such a mobile/sedentary interface has often been a factor of crucial relevance in the history of China, for example.[22]

The Great Wall itself was built with this intention and in general the boundary did not penetrate very far into imperial China itself. On occasions, of course, the interface moved so far east that the result was one of élite domination: the outcomes were the Yuan dynasty of the Mongols, and later the Manchu dynasty.

Donor/Recipient Population Systems

Another interesting model is of relevance to one particular kind of élite displacement. In his influential article on the origins of agriculture, entitled 'Post-Pleistocene adaptations', Lewis Binford[23] discussed the position when there are 'two or more different kinds of sociocultural systems which occupy adjacent environmental zones'. Here, however, we are not thinking of changes which cause a displacement in the boundary between the two: that might in some cases lead to the Sedentary/Mobile Boundary Shift just discussed. Instead it is worth considering the circumstances if the more rapidly growing group and its economy cannot move into neighbouring territory. In such a situation, as Binford shows, the more rapidly growing group becomes, often over a long period, the donor group in terms of population, and the other the recipient. The result is the steady intrusion of an immigrant population into the less dynamic zone.

Whether or not this process lies at the source of the origins of agriculture in the Near East, as Binford at that time suggested, there is a case for seeing the development of the Semitic languages[24] in the Near East, over a long period of time, as the result of such a process. The donor zone in this case would be, speaking approximately, the Arabian peninsula, and the recipient one, Mesopotamia. It can certainly be argued that from the third millennium BC onwards, there were frequent and sometimes steady influxes of Semitic-speaking groups into Mesopotamia, who settled there and ultimately came to outnumber the Sumerian-speaking population. In such circumstances, the language of the majority may well become dominant during a period of instability, as indeed occurred with the emergence to power of Sargon of Agade.

It is not my argument here that this is what happened in Europe. On the contrary, there is no evidence that such processes occurred there during the periods in question. As far as the steppe lands of western Russia are concerned, the former model of Sedentary/ Mobile Boundary Shift is quite sufficient to explain the limited archaeological evidence which is relevant. But it is pertinent to note that such a model is possible, and that it may have a bearing on the rise to dominance of the Semitic languages. In this way there should be no suggestion that a special case is being argued for either problem.

Now we have examined some of the processual mechanisms underlying language change we can turn to a specific case, the Indo-European problem. In doing so I will try to follow the principles outlined in this chapter, which apply with equal force anywhere in the world when we are considering the archaeology of language.

7. Early Language Dispersals in Europe

In the previous chapters a position was taken which is critical, directly or by implication, of nearly every attempt so far to solve the Indo-European problem. Does this mean that the problem is incapable of solution? I think not. I believe it is possible to offer a plausible explanation for the existence of related languages across almost the whole of Europe which does not make the erroneous assumptions criticised earlier. Quite how we can proceed to test this explanation is a more difficult question.

1 Language and Farming

If we look at the distribution of the Indo-European languages of Europe when we first see them in the centuries shortly before or after the beginning of the Christian era (or, in the case of Greece, a thousand years earlier), virtually the whole of Europe seems to have been Indo-European-speaking. The only clear exceptions are the Etruscan language of central Italy, and presumably the ancestor of the Basque language of northern Spain, with Iberian at the east of the peninsula. This is a vast area for such a degree of uniformity.

The possibility advanced by Trubetskoy has already been discussed, that this uniformity is simply the result of convergence. That is to say that languages in different areas which were not themselves necessarily related, became 'Indo-Europeanized' through processes of contact. The conclusion was reached instead that, as most scholars have argued, some common origin for the languages must be accepted. This means that the family tree model has to apply, at least in part, to explain some of the observed uniformity. That does not exclude the operation of the wave model, and indeed it is likely that the present pattern is a veritable palimpsest of ancestral influences overlain by loan-words and by subsequently adopted common grammatical forms over succeeding millennia.

What historical reality lies behind the common ancestral origin of

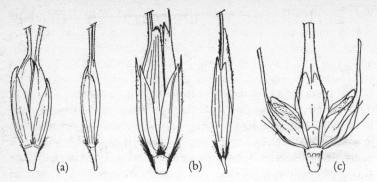

FIG. 7.1 (a) Emmer wheat, (b) einkorn and (c) six-row barley: the basic ingredients of the neolithic revolution in Europe and the Near East (*after J. M. Renfrew*).

all these languages? We have rejected the 'Kurgan' theory of a dispersal around 3500–3000 BC, and with it those for Corded Ware and for Beakers (c. 2900 to 2000 BC). The same arguments apply for the later unities, the culture complexes which one may recognize, such as the Urnfields of the late bronze age. Even if each of these culture complexes *was* recognized as implying linguistic uniformity, none of them is large enough to apply to the whole of Europe. The Urnfields could not possibly do, for they could not explain the arrival of people speaking an Indo-European language in Greece before 1500 BC. The Beaker complex is likewise not relevant to south-east Europe: there are no Beakers there. There is, indeed, precious little Corded Ware in Greece, and none in Italy. So only a rather embracing theory where Kurgan cultures, Corded Ware and Beakers are all brought into play, as in the wider ramifications of Professor Gimbutas's Kurgan hypothesis, would do.

The alternative, then, is to go earlier. In doing so, we do indeed come upon one major process which undoubtedly radically affected the whole of Europe. This was the adoption of farming.

It is widely accepted today that most of the major plant domesticates and probably some of the animals also, which formed the basis for the early farming cultures of Europe, were ultimately imports into the area. In her book *Palaeoethnobotany*, Dr Jane Renfrew[1] has reviewed the evidence for the plants, and although there remains the possibility that wild prototypes for some of the cereal plants were available in parts of south-east Europe, the overall conclusion is that the economy of agriculture was in the main an imported one. There are just a few intriguing indications of cereal grains from much earlier levels in the Franchthi Cave in Greece.[2] But at present it seems safe to say that the first farmers of Europe were settled in Greece (and Crete) before 6000 BC. They had a mixed economy based upon the cultivation of emmer wheat and einkorn wheat along with pulse crops such as peas and vetch. Their livestock were mainly sheep and goats; cattle and pigs were also known, though perhaps not domesticated at the outset. This is well-documented from research at such thoroughly investigated sites as Nea Niko-medeia in Macedonia, Argissa Maghoula in Thessaly, Knossos in Crete and the Franchthi Cave in south Greece.[3]

It is possible to trace the spread of farming throughout much of Europe back to its Greek origins. That does not mean that there was any dispersal of people. It is quite conceivable that the existing, rather sparse, hunter-gatherer population of Europe acquired the necessary plant and animal species from their neighbours to the south-east and took up farming gradually themselves. That would

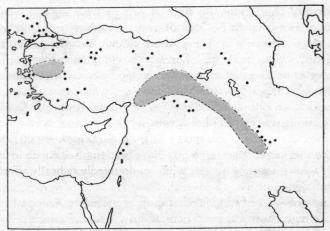

FIG. 7.2 Modern distribution in the Near East of the wild prototype *Triticum boeoticum* for domesticated einkorn (*after Zohary and J. M. Renfrew*).

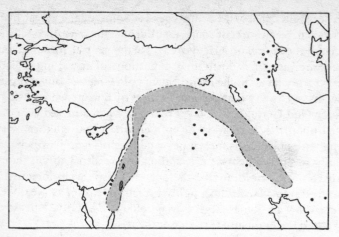

FIG. 7.3 Modern distribution in the Near East of the wild prototype, *Hordeum spontaneum*, for domesticated barley (*after Zohary and J. M. Renfrew*).

represent a process of what the anthropologist terms 'acculturation'. Instead I suggest that the spread of farming in Europe took place by a process much like the wave of advance described in Chapter 6. This implies that the bulk of the population in each new area which comes to practise a farming economy is not of local ancestry. In the main this is not an indigenous, acculturated population, but one where the children, in most cases, were born perhaps twenty or thirty miles away from the birthplaces of their parents. There is absolutely no need to suggest any organized migrations: no individual on this model needs to have moved more than forty to sixty kilometres in his or her entire life.[4] Yet gradually, because of the great increase in population which the development of farming allows in an area, the result would have been to fill Europe not only with a new, farming economy, but to a large extent with a new population.

The process of bringing a farming economy to Europe began somewhere shortly before 6000 BC in Crete and Greece. To be more accurate we should probably try to use a calibrated radiocarbon chronology. If we do so, we should say that farming reached Greece sometime before 6500 BC. It had reached the Orkney

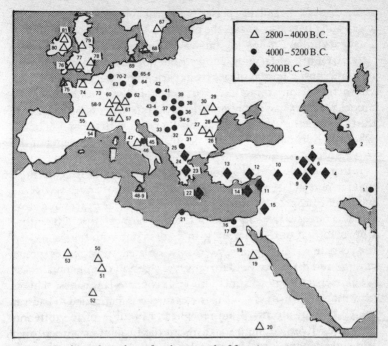

FIG. 7.4 Radiocarbon dates for the spread of farming economy to Europe. The map indicates the earliest sites of farming settlements, as determined by radiocarbon analysis for results published up to 1965. Dates are in uncalibrated radiocarbon years (*after J. G. D. Clark*).

Islands, at the northern tip of Scotland, and the rest of Europe also by about 3500 BC.[5]

It is perfectly reasonable to view the coming of farming to Europe as a single process, albeit one with many phases, with pauses and sudden advances. For if we were to take the wheat sown in Orkney in the neolithic around 3000 BC, and ask where each year's seed corn had itself been reaped, we would trace a line across the map of Europe that would inevitably lead us back to the Greek early neolithic, and from there back across to western Anatolia. This is a crucial point. It is by no means so certain that the same would be true of the ancestry of human beings; although that is broadly what I am in fact arguing here. However, for the wheat and some of the other plant species (and probably the ancestry of the sheep and goats also) that is the position.

My argument, following the wave of advance model, is that the new economy of farming allowed the population in each area to rise, over just a few centuries from perhaps 0.1 persons per square kilometre to something like 5 or 10 per square kilometre. As the model predicts,[6] with only small, local movements of twenty or thirty kilometres, this would gradually result in the peopling of the whole of Europe by a farming population, the descendents of the first European farmers.

If that was the case, we would expect that the language of those first farmers in Greece around 6500 BC would be carried across the whole of Europe. Of course it would change in the process. In areas close to Greece, the language of the first farmers would be rather similar to that of their farming ancestors. But with the passing of the years, if the two regions were now isolated, divergences would emerge and dialects would form. Over a period of millennia, these would separate into distinct although cognate languages. This is very much the process which, as we have seen, happened to Latin at the end of the Roman Empire, where a number of the different provinces diverged linguistically with the formation of their own Romance languages.[7] Further to the north-west, and many centuries later, the language of the first farmers as they arrived might already be rather different from their ancestors in Greece, and even more so from their distant cousins in Greece at the same point in time. There is no difficulty, then, in imagining the development of a whole series of different languages, and ultimately of language families in the different parts of Europe.

So far, however, we have completely ignored the pre-existing, hunter-gatherer, the 'mesolithic' population. On one view we might disregard them, suggesting that they exploited a rather different ecological niche from that used by the first farmers, as Ruth Tringham[8] has indeed argued. If they kept themselves to themselves, so to speak, they would soon come to represent a small linguistic minority representing perhaps no more than 1 per cent of the population in most areas. Gradually they might have been linguistically assimilated, although contributing words and perhaps grammatical features to the language of each area.

In cases where the mesolithic population was much denser – perhaps in Brittany or on the shores of Portugal,[9] where the shell middens suggest a fairly flourishing mesolithic community, their contribution might have been larger, and where the local mesolithic population actually took up farming itself, it too would undergo much the same increase in population density. In such a case its language would have a greater probability of surviving. On this model, that could be the explanation for the occasional pockets of non-Indo-European languages which survived into historic times, such as Etruscan or Basque, and no doubt many others which survived for a while but are now extinct.

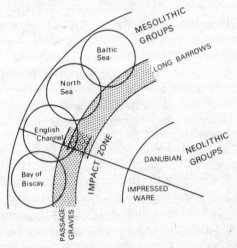

FIG. 7.5 The impact of farming on the existing mesolithic communities of north-west Europe along the 'Atlantic façade' (*after Kinnes*).

That then is the model in outline. It predicts that if we see a very wide uniformity in language, we should seek a demographic and economic explanation. The Indo-European languages of Europe would thus be traceable back to the first farmers of Greece who would themselves have spoken an early form of Indo-European.

It should be noted that this correlation between European mixed farming and the Indo-European languages applies equally to very large areas of the globe. Precisely the same process took place in Australia, when the first European settlers, with their domesticated plants and animals, spread rapidly across a sub-continent until then occupied exclusively by hunter-gatherers. In the rest of the world (and indeed in Australia too) the model is mixed with the other major process outlined in Chapter 6: élite dominance. In the Americas and in New Zealand, where there were already native farming economies, the new European arable farming system, with its domesticated animals, was propagated by force of arms. However many of the features of the original model still apply. The wave of advance can be traced as the American frontier, and it crossed what is now the United States in just a few centuries. The result has certainly been a vast increase in population density. Much the same is true for some of the countries of South America, although naturally in lands such as Peru, which already had a highly developed economy and social organization, the picture is more complicated, as it is in Central America. The equation between mixed cereal and livestock farming and the Indo-European languages is a striking one, although not of course universal: many Semitic speakers are mixed farmers too, and the correlation is a product of the processes which I have described.

2 The Spread of Farming in Europe

To say that the first farmers of Europe spoke an early Indo-European language or languages is sheer hypothesis. The alternative, that the linguistic unity might extend yet further into the past, we will examine in Chapter 11. Following this first hypothesis, let us explore in more detail the process by which Europe came to adopt farming. The progress of archaeology in recent decades allows a very detailed picture to be built up.

In the first place, we should realize that although the origins were shared, there was nothing stereotyped about the process. In some areas there were already settled communities before the advent of farming, sometimes with a well-established village life. The site of the Lepenski Vir[10] on the Danube, above the Iron Gate, in what is now Yugoslavia, is one of these. There was a village of at least forty houses, and the art of the time, around 5000 BC, had a coherent style of its own. This was a community based mainly upon the fish resources of the Danube and one which operated therefore upon what we should regard as a 'mesolithic' subsistence base.

The late Eric Higgs looked at farming adaptations in an original way, and he was among the first to point out that Europe made many contributions of its own to its farming economy.[11] Thus cattle, and pigs, may have been separately domesticated in Europe. It has also been argued that there may have been a separate centre in southern France for domestication of sheep.[12]

Thus while the first immigrant farmers of Greece may have brought with them the plants and animals which made farming there possible, they worked out their own adaptations to their special circumstances. Robert Rodden, the excavator of the early farming village of Nea Nikomedeia has shown how the houses there were built with a timber frame, and the walls were then completed by plastering with mud in a manner not unlike the wattle and daub method in medieval Britain.[13] This differs from the use of plain mud brick that was used in some farming communities further east, such as Çatal Hüyük in Anatolia. In Europe, as he points out, farming villages were on an open plan, with separate free-standing houses. Often in the Near East, the settlement was 'agglomerate', with inter-linking rooms and houses.

John Nandris, of the University of London, has written about the First Temperate Neolithic,[14] stressing that the early farming settlements of temperate Europe, in Yugoslavia and neighbouring lands, were different in many ways from those of Greece. Andrew Sherratt has recently made this point in relation to the Hungarian Plain,[15] and both have stressed that groundwater and flooding are relevant factors in those areas, which they rarely are in Greece. So there was nothing routine about the adoption of farming techniques in each area. In a way the occupants of each new piece of territory had to rediscover for themselves the nature of farming, and what was appropriate to that area. They generally had available to them the plants and animals which their fathers had used, and many of the relevant skills, but they had to work out adaptations for themselves. They experimented with new techniques, and with different plant and animal species. They hunted the wild fauna of the area, and ultimately transformed their farming practices, so that the neolithic of northern Europe was very different from that of Greece. But the

culture and the farming economy of each territory was recogniz-
ably a *transformation* of the parent economy of its neighbour. Rather
than seeing the wave of advance as a mechanical, indeed passive,
process we should view it as a whole series of transformations in
which the farming populations actively participated. This may have
implications for their languages too, but it does not alter the
circumstance that each economy was a transformation of its
predecessor in a long series traceable back to early Greece.

The archaeologist is concerned not only with the economy but
with the material culture of the communities with which he is
dealing, and where possible with their social structure and ideology
also. In Greece the early farmers had stone tools – chipped stone
blades and polished stone carpentry tools and axes. After a brief
period without pottery they invented or acquired the techniques of
pottery making. They were probably already weaving, and, of
course, they were building houses. Small baked clay figures or
'figurines' in early neolithic Greece, which are found also in the first
temperate neolithic of the Balkans, have been taken as indications of
cult practice. I share this view, although other interpretations are
possible. There are occasional finds of bits of copper from very
early farming times, although the use of copper to make artefacts
has not yet been documented from the Greek early neolithic, as it
has in that of Anatolia. The use of boats is certainly implied by the
importation of obsidian, a volcanic glass useful for making chipped
stone tools, from the island of Melos, even before the farming
economy began. If we examine the protolexicon, as set out by
Gordon Childe (see page 83) we can document or predict nearly all
the components except the words relating to the wheel and the
chariot, which were certainly not yet known. Although there are no
grounds for speaking of a ranked society at this time, it is perfectly
possible that the village could have had a head man who might fit
the role of the simple predecessor of the *rex* or *raja*. Of course the
Greek environment lacks many of the trees and some of the animals
which are seen in the Indo-European language of more northerly
lands, so that the absence of words for these species in the Indo-
European languages of southern Europe is to be predicted.

It is possible, with the aid of radiocarbon dating, to trace the
spread of the farming economy through Europe. From Greece in

6500 BC the same type of farming economy was well established in Yugoslavia by around 5000 BC. Stuart Piggott has given a simplified map[16] of this process.

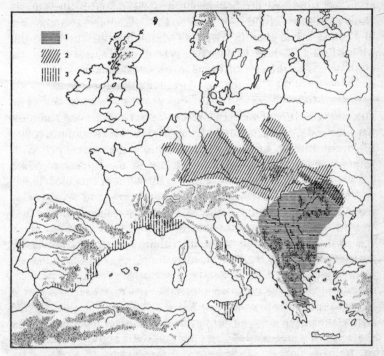

FIG. 7.6 The early spread of farming in Europe, 1. Starčevo and allied; 2. Linear pottery; 3. Impressed pottery (*after Piggott*).

The cultures of the first temperate neolithic take different names: Starčevo in Yugoslavia, Körös in Hungary, Criş in Romania and Karanovo in Bulgaria. They have much in common. It was from the Körös culture that a transformation took place, producing a new adaptation which is seen from Hungary and Czechoslovakia right up the Danube to Germany and north to the Low Countries. This is termed the Linear Pottery culture, which we have already met in the writings of Kossinna. The house form here was a very different one. These were long, timber-frame houses, much more suited to the winters of central and northern Europe than were the mud houses of Greece. By 4000 BC we find this culture almost on the shores of the English Channel. By 3000 BC a new transformation has produced the first neolithic of Scandinavia, the Funnel Beaker Culture (TRB), mentioned in the last chapter, and seen first in Denmark and then in Sweden. Meanwhile the spread of the Linear Pottery culture to the east has resulted in a new transformation across to the east of the Carpathian Mountains, where the early phases of the Cucuteni and Tripolye cultures emerge.

In the Mediterranean an analogous process was at work.[17] The farming economy of western Greece reached Italy by sea, and soon Sardinia and Corsica, southern France and the Mediterranean coasts of Iberia. In each of these areas there is pottery decorated with impressions which has given its name to the Impressed Ware cultures. Farming was soon practised throughout much of Iberia, and in central and northern France. From there, and perhaps also from the Low Countries, the first farmers reached Britain and Ireland. This is of course an absurdly compressed account, which covers in a few pages what many volumes and many university courses treat in much greater detail, over many chapters and many lectures.

It should be noted at this point that the view that the techniques of farming spread from south-east Europe to north and west, carried by the expansive movement of a farming population, as argued by the wave of advance model, has not gone unchallenged. It was one of the great merits of the approach of the late E. S. Higgs to questions of prehistoric economy that he was very willing to question earlier assumptions. One of these was the view that the origins of farming reflected a sudden revolution. Instead he argued for a long symbiosis between humans and animals which resulted in the development of domesticates, and which took place over a very wide area. A number of his former students[18] have argued not only that farming practices were adopted in the main by local hunter-gatherer populations who acquired those domesticates that were not locally available through trade and exchange, but also that most of the domesticates were in fact locally available. This case, however plausible it may be for cattle and pigs and for some of the pulse and other crops, does not work very well for precisely those species which were the first staples of the farmers of southern Europe: wheat and barley, and sheep and goats.

Both Robin Dennell and Graeme Barker have sought to argue that barley and einkorn wheat might be native to Europe, and hence locally domesticated there, while conceding that this can hardly be so for bread wheat and emmer. Although indications of wild barley have indeed been found from upper palaeolithic levels of the Franchthi Cave in Greece, there is no evidence that it underwent domestication there, and most palaeobotanists accept that the domestic cereals of Greece were indeed imported. No evidence has yet been put forward in a systematic way to argue that cereals were independently domesticated in other parts of Europe. The essential basis of European agriculture – cereals – was an imported one.

The most important stock animals in early Mediterranean Europe were sheep and goats. It is indeed the case that wild ovicaprids are known from some parts of the area already from the mesolithic and earlier periods. Much has been made of the evidence for this from early sites such as Châteauneuf-les-Martigues in southern France. But it is far from clear that these were the prototypes and ancestors for the domestic animals which were used there in neolithic times. As Geddes[19] has written:

> On the basis of cytogenetic and palaeontological evidence, it now appears improbable that the late Mesolithic sheep of southern France were domesticated *in situ*, or were themselves wild. These domestic sheep, whose ancestry must be traced ultimately to south-western Asia . . .

To insist that the main plants and animals were imported to Europe is not, however, the same as to demonstrate that the early farmers were themselves immigrants. It is perfectly possible to argue that exchange systems between the local, mesolithic population and their farming neighbours could have provided the former both with the necessary domesticates and with the stimulus to use them.

However the critics of the wave of advance model often seem not to have understood it too well. Barker goes so far as to argue:[20]

> There is remarkably little hard evidence for any colonization movement. In particular, not a shred of evidence has ever been

produced (or apparently thought necessary) to demonstrate the existence anywhere in Europe or in the putative homelands outside Europe of the kind of seething population sump predicted by the model in order to provide ever more land-hungry colonists for service at the expanding agricultural frontier.

To speak in these terms is to misunderstand the model at a rather basic level. Dennell[21] has quite rightly pointed out that the population density of the first farmers, once their settlements were well established, was not particularly high – but it does not need to be for entirely virgin land nearby to seem attractive. He has also stressed that the early farming cultures of Europe were regionally distinctive. That point is noted above, where it is argued that we may speak in terms of a number of transformations of the early farming package. These transformations were there viewed as adaptations to the new environments gradually brought about by the first farmers as they moved into them and developed their own farming systems. Interestingly Dennell himself speaks of the Linear Pottery people as colonists, and it is difficult to see why the same perspective is not applicable in south-east Europe and in west Mediterranean Europe also. Ammerman and Cavalli-Sforza further adduce in support of their wave of advance maps[22] for the distribution of various blood groups in Europe, suggesting genetic affinities which they feel are best explained by their model. I think experience has shown that genetic arguments in relation to language and culture quite readily lend themselves to misleading interpretations. So that although the blood group data could indeed be used to reinforce the case presented here, I feel it would be wiser to await further assessment of the arguments relating to these data, which have not yet been thoroughly reviewed.

The case for the arrival of a farming economy in several areas of Europe has, however, been well made, and I do not yet find the alternative assertions very persuasive.[23] This does not mean that the wave of advance model has to be applied in an inflexible or mechanical way. Of course there were local variations, and changes of pace, with quite long periods of stability in order for a farming population to become established and grow in numbers within a given area, before some individuals thought it preferable to seek farming land a little further afield. There was, then, nothing uniform about this process. In some cases, as with the Linear Pottery culture, farming seems to have spread rapidly. In others, as with the first neolithic of Scandinavia, it took rather a long time to get going. The archaeological record is becoming clearer all the time.

3 The Ancestral Languages of Europe

If the spread of farming was indeed responsible for the initial dispersal of the Indo-European languages in Europe, we should be able to make certain inferences about the relationships between the early languages in each area. Of course these will have been affected by many processes and circumstances before resulting in the modern languages of Europe, but there may be predictions which we can make which might be used to test the validity of the proposed explanation.

It does not, of course, follow that the first farming population of Greece all spoke the same dialect or even the same language. Be that as it may, we can list the transformations schematically as follows:

1 Anatolia to Greece (Thessaly and West Macedonia)
2 North Greece to First Temperate (Starčevo/Körös/Karanovo)
3 First Temperate (Körös) to Linear Pottery
4 Linear Pottery to Proto-Cucuteni and Proto-Tripolye
5 Linear Pottery to Scandinavia (TRB), and westwards into North France
6 West Greece to Impressed Wares (Mediterranean Coasts)
7 Impressed Wares to Iberian Neolithic
8 Impressed Wares to Central and North France
9 North France and Low Countries (Linear Pottery) to Britain and Ireland.

These relationships are set out in Fig. 7.7.

For the purposes of analysis, it may be interesting to see what linguistic patterns would emerge if we made the probably unwarranted assumption, that the languages of Europe as we know them from around the beginning of the Christian era derived from

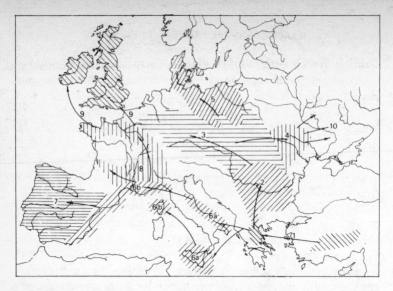

FIG. 7.7 Hypothetical sequence of cultural and linguistic transformations during the early spread of farming in Europe. The initial transformation (1) is from the early neolithic of Anatolia to that of central Greece where the language was ancestral to the Greek language. Transformation (10) indicates the change from East European settled farming to the first pastoral-nomad economy of the steppe lands.

those of the first farmers in each of the regions under consideration. The experiment at least has the merit of maximal simplicity.

Transformation 1 would lead ultimately to the Proto-Greek language.

Transformation 2 would lead to Proto-Illyrian, and perhaps Proto-Thracian and Proto-Dacian in the east.

Transformation 3 would lead to a language of Central Europe relevant perhaps to Proto-Celtic and Proto-Germanic.

Transformation 4 would lead to languages in those lands where the Slav languages are now spoken.

Transformation 5 would lead to the early, presumably Proto-Germanic, languages of Scandinavia.

Transformation 6 would lead to the Proto-Italic languages (but not non-Indo-European Etruscan).

Transformation 7 would lead to the early languages of Spain and Portugal (but not non-Indo-European Basque and Iberian).

Transformation 8 would lead to the early Proto-Celtic (or pre-Celtic) languages of France (to which Transformation 5 would contribute).

Transformation 9 would lead to the early languages of Britain and Ireland, including Proto-Celtic (or pre-Celtic) and perhaps Pictish, if this is an Indo-European language.[24]

Transformation 10 would lead to the first Proto-Indo-European languages of the steppe lands.

There is in fact no reason to suppose that so simple a picture could be valid; for there are no doubt many cases of language replacement which we ought to be considering, as well as other more complex linguistic processes. In the first place they take no account whatever of the pre-existing languages of the hunter-gatherer populations of those areas. We are aware today only of Basque, Iberian and Etruscan as the long-standing non-Indo-European languages of Europe, but there may well have been many more.[25] Although they have not survived as living languages, nor been recorded in inscriptions, they may well have had their influence upon the Indo-European languages which survived.

Secondly, it is not clear from this model to what extent the language of the first farmers of Greece was modified during the wave of advance phase. On the one hand one might imagine that there was little change initially, so that a somewhat similar Proto-Indo-European language might have been spoken from Greece right through to Scandinavia with only dialectal variations at the outset. The differentiation into the various Indo-European branches would then have been a subsequent process. On the other hand, linguistic change might have been quite fast during the dispersal phase, so that the language of the very first Scandinavian farmers, or even of the first Linear Pottery farmers, might already have been very different at the outset from the early farmers of Greece.

An intermediate position between these two extremes is

suggested by the work of the German linguist Hans Krahe.[26] He pointed out in 1957 that the river names of central Europe preserved many similarities which might indicate the presence in the area of an early stage of development of the Indo-European languages which he termed 'Old European'. For instance rivers named Alba appear in Spain, France, Switzerland and Germany; and rivers named Ara are found in Germany, Holland, England, Scotland and Spain. On the model proposed here it would be easy to see in these names a survival of the early group of dialects or languages existing across central and northern Europe before the process of differentiation had resulted in the different Indo-European branches, few of which retained such word forms.

On this model also we would expect various new words to arise along the way, so to speak, so that the innovations would be seen in languages diverging from the line of development from early Greece after a given point but not prior to that point. This would tie in with Krahe's observation that the European words for 'sea', 'forest', 'oak', 'apple', etc., are found in the languages of central and northern Europe – in general north of the Alps – but not further south. In the same way, a number of the other special words for species occurring in temperate and northern lands, but not in the south, would be expected to develop. Some might borrow pre-existing words in the language and give them a more specialist meaning. Others would be entirely new words. In this way, for instance, many of the Proto-Indo-European names for trees may have come about. Krahe concludes his 1957 article with a view which would harmonize with the model proposed here:[27]

> Finally, as a further reward we should observe that the recognition of 'Old European' – at least for the west Indogermanic languages – has made evident a prehistoric *intermediate stage* in the development. On the one hand this lies chronologically long *after* the period of a still relatively unitary general-Indogermanic root language. On the other hand it lies far *before* the earliest emergence of the separated individual languages.

A further limitation implicit in this simplistic presentation of the basic model is the lack of consideration of possible language replacements occurring between the pattern thus established around

4000 BC and the beginning of the present era. As we know that since that time the spread of the Latin language was responsible for the subsequent pattern of the Romance languages, is it reasonable to suppose that similar developments were not taking place earlier? In the same way, it is well established that the Hungarian language was introduced into central Europe around the ninth century AD – so why not similar events earlier? However the model is perfectly open to elaboration of that kind. The process outlined here might well have been succeeded by other processes which would have the effect of complicating the linguistic picture. That would not in itself invalidate the wave of advance approach.

Moreover, it does not follow that simply because the Romans and the Magyars effected successful language replacements other such replacements must necessarily have happened in earlier times. It should be noted that the historically attested language replacements in Europe do not fall within the Demographic/Subsistence category discussed in Chapter 6. That is relevant only to substantial changes in population density brought about by changes in subsistence practices, and we have very little evidence for such demographic changes after the initial spread of farming. To be sure, there were continual processes of intensification, including the 'secondary products revolution' with its greater emphasis on live-stock, but there is no reason to think that they were generally associated with substantial movements of people. On the contrary, the language replacements to which we can point fall within the Élite Dominance model. Such a model is entirely appropriate to the practice of military power by an empire like that of the Romans. It is appropriate also to a chiefdom society, such as the Magyars, when this is supported by a new military technology – in this case the technology of mounted warfare aided by the use of the stirrup. The first of these circumstances is simply not applicable in Europe before the time of the Romans. The second – chiefdom society coupled with developments in military technology – may have been. It is possible that the use of the horse in the first millennium BC by mounted warriors (although without the full possibilities of a heavy cavalry made possible by the stirrup) may have been significant in this way. In this case the impact of the Scythians and the Cimmerians may have been influential in eastern Europe, and this may have an important bearing upon our understanding of the Slav languages, and perhaps upon other aspects of the language pattern of east-central Europe.

Apart from these events, however, it is at present difficult to see indications of major episodes of élite dominance by outside groups in the prehistory of Europe such as might have resulted in significant language displacements. Some are, it is true, historically attested on a more limited scale. The origin of the kingdom of Dalriada in western Scotland, which is quite plausibly credited with the introduction from Ireland of the Gaelic language to its territory, and ultimately to Scotland as a whole, was probably one of these. A similar case can be made for the early origins of the Breton language from south-west England – although both these cases should be critically examined. But before the development of 'chiefly' tribal societies of heroic mould in the European iron age, such episodes are less likely. It is possible, therefore, that the language pattern of Europe was a fairly stable one between 4500 and 1000 BC. The Celts are discussed further in Chapter 9.

To say this does not in any way question the likelihood of border adjustments – of shifts over time in the position of linguistic boundaries. We must expect also the usual processes of linguistic evolution over time – convergences between some neighbouring languages, ultimately perhaps resulting in assimilation, and in other cases divergences resulting in the separation of distinct dialects and even languages. These would be no doubt determined in part by the extent of interaction between neighbouring areas, so that natural barriers such as mountains, and sometimes seas, would be expected to emerge also as linguistic boundaries. Thus it is likely that Iberia will have had a fairly stable linguistic history – although interactions across the Straits of Gibraltar may have played a significant role. Italy may also have been a stable area (although probably prone to regional variants), and we have some evidence that Greece was too. The case of eastern Europe may, however, be very different, and a more complex linguistic history is to be predicted there.

The advantage of this hypothesis is that it allows us to see the development of the European languages in time depth. We have already seen how it harmonizes with the hydronomy (river name) approach of Krahe. The Bulgarian scholar, Vladimir Georgiev, has also stressed the importance of place names[28] in revealing an earlier stage of linguistic development, and it may be that some of those which are often classed as 'Pre-Indo-European' by some scholars may instead represent an intermediate stage, as Krahe suggested, before the differentiation of the different language branches.

4 The Question of Time Depth

There is no doubt that the date proposed here for the dispersal of farmers speaking an early Indo-European language is very much earlier than most scholars have suggested, with the exception of Herbert Kühn and Pedro Bosch-Gimpera. (Kühn's ideas are discussed in Chapter 11). What is proposed here does in fact have much in common with Bosch-Gimpera's theory,[29] except that modern research shows very clearly that farming spread to the rest of Europe from Greece, and to Greece from Anatolia. These suggestions have more in common with the ideas of Bosch-Gimpera than with those of Kossinna or Childe – but Childe's emphasis on the importance of chariotry and horsemanship are again particularly apt for later episodes of élite dominance.

On the other hand it is difficult to see how most linguists have felt able to suggest that the Indo-European dispersal took place as recently as the third millennium BC or a little later (although their chronology has been set a few centuries earlier in the light of the calibration of radiocarbon dates). It is easier to see how the enthusiasts for glottochronology arrived at a relatively late date following these assumptions, but these have been widely criticized by many linguists.

My analysis of the literature suggests that the date of c. 2500 BC often cited for the 'dispersal' is based upon a circularity of reasoning. Archaeologists often quote it as being based upon linguistic evidence, and can indeed refer to linguists who give this impression. The linguistic argument seems to be a two-fold one. In the first place the absence of common words for 'iron' and 'bronze' among most Indo-European languages is taken as an indication that these were not part of the protolexicon and were thus not known in the homeland. And they point to the Latin *aes*, the Germanic *aiz* and the Sanskrit *ayas*, etc. meaning variously 'copper', or 'bronze' or 'ore' or 'metal', as an indicator that metallurgy of some kind was already underway in the homeland before the dispersal. Hence, they conclude, the dispersal took place towards the end of the neolithic period or early in the copper age. This ignores the circumstance that even the neolithic population of Europe must have been familiar, in many areas, with native copper, and in many others with copper and other metallic ores, which often have either a brightly-coloured or metallic appearance. The existence of a word for 'ore' or for 'copper' is no proof of copper metallurgy. In any case we are now very familiar with indications of very simple copper metallurgy in quite early neolithic contexts, in Greece and in the Near East[30] (Çatal Hüyük, Çayönü, Ali Kosh etc.). This argument, then, in no way militates against an early neolithic, or indeed earlier, date.

The circularity is yet more apparent in the second argument. Basically this takes the supposed finding of linguistic palaeontology leading to a homeland in south Russia or in central Europe, and accepts the conclusions either of the Kossinna school or of the early Childe and of Gimbutas in favour of a late neolithic dispersal. The dispersal is thus set around 2500 BC. This date is not based on any clear linguistic argument; it is not really a linguistic argument at all. It is a conclusion based upon consensus. Yet it is taken by archaeologists as linguistic evidence, and is used by them to support that very consensus. There is therefore a complete circularity. And in this case it would appear that the consensus may be in error.

Another, linguistically much more interesting, argument relates to the speed with which languages change and diverge. It will no doubt be argued that six thousand years is too long a time for the process of divergence resulting in the modern languages of Europe, and that the notion of a very early form, in Greece, eight and a half thousand years ago is unreasonable. However this view may not sufficiently take into account the implications of the decipherment of the Linear B tablets with its revelation of Mycenaean Greek; for Mycenaean Greek can be understood in many cases as if it were classical Greek. There are a few phrases where the resemblance is close, so that the transliterations of those parts of the tablets begin to make some sort of sense even in modern Greek. Admittedly there are many other cases where the Mycenaean Greek cannot be

understood at all, even with the aid of Classical Greek. But there are
some phrases, now 3,300 years old, which may still be recognized
as Greek (although of course the decipherment itself has not gone
unquestioned). I think it can be reasonably asserted that Mycenaean
Greek stands closer to Modern Greek than it does to Latin.
Mycenaean Greek and Latin must have come a long way, through
many processes of divergence, since the first notional 'dispersal'. So
that from that perspective the time depth suggested here is not
implausible.

Of course this is precisely the area where the procedures of
glottochronology should be most relevant. Its original exponent,
Morris Swadesh, following calculations by Roberto Escalente,
produced a table,[31] on which Fig. 5.4 is based, suggesting that Greek
and Latin became separate branches some twenty centuries before
the thirteenth century BC, i.e. c. 3300 BC, and that Hittite separated from Greek c. 4500 BC. These tables do not in general produce a pattern entirely consistent with the branching family tree
model upon which they are based. The main point to be made is that
there is no good ground for thinking that the rate of word loss in
one language need be the same as in another. If we were to alter
Swadesh's rate of loss by a factor of about two we might obtain
results more consistent with the datings which have been reliably
established by radiocarbon for the spread of farming in Europe.

Glottochronology, with its rather dubious claims for chronological precision, should be treated with caution, but the closely
allied approach of lexicostatistics is based on far less narrow
assumptions. If we are content simply to use the tables offered as a
measure in some sense of the closeness or similarity between pairs
of languages, as measured from their vocabularies, we may obtain a
more useful picture – unfortunately it is not a consistent one. The
reason for this may be simply that many of the branches have
diverged so far from each other that the numerical score of similarities between them is not many times more than the 8 per cent
which Swadesh predicted would arise by chance alone, between
entirely unrelated languages. With the very early divergences
which I am proposing, going back some eight thousand years, we
are beginning to approach the notional limit of 11.7 thousand years.
Swadesh suggested that when two languages diverged from a

common parent language as long ago as that, the word losses from them would have been cumulatively so great that the remaining 8 per cent of similarities which his method would predict would in fact be no more than the figure to be expected from chance similarities. So there are, in Swadesh's own view, serious difficulties in using this method for early periods.

I believe, in short, that the methods of lexicostatistics can usefully summarize what vocabulary can tell us about similarities between languages. They cannot be used mechanically to reconstruct a supposed historical picture.

It does not appear, therefore, that the claims of glottochronology are sufficiently firm to rule out the pattern of events proposed here. On the contrary, these events might usefully be used in a re-examination of some of the principles upon which glottochronology itself rests. The stability seen in some languages, notably Greek, does suggest that in many cases the pace of language change may be no faster than is proposed here. In general, I feel lexicostatistics is more likely to be helpful in illuminating the general relationships between languages than in establishing a precise chronology for language change.

5 Before Greece, Anatolia

There can be little doubt that the principal plant domesticates, and some of the animals too, came to Greece from Anatolia. It is likely that they were brought by immigrant farmers travelling in small boats across the Aegean sea. We need not think of this as an organized 'migration'. There is plenty of evidence that already in pre-farming times the early inhabitants of southern Greece were travelling by sea. This is documented for us by the finds of obsidian, shown by analysis to have come from the island of Melos,[32] which is found in early Greek sites, and particularly in mesolithic and even in late upper palaeolithic levels of the Franchthi Cave in the Peloponnese. It must be assumed that the early inhabitants of the Aegean coasts of Anatolia were travelling in the same way, although this is not yet clearly documented.

In the case of Crete we can be sure that the techniques of farming were indeed introduced by new settlers, since there are at present

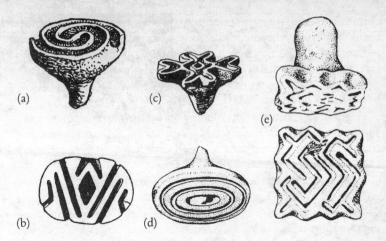

FIG. 7.8 Stamp seals ('pintaderas') from Anatolia and Europe: (a) (b) and (c) from Çatal Hüyük, Anatolia (d) from Maliq, Albania (e) from Tečić, Yugoslavia (*after Mellaart and Makkay*).

very few indications there of an earlier, hunter-gatherer population. Precisely where these small groups of immigrants came from is not yet known, but one presumes it was from early farming settlements yet to be discovered, on the southern coasts of Aegean Anatolia. We certainly have a clear indication of the way of life which they brought with them revealed in the lowest levels at the site of Knossos in Crete.

Most workers agree that the first farming practices of mainland Greece were also introduced by small groups of immigrants. The process need have been no more than a marine version of the wave of advance model. We can imagine people who were already used to travelling by boat, and who may in previous years already have crossed the Aegean on short visits, deciding to make a permanent move to exploit the rich potential of the farmlands of Thessaly, Central Greece and the Peloponnese. So far there are almost no indications of early farming settlements along the north Aegean coast, in what is now East Macedonia and Thrace. So all the evidence does support a sea-crossing, rather than a wave of advance movement along the northern coastlands.

FIG. 7.9 The original area of the Anatolian early farming culture (shaded), and the cultural similarities between the early Greek farming site of Nea Nikomedeia and other early sites. Specific similarities are indicated by numbers (see key). Karanovo is typical of early farming sites in Bulgaria, Soufli Magoula of many early farming sites in Thessaly in central Greece (*after Rodden and Mellaart*).

COMPARISONS WITH NEA NIKOMEDEIA

ARCHITECTURE
1 Square house plan
2 Wood frame and mud wall
3 Open settlement plan

SUBSISTENCE
4 Cattle?
5 Pigs?

ADORNMENT
6 Studs and nails
7 Clay stamps ('pintaderas')
8 Belt-fastener

POTTERY DECORATION
9 White-painted and finger impressed
10 Red-on-cream painting
11 Modelled face

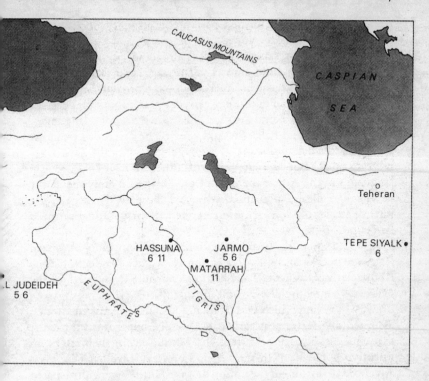

We do not have much idea of the language of neolithic Crete, since its bronze age successor, as documented by the Minoan Linear A tablets, remains undeciphered. But if the earliest farmers of mainland Greece spoke an early form of Indo-European, so did their parents in the early farming settlements of Aegean Anatolia. None of these has yet been investigated, but in view of the very early farming sites further east, there is no doubt that they must have existed.

It is likely that the first farmers of west Anatolia did not develop farming there, on the spot, from wild prototype species, and we should imagine the wave of advance beginning rather further to the east, perhaps in the Konya Plain, where the site of Çatal Hüyük[33] is located, or further east still. The question is one of determining where there was a substantial hunter-gatherer population that either adopted farming through contact with farmers in neighbouring territories or actually formed part of the primary nuclear zone where early farming developed.

On the model presented here, it is altogether unsurprising that Hittite should be an Indo-European language. Like its contemporary to the west, Mycenaean Greek, it would represent the successor within its own region of its very early Indo-European predecessor some five thousand years earlier. The other Anatolic languages, notably Luwian and Palaic, would likewise be descended from the same Anatolian neolithic predecessors, along with other languages now extinct. But the presence of other, non-Indo-European languages in the area at the time of the Hittites, mainly the Hattic language, indicates perhaps that not all the early farmers in the nuclear zone of domestication spoke an early Indo-European language.

It would of course be possible to see these non-Indo-European language-speakers as intrusive in some way, the product of some language displacement. They could have come from north of the Caucasus, or from the areas east of Anatolia. But there seems to be no way of telling which was 'earlier' – Hittite or Hattic. It is often assumed that Hattic was earlier in Anatolia, but that is simply the consequence of assuming that the Hittites were themselves an intrusive population. In reality, no good evidence has ever been advanced to document the notion that the Hittites were intrusive to Anatolia. It is true that the archaeological record is not very complete yet in Anatolia, and any number of surprises may emerge. I am not personally convinced by the arguments advanced by James Mellaart, one of the leading authorities on prehistoric Anatolia, for widespread destructions associated with movements of people and languages, during the early bronze age.[34] Again it is difficult to see why people would move in large numbers at that time from south-east Europe, the region that is now Turkish Thrace, into Anatolia. I would prefer to see Hittite as a language indigenous to Anatolia, growing from an early Indo-European base there.

How far east do we hope to trace this westward-moving wave of advance? The answer to that question must come from our knowledge of the origins of farming itself. At present it is widely agreed that the 'nuclear zone' may be approached by a study of the distribution of the prototype plant species. In the absence of good distribution maps for the early prehistoric period, modern maps for the relevant species[35] give the best indication.

The nuclear zone, on the 'hilly flanks of the fertile crescent', to use the terminology of Robert Braidwood, may be subdivided into three lobes.[36] The first, in the Levant, is represented by such early sites as Jericho and Tell Ramad. Its hunter-gatherer predecessor was the Natufian culture of Palestine. The second lobe, represented by such early farming sites as Jarmo and Ali Kosh, was preceded by the hunter-gatherer groups which are today named after the cave of Karim Shahir in the north Zagros. The third lobe is in south-east Anatolia, with such sites as Cayönü and Çatal Hüyük. The hunter-gatherer groups in this region, which are of special interest to us, are less well known. It should be noted, moreover, that Soviet archaeologists might claim a fourth lobe for this nuclear zone lying east of the last, and extending into Turkmenia,[37] with sites such as Djeitun and Togolok Tepe.

There were of course other centres of early farming, other nuclear zones, for instance in China. Our concern here is primarily with the range of plant and animal species which accompanied the specific wave of advance under review, and which formed the basis for the mixed farming economy of Europe and western Asia. Whether or not the development of early farming in India and Pakistan represents an entirely independent farming origin, like that of China, we will consider next (see Chapter 8). The alternative hypothesis could be advanced that the relevant areas formed part of a further lobe of the nuclear farming zone of western Asia.

The logic of the argument thus leads us to conclude that the first farmers in the east Anatolian part of the nuclear farming zone were probably speaking an early form of Indo-European.[38] We shall see that the same might conceivably be argued for some of the early farmers of the Zagros area. But in the southern part of the Zagros we are close to the two areas, Sumer and Elam, where in very early historic times, not long after 3000 BC, we have clear written evidence for the existence of two non-Indo-European languages, Sumerian and Elamite. In the Levant, the earliest known inscriptions certainly give us no indications of Indo-European languages: it is not clear whether early Semitic languages may have been spoken in the area so early as this. The language of Ebla in north

Syria in the third millennium BC is related to the Semitic languages. Displacements by later Semitic languages, such as Arabic, indicate that these originated further south, in Arabia, and a case can be made for a Semitic 'homeland' in that area. It seems difficult, therefore, to hazard a guess about the language of the Natufians of Palestine.

All these are hazardous postulates, about a time so early that we cannot possibly have direct linguistic evidence for it. However the logic of the model identifies east Anatolia as part, although not necessarily all, of the early 'homeland' of people speaking a very early form of Indo-European, around 7000 BC.

6 Implications

The implications of this model are of course highly significant, both for our understanding of the Indo-European languages, and for the prehistory of Europe and much of Asia. For Europe the picture which results is one of much greater time depth, much greater stability, than has hitherto been widely recognized. (The implications of this for north Europe, and specifically for the Celts, are looked at in Chapter 9.) In general, what we begin to see is that the prehistory of the different regions of Europe shows, with some significant exceptions, considerable continuity, from the time of the first farmers onwards. It is already widely accepted that the old idea of immigrant megalith builders, for instance, can be unhesitatingly discarded, in favour of local origins. Similarly the origins of copper metallurgy may now be seen independently in at least one area of Europe (i.e. the Balkans), and there is no reason to think in terms of any large-scale movement of people in association with the spread of metallurgical practices.

We have argued that the Beaker complex came about as a result of a network of interactions and exchanges rather than through any population movements or élite displacements, and similarly for the Corded Ware/Battle Axe complex. In Chapter 9 a similar case will be made for the Urnfield complex and for the iron age La Tène culture.

This point of view does not imply any exaggerated claims for the isolation of Europe, nor any extreme arguments in favour of 'independent invention'. It can harmonize quite happily with theories of what used to be called 'diffusion' – the gradual spread of new ideas and techniques. Those scholars who like to think in terms of 'world systems' may see Europe as simply the periphery to the Near Eastern core of a larger world system. None of that would contradict the continuities which are here proposed, nor the linguistic stability for which I am arguing.

What they imply, however, is that we should look in each area for its own roots – unless we have clear reason to do otherwise. There need be no prior assumption that things must have changed a good deal with the 'coming' of the Indo-Europeans. As an example of this new freedom to 'think local', it is worth turning again to the old problem of 'The Coming of the Greeks'.

7 Who were the Greeks?

As we have seen, until the Linear B tablets were shown to be written in an early form of Greek, it was often thought that the Greeks entered Greece during the dark ages at the end of the Mycenaean civilization. The writings of early historians such as Thucydides could be interpreted as suggesting, (although they did not actually say so), a Dorian invasion from right outside Greece, one among successive 'waves' of invaders, later to be responsible for the various dialects of classical times.

Already before the decipherment, there were many who recognized the elements of continuity from Mycenaean to classical times and earlier indications of entry were therefore sought. One of the favourites was placed at the beginning of the middle bronze age, when the wheel-made gray Minyan ware made its appearance. Childe was among the first to comment upon its possible significance[39] – now the significance of a single pottery type is widely discounted. Instead some scholars look to an earlier phase during the later part of the early bronze age, around 2200 BC, when an assemblage of pottery is found on a number of maritime Greek sites which does indeed resemble pottery from north-west Anatolia. This would be a possible candidate for replacement by élite dominance. While such pottery is found in some areas, it is not seen in other parts of Greece, and it is possible to exaggerate its importance.

Other than that, it is difficult to find any major assemblage of finds from prehistoric Greece which shows an outside origin, such as would indicate a displacement of people. The one significant exception occurs in east Macedonia, where at sites like the one which Marija Gimbutas and I excavated at Sitagroi, pottery and other finds closely resembling those from sites in Bulgaria to the north, twice occur. The first time is during the copper age, around 4500 BC, and the second is during the early bronze age, two thousand years later. This area, although firmly now part of Greece, has sometimes been a marginal one, and may at times have owed allegiance in different directions through a process of boundary displacement. It was indeed occupied in early classical times by Thracian tribes, barbarians who did not speak the Greek language. No doubt they did indeed speak a Thracian language akin to that in what is now Bulgaria, whose origins were suggested earlier.

The story in Greece, although there are several gaps in our present understanding, seems to be one of substantial continuity, with some occasional displacements. The economic decline at the end of the neolithic period, and the system collapse at the end of the late bronze (Mycenaean) period may both have produced some boundary displacements in border areas, but there is no need to suggest anything more radical.

These archaeological observations harmonize quite well with recent thinking by historical linguists. One of the most notable, John Chadwick,[40] the collaborator with Michael Ventris in the decipherment of Linear B, has written:

> My own opinion, advanced with due caution but firmly held, is that the question 'Where did the Greeks come from?' is meaningless. We can only begin to speak of Greeks after the formation of the Greek language as a recognizably distinct branch of Indo-European . . . the study of place-names and loan-words is rather more complicated than (many) have thought; and the certain facts are few. The only certain historical conclusions to be drawn for Greece from linguistic evidence of this type are these: at least one language was spoken

there before Greek; Greek is the product of the engrafting of an Indo-European idiom on non-Greek stock; Greek was already spoken in Greece in the Mycenaean age; and finally, the distribution of the Greek dialects within Greece was radically changed by the events which followed the collapse of the Mycenaean civilization.

Now it is true that in the passage quoted, Chadwick suggested that the process of formation of the Greek language took place 'during the first half of the second millennium BC', so that the arrival of Indo-European-speaking peoples in Greece would presumably be set by him somewhere around or a little before 2000 BC. But it is not clear to what extent Chadwick is influenced by the widely-held assumptions which we have already discussed about the 'coming of the Indo-Europeans'. Any independent arguments about date would presumably have to be based on general notions about the rate of which languages change. I have already given reasons for thinking that Mycenaean Greek probably differed at least as much from its Indo-European neighbours of the time as it does from modern Greek.

Apart from this debateable, although very important, point about dating, the linguistic views of Chadwick harmonize perfectly with the archaeological arguments put forward here. In the words of Sir John Myres:[41] 'the Greeks were ever in process of becoming'. The same may be said of several of the other languages of Europe.

8. The Early Indo-Iranian Languages and their Origins

The model for early Indo-European origins set out in the last chapter outlined a basic process which could be used to explain the fundamental underlying relationships between the major Indo-European languages of Europe and of Anatolia. But so far, nothing has been said about their relationship to the Indo-European languages of India, nor to the whole group of Iranian languages. There remains also the problem of the so-called Tocharian languages of Chinese Turkestan, and of various other more limited indications like the several Indo-European words recognized both in the Hurrian language and in the names of the rulers of their land of Mitanni where it was spoken. Let us start with India.

1 The Aryas

The *Hymns of the Rigveda*, which preserve the oldest form of Indian language which has come down to us, Vedic Sanskrit, were not written down until very much later. The earliest actual inscriptions from India come from the time of the great ruler Ashoka, dating from the third century BC. They are classified generally as 'Middle Indo-Aryan'. Early Sanskrit literature, although much of it was set down after that date, was written in accordance with the Sanskrit language of the fifth century BC, as codified by the celebrated grammarian Panini, who lived in north-western India about that time. As the linguist M. B. Emeneau[1] puts it:

> Classical Sanskrit is a literary language written according to the book – that is, Panini's grammar, and following it more or less correctly. We find in it no dialects, no chronological development, except loss and at times invasion from the vernaculars of the users, and no geographical divergences. Vedic Sanskrit, however, is different. It is anything but a unified language, a language of one dialect only . . . the Rigvedic dialect then is not the direct ancestor of classical Sanskrit. There must have

been several related dialects in the period of the *Rigveda* composition, one of which is the basic dialect of this text, another of which is basically the ancestor of the classical language of some centuries later.

Opinions differ about the difference in date between classical Sanskrit and the Vedic Sanskrit of the *Rigveda*. Emeneau quotes a difference of between one and five hundred years and suggests a date of about 1200–1000 BC for the composition of the hymns, but the estimation of the rate of linguistic change from internal evidence alone is very hazardous, and an earlier date is perfectly possible.

The *Hymns of the Rigveda* form an extraordinary body of literature. In general they are dedicated to specific deities, among whom the following occur very frequently:

Indra, God of the Blue Sky, the Thunderer,
Agni, the God of Fire and Light,
Varuna, Chief of the Lords of Natural and Moral Order,
Mitra, a Light God,
Surya, the Sun God,
the Asvins, the two horsemen, twin heralds of Dawn,
and the Maruts, who are storm gods.

The rituals described or alluded to again and again include the drinking of Soma, the deified juice of a plant of the same name which, strangely, later scholars have not identified precisely.

It is worth quoting one of these hymns taken from the great corpus of more than one thousand which form the ten books of the *Rigveda*. I have chosen one dedicated to Indra, which mentions in verse 8 the Aryas, the people who speak the Vedic language. As so often, the god is shown in warlike mood, destroying the strongholds of the enemies of the Aryas. (Puru and Divodasa/Atithigva are princes favoured by Indra; Sambora is a demon of air, and Ahi of drought.)

Book 1, Hymn cxxx[2] ~ *Indra*

1 COME to us, Indra, from afar, conducting
  us even as a lord of heroes to the
  gatherings, home, like a King, his heroes'
  lord.

We come with gifts of pleasant good, with
  juice poured forth, invoking thee,
As sons invite a sire, that thou mayst get
  thee strength, thee, most bounteous, to get
  thee strength.

2 *O Indra, drink the Soma juice pressed*
    out with stones, poured from the reservoir,
    as an ox drinks the spring, a very
    thirsty bull the spring.
  For the sweet draught that gladdens thee,
    for mightiest freshening of thy strength.
  Let thy Bay Horses bring thee hither as
    the Sun, as every day they bring the
    Sun.

3 *He found the treasure brought from heaven*
    that lay concealed, close-hidden, like the
    nestling of a bird, in rock, enclosed in
    never-ending rock.
  Best Angiras, bolt-armed, he strove to win,
    as 'twere, the stall of kine;
  So Indra hath disclosed the food concealed,
    disclosed the doors, the food that
    lay concealed.

4 *Grasping his thunderbolt with both hands,*
    Indra made its edge most keen, for
    hurling, like a carving-knife for Ahi's
    slaughter made it keen.
  Endued with majesty and strength, O
    Indra, and with lordly might,
  Thou crashest down the trees, as when a
    craftsman fells, crashest them down as
    with an axe.

5 *Thou, Indra, without effort hast let loose*
    the floods to run their free course down,
    like chariots to the sea, like chariots
    showing forth their strength.

> They, reaching hence away, have joined
>   their strength for one eternal end,
> Even as the cows who poured forth every
>   thing for man, yea, poured forth all
>   things for mankind.

6 Eager for riches, men have formed for thee
    this song, as a skilful craftsman
    fashioneth a car, so they have wrought
    thee to their bliss;
  Adorning thee, O Singer, like a generous
    steed for deeds of might,
  Yea, like a steed to show his strength and
    win the prize, that he may bear each
    prize away.

7 For Puru thou hast shattered, Indra!
    ninety forts, for Divodasa thy boon
    servant with thy bolt, O Dancer, for
    thy worshipper.
  For Atithigva he, the Strong, brought
    Sambara from the mountain down,
  Distributing the mighty treasures with his
    strength, parting all treasures with his
    strength.

8 Indra in battles help his Aryan worshipper,
    he who hath hundred helps at hand in
    every fray, in frays that win the light of
    heaven.
  Plaguing the lawless he gave up to Manu's
    seed the dusky skin;
  Blazing, 'twere, he burns each covetous
    man away, he burns, the tyrannous
    away.

9 Waxed strong in might at dawn he tore
    the Sun's wheel off. Bright red, he
    steals away their speech, the Lord of
    Power, their speech he steals away from
    them.

> *As thou with eager speed, O Sage, hast*
> *come from far away to help,*
> *As winning for thine own all happiness of*
> *men, winning all happiness each day.*

> 10 *Lauded with our new hymns, O vigorous*
> *in deed, save us with strengthening*
> *help, thou Shatterer of the Forts!*
> *Thou, Indra, praised by Divodasa's clansmen,*
> *as heaven grows great with days,*
> *shalt wax in glory.*

This hymn is typical in its reference to Soma juice, and in its association of horses and chariots with the heroic practice of war.

Even a superficial reading of the Vedic hymns gives a clear, if no doubt a partial impression of the world of the Aryas. (It should be noted that the people are the Aryas, and 'Aryan' is the adjective derived from their name).

Many scholars have pointed out that an enemy quite frequently smitten in these hymns is the Dasyu. The Dasyus have been thought by some commentators to represent the original, non-Vedic-speaking population of the area, expelled by the incursion of the warlike Aryas in their war-chariots. As far as I can see there is nothing in the *Hymns of the Rigveda* which demonstrates that the Vedic-speaking population were intrusive to the area:[3] this comes rather from a historical assumption about the 'coming' of the Indo-Europeans. It is certainly true that the gods invoked do aid the Aryas by over-throwing forts, but this does not in itself establish that the Aryas had no forts themselves. Nor does the fleetness in battle, provided by horses (who were clearly used primarily for pulling chariots), in itself suggest that the writers of these hymns were nomads. Indeed the chariot is not a vehicle especially associated with nomads. This was clearly a heroic society, glorifying in battle. Some of these hymns, though repetitive, are very beautiful pieces of poetry, and they are not by any means all warlike.

Archaeology gives very little help in broadening the context for these hymns, since there is no clear archaeological link – the hymns themselves are not dateable other than on general linguistic grounds, perhaps to around 1000 BC, perhaps rather earlier. Their importance should not to be underestimated. They stand at the head of the whole body of Indian literature, and at the very sources of the Hindu religion; that is not to say that we can see the Hindu religion in them with any degree of clarity. The principal deities of Hinduism are the Lords Brahma, Vishnu and Shiva. Brahma and Vishnu do appear in the Vedic texts, but not Shiva. On the other hand, many of the principal divine figures of the *Rigveda* continue to play a role in the Hindu religion, albeit a more minor one. Amongst these are Surya (the sun god), Indra and Mithra.

2 The Indus Valley Civilization and its Aftermath

When Sir William Jones first spoke of the early literature of India he had absolutely no idea of the antiquity of Indian civilization. For many years, the material record did not go back much before the time of King Ashoka in the third century BC, and the brief accounts of north India left by the commentators upon Alexander the Great's travels and conquests in the previous century. It was not till the year 1921 that Sir John Marshall[4] (with R. D. Banerji) made his great discovery of the Indus Valley civilization, with the investigation of two of its great cities at Mohenjodaro and Harappa. He found huge, brick-built cities in the fertile flood plains of the river, with well-planned street layout and many of the features of urban life with which scholars were already familiar from the discoveries in Mesopotamia. Amongst these were a well-developed craft specialization – for instance in pottery and bronze – and no doubt a highly structured social organization, reflected in the citadel at each site, with its large public buildings. The civilization was already flourishing shortly after 3000 BC, but had gone into irreversible and rather rapid decline by 1800 BC.

This was a literate civilization. Most of the inscriptions are preserved upon sealstones, generally with only a few characters each. This has allowed very thorough studies of the script, in which some four hundred signs were found, fifty-three of them used commonly. This suggests that it must be a mixed hieroglyphic and syllabic script rather than a pure syllabic script like Minoan Linear B. There are of course too many signs for an alphabet, yet not enough for a true pictographic script like that of the Egyptian

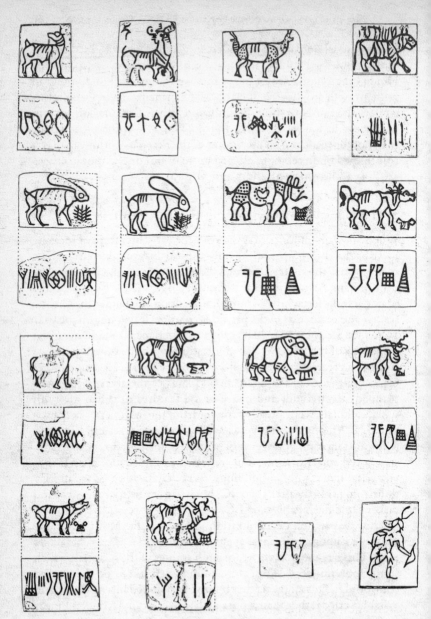

FIG. 8.1 The Indus script on copper tablets from Mohenjodaro (*after* Marshall).

hieroglyphs or the Chinese script. Various efforts have been made to decipher this script, and the Finnish scholar A. Parpola[5] has produced an impressively lucid analysis. At present, many specialists favour an interpretation using the assumption that the language of the sealstones is related to the Dravidian languages. These are the languages of modern central and southern India, constituting a different language group from the Indo-European. But this again rather follows the assumption that the Indo-European languages are intrusive into the north of the Indian sub-continent, and that the Dravidian languages were already there when they came. Other attempts at decipherment have been made on the alternative assumption that the script is related to proto-Elamite, the language of the inscriptions of south-east Iran at the time the Sumerian civilization was flourishing in southern Mesopotamia. This again is perfectly plausible, especially since proto-Elamite tablets have been found at the important site of Tepe Yahya on the south Iranian plateau. Still other efforts to decipher the inscriptions have been made, assuming instead that the language of the Indus Valley sealstones is in fact an early form of Indo-European. In my view, it is difficult to feel that any of these decipherments has yet been particularly successful, not even that of Parpola or the Russian scholars[6] who have claimed the inscriptions as early Dravidian. The difficulty is that in each case, for a successful decipherment, one needs to start with something that is known. So far, unfortunately, there are no bilingual inscriptions involving the Indus script, nor can any proper names yet be recognized in it. So the present decipherments consist in *assuming* a solution, and then trying to show that the results are plausible. This can lead to positive results, but again it can easily be an exercise in self-deception, and it is not clear that convincing progress has been made of the interpretation. This is not, however, to belittle the very important work which scholars have conducted in preparing a computer-based corpus of inscriptions, and an analysis of the occurrences and co-occurrences of the individual signs.

The great question for us is, of course, are the Indus Valley sealstone inscriptions in an early form of Indo-European?[7] In a sense this would not be surprising, since the earliest written records from the area which can now be interpreted are the *Hymns of the Rigveda*.

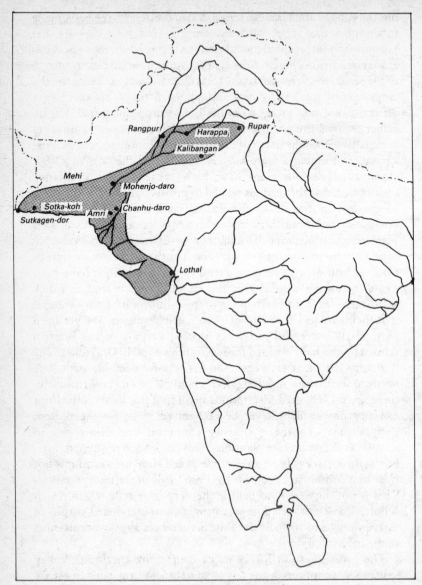

FIG. 8.2 Map of India indicating sites of the Indus Valley civilization
(shaded) (*after J.G.D. Clark*).

But the weight of scholarly opinion has in the past been against such an interpretation. It is important to analyse why.

In the first place, it has generally been assumed that the speakers of Indo-European were immigrants to India. This led to the further assumption by many scholars that the Indus Valley civilization was pre-Indo-European and perhaps Dravidian in its speech. Given that the Indus Valley civilization came to a rather sudden end, which extinguished urbanism in India for a millennium, it is not surprising in the migrationist climate of the earlier part of this century that scholars should have thought in terms of 'destroyers'. And who more natural than the warlike, battle-axe-using Indo-Europeans, already familiar from European prehistory, who could of course be linked with the warlike, chariot-riding Indo-Aryans of the *Rigveda*? This was the view advanced, for instance, by Sir Mortimer Wheeler, who assumed that various groups of skeletons found during the excavations at Mohenjodaro were the remains of those who had been killed in the cataclysm which befell the city:[8]

The Aryan invasion of the Land of the Seven Rivers, the Punjab and its environs, constantly assumes the form of an onslaught upon the walled cities of the aborigines. For these cities the term used in the *Rigveda* is *pur*, meaning a 'rampart', 'fort' or 'stronghold'. One is called 'broad' and 'wide'. Sometimes strongholds are referred to metaphorically as 'of metal'. Autumnal forts are also named: this may refer to the forts in that season being occupied against Aryan attack or against inundations caused by overflowing rivers. Forts 'with a hundred walls' are mentioned. The citadel may be made of stone; alternatively, the use of mud-bricks is perhaps alluded to by the epithet *ama* ('raw', 'unbaked'). Indra, the Aryan war-god is *puramdara*, 'fort-destroyer'. He shatters 'ninety forts' for his Aryan protégé, Divodasa. The same forts are doubtless referred to where in other hymns he demolishes variously ninety-nine and a hundred 'ancient castles' of the aboriginal leader Sambara. In brief he 'rends forts as age consumes a garment'. Where are – or were – these Citadels? It has in the past been supposed that they were mythical, or were 'merely places of refuge against attack, ramparts of hardened earth with

palisades and a ditch'. The recent excavations of Harappa may
be thought to have changed the picture. Here we have a highly
evolved civilization of essentially non-Aryan type, now
known to have employed massive fortifications and known
also to have dominated the river-system of north-western
India at a time not distant from the likely period of the earlier
Aryan invasions of that region. What destroyed this firmly
settled civilization? Climatic, economic, political deterioration
may have weakened it, but its ultimate extinction is more
likely to have been completed by deliberate and large-scale
destruction. It may be no mere chance that at a late period of
Mohenjo-daro men, women and children appear to have been
massacred there. On circumstantial evidence, Indra stands
accused.

This interpretation is rooted entirely on assumptions which, as
we have seen, are not necessarily valid. When Wheeler speaks of
'the Aryan invasion of the Land of the Seven Rivers, the Punjab', he
has no warranty at all, so far as I can see. If one checks the dozen
references in the *Rigveda* to the Seven Rivers, there is nothing in any
of them that to me implies invasion: the land of the Seven Rivers is
the land of the *Rigveda*, the scene of the action. Nothing implies that
the Aryas were strangers there. Nor is it implied that the inhabitants
of the walled cities (including the Dasyus) were any more aboriginal
than the Aryas themselves. Most of the references, indeed, are very
general ones such as the beginning of the Hymn to Indra (Hymn 102
of Book 1):[9]

> To thee the Mighty One I bring this mighty Hymn, for thy
>   desire hath been gratified by my praise
> In Indra, yea in him victorious through his strength,
>   the Gods have joyed at feast, and when the Soma flowed.
> The Seven Rivers bear his glory far and wide, and heaven
>   and sky and earth display his comely form.
> The Sun and Moon in change alternate run their course,
>   that we, O Indra, may behold and may have faith . . .

The *Rigveda* gives no grounds for believing that the Aryas
themselves lacked for forts, strongholds and citadels. Recent work
on the decline of the Indus Valley civilization shows that it did not

have a single, simple cause: certainly there are no grounds for blaming its demise upon invading hordes. This seems instead to have been a system collapse, and local movements of people may have followed it. Furthermore the chronology for the Aryan invaders theory is decidedly shaky. The decline of the Indus Valley civilization can now be put about 1800 BC. Yet we have seen that many scholars would set the date of composition of the *Rigveda* around 1000 BC. Certainly one could argue for an earlier date than this, but it is scarcely sound to do so in order that the date should come close to the end of Harappa and Mohenjodaro, and then to go on to claim that the closeness in date suggests that the one caused the other! This is what some arguments have done.

There is at least one other good example of the production of this kind of heroic poetry after a system collapse: the poetry of Homer. But Homer was writing sufficiently soon afterwards to have some memory of the pre-collapse Mycenaean age, probably because he was setting down what by then had become a strong oral tradition in poetry. The *Rigveda* could well stand in the same position in relation to the Indus Valley civilization, except that, perhaps taking shape rather longer after the collapse, it does not really hark back to the golden age before it. A much closer parallel for it in this respect than the Greek epics would be the Homeric Hymns, which in some ways are quite similar to it. They too relate primarily to their own time, and little in them refers back to the civilization of the earlier literate age.

3 Hypothesis A: Neolithic Aryas?

The time has now come to grasp the nettle. I can suggest one interesting way of relating the early languages of India and Iran to those of Europe. As we shall see, the evidence is not completely persuasive, and it is necessary to think of an alternative hypothesis, which is set out in section 4. However, both have the merit of offering some mechanism for the language displacement involved.

The first, and in some ways the simplest answer, is to suggest that the arrival of Indo-European speakers in the Indian sub-continent was very much analogous to that in Europe. Recent archaeological work in Pakistan has given very early evidence for farming there of a kind simply not previously available. The French archaeologist, Jean-François Jarrige, has conducted an outstandingly successful excavation at the site of Mehrgarh in Baluchistan (west Pakistan),[10] and there is now evidence for the cultivation of cereal crops (six row barley, einkorn, emmer and bread wheat) preceding 6000 BC.

It is not yet altogether clear that Baluchistan lay outside the primary zone for the domestication of these and other species. It would be perfectly possible to argue for the Zagros Mountain loop of the four primary zones to extend eastward to west Pakistan. It is possible instead that some sort of wave of advance operated to south and east as well as to north and west from the primary zones in and near east Anatolia, although of course modified by the terrain. We have already seen how rapidly Europe adopted farming under the influence of this wave of advance. In this way it might be argued that, from the very earliest farming times, as represented by Mehrgarh and by other sites later, an early Indo-European language was spoken in the Indus Valley and in areas to the north and west.

Despite Wheeler's comments, it is difficult to see what is particularly non-Aryan about the Indus Valley civilization, which on this hypothesis would be speaking the Indo-European ancestor of Vedic Sanskrit. Certainly there are elements of continuity from the Indus civilization on to its aftermath. The main disruption was the ending of urban life, but as Raymond Allchin has emphasized,[11] the rural life of northern India, and what is now Pakistan, carried on little changed.

There are, in particular, some suggestions that the religion practised in the Indus Valley may have had its effect on the later Hindu religion. The 'great bath' at Mohenjodaro may well have had ritual purposes,[12] which reminds us today of the various Hindu ceremonies of purification. Among the few major stone objects from the Indus Valley sites are shaped stones, which many observers have pointed out may hold a phallic significance,[13] but they also resemble quite closely the *lingam*, the sacred stone dedicated to the Lord Shiva in modern Hindu practice. There are other indications, for instance the seated figure, in *yoga* position, seen on an Indus Valley sealstone[14] has been equated by some with representations of the Lord Shiva himself. Of course continuity of cult need not indicate continuity of language, but there is no inherent reason why the people of the Indus Valley civilization should not already have been speaking an Indo-European language, the ancestor of the *Rigveda*.

Raymond and Bridget Allchin have recently considered the case for 'pre-Vedic' movements into the plains of India and Pakistan, pointing to distinctive fireplaces at the site of Kalibangan,[15] which may be interpreted as ritual hearths:[16]

> Such 'ritual hearths' are reported from the beginning of the Harappan period itself. It has been suggested that they may have been fire altars, evidence of domestic, popular and civic fire-cults of the Indo-Iranians, which are described in detail in the later Vedic literature. It may then be an indication of culture contact between an early group of Indo-Aryans and the population of the still flourishing Indus civilization.

The Allchins do not suggest that the Indus civilization itself should be regarded as Indo-European-speaking, simply that elements within it may already be recognized which are later characteristic of Indo-Aryan culture, as seen in the *Rigveda*. Their arguments in favour of Indo-Aryan features back in the Harappan period could certainly be taken in support of Hypothesis A.

Since the development of the civilization can quite plausibly be traced right back to early roots in the finds at Mehrgarh, the origin of the neolithic there is of the greatest relevance. The difficulty, of course, is that the area in question is a long way south and east of the recognized early farming centres in the Zagros.

This view would certainly have the merit of linking the spread of the Indo-European languages to the south-east with the same basic mechanism as in the north-west. And of course the Old Iranian language is also Indo-European. One difficulty, of real significance, is that there are said to be very few loan-words which might be identified as Indo-European in the early languages recorded in Mesopotamia. Had there been such early contact between them and these early Indo-European languages to their east, then there might have been indications already in them. The proto-Elamite tablets from the south Iranian site of Tepe Yahya are likewise a counter-argument to early Indo-European being spoken in that area, although proto-Elamite may have been a later introduction there.

On the other hand the Soviet archaeologist, V. M. Masson,[17] has suggested that the seals which he recovered from the site of Altyn-Tepe in Turkmenia, far up north near the Caspian Sea, are of proto-Indian type. Since he accepts the Russian decipherment for the Indus Valley script, which claims that the language is Dravidian, he comes to a very different conclusion from the one put forward here. But if we accept the observation that the Altyn-Tepe seals and those of the Indus are similar, and that this has linguistic implications, we could certainly take the alternative view that the accompanying language in each case was proto-Indo-European. This is not difficult to accept for the sites in Turkmenia, for there one sees a good degree of continuity back to the period of the earliest farming at Djeitun, and there are indications that these farming origins are related to those further to the west including those of our Indo-European-speaking farmers in East Anatolia. As the Soviet authors V. M. Masson and V. I. Sarianidi put it:[18]

> It has now been established beyond any doubt that the people who adopted the Djeitun culture maintained connections with the early agriculturalists of the Near East . . . In the Iraqo-Iranian zone the best documented [area] is the Zagros Mountain region – Jarmo, Sarab and Tepe Guran: this offers the clearest analogies to the Djeitun culture, especially in flint implements and pottery, though there are also important differences which distinguish the two cultures.

Hypothesis A, then, would carry the history of the Indo-European languages in north India and Iran back to the early neolithic period in those areas. The decisive process of dispersal would, as in Europe, be the demographic changes which accompanied the development of early farming. It might be possible also to link early Turkmenia with this process.

All of this, it must be admitted, is very hypothetical indeed. A much more comprehensive view is needed of the contemporaries of early Mehrgarh, and of the early neolithic in Baluchistan generally, before the hypothesis can be further advanced. If Baluchistan itself turns out to be within the primary zone of early agriculture, as is perfectly possible, the argument may become more difficult.

It should be noted, moreover, that the Old Iranian language as seen in the *Avesta*, and Vedic Sanskrit, as seen in the *Rigveda*, are very close: so close that they are generally considered to belong to a single, Indo-Iranian branch of the Indo-European family. Without placing too much reliance on the actual absolute figures produced by glottochronology, we may note that the lexicostatistician, Norman Bird,[19] has reported a strong co-occurrence of Indic with Iranian words: 85 per cent of Iranian words from his list have Indic equivalences. At first sight this is an exceedingly high figure – although we should note that 77 per cent of Hittite words in the list have co-occurrences with Indic roots also. If Vedic Sanskrit and Old Iranian are really to be considered as very closely related, this would imply a higher degree of recent interaction than might result from the straightforward pattern of an early wave of advance spread of agriculture. Some degree of continuing contact after the spread of early farming would be necessary to produce this degree of linguistic affinity. Fortunately the various links between the cultures of the Iranian plateau in the succeeding periods are becoming increasingly clear. There are indications of settlements of the Indus Valley culture on the banks of the Amu Darya river in northern Afghanistan, and graves of bronze age Turkmenian type have been reported from near the site of Mehrgarh in Baluchistan.[20] Of course these are some four thousand years more recent than the earliest farming discoveries there. But it is clear that there were continuing interactions in Afghanistan and on the Iranian Plateau, and a continuing community of Indo-European languages in that area is not improbable. It would be from this complex that, at a rather later date, the horse-riding nomads responsible for the presence of Indo-European languages in Chinese Turkestan (i.e. the Tocharian languages) would ultimately derive, and the chiefs of the Land of Mitanni in the mid-second millennium would originate from this same complex. (In view of the reported scarcity or non-existence of Indo-European loan-words in the early languages of Mesopotamia, we must assume that until the mid-second millennium BC, these people on the east of the Zagros Mountain range kept themselves to that area). There were of course numerous trading contacts between the Iranian plateau and Mesopotamia – already in the Sumerian period there are attractive, carved, greenstone vessels in Mesopotamia, made of chlorite schist, which must have originated on the plateau – but if we are following the present hypothesis, these contacts would not have had much linguistic impact. Much more work will have to be carried out on the archaeology of Central Asia before this hypothesis can be properly investigated, but it is perfectly conceivable that by the early second millennium, the languages of the Iranian plateau and of the Indus Valley, as well as of Turkmenia, were predominantly Indo-European.

The adoption of the horse and the techniques of chariotry may for a while have given some of these people some degree of military advantage over the populations in the Mesopotamia plains, and this may account for the various Indo-European names and words which we find from around 1500 BC onwards. Certainly, the adoption of horse riding transformed the economy of the steppe lands, and the various mounted nomad groups of the first millennium BC – the Saka and the Scythians, the Cimmerians, the Medes and the Tocharoi, all speaking Indo-European languages – developed military technology. The so-called Tocharians of Chinese Turkestan may have reached that area at this time. It is interesting, too, that although most of the military activity reported in the *Rigveda* was conducted from a horse-drawn chariot, as indeed was that of the Hittites and the Hurrian-speakers of Mitanni, there are passages in the Vedic hymns which strongly suggest that by the time of their composition horses were also being ridden.[21] This suggests a rather later date for the *Rigveda*, and reminds us that at this time there were renewed possibilities for contact between all the lands bordering upon the Iranian plateau.

Much here is hypothetical, but at least a coherent picture can be set out, which explains the observed language distributions (when they enter the light of history) in terms of readily intelligible processes of culture change. It remains to be seen whether so prolonged a separation as this implies between the western Indo-European languages of Europe and the eastern Indo-European languages of Iran and India is a feasible background for the various linguistic resemblances between them. That is a linguistic problem whose outcome will have an important bearing upon the viability of Hypothesis A. It should be remembered that with the increased intensity of interaction from the first millennium BC, when horse riding became widespread, there is the definite possibility of shared language developments of a wave-theory type extending across the steppe lands, between the Slavic languages in the west, the Anatolian languages (and Armenian) and the Iranian and Indic languages. This perspective of a very long time depth for the Indo-Iranian languages should not be lightly dismissed. Certainly the assumption that the Aryas were recent 'immigrants' to India, and their enemies were 'aborigines', has done much to distort our understanding of the archaeology of India and Pakistan.

It may be permissible at this point to draw a very general parallel between the transition in Greece from the Mycenaean to the Classical periods on the one hand, and the passage in north India and Pakistan from the Indus Valley civilization to the Vedic period, already implied when we compared the Homeric Hymns[22] of early iron age Greece with the *Hymns of the Rigveda*. Neither gives any clear hint of the urban civilization which flourished in the relevant area some centuries earlier and then collapsed.

I have recently argued that, in the case of the Greek religion, we see a whole series of transformations from that of the Mycenaean late bronze age of around 1500 BC to the religion of the classical Greeks a millennium later. The Mycenaean religion and the Greek religion were very different belief systems, or at least their material manifestations were fundamentally different. But the Greek religion did not replace the Mycenaean as a result of the immigration of 'Greeks'. That is the old view which we can now confidently dismiss: instead we see a succession of stages when new elements emerged, most but not all of them of local origin.

If we apply the same line of reasoning to the transformation from Indus civilization to its non-urban aftermath of a millennium later, we can trace the emergence of a number of elements, few of which need to be of foreign origin. Certainly there are some outside elements – the use of the horse to pull a war chariot is one of these. Precisely the same innovation is seen in Mycenaean Greece, at about the same time, and it is now clear that this happened in Greece without a significant change in population from immigration. Some centuries after the chariot, horse riding in association with new military techniques is seen in both areas. It is not surprising that both innovations had a greater impact in India and Pakistan, where the open terrain offers more scope for the horse (and indeed for the chariot) than does the rocky and mountainous landscape of Greece. There is nothing which forces us to associate these innovations in India with a new population, or with immigrants, any more than in Greece. The adoption of new military techniques will only entail language displacement if they are associated either with significant population change or with new élite dominance.

What we may be seeing at this time is the development of a new ideology, which finds its finest expression in the *Hymns of the Rigveda*, and indeed of the *Avesta*, and this may be reflected in the pottery of Cemetery H at Harappa,[23] which has handsome decorated vessels depicting horses, and departs from the geometric tradition of the pottery decoration of the Indus Valley civilization. (Much the same can, of course, be said of the pictorial pottery of Geometric Greece, where the Homeric heroes are first represented silhouetted in black against the yellow clay.)

We should, in other words, consider seriously the possibility that the new religious and cultural synthesis which is represented by the *Rigveda* was essentially a product of the soil of India and Pakistan, and that it was not imported, ready-made, on the back of the steeds of the Indo-Aryans. Of course it evolved while in contact with the developing cultures of other lands, most notably Iran, so that by a process of peer polity interaction, cultures and ideologies emerged which in many ways resembled each other. It is not necessary to suggest that one was borrowed, as it were, directly from the other.

This hypothesis that early Indo-European languages were spoken in north India with Pakistan and on the Iranian plateau at the sixth millennium BC has the merit of harmonizing symmetrically with the theory for the origin of the Indo-European languages of Europe. It also emphasizes the continuity in the Indus valley and adjacent areas from the early neolithic through to the floruit of the Indus Valley civilization – a point which Jarrige has recently stressed. Moreover the continuity is seen to follow unbroken from that time across the Dark Age succeeding the collapse of the urban centres of the Indus Valley, so that features of that urban civilization persist, across a series of transformations, to form the basis for later Indian civilization. A number of scholars have previously developed these ideas of continuity.

The hypothesis has, however, what may be a damaging weakness. It requires that the first farmers in the area, at sites such as Mehrgarh, should have reached there with their farming economy by the sort of wave of advance process which has been postulated for neolithic Europe. What works in Europe does not necessarily apply so well for the transmission of farming across or along the western flanks of the Iranian plateau from some nuclear farming area to the north. It remains to be seen whether the wild predecessors of the plants and animals found domesticated at Mehrgarh were already native to the area. If they were not, Hypothesis A may find some support. If they were, it is surely more likely that the process of domestication took place locally, and the theory of an incoming wave of advance is not necessary. In these circumstances we have to look for another explanation.

4 Hypothesis B: Mounted Nomads of the Steppe

This hypothesis outlines an alternative. Let us admit at the outset that it resembles the old and traditional view in relying on pastoral nomad invaders, but in other ways it is very different. It accepts the likelihood of local farming origins and that the arrival of the Indo-European languages is associated with the arrival of mounted warriors whose original way of life was one of nomad pastoralism; that is to say a process of élite dominance.

The Development of Central Asian Nomad Pastoralism

In order to reach some understanding of the second and first millennia BC in this area, it is essential to look at the origins of nomad pastoralism.[24] This is a difficult theme, since the archaeological traces of pastoral nomads are notoriously less substantial than those of settled farmers.

i *Development of a primarily pastoral economy.* In Central Asia and the European steppes, the principal domestic animals exploited were generally sheep and goats, and horses were herded for their products (milk, meat) as well as their usefulness for traction or as beasts of burden. The essential point is that some arid steppe lands are appropriate for grazing but not for the growing of cereal crops.

The pastoral economy is usually symbiotic with the agricultural one as it has been shown that a major component of the diet of these pastoralists was bread. The practice of agriculture is thus a pre-condition of a pastoral economy. In general a nomadic way of life may often have developed from the more limited mobility of a transhumant one.

ii *Use of equids as pack animals.* There is only limited evidence for this practice of using horses, mules, donkeys and onagers prior to subsequent stages of development, but the ability to transport a certain amount of equipment by animal, including tents, is a fundamental element in most nomadic economies.

iii *The use of wheeled carts.* The use of the four-wheeled cart[25] is archaeologically attested both in Europe and in Asia before that of the two-wheel chariot with spoked wheels. In many cases the draught animals seem to have been equids,[26] but in some areas cattle were also used. This seems to have been the case, for instance, in the Indus civilization[27] (although the economy there was not of course based on pastoral nomadism). In some cases two-wheeled carts are more common, but in the earlier phases of development the wheels were solid or composite, not spoked.

iv *Development of the war chariot with two spoked wheels and drawn by horses.* This is not reliably attested anywhere before about 1800/1600 BC. Such war chariots can be seen on Mycenaean[28] gravestones dated from about 1600 BC, in late Hittite reliefs[29] and in scenes of battles from before the Amarna period in Egypt.[30] The Hurrian called Kikkuli from the Land of Mitanni wrote a treatise in the Hittite language on the training of chariot-horses for the Hittite rulers of Hattusas. And the *Hymns of the Rigveda* make frequent reference to war-chariots.

v *Fully mobile nomad pastoralism and the military use of mounted horsemen.* Surprisingly perhaps we have little evidence that horses were ridden until long after they were used to pull chariots. The earliest representations of horse riding nearly all seem to come after about 1200 BC. That is certainly true in Greece – we have no pictures of Mycenaean horse riding[31] – and it is also true of the Hittites, the reliefs showing mounted warriors all come from the time of the Late Hittite period.[32] The art of the Scythians, and of Mesopotamia, where there are palace reliefs of the Assyrian kings, are the earliest representations we have of horse riding. (There are Egyptian reliefs of an earlier date which do in fact show horses being ridden,[33] but these early depictions are not of mounted warriors.)

The development of the bit seems to have been an essential innovation for riding, and chariot horses were not initially controlled in this way. Finds of bronze and iron horse-bits offer the most abundant archaeological evidence of horse riding, and they occur by 1500 BC in the Near East, earlier on the steppes, and in Europe and in China after 1000 BC.[34]

Claims have been made that perforated bone objects found very much earlier in central Europe were in fact horse-bits,[35] but they are not numerous, and the innovation (if such it was) did not become widespread nor is it certain that they were used in this way.

FIG. 8.3 Decorated antler cheek-pieces for horse-bits from the Carpathian basin, c. 2000–1800 BC (after Piggott).

vi *The military use of heavy cavalry, using the stirrup.*   Rather surprisingly, once again, the all-metal stirrup[36] seems to have been a
late invention made in China in the fourth century AD and first seen
in Europe in the seventh century. It allowed the use of much more
formidable weapons, notably the lance, since the horseman could
now avoid being unseated during the heavy impact of battle. The
barbarian invasions of Europe after the Dark Ages are said to have
owed much of their effectiveness to this.

This very schematic outline distinguishes between pastoralism as a
new form of adaptation to the steppe lands (allowing them to be
exploited for the first time), fully mobile nomad pastoralism based
on horse riding, and the warlike, expansionist behaviour which we
often associate in our minds with pastoral nomads. This aggressive
behaviour of the mounted warrior only becomes a significant
feature in the history of Europe and Asia after about 1000 BC. The
suggestion that the Corded Ware/Battle Axe people of central and
northern Europe behaved in this way was based largely upon the
fundamental misunderstanding of ignoring these distinctions.
Likewise the Kurgan peoples of the south Russia steppes need not
be regarded as formidable warriors until they were capable of
fighting upon horseback. One very relevant factor here may well
have been the development of suitable breeds of horse large enough
to serve as chargers.[37] The considerable delay between phases (ii)
and (iii) on the one hand and phases (iv) and (v) on the other may be
due largely to this.
    One of the main ideas constituting Hypothesis B is that, with the
development of chariotry and then of military horse riding, a new
possibility for élite dominance emerged. This would be the basic
underlying mechanism for the process of language replacement
which took place during the later second millennium BC. But
precisely where did these important innovations take place? That
question is not an easy one to answer, although it is clear that the
development is likely to have occurred amongst people who were
already using the horse intensively both as a pack animal and for
traction – and this brings us back to the steppes of Eurasia.
    It would seem that the horse was not used for traction on the
Iranian plateau until rather later than on the steppe lands to the

north. Certainly we find cattle, not horses, yoked to the model carts found in the Indus civilization. In Turkmenia there are comparable models, but with camels[38] pulling the carts, found in what is termed the Namazga IV period, dateable from about 3000 to 2600 BC. In Mesopotamia on the famous standard from Ur[39] just a little later, the animal pulling the cart is sometimes considered to be an onager, and the horse may not yet have been introduced.

Given then that the predominantly pastoral economy of the steppe lands must have developed in the first place from a mixed farming economy on the more fertile steppe margins, can we determine more precisely where this took place? This is one of the most interesting questions of Eurasian prehistory. Consideration of the map suggests that there are really only four possibilities:

(a) the south Russian steppe margins, at the west of the great Eurasian steppes, in the Ukraine area. There the point of agricultural origin would be the neolithic cultures of eastern Europe, termed Cucuteni and Tripolye.

(b) the lands north of the Caucasus Mountains, between the Black Sea and the Caspian Sea. The local farming cultures there have been studied by Soviet archaeologists, but are not yet well dated.

(c) the farming areas of Turkmenia, along the line of the Kopet Dag, east of the Caspian Sea. The Djeitun culture represented the first farmers in that area. (Most of Central Asia was dominated during the period of the Turkmenian neolithic by what has been called the Kelteminar culture, which has a characteristic range of pottery and flint types. In many cases the settlements are located on the banks of lakes and small rivers, and it has been suggested that fishing as well as hunting were of considerable economic importance).

(d) any other areas of early farming further east. No other such centres are in fact known at present until one reaches China and the Yangshao culture of Honan province.

It seems likely at present that the fully mobile pastoral economy of the Eurasian steppeland developed either in area (a) or (b). We are thus talking of the range of cultures which go under the name of *yamno*[40] (Pit Grave) or Kurgan (burial mound) cultures. Radiocarbon dates do not yet provide unequivocal evidence to decide between them, but it is an integral part of Hypothesis B that the Eurasian steppelands were colonized by nomadic pastoralists from the west (i.e. from the Ukraine). This theory was put forward by Ward Goodenough in 1970 and this somewhat technical archaeological discussion opens up wide vistas.

The development of pastoralism in the steppe lands had consequences in their own way as significant as the introduction of farming to south-east Europe. For here now was a new economic basis which could spread with its own wave of advance. The language of the first nomad-pastoralists could spread, by a process analogous to adaptive radiation, with the same dynamic demographic basis which underlay the rapid spread of farming across Europe. Just as in Europe, the language of the first farmers (of Greece) had an adaptive advantage (its farming basis) which allowed it to spread throughout the area, so on the steppe lands the language of the first effective nomad pastoralists had the opportunity to spread across the region.

I suggest that this is precisely what it did. Sandor Bökönyi,[41] in his study of the prehistory of the horse, has shown that the horse was already known and exploited (presumably for food) in the south Russian steppes at the outset of the period in question. The context there is in the early farming Tripolye and Cucuteni communities of the eastern Balkans. It was the spread, from west to east, of the *yamno* or Kurgan cultures of the first true steppe neolithic which gave the steppe lands of Europe and Central Asia their first cultural unity. I suggest that the language of these early steppe pastoralists, who were not yet driving chariots or perhaps riding horses, was already Indo-European. Moreover we can be more specific than that. The language must indeed have been derived from that of those Cucuteni and Tripolye peasants who, with their mixed farming economy, were at the beginning of the transition to nomad pastoralism on the steppe margins. The transformations by which this culture and its accompanying language developed from its earlier European antecedents were discussed in Chapter 7. The Slavic language group may represent the much later development within the same area of the language spoken by the descendants of those Tripolye and Cucuteni peasants.

This solution of the problem is rather better substantiated archaeologically at the present time than is its Caucasian alternative. It is also linguistically more convenient, because the contemporary languages of the Caucasus region do not belong to the Indo-European group. The Caucasian languages are numerous and varied, and there is no reason to think of them as a recent importation to the area. They appear on the map, indeed, to form a sort of linguistic barrier between the early farmers of Anatolia and the steppe lands to the north.

Once it is accepted that the first nomad pastoralists of the steppes were already speaking an Indo-European language, derived from south Russia and points west, the rest of the picture is clear enough. The succeeding culture of much of the steppes, which is termed the Andronovo culture, shows considerable unity over a very large area, and it persists to bronze age times. There can be no doubt that the horse was being used to pull the carts of the steppe population before this time, and maybe it did begin to have a military significance. At any rate, one may suggest that at this time the steppe nomad economy began to have an impact upon Turkmenia and the Iranian plateau. As Masson and Sarianidi write in their consideration of Turkmenia:[42]

The migration of tribal groups to the south is an almost established fact. The second millennium BC was a period of great migrations and population changes, possibly as a result of the 'population explosion' in the Euro-Asian steppes following the adoption of nomadic stock-breeding and primitive agriculture which followed the archaic Neolithic economy. At all events, the archaeological material at our disposal leaves no doubt as to the spread of a population with Andronovo and Timber-Grave characteristics. There were two main movements of these steppe tribes into Western Central Asia . . . This should, of course, be studied in conjunction with the problem of the diffusion of tribes of the Indo-Iranian linguistic group.

I would myself differentiate between the initial population explosion associated with the adoption in the steppes of the nomad pastoral economy and the later movements south, which I imagine as being related more to the élite dominance model. But from this point on, Hypothesis B accords with much of the standard archaeological interpretations for the area.

There can be no doubt that when the peoples of the steppes, then termed, amongst other things, Cimmerians, Sarmatians and Scythians, first entered the light of history about a thousand years later they spoke Indo-European languages.[43] The same is true of the peoples of the Iranian plateau – the Medes and Persians, and the Saka (i.e. the Scythians once again). The Iranian languages are thus naturally to be seen as Indo-European through the dominance of the Iranian plateau by horse-using steppe-nomads from the north. How far east this unity extended is difficult to determine, but the later existence of Indo-European languages in the Turfan depression of Chinese Turkestan suggests that it may have been a long way. Of course by the time it is recorded, in the eighth century AD, Tocharian already formed an Indo-European enclave amongst nomadic pastoralists speaking Ural-Altaic languages.[44]

It is clear that at some point during the first millennium BC there were very significant developments in the eastern part of the Eurasian steppe which resulted in the dominance of populations speaking Ural-Altaic languages over much of the area. Just as initially, in Europe and Central Asia at least, the economy of nomad-pastoralism was associated with Indo-European speakers, so later the nomads were predominantly non-Indo-European in speech, with the exception of just a few pockets, like the speakers of the Ossetian language.[45] The underlying economic or processual reasons for these later changes are not at all clear to me: one is reluctant to blame all of this simply upon the invention of the stirrup. But that problem takes us beyond the time scale of the present inquiry – it is, of course, entirely relevant both for the later language displacements in Anatolia, which led to the adoption of Turkish and the extinction there of Indo-European speech, and for the incursion of the Finno-Ugrian languages into Hungary, and Estonia in the first millennium AD.

Turning once again to the Indus, there is no reason to imagine that our 'nomadic warriors' were responsible for the demise of the Indus civilization – that was probably a case of system collapse. But these well-organized and mobile tribal groups, with a chiefdom organization, may have profited by the disorder in the Indus to achieve a measure of élite dominance, and hence to bring about an effective language displacement. Thus the early language of eastern Europe, transformed no doubt in its transition to the Eurasian steppes, and transformed again in its adoption to the Iranian plateau and to Afghanistan, would have come to the Indus.

5 The Choice of Hypotheses: A versus B

At present it is not easy to see how one should choose between these two hypotheses. Both accept the major premise of this book that central and eastern Anatolia was the key area where an early form of Indo-European language was spoken before 6500 BC. From there the distribution of the language and its successors into Europe was associated with the spread of farming.

Hypothesis A suggests that the zone of early farmers speaking Proto-Indo-European extended east to northern Iran and even to Turkmenia at the outset. The spread of Indo-European speech to the south, to the Iranian plateau and to north India and Pakistan, can then be seen as part of an analogous dispersal, related to the demographic changes associated with the adoption of farming.

Hypothesis B does not take this view. It suggests instead that the crucial development for the eastern area was the development in the Eurasian steppes of nomad pastoralism, and that this took place first at the western end of the steppes. In this way, it was argued, the nomad pastoralists of the steppes spoke an Indo-European language at the outset. Their later dominance in Iran and in the Indus is then ascribed to their military effectiveness, based largely upon the use of the horse.

It is of course possible to blend these two hypotheses. Even if we accept Hypothesis A, it is still likely that the first steppe nomads did indeed speak Indo-European languages, and that their adaptation to the steppes first took place in the Ukraine. If we accept Hypothesis B, it is perfectly possible that Indo-European languages were spoken in north Iran and Turkmenia from the time of the first

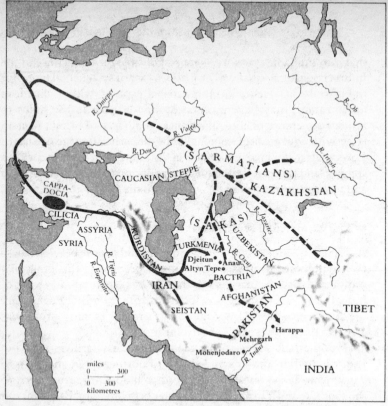

FIG. 8.4 Proposed alternative origins for the Indo-Aryan languages. *Hypothesis A* (indicated by continuous line). Spread of farming economy and early Indo-European speakers eastwards from Anatolia during the sixth millennium BC. And/or *Hypothesis B* (indicated by broken line). Incursion of a pastoral nomad economy, with pack-animals, carts and possibly horse riding, from the Russian steppe-lands to the Iranian plateau and to north India during the second millennium BC.

farmers there: the first Indo-European speakers in India would be very much later.

From the linguistic point of view, however, the two hypotheses are very different. The first implies that the Indo-European languages of Iran and India and Pakistan derive from precursors in eastern Anatolia and further east, just as the first Indo-European languages of Europe derived at the same time from precursors in central and western Anatolia. The successors of the western Anatolian languages are the Indo-European languages of Europe;

the successor of the central Anatolian languages was Hittite; and the successors of the eastern Anatolian languages were thus the Indo-Iranian languages. We might expect, then, a number of resemblances between Hittite and the Indo-Iranian languages. On the other hand, the languages of eastern Europe would originally have born little affinity with the Indo-Iranian languages, although convergences could occur as a result of steppeland influences on Iran and India at a later date. The original separation would have taken place by 6500 BC.

On the other hand, Hypothesis B implies that the relationship between the Indo-Iranian languages and those of eastern Europe would be very much closer, with a common origin around 4000 BC. There are some indications which might support such a view, for instance the old classification of the Slavic languages within the eastern or *satem* group – but little emphasis is placed these days upon this simplistic distinction.

Archaeologically speaking, a conclusion is not at present any easier. The decision which has to be made is whether or not the development of the early neolithic of the Iranian plateau, and especially of Baluchistan was initially, in large measure, the result of a 'spread' of farming there, on a wave of advance model, or instead primarily a local development. A further crucial question is whether or not there is really convincing evidence in the Indus for an episode of élite displacement, with the new élite coming from well to the north, outside the area, somewhere around the middle of the second millennium BC. This has often been suggested. But there are only a few finds which might indicate the arrival of an élite from the north. There are in fact some finds near Mehrgarh[46] in the Indus valley which closely resemble the culture at the site of Namazga much further to the north in Turkmenia. The famous Cemetery H at Harappa, with its painted pottery, would make an interesting focus of study. Can we regard it as a late development of the Indus civilization, a transformation from it, in a society which was becoming or had become non-urban? Or do we have to see it as the result of an immigrant group, bringing with it a whole new range of material equipment by which its source can unequivocally be identified? One cannot be sure, but present evidence might suggest the former.

As a tentative conclusion, however, I feel that it is useful in considering the Indo-Iranian languages, to see their distribution as the result of the working out of at least three cultural and economic processes. The first would indeed be the colonization, by early peasant farmers, of tracts of potential farmland in Iran, perhaps as far south as Pakistan (including Mehrgarh) on a variant of the wave of advance model adapted for the environment of the terrains in question. This draws heavily upon the arguments considered for Hypothesis A. The area of origin would be eastern Anatolia, and those areas to the east which one can regard as participating within the original 'nuclear zone' for the initial domestication of plants and animals. At present, however, it seems that the area to the west of the Zagros mountains, including Mesopotamia and most of the Levant, had an early farming population which was not Indo-European speaking.

The second process of importance is the development of nomad pastoralism in the steppe lands of Russia, and the wider spread of such nomad pastoralism. The evidence at the moment seems to show that the domestication of the horse took place at the western extremity of the Russian steppes, and that the spread of the nomad pastoral economy took place from west to east. Naturally one should consider whether comparable processes leading to nomad pastoralism were independently under way in other areas. At present it is possible to consider a nomad pastoralist presence in central Asia from the third millennium BC as a result of this second process.

The third process is that of élite dominance, where well organized communities of mounted nomad pastoralists, with a ranked social organization, achieved dominance in certain areas by force of arms. We are talking here of events in the first millennium BC, and perhaps back into the second millennium BC, but not earlier, for we have no evidence for mounted warriors at an earlier time.

The situation in each area was no doubt the product of these and other processes. In central Asia, the second process is likely to have been the most important, at least initially, and in this context the later work of Henning on Tocharian origins is highly significant. He argues for an equation between the Proto-Tocharians and the

Guti, who are documented in Babylonia at the end of the third millennium BC. He observes that[47] 'if we regard the Guti as "Proto-Tocharians", their nearest relatives among the Indo-Europeans would be the Hittite nations of Asia Minor', although my arguments would lead to a closer relationship with the early nomad pastoralists of the European steppe lands. There may be other problems, at a detailed level, with some of Henning's proposals, but as he says,[48] 'This is the heart of the theory that I wish to propound. Possibly the archaeologists may welcome a theory that involves considerable movement of people from Persia to the limits of China as early as the close of the third millennium BC.' That is indeed welcome, as an observation formulated on linguistic grounds, so long as it can be tied up with the processual realities which we are endeavouring to establish.

In the case of India and Pakistan the present dilemma remains the decision as to how much emphasis to place on the first of these processes, the farming wave of advance, and how much on the succeeding two. It is at least useful to stress that the situation may not be adequately explained by laying weight upon a single one of these processes. The balance of the evidence, as recently usefully reviewed by Shaffer,[49] is in favour of the presence of an Indo-European speaking population during the Harappan civilization, and not exclusively later. At the same time the strong continuities between that Harappan civilization and its antecedents, right back to the earlier neolithic, are becoming more and more evident.

The main difficulty for the Indian evidence arises from the extremely close affinities between Vedic Sanskrit and the Old Iranian language of the *Avesta*. This clearly argues for relatively recent processes at work relating the two areas. One is tempted, then, to suggest that some phenomena of élite dominance were indeed at work during the first millennium BC, or rather earlier, and that the élites of the two areas were closely related. But it is important to observe that this does not militate against the presence of Indo-European speech in north India and Pakistan at a somewhat earlier period. Some sort of 'two wave' hypothesis of this kind may do more justice to the complexity of things for the Indian subcontinent than any simpler explanation.

Above all we need to know very much more about the early

archaeology of nomad pastoralism. We need to see whether the sequence of six stages outlined above does really correspond to the reality. These are questions for the future. Meanwhile it is useful to bear both hypotheses in mind. By doing so, and by admitting that at present both have a certain degree of plausibility, we are helpfully reminded how little we at present know. These questions are not in principle unanswerable. When we consider how much we have learnt in recent years about the origins of the Indus civilization,[50] and when we recall that the important evidence now available from Turkmenia is mainly the result of fairly recent work by Soviet archaeologists, there are certainly grounds for optimism.

9. Ethnogenesis: Who were the Celts?

The whole race, which is now called Gallic or Galatic, is madly fond of war, high spirited and quick to battle, but otherwise straightforward and not of evil character. And so when they are stirred up, they assemble in their bands for battle, quite openly and without forethought, so that they are easily handled by those who desire to outwit them; for at any time or place and on whatever pretext you stir them up, you will have them ready to face danger, even if they have nothing on their side but their own strength and courage.

Strabo[1] IV.IV.2

Physically the Gauls are terrifying in appearance, with deep-sounding and very harsh voices. In conversation they use few words and speak in riddles, for the most part hinting at things and leaving a great deal to be understood. They frequently exaggerate with the aim of extolling themselves and diminishing the status of others. They are boasters and threateners and given to bombastic self-dramatization, and yet they are quick of mind and with good natural ability for learning. They also have lyric poets whom they call Bards. They sing to the accompaniment of instruments resembling lyres, sometimes a eulogy and sometimes satire. They also have certain philosophers and theologians who are treated with special honour, whom they call Druids.

Diodorus Siculus[2] V. 31

I think it would be helpful now to return to Europe and select one major area and one important problem for examination in rather greater detail. I have chosen to consider the so-called Celtic languages because the issue of their origin has become almost inseparable in the literature from that of the origin of the Celts themselves. To the extent that the two questions can indeed be distinguished, the first is linguistic and the second relates to a people or peoples: it is ethnic. The discussion thus offers the opportunity of considering one of the most interesting and currently neglected of topics in the whole field of prehistoric archaeology (neglected, that is to say, in the West although not by our Russian colleagues[3]): that of ethnogenesis.

The Celts

The image of the warlike Celt or Gaul (since the two terms are almost interchangeable among the classical authors) is a familiar one, graphically illustrated by a number of statues[4] of the same period of the 'Dying Gaul' displaying a memorable mixture of fierceness and manly pathos. The Celts and Gauls were well described in their homelands by the authors quoted and by others including Julius Caesar. Several of the languages of those Celts, or those immediately descended from them, survive today, including Irish, Welsh, the Gaelic spoken in Scotland, and Breton, while others such as Manx and Cornish were still current until a few centuries ago. The term 'Celtic' has several other overtones, referring also to the Celtic church, notably in those western lands which had never been conquered by the Romans, during the first millennium AD. With the Celtic revival in the nineteenth century came a new awareness of Celticity, and a determination to value and safeguard the Celtic heritage. The Welsh festival, the Eisteddfod, dates from that period.

Archaeology and linguistics were not slow to document the Celts and to consider their origins. Serious efforts were made to record the languages in the seventeenth century, by such scholars as Edward Lhwyd, and in the eighteenth century it was realized that the languages spoken by the Celts and Gauls in classical times were related to the more recent languages in those lands, and these to each other, so that it is meaningful to speak of a Celtic language group. Not long after the existence of an Indo-European family of languages was recognized, it was perceived that the Celtic languages belonged as a group within the family of the same general kind as the Romance languages or the Germanic languages and so on.

The origin of the Celts was naturally sought, and this was rightly seen to be both a linguistic and an archaeological problem. The prevailing model for culture change at the time was essentially a migrationist one, so it was inevitable that archaeologists should speak of 'waves' of migrating Celts. The Celtic languages had been classified into P-Celtic (including Welsh and Breton) and Q-Celtic (including Irish and Scottish Gaelic), and therefore these were seen as the result of successive waves of invaders. It was generally recognized that the Hallstatt culture, which preceded La Tène, was represented by Celtic-speaking peoples. The question then arose as to whether its late bronze age predecessor, often described as the Urnfield culture, was an immigrant one, bringing the first Celtic speakers to western Europe, or whether much earlier archaeological cultures in the area, perhaps the Corded Ware culture, should instead be regarded in this way.

These questions look very different today and it is interesting to try to see how a processual approach would cope with the problem. Moreover the perspective developed in the previous two chapters, arguing for a much earlier presence in Europe of people speaking an Indo-European language than has been generally thought,

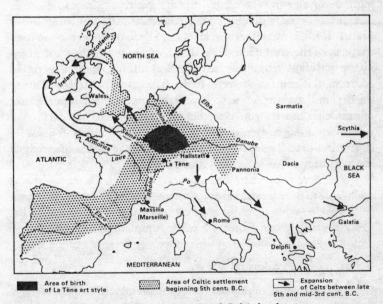

FIG. 9.1 Map by Duval indicating notional Celtic lands.

is clearly relevant. We shall see that in the case of the Celts it harmonizes rather well with ideas which have been developing recently in the field of historical linguistics.

First it is necessary to ask rather more precisely, who were the Celts? That is to say what do we mean by that term, and what did the classical authors mean? This brings us at once to the very interesting and very difficult concept of ethnicity. What do we mean by an ethnic group? And how far may such groups be recognized archaeologically? The question is clearly a very important one when we are discussing the archaeology of languages, especially since language is often one of the defining elements of the notion of ethnicity.

In the case of the Celts, the term 'Celtic' has clearly come to mean many things: we can define at least eight senses in which it is used. In the first place it refers to people whom the Romans designated by that name. Second it can indeed refer to people who called themselves by it. Third it can designate a language group, as defined by contemporary linguistics. Fourth, it has come to label an archaeological complex in west central Europe which embraces a number of archaeologically defined cultures, such as the Marnian of north France. Fifth, it can refer to an art style. Sixth, the term is often used to speak of the warlike, independent spirit of the Celts, as reflected in the passages from the two classical authors quoted here. In addition, it is common to refer to the elaborate art of Ireland during the first millennium AD as Celtic, in the same sense that one speaks of the Celtic church. And then there is the whole series of uses of the term within our contemporary society, where it refers to qualities or features broadly supposed to derive from the earlier ones which we have been discussing: the Celtic heritage.

We are here concerned with the ways in which the term Celtic is applicable to peoples and lands at the time of the Greeks and Romans, and to ask to what extent it is permissible to speak in terms of 'the Celts, the first great nation north of the Alps whose name we know'.[5]

Ethnicity – a Processual View

One of the most notable features of the prehistoric archaeology of the earlier part of this century, was to develop a perspective which laid stress on regional variations, which was interested in the archaeological record in terms of space as well as of time. This was an important part of Gordon Childe's methodology who, (as we saw in Chapter 2), applied it some sixty years ago to the Indo-European question.[6] He defined the term 'culture' in a technical, archaeological sense, as a 'constantly recurring assemblage of artefacts'. He then went on to take a further, deceptively simple step, which lies at the root of many subsequent problems, in equating the notion of culture, so defined, with that of 'people'. He never defined with complete clarity just what was meant by 'a people', but it is clear that he had much the same in mind as was meant by many anthropologists of his day, namely what today – and sometimes already then – would be termed an ethnic group.

In general, as we have seen, Childe distinguished carefully between these ideas and any notion of genetically determined physical characteristics. There is no confusion here with the question of race, and this can be set to one side – although it is inconveniently the case that the terms 'ethnicity' and 'ethnic' are often used in the modern world in a racial sense rather than in a social one.

At this point it is necessary to make several important distinctions in terms of ethnicity, language, religion, political organization and material culture. They do not necessarily co-vary, nor need they be expected to.

The political organization or polity may be defined as a self-governing group of people, generally occupying a well-defined area. This does not mean that they define the group in territorial terms – often the group is defined rather in terms of kin relationships. When we are speaking of a polity we are not necessarily thinking of a sedentary group: a hunter-gatherer band may be regarded as a polity as much as a city state or an empire, so long as it functions as a unit and does not fall within the jurisdiction of a larger group for administrative or legal purposes.

Ethnicity is something rather different, although in the modern world of nation-states the effective polity (the state) is often in effect an ethnic group also: we tend to speak of the French or the Germans or the Swiss without really thinking carefully whether we are speaking of nationality or ethnic affiliation. On the other hand, we are very clear that it is still meaningful to speak of the Welsh, or even of the Welsh nation, while not imagining or suggesting that we are dealing with a separate political unit. Ethnicity and political organization do not always coincide, although they often may. Many polities may together form a single ethnic group – as for instance in the case of the Greek city states. Equally a large polity such as the Roman empire can embrace many ethnic groups.

In talking of ethnic groups,[7] then, we mean groups of people who recognize themselves as distinct, and who see this distinction as part of their birthright. Many definitions have been offered in the anthropological literature: one of the most convenient was quoted by the British ethnologist Dragadze:[8]

> Ethnos . . . can be defined as a firm aggregate of people, historically established on a given territory, possessing in common relatively stable particularities of language and culture, and also recognizing their unity and difference from other similar formations (self-awareness) and expressing this in a self-appointed name (ethnonym).

This seems to me a very convenient definition: it refers to the historical realities of kinship and descent, to the spatial aspect, the community of language, and to other features which will often include religion. Then it rightly stresses that for a group to be a real ethnic group, it must be aware of itself as such. The group will therefore have a name for itself – an ethnonym.

Since we are particularly interested in linguistic questions, it should be noted that language and ethnos are not equivalent. Different ethnic groups can speak the same language – for instance the different peoples in the world today who speak Arabic, some of whom have very different histories and backgrounds and would not necessarily consider themselves as one. It is also possible, although less common, for a single people to contain within it groups speaking different languages. That would be true for nobles and commoners in traditional Tonga in the Pacific, or for the Royal Family and the commoners in Hanoverian England.

Where Childe may have erred in discussing these matters is in too readily equating the 'cultures' which he defined with 'peoples' – that is to say, with ethnic groups. Material culture embraces all the artefacts made and used by humans, and it cannot always be broken down into discrete spatial units, as Childe tried to do. In some cases, when the prehistoric map is divided up by the modern archaeologist into 'cultures', he or she is making a series of arbitrary decisions. In some cases the archaeological cultures supposedly identified are simply the result of the taxonomic efforts of the archaeologist: they need have no further reality than that. So these 'cultures' may not have had any great reality at the time in question.

Moreover it should be noted that *ethnicity is a matter of degree*. Some ethnic groups are very conscious of their separateness, and emphasize it in all manner of ways, some of them involving dress, and distinctive jewellery and distinguishing decoration, which can sometimes be observed archaeologically. Others are less aware of 'belonging' and take no special care to distinguish themselves from other groups. They may indeed not be aware of the existence of languages apart from their own, and may have no special name to distinguish what outsiders – such as colonial administrators or visiting anthropologists – regard as an ethnic group. The British anthropologist, Jack Goody,[9] described one such group in Africa, known as the LoWiili, who do not really think in these terms: the name by which they are known is not their own name for the group, because they don't have such a name, nor is there in fact any stable and well defined group. This is, then, a good example of what seems to be, to a large extent, an externally bestowed ethnicity.

There are, of course, plenty of examples of real ethnicity in early times. Ancient Greece offers an excellent case, where the independent city states recognized that together their people were Hellenes, although Hellas as a territorial-political concept was not achieved until much later. Only Greeks for instance were allowed to compete together at the Olympic Games. There can be no doubt that the concept of Greekness did play a crucial role in influencing social and political development in the Aegean.

We should note too that ethnicity can work at more than one level. In Greece, the citizens of many of the city states were fiercely loyal to their city, and it is quite appropriate to think of the Athenians or the Naxians as in some sense ethnic groups. In other parts of Greece, where city states had not developed, there were tribal units, for which the Greek word is the one from which the modern concept of ethnicity comes – *ethnos*. But the members of these *ethne* were conscious too that they were Greeks, and at the time of the Persian invasions, were willing to go to war in support of this concept.

This may seem rather a lengthy discussion of a single concept, but it does have a bearing on how we think about the Celts. Moreover the whole question of ethnic formation is an increasingly important one for archaeology, and it also affects the linguistic questions. It is a necessary preliminary to look at the way the Greeks and Romans spoke of the Celts, since there is no reason to think that they were any more clear-minded or rigorous in their handling of ethnic questions than more recent writers.

The Celts as seen by the Greeks and Romans

The earliest accounts which we have of the people who inhabited the Celtic lands – whatever one may mean by that term – come from the classical historians and geographers. In the last century these accounts were often taken at their face value, without any careful consideration about what these writers were setting out to do, or what their sources were.

To write a systematic geography, with an account of lands and peoples, is no easy task. Our understanding of the geographical descriptions of the ancients is very much enhanced by considering the formation of the Greek ethnographic tradition, as the Irish classical scholar J. J. Tierney[10] has done with particular reference to the Celts. The *Histories* of Herodotus, written in the fifth century BC, represent the first extended geographical descriptive treatments which have come down to us. It is necessary to keep this background in mind, since we are interested in the meaning of such terms as Keltoi/Celtae and Galatai/Galli in their Greek and Latin forms respectively. To quote Tierney:[11]

> But if we wish to envisage this question clearly it is necessary to realize that the distinct ethnographic unit is rather like the chameleon, that in fact, these entities do not exist . . . But nevertheless, the ancients had to use names, group names, to denote the various barbarian tribes surrounding the Mediter-

ranean basin, and it was on the basis of such group names, established on however slender foundations, that Greek ethnographic writing grew and developed. We should then make a primary distinction between the actual ethnographic situation on the one hand, which may be described in the most general terms as a gradual shading off from civilization and culture to barbarism, and on the other the rather schematic representation (or lack of representation) of these facts in the generalized statements and more or less well-founded assertions of ethnographers.

It seems, in fact that by some earlier geographers, notably Ephorus, the barbarian world was conceived descriptively as divided into four, corresponding to the points of the compass, as seen from Greece. To the north were the Scythians, to the east the Persians, to the south the Libyans and to the west the Celts. This point is well made by Tierney in his discussion of the emergence of the Germans in the ethnographic writing of the first century BC as a distinct ethnographic unit:[12]

> In Pytheas the Scythians extend as far west as the Baltic and the North Sea, and this is the universal view of later writers. To Posidonius, when giving an ethnographic sketch of Northern Europe, therefore, the only question which would occur in regard to such tribes as the Cimbri and Teutones or the Germani would be whether their affiliations were rather Celtic than Scythian.

The whole question is an interesting one, because it has been conclusively shown that the main descriptive accounts which have come down to us from geographers such as Strabo and Diodorus Siculus and even Caesar, were drawn largely from the earlier account, which has not survived in its entirety written by Posidonius in Book 23 of his *History*. Posidonius lived from 135 to 51 BC and the detailed information which we now have available comes to us in passages written after that date.

It follows from this discussion that for some geographical writers, and perhaps for all of them, the term Celtic was in the first place a rather broad geographical designation, relating to all the inhabitants of northern and western Europe, whatever their nature. It later came to have a much more precise geographical designation, equating with the Roman province of Gaul, so that in this later sense the Galli or Keltoi were distinguished from the inhabitants of Iberia and from those of the islands of Britain and Ireland. We may question whether the early writers saw anything very inherently 'celtic' about them: they were just describing the natives of the region, following the rather standard descriptive order[13] as established by Herodotus:

  I The Country, including (1) Boundaries, Measurements, Shape, (2) Nature of the Land, (3) Rivers, (4) Climate, (5) Animals;
 II The People, including (1) Population, (2) Antiquity and Ancient History, (3) Way of Life, (4) Customs;
III The Wonders of the Country.

It should be noted that language as such did not loom large in the description. As T. G. E. Powell remarked: 'Languages, other than their own, were not esteemed by the Greeks and linguistic distinctions between the barbarians would therefore not have come into consideration'. However, it is necessary to disagree in part when Powell goes on to say:[14]

It seems reasonable to suppose that the Celts were distinguishable to Herodotus on descriptive grounds, even if he never saw any representatives, in the same way as other barbarian peoples might be identified. The term *Celts* is therefore justifiable in a proper ethnological sense, and should not necessarily be restricted to mean Celtic-speaking, which is a concept of academic thought of quite modern times.

His point about language is undoubtedly true, but it is open to doubt how far the Greeks or Romans really saw the Celts as an entity with a meaning beyond the designation of the inhabitants of certain lands in the north-west. What really interests us, of course, is what Tierney would term 'the actual ethnographic situation': what were the ethnic groups in the area at the time in question. Here what concerns us is how the people whom we are discussing viewed themselves, 'recognising their unity and difference from other similar formations and expressing this in a self-appointed name (ethnonym)', as our definition of ethnicity puts it. There is no doubt that the classical authors report a number of tribal names which are probably perfectly accurate. What is open to question is whether the inhabitants of these areas themselves had any notion of a larger unit than their own local tribe. As the distinguished student of the Celts, Henri Hubert, wrote of the Irish:[15]

> Did the islanders really call themselves Celts? That is another question and was probably not asked. It is extremely doubtful whether the inhabitants of Ireland ever gave themselves a name of the kind. Moreover the Irish seem to have exhausted the resources of their ethnographical sense when they described themselves in reference to themselves and distinguished the elements of which they were composed.

It is now appropriate to turn briefly to the terminology used in the three systematic descriptions which have come down to us. As we have seen, each is thought to have been based largely on the *History* of Posidonius.

The first of these is Caesar, writing in Latin in the middle of the first century BC. His concern is with Gaul and Britain, and so he offers no description of Iberia. As is well known, he begins his work as follows:[16]

> Gaul is a whole divided into three parts, one of which is inhabited by the Belgae, another by the Aquitani, and a third by a people called in their own tongue Celtae, in the Latin Galli. All these are different one from another in language, institutions and laws. The Galli are separated from the Aquitani by the river Garonne, from the Belgae by the Marne and the Seine.

In a later passage, in Book VI, he gives a systematic description of the customs of Gaul and Germany, but this does not offer much further insight into the definition of the broader ethnic units.

Diodorus Siculus, writing in Greek shortly after Caesar, deals first with various islands, including Britain. There is no suggestion that Britain is Celtic or Galatian:[17]

And Britain, we are told, is inhabited by tribes which are autochthonous and preserve in their ways of living the ancient manner of life.

In his description of the nearby mainland he first tells one of those agreeable little genealogical tales[18] by which the Greeks overcame difficulties of nomenclature. He speaks of the region Keltika, which was visited by the hero Herakles, who fathered a child by the daughter of its ruler. The son was called Galates, and he called his subjects Galatai after himself 'and these in turn gave their name to all of Galatia', Galatia being the Greek equivalent of the Latin Gallia or Gaul. Diodorus goes on to say that 'Gaul is inhabited by many tribes of different size; for the largest number some two hundred thousand men, and the smallest fifty thousand'. He gives a description of the ways of the Galatai (Gauls), but includes one interesting passage when he returns again to this question of nomenclature:[19]

And now it will be useful to draw a distinction which is unknown to many: The people who dwell in the interior above Massalia, those on the slopes of the Alps and those on this side of the Pyrenees mountains are called Celts (Keltoi), whereas the peoples who are established above this land of Celtica in the parts which stretch to the north, both along the ocean and along the Hercynian Mountain, and all the peoples who come after these, as far as Scythia, are known as Gauls (Galatai); the Romans, however, include all these nations together under a single name, calling them one and all Gauls (Galatai).

In making this distinction, Diodorus may be following Caesar, but it is interesting that he makes no mention of the Germans. When he comes to Spain he has another interesting point about nomenclature:[20]

Now that we have spoken at sufficient length about the Celts we shall turn our history to the Celtiberians (Keltiberes) who are their neighbours. In ancient times these two peoples namely the Iberians (Iberes) and the Celts (Keltoi) kept warring among themselves over the land, but when later they arranged their differences and settled upon the land altogether, and when they went further and agreed to intermarriage with each other, because of such inter-mixture the two peoples received the appellation given above.

The third and most lengthy description is that of the geographer, Strabo, writing in Greek around the time of Christ. In western Europe, he deals first with Iberia, in a long description rich in interesting detail, in which mention is made of the Celtiberians, seen as the end product of an incursion of Celts into the country. After dealing with Iberia in Book III, he turns to Transalpine Celtica in Book IV, and repeats the division into Aquitani, Belgae and Celtae. Later he makes a specific and important point about nomenclature:[21]

> This then is what I have to say about the people who inhabit the dominion of Narbonitis, whom the men of former times named 'Celtae' (Keltai); and it was from the Celtae, I think, that the Galatae (Galatai) as a whole were by the Greeks called 'Celti' (Keltoi) – on account of the fame of the Celtae, or it may also be that the Massiliotes as well as other Greek neighbours, contributed to this result on account of their proximity.

This interesting passage perhaps offers the clue to the wider use of the term Celt. It is perfectly plausible that the first barbarians with whom the Greek population of the colony of Massalia (Marseilles) came into contact belonged to a tribe with the ethnonym 'Keltoi' or the equivalent, and that the Greeks used this term to designate all barbarians from the region in general. The story does carry the implication that the inhabitants of the region in general did not apply the term 'Celts' to themselves, but that this was an externally imposed ethnonym.

From this brief inspection of the principal classical sources, we can draw a number of important conclusions. Many of them are in a sense negative, since the classical authors were not primarily interested in native perceptions of ethnicity, nor in linguistic variation, but they are still important because many prevailing views about the Celts today come from precisely these written sources.

In the first place, there is no evidence that the inhabitants of Britain or Ireland ever called themselves Celts or Gauls. When Strabo speaks of Britain he clearly distinguishes between its inhabi-

tants and those of the mainland:[22] 'The men of Britain are taller than
the Celti . . .' And Caesar, in another famous passage, states:[23]

> The inland part of Britain is inhabited by tribes declared in their
> own tradition to be indigenous to the island, the maritime part
> by tribes that migrated from Belgium (*ex Belgio*) to seek booty
> by invasion. Nearly all of these latter are called by the names of
> the states (*civitates*) from which they sprang when they went to
> Britain.

Once again we find the natives operating at tribal level, in terms of
nomenclature. As Anne Ross has put it:[24]

> There is no evidence that the inhabitants of Britain ever called
> themselves Celts, and Caesar only reports Celtae in one third
> of France.

Caesar himself, although referring to Celtae in one third of
France, does not suggest clearly that there was, in the eyes of the
natives themselves, a single ethnic unit of Gauls or Celts occupying
the whole province. Strabo, in the interesting passage quoted above
offers what is perhaps the clue to the problem in suggesting that it
was the first Greek settlers in the south of France, at Massalia, who
took the name of the local tribe, the Keltoi, and applied it to the
entire barbarian hinterland. As the Irish linguist, David Greene,
conveniently sums up the matter:[25]

> We cannot even be sure that Celtic-speaking peoples are meant
> when Classical writers use the names *Keltoi* or *Galatae*, for
> these ethnic names were used with considerable looseness –
> indeed we do not know what *Keltoi* and *Galatae* meant origi-
> nally, but there is no evidence that they are Celtic words, or
> that any Celtic-speaking peoples ever called themselves by
> those names.

The conclusion must thus be the strong suspicion that the term
'Celts' is not a proper ethnic term, in the sense derived earlier, but
was imposed on a wide variety of barbarian tribes by classical
geographers, following Posidonius. The outcome of the discussion, then, is not to deny that there was indeed a language group,
which since the eighteenth century has been termed 'Celtic', nor
that there are significant archaeological observations to be made

about the material culture and way of life at the relevant places and times. But these different and valid perceptions should not be confused by lumping them all together as 'Celtic'. As the philologist, Myles Dillon, has said:[26]

> By Celts I mean people who spoke a Celtic dialect, not people who buried their dead in urn-fields or had leaf-shaped swords or any particular kind of pottery. Language is the test. This is not an infallible statement of known truth; it is merely an agreed use of the term upon which linguists insist.

The Celtic Languages

The foregoing discussion has led to the conclusion that the archaeology and the linguistic evidence must not be allowed to become confused through the too-ready application of a terminology, borrowed rather trustingly from the classical writers writing in the tradition of Posidonius. If we focus now on the linguistic evidence, especially as it relates to the end of the first millennium BC and the beginning of our era, a good deal is known.

From central Europe westwards, across the whole territory north of the Alps, Celtic languages were apparently spoken. The position in the Alpine region was more complicated, although it is clear that a Celtic language was spoken in northern Italy. The eastern extent of the distribution of Celtic speakers is also rather difficult to define. In the north, in Scandinavia, we have very little clear evidence, but it is in that region that the Germanic languages later make their appearance. The distinction between Gauls and Germans seems to have first been made by the early geographers around 70 BC, but there were no doubt linguistic distinctions to be drawn earlier.

In Iberia it is clear that the central and western part of the country was inhabited by people speaking a Celtic language, and these have been convincingly equated with the Celtiberians of the classical writers. In the north, however, there seem to have been the ancestors of the modern Basques, speaking a non-Indo-European language. And in the lands along the eastern seaboard of the peninsula coins and other inscriptions have been found indicating the presence of people speaking another, and probably non-Indo-European, language, Iberian.

It is perhaps paradoxical that the Celtic languages which we know best, namely those which survive today, or at least did so until recent times, are those of which we know least from classical times. The explanation, however, is a simple one, and it relates to the spread of literacy. It was precisely in those lands which first became literate, namely Iberia and Gaul, that Roman influence predominated. So did the Latin language, and they speak today Romance descendants of Latin.

The Celtic languages survived best in the areas which the Romans did not reach, or at least did not dominate. So that the languages of the Continental Celts, as they are termed, are known to us only from a limited number of inscriptions. The languages of the Insular Celts are much less well attested for the very early period, but are richly documented today, and in the case of Ireland have yielded a fascinating literature, first set down in writing in the sixth century AD, but with roots stretching far back beyond that time.

Very little would be known about the Celtic languages, in fact, if it were not for the British Isles, which were dominated at the time of the Romans by Celtic speakers. At that time British was spoken in Britain and Irish in Ireland,[27] although scholars prefer to use the terms Brithonic and Goidelic respectively, and they can to some extent be reconstructed from the modern languages which have descended from them.

The Goidelic dialects of more recent times are Irish, Scottish Gaelic and Manx, although the last two have a separate history only since the sixteenth century. It should be noted that Scottish Gaelic is thought to have come to be spoken, first in western Scotland and then more widely, as a result of a movement of a band of settlers from north Ireland in the fifth century AD. They are credited with setting up the Kingdom of Dalriada, so this might correspond to a language displacement caused by élite dominance.

The inhabitants of Scotland, until the wider dispersal of Gaelic, are generally referred to as Picts, following a number of references in late classical and subsequent writers. Much has been written about them, but once again there can be serious doubts about their nature and indeed their unity. The simplest interpretation is that this term was used for convenience to designate much of Scotland

and its inhabitants, and that it does not have any very special ethnic significance. What language was spoken in Scotland, or what languages, is far from clear. We have evidence of personal names, and of place names, as preserved by classical writers and in early medieval sources (including the Pictish Chronicle, a list of kings in a Latin text put together in the middle of the ninth century), and in the place names of more recent times. There is some evidence to be derived from these sources which would not contradict the view that they represent a northern dialect of Brithonic, perhaps not unlike that spoken further south before the dominance of the Romans.

There is, however, an interesting series of very short and difficult inscriptions, also termed Pictish and mainly written in the Ogam alphabet, which was probably invented in Ireland in the fourth century and imported to Scotland with the Dalriadic settlers in the fifth. These have been interpreted in all manner of ways, sometimes as Celtic, and sometimes as written in a language which is not Celtic but nonetheless Indo-European. The leading living authority, K. H. Jackson,[28] has however written:

> The inscriptions, of which some certainly, probably all, date from the late-Pictish period, appear to be written in a quite unknown language, not Celtic and evidently not Indo-European at all, though they contain some Celtic names and two Gaelic loan words.

He is led to the conclusion that:

> There were at least two languages current in northern Scotland before the coming of the Irish Gaels in the fifth century. One of them was a Gallo-Brittonic dialect not identical with the British spoken south of the Antonine Wall, although related to it. The other was not Celtic at all, nor apparently even Indo-European, but was presumably the speech of some very early set of inhabitants of Scotland.

Any evidence for a non-Indo-European language is of particular interest in our consideration of Indo-European origins, and this conclusion of Jackson's can be shown to harmonize rather well with the view of Indo-European origins proposed here.

Whereas the Pictish language remains something of an enigma, the rich Irish sources constitute our principal source of information about the early Insular Celtic languages. The earliest manuscript texts written entirely in Irish date from the twelfth century onwards, but an earlier form, termed 'Old Irish' is seen in the glosses written into Latin manuscripts of the eighth and ninth centuries, nearly all preserved on the continent. Prior to these there are some three hundred Irish inscriptions, written in the Ogam alphabet, dating from about the fourth century AD. They are in an earlier form of the language, sometimes termed 'Primitive Irish', and as Dillon puts it: 'They are in a form of language still close to Latin, and quite different from the earliest manuscript form, in which the original final syllables have been lost or reduced.' We should note, however, that the supposed relationship with Latin depends on an interpretation[29] of the development of the Indo-European groups in which there was an 'Italo-Celtic' stage of evolution, prior to the separation of the two, a view which is now not so widely held.

The earliest preserved Irish poetry dates from the sixth century. It is in verse, generally written in praise of famous men. A common origin has been claimed for this Irish heroic verse with the metres of Greek and Vedic, and that it therefore represents an ancient Indo-European inheritance,[30] although that view has met with criticism. Be that as it may, the poems certainly reflect a heroic society, glorying in feats of arms. The following quatrain[31] refers to Bran Berba whose death is set in 795 AD:

> Bran the Brown, protection of the host, a fierce raider;
> harsh spear, glorious one, strong by heredity;
> heir to wisdom, sun of warriors, full tide;
> a bloody wolf, dog of the pack, who does not wrong.

And again, for Fedlimid, who died in 847:

> Fedlimid the king
> > for whom it was the work of a single day
> To leave Connacht kingless without a battle,
> > and to lay Meath in ruins.

The Brithonic dialects are Welsh, Cornish and Breton. Cornish and Breton can be distinguished from Welsh in the few documents which survive from the eighth to the eleventh century, but it is only much later that Breton and Cornish are found in texts of any length.

The Welsh literature, like the Irish, is notable. The most famous of the early poems is 'The Gododdin', preserved in a manuscript of thirteenth century date, but dated by scholars either to the seventh or the ninth century. It begins with a splendid lament[32] for a young warrior, whose name we are not told:

> A man in courage but a boy in years
> Brave in the din of battle
> Swift horses with long manes
> Under the graceful youth
> A light broad shield
> On the crupper of a swift horse.
> Clean blue swords,
> Fringes of fine gold.
> Before his wedding-feast
> His blood streamed to the ground.
> Before we could bury him
> He was food for ravens.

The principal early sources for the Goidelic and Brithonic languages are thus Irish and Welsh respectively. Very little is known of the Brithonic language spoken in England prior to the Romans and the Saxons, the principal source of information being in the place names surviving into later times.

The two groups, Brithonic and Goidelic, are sometimes termed P-Celtic and Q-Celtic, since in Brithonic the sound *qu-* appears as *p-*, whereas in Goidelic it remains as *q*, later becoming *k*. Thus the numeral 'four' and the pronoun 'who' appear in Welsh as *pedwar* and *pwy*, and in Irish as *cethir* and *cia*.

Inevitably there has been much speculation about the origins of the two groups, and most scholars have spoken in terms of successive migrations. These were conventionally set in the first millennium BC, often equated with the supposed immigrants responsible for the inception of the Iron Age in the islands, but, as we shall see, this view has lost ground with the general rejection of such a migrationist inception for iron working and other contemporary developments in Britain and Ireland.

Continental Celtic is a series of languages which had no survivors after the early first millennium AD. The sources of information are therefore exclusively of two kinds: inscriptions and names. Thousands of proper names have been preserved, local and ethnic, divine and personal, from a series of different sources, including the classical authors and words preserved or quoted in other European languages. Numerous inscriptions have been preserved in Ancient Gaul, as well as in north Italy and Iberia. The lack of long literary texts has made the progress of research difficult, and one Irish scholar, Prionsias MacCana, has been rather dismissive of the entire enterprise:[33]

> Here survive only the merest vestiges of the language and its linguistic culture and yet the student finds that a surprisingly numerous succession of eminent scholars have laboured to save what, in the nature of things, can be only a meagre harvest, assiduously sifting and re-sifting the same slender and highly ambiguous materials, dotting each other's *is* and crossing – and occasionally uncrossing – each other's *ts*.

But this judgment singularly fails to do justice to the systematic nature of the enterprise. For Gaul we have the major survey by Joshua Whatmough, *The Dialects of Ancient Gaul*,[34] for northern Italy a number of important studies on the so-called Lepontic languages,[35] and for Iberia a series of works, notably by Antonio Tovar,[36] following the decipherment of the Iberian script more than sixty years ago by Manuel Gomez-Moreno.

The inscriptions of Gaul are numerous and informative: some, like the calendar of Coligny,[37] have been known and quite well

FIG. 9.2 The Botorrita tablet, a long inscription in the Celtiberian script.

understood for some time, and others are continually coming to light. Gaulish is recognized by most authors as having affinities with Brithonic. It is P-Celtic, although the importance of that specific classificatory criterion should not be over-stressed.

In Iberia, the picture is very much more complicated and there have been scholars who have doubted the Celticity of Hispano-Celtic (as Celtiberian is more logically termed). Such doubts have been laid to rest, however, by the discovery of a bronze tablet at Botorrita[38] in north-central Spain, twenty kilometres south of Saragossa, bearing on both faces a long inscription written in the Celtiberian script. The interpretation is not entirely clear: it may be the text of a contract relating to land ownership or land-tenure, but the discovery of so long a text has had a major impact on the understanding of Hispano-Celtic, establishing it as a further major branch of Continental Celtic.

The linguistic situation in Iberia is a complicated one which is

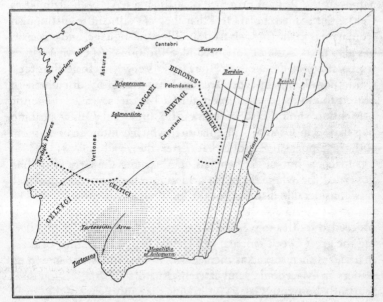

FIG. 9.3 The early linguistic population of Iberia, showing areas occupied by speakers of non-Indo-European Iberian (shaded) and Tartessian (stippled). Celtic names are in capitals (*after Tovar*).

worth discussing a little further.[39] In addition to Hispano-Celtic in the centre and west, a further language, Lusitanian, which is Indo-European and perhaps Celtic, is known from the north-west. Basque,[40] which is not an Indo-European language, survives to this day in the north of the peninsula. At the extreme south-west, in the Algarve in southern Portugal, there are a number of inscriptions of a rather different form than the Iberian, and perhaps older. These are sometimes termed Tartessian and may conceivably represent a further non-Indo-European language. Such is certainly claimed for the Iberian language, known from inscriptions and coins found along the eastern coasts of Spain; there is now enough material available to allow some comparison of grammar and morphology, and the old idea that this was an early predecessor of Basque is no longer maintained.

Looking to the eastern Celtic area, it is difficult to say much about Celtic-speaking groups very far east of the river Rhine.[41] Place names in the Roman province of Dalmatia have been claimed as Celtic, but some scholars feel that they are difficult to distinguish from names in the (Indo-European) Illyrian language, and criticism has also been made of supposed identifications of personal names from Pannonia, the modern Hungary.[42] Very often the claims for a Celtic population in those areas are backed up by discussion of objects found there which are in the La Tène art style.

Mention should also be made of a supposed Celtic-speaking population in Galatia,[43] in Anatolia, which a number of classical authors report. It is told that, after the death in 281 BC of Lysimachos, one of the generals of Alexander the Great who had governed the whole Thracian area after Alexander's death, there was considerable disorder, of the kind which one might today be tempted to term a system collapse. It is reported that Celtic bands proceeded south and were only narrowly prevented from plundering the great Greek sanctuary of Delphi in 279 BC. Some of these marauders then served as mercenaries in the armies of contending leaders in Macedonia, and later in Anatolia, in the region subsequently known as Galatia (following the equivalence of the Greek terms Keltoi and Galatai). The linguistic significance of the travels of these bands of freebooters and mercenaries has been disputed. As Greene[44] puts it:

That the Galatians were at one time Celtic-speaking is testified to only by a handful of proper names, for their few surviving inscriptions are in Greek, and it is difficult to take seriously the statement of St Jerome that the Galatians of his time spoke a language which was almost the same as that of the Treveri, who gave their name to Trier in the Rhineland; it is hard to believe that this was not a purely historical statement, since it will be remembered that St Jerome was writing in the fourth century AD, when the Celtic dialects were on the point of extinction everywhere on the Continent of Europe.

Whatever the status of the Galatian Celts, they have little significance for the origin of the Celtic languages, since it has never been suggested that a Celtic language was spoken in Anatolia prior to the supposed arrival of these intruders in the late third century BC.

The picture which we thus have of the Celtic languages, when they first become known to us, is of a major linguistic group in central and western Europe. In Iberia certainly, and perhaps in Scotland, we glimpse peoples speaking languages which were non-Indo-European, and who are generally supposed to have been already in those lands prior to the arrival of the first Celtic speakers.

The Art and Archaeology of the Celts

We have seen that it is perfectly possible, using the available linguistic evidence to indicate the territories which were occupied by peoples speaking Celtic languages at about the time of Christ. It is consequently quite a simple matter to study the material culture[45] of those times and places, and to take particular note of the remarkable art style which we find there. There is no doubt that 'Celtic' art is one of the great glories of prehistoric Europe.[46] It can only be fully appreciated if we are willing to set aside the representational canons of classical Greek art, or indeed of Roman art, and to respond visually to a style which is more imaginative and decorative than these, and which delights in flowing line to the exclusion of careful depiction. The art of these northern barbarians certainly does have a coherence and integrity which many today find at least as appealing as the more measured achievements of the Romans.

To the extent that much of it was produced by people speaking Celtic languages, it is perhaps permissible to call it 'Celtic'. But there is no guarantee that all of it was produced by Celtic-speakers: some quite famous pieces, often claimed as 'Celtic', such as the famous Gundestrup[47] cauldron, may have been produced far to the east, among Thracians and Dacians. Nor is it the case that all the regions which we know to have been Celtic-speaking were producing fine works in the La Tène art style. These points are not mere pedantry, if we are considering Celtic origins, because the origins of the languages and the origins of the material culture and the origins of the art are not necessarily the same. That is why it is necessary to take issue with Stuart Piggott, when he writes in his excellent book *The Druids*:[48]

> That this was a unit not only in the sense of sharing a common language, or variant dialects of a single tongue, is shown by the recognition of the Celts as a 'people' by the classical world (as distinct as, for instance, Scythians or Ethiopians), and by the evidence of common traditions in material culture perceivable to the archaeologist today.

This is an oversimplification as dangerous in its consequences as that of laying great emphasis on the supposed 'Celtic spirit' of those supposedly warlike peoples, which has recently been very effectively questioned by the British archaeologist N. Merriman.[49]

One of the most obvious features of the archaeology of central Europe in the iron age is the emergence of a prominent élite in south Germany and in southern France, documented most clearly by a splendid series of 'princely graves'. These are very notable in what archaeologists term the Hallstatt C and D periods, from about 700 to 500 BC. Major fortified hill forts are found at the same time, and it has been plausibly argued that one of the factors favouring the development of these chieftain societies was contact with the already quite highly civilized lands to the south:[50] contacts with Etruria and with the Greek colony of Massalia, founded about 600 BC. It has been suggested that local petty chieftains managed to control the supply of prestige luxury goods deriving from these centres, and through this dominance over trade were able to enhance their own positions, and to accumulate much wealth as well as influence, reflected in the rich gravegoods (containing many imports) accompanying their burials.

There seems to have been some sort of recession after 500 BC, but in the La Tène period which followed we again see princely graves, and by this time many of the prestige goods are of local manufacture, some of them masterpieces in that very non-classical art style which we have come to call La Tène. Eminent scholars such as Jacobsthal have discussed the development of this art style in considerable detail, and although it owed much to classical influences from the south, and perhaps something to the animal art of the steppe lands far to the east, it really does seem to be a local development.[51] We can discern beautifully incised, elegant linear decoration for instance on the backs of the polished bronze mirrors of south Britain, which is very much further afield. There is no doubt that it was significantly influenced by the earlier art of the south German homeland area.

When we come to examine the origins of this art and this material culture, we find them both to be locally rooted. The Hallstatt iron age can be seen to have evolved from the late bronze age Urnfield cultures of the same area, which are also widely seen in southern France and in eastern Europe. It has been traditional among many archaeologists to account for these urnfields in terms of some sort of migration, perhaps from further east. But the evidence for this has never been very satisfying, and most archaeologists would discount it today. There is no doubt that, during the developed bronze age the then very widely prevalent custom of inhumation burial, often under a burial mound or tumulus, was replaced by one of cremation, where the ashes were placed within an urn, and the cremated and inurned remains of the community buried in cemeteries or urnfields. This change in burial custom occurred over a very wide area, and there is no reason to think that changes in one area took place quite independently and in ignorance of changes in others. These regions were in contact at the time – our evidence of prehistoric trade demonstrates this. Changes of belief and custom in one area would no doubt be influential in others, but this does not need to imply any significant movement of people, other than in the normal course of trading and other contacts. Certainly there is no reason to suggest any significant process of language displacement of the kind discussed in Chapter 6. Archaeologists today are much more inclined to think in terms of models of interaction, where contact between neighbouring and politically independent communities proved influential for the development of customs and beliefs. Such peer-polity interactions[52] were probably responsible for the development of the networks of contacts which facilitated the custom of using beaker drinking vessels as prestige objects around 2300 BC. This is seen today as a more acceptable explanation than migrations of 'Beaker Folk', for which in reality there is no good evidence.

In recent years the earlier view that the British Isles were profoundly influenced during the iron age by a series of migrations from the continent has been almost universally abandoned. There is no good archaeological evidence for such migrations, although there were clearly important cross-channel political and trading contacts which had significant effects. The local insular development of the British variant of the La Tène art style no doubt came about through the effect on the islanders and their smiths of the prestige objects in the La Tène style which were traded to Britain. It is not necessary to go further than this.[53]

Turning now to Iberia, the presence of Celtic-speaking people there has often, similarly, been explained in migrationist terms. The great Spanish scholar, Pedro Bosch-Gimpera, forty-five years ago wrote an influential paper,[54] 'Two Celtic waves in Spain', in which the first wave, thought to arrive around 900 BC, was to be associated with what he called the urnfield culture seen in Catalonia. The second wave was linked with the Hallstatt cultures of the iron age of France and Germany which, as he correctly observed, could be seen as the ancestors of the La Tène culture in those areas.

These ideas seem less plausible today than they did when they were first put forward – but they have not yet been subjected to the same severe reassessment that the comparably migrationist ideas once applied to the British Isles have experienced. It may be that when they are more rigorously scrutinized they will fare no better. Certainly from the artistic standpoint, Iberia is very different. There, on the Mediterranean coastland in the region which we know to have been the home of the non-Celtic-speaking Iberians, there are remarkable artistic developments,[55] which are associated in part with the trading activities of the Phoenicians. Much of the artistic and cultural originality of iron age Iberia can be interpreted in this way, and La Tène art is not prominent there, not even in the lands which we know, from the distribution of inscriptions and from the study of place names, were occupied by people speaking the Hispano-Celtic language.

This point simply emphasizes again that language and art style should not be too readily equated, and that their origins are likely to be very different one from another.

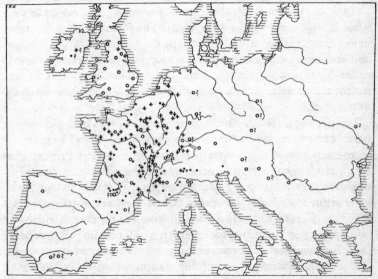

FIG. 9.4 The evidence of Celtic place names: names ending in -*dunum*. ○ indicate those attested from Antiquity, L those of Roman date, + those attested from the Middle Ages, ● those documented only more recently (*after Rix*).

Celtic Origins

The question 'Who were the Celts?', for all its apparent, indeed deceptive, simplicity has turned out to be a rather complicated one. I will now try to draw together the various strands and relate them to the theory of Indo-European origins proposed in Chapter 7. There it was suggested that the first persons to reach Europe speaking an early Indo-European language were the first farmers, and that the spread of early Indo-European speech was to be equated with the gradual but steady spread of farming throughout Europe. The various enclaves of non-Indo-European languages which survived are mainly to be interpreted as having been spoken by pre-farming groups already in Europe who came to adopt the farming economy and who subsequently retained their own speech. Etruscan and Iberian (and possibly Pictish) would represent the descendants of such groups into classical times, and Basque as far as our own day. Nothing which has been said so far about the Celts is dependent upon this theory, however, and only parts of what follow make such assumptions. The essential point, that we have to distinguish carefully between the Celtic languages, the art and archaeology of the time, the ethnic designations of the Greek and Roman geographers and the real ethnic perceptions of the people themselves, should be applicable to any systematic analysis of the problem.

It is my argument that most previous treatments of this question have been bedevilled by the assumption that the Celts had to come from somewhere else, or at least that their parent Proto-Indo-European language must have arrived as recently as the end of the neolithic period, as so many scholars from Schrader to Gimbutas have argued. Recently a number of historical linguists, including Antonio Tovar, Karl Horst Schmidt and Wolfgang Meid have taken an altogether more processual view of Celtic linguistic formation. But even they have had, perforce, to rely upon what have been said to be the findings of archaeology, namely the familiar theory of the incursion of groups of Indo-European speakers during the third millennium BC, deriving from the west Russian steppes. As we have seen, this theory cannot be regarded with confidence today as representing 'the findings of archaeology', although it is of course entitled to as much serious consideration as any other. My own theory will certainly not be welcomed by all archaeologists as an acceptable and well-documented one, and there are several problems in historical linguistics to be overcome before it will satisfy many of them. It may nonetheless claim to represent 'the findings of archaeology' as much as the Kurgan theory. I believe that historical linguists would be very much wiser to proceed as far as they are able in interpretation within the framework of their own discipline before relying too heavily upon any supposed archaeological consensus: for at present there is none.

To illustrate this problem, and to begin our analysis of the question of origins, it is convenient to quote at length from one of the best recent surveys of the Continental Celtic languages, by Karl Horst Schmidt. Naturally I have no criticism to make of his philological arguments, but it is permissible to point out that, in common with most other historians of the Celtic languages, he bases his discussion at a very early stage on a specific archaeological interpretation:[56]

According to Archaeology and Prehistory, the Celts descend from a mixture of the Bronze Age Tumulus Culture (1550–1250 BC) and the Urnfield Culture (thirteenth century BC). Originating in what is now Eastern France, North Alpine Switzerland, and South-Western Germany, they spread over the whole of Europe and Asia Minor during the Hallstatt (from the eighth century) and La Tène (from the fifth century) periods of the Iron Age. The date of the first Celtic settlement in Ireland is uncertain; in N. K. Chadwick's opinion it may go back to the Bronze Age before 1000 BC. The first immigrations to the Iberian Peninsula, to the English Channel, and probably to England as well, took place during the Hallstatt period in the eighth/seventh century BC. The latest Hallstatt chieftains' tombs and the early La Tène culture, expanding to the north into the territory between Champagne and the Rhine, Nahe and Mosel are followed by La Tène B–C Culture (fourth to second century BC) with so-called 'Flachgräber-friedhöfen.' or 'flat' cemeteries. This period is characterized, as Kimmig has expressed it, by 'unity of cultural occupation over wide areas, displaying contemporary links with historical observations on the ethnic affiliations of the cultural material'. This period is marked by the widest expansion of the Celts, who had invaded Italy, the Balkan Peninsula, and Asia Minor and had settled in Bohemia, Upper Silesia and Hungary. The conquest of France is reflected in its name, Gaul. Celtic migrations of the La Tène period reached Britain, Ireland and Spain, encountering older Celtic strata in the population in Ireland and on the Iberian Peninsula.

It should be noted that there is no criticism to be made of the archaeology as such quoted in this passage. Wolfgang Kimmig is one of the most distinguished archaeologists for the period, and his views[57] of the development of the Hallstatt and La Tène cultures may be followed with the greatest confidence. The difficulty comes with the equation of the archaeological and linguistic data.

No one really disputes, I think, that the primary meaning of the terms Celt and Celtic for the modern scholar must be linguistic ones. As Myles Dillon[58] writes:

> The Celts were distinguished in various ways, by social organization, dress, methods of warfare, for these are matters of which early historians took account, but the main distinction, then, as now, will have been that of language . . . Indeed this definition by language is the only useful one, for by reference to it we can speak meaningfully of Celtic archaeology or Celtic religion. But if we do not admit language as the criterion, these terms involve a circular argument.

This advice has been lost sight of in many treatments. For while archaeology does indeed tell us that at the time Celtic was spoken in eastern France, north alpine Switzerland and south-western Germany in the first century BC the material culture known today as La Tène was in use in those lands, it does not *and cannot*, by its nature, assign any special priority to the La Tène cultural assemblage in this matter. Celtic languages were spoken over a wide area at this time, and not all of these lands display the same material culture as seen in that particular region. Kimmig is quite right, according to our present knowledge, in tracing Hallstatt and La Tène antecedents back to the Urnfield cultures and so back to the Tumulus cultures of the bronze age. The archaeology is impeccable. But we may ask what logic leads to the assertion that the Celts originated in the Tumulus cultures of these or neighbouring areas. There is absolutely nothing in the linguistics, so far as I know, to confer priority on the east France/north Switzerland/south-west Germany region. From the archaeological standpoint it is indeed a special region, the home of the richest iron age chieftains' graves, and very possibly in addition the original home of the La Tène art style. However our picture of the development and indeed the spread of that art style now has very little to do with the movement of significant numbers of people. We no longer think of it as transported across Europe or to Britain, or indeed to Ireland, by a series of migrations, nor even of smaller bands of warrior élites, intent on subjugating their neighbours. There is therefore no particular case for associating the people of that region with any impetus towards the displacement of the languages spoken by their neighbours, though there is no doubt that they were influenced by them. The La Tène art style was indeed transmitted; but by a process of trade and of emulation, with smiths in one region no doubt eagerly copying the latest achievements of others.

There is equally no warranty today for the statement that the first Celtic immigrations to England took place during the Hallstatt period in the eighth or seventh century BC. Twenty years ago, Grahame Clark in a celebrated article entitled 'The invasion hypothesis in British prehistory',[59] questioned the migrationist view of British prehistory, and the iron age scholar, F. R. Hodson,[60] held up for examination the then prevailing view that there had been three waves of immigrants to Britain during the iron age. Such a position has now been almost universally abandoned. Its former champions, of whom the most notable is Christopher Hawkes, have proposed more subtle models for the changes which took place. He has spoken of a process of 'cumulative Celticity',[61] involving peaceful contacts over a very much longer period. Similar comments may be made for the Celts of the Iberian peninsula.

In north Italy possibly the case may be different: there is direct historical evidence (mainly in the work of the Roman historian, Livy[62]) for an invasion of north Italy by Celtic tribes. In my own view, this too might be held up to question, but it is not necessary to do so here, and for present purposes his story, like that of the incursion of Celtic groups into Greece with their attack on Delphi, and ultimately to Galatia in Anatolia, may be accepted. Whether Celtic-speaking people ever settled in significant numbers in eastern Europe, including Hungary, still seems a matter for discussion. There is plenty of material there referable to the La Tène culture in archaeological terms, and plenty of works of La Tène art. However there is no principle which says that those who employed a La Tène material culture were necessarily Celtic-speaking, and the linguistic evidence from the area is not yet completely clear. As for the 'conquest of Gaul' by Celts, it is surprising to see so naïve an interpretation of the archaeological evidence accepted by so clear-sighted a philologist as Schmidt. There is nothing in the archaeology which puts Gaul in a secondary or derivative position in the field of Celtic speech.

It was suggested in Chapter 7 that the first people speaking an early Indo-European language reached western Europe at the time of the first farmers. The Celtic languages would all be descended from this early Indo-European language or languages. There are radiocarbon dates associated with early farming in southern France around 6000 BC, associated with the so-called 'impressed ware', which is a widespread feature of early neolithic settlement in the west Mediterranean, and there are early dates for farming in Spain around 5500 BC, but the picture there is not yet a very complete one, and earlier dates are to be expected. The farming economy reached north-western France by shortly after 5000 BC, and south Britain by 4500 BC. Farming is also documented in Ireland by 4500 BC, and in the Orkney Islands, at the extreme north of Britain, by 3500 BC. At the same time, the spread of farming by the 'eastern route' up the Danube valley was occurring. Farming sites of the Danubian I culture (or Linear Pottery culture) are found in northern France by about 5000 BC, and are common in Germany and Holland by that time. It is not at present clear whether the first farmers seen in England should be traced back to this tradition or to the farmers of western France, whose domestic plants and animals may have been the lineal descendants of stock which had once grown in the west Mediterranean. Linguistically, however, if we follow this broad picture, it might be logical to expect some differences between this west European group and the central European. Both derived, of course, from the early farmers of Greece back around 6500 BC, but different cultural and linguistic traditions had no doubt been established over the succeeding fifteen hundred years. We must therefore expect that the farmers using Linear Pottery must, when they entered France, have been speaking a rather different dialect from that of their western cousins, whom they will soon have encountered. As we shall see, there are some points in our understanding of the linguistic background which might correlate with this picture.

It is first worth noting, however, that several historical linguists have, recently, been able to adjust their thinking to a much earlier origin for the Celts than that set out above by Schmidt, who was following the archaeology of Kimmig. The move away from migrationist explanations in Britain, as we have seen, led Grahame Clark twenty years ago to question the validity of any of the supposed invasions to Britain between the coming of the first farmers and the Romans, with one single exception. That exception was the Beaker phenomenon, which at that time was still seen in migratory terms: it was still permissible to speak of 'Beaker Folk'. This interpretation of the beaker phenomenon is no longer accepted in England, and most archaeologists do not now think in terms of beaker-bearing immigrants on any scale. For at least a decade, however, the 'beaker immigrant' hypothesis remained in favour, while the iron age waves of immigration had been rejected.

The possible association of Indo-European speech with the introduction of beakers to the British Isles was adopted by Stuart Piggott, among other archaeologists, and taken up by Dillon, among other philologists. In 1972 he wrote:

> The Celtic settlement of the British Isles is more difficult to trace. It now seems that we must choose between two extremes. About 2000 BC came Bell-beaker people, whose burials are in single graves, with individual grave-goods. The remarkable Wessex Culture of the Bronze Age which appears about 1500 BC is thought to be based upon this tradition. The grave-goods there suggest the existence of a warrior aristocracy 'with a graded series of obligations of service . . . through a military nobility down to the craftsmen and peasants', as in the Homeric society. This is the sort of society which is described in the Irish sagas, and there is no reason why so early a date for the coming of the Celts should be impossible. As we shall see, there are considerations of language and culture that rather tend to support it. From the middle of the sixth century BC the Early Iron Age people, builders of the

hill-forts so characteristic of the insular Celtic world, begin to appear. From then until the Belgic invasion, to which Caesar refers as having occurred not long before his time, there were successive waves of Celtic immigration into Britain. But the common opinion among archaeologists seems now to be that there were no large scale immigrations into the British Isles between 2000 and 6000 BC.

I have quoted this passage at length because, although published seven years before the article by Karl Horst Schmidt, quoted earlier, it represents a development in the chronological argument, and is interesting too because it refers to social interpretations. It derives from the currently anti-migrationist (or at least no longer pro-migrationist) tradition of the British archaeological school, whereas Schmidt is relying on the more traditional archaeological position largely maintained today by the continental school of archaeology. It should be noted that the author still puts some emphasis on the supposed 'successive waves of Celtic immigration' in the early iron age, a concept which around that time was being replaced by Christopher Hawkes's more flexible concept of 'cumulative Celticity'.

What is so interesting about Dillon's treatment, however, is that this reassessment of the chronology leads to a very interesting change in the linguistic position:[63]

If the earliest Celtic settlements date from the Bronze Age, the question whether the invaders were Goidels or Brythons does not arise. Linguistic features that distinguish the Brythons may be much later, some of them innovations ($u > i$; $qu > p$) which spread from a centre on the Continent and never reached the 'lateral' areas of Ireland and Spain.

This line of reasoning opens up an entirely new perspective, and one where we begin to conceive of many of the fundamental linguistic changes occurring *in situ*, as it were, in the lands where we en-counter the languages in historical times. Dillon is, in effect, here beginning to develop a theory for the differentiation between Q-Celtic (Goidelic, with Hispano-Celtic) and P-Celtic (Brithonic, with Gaulish) which does not depend on migrations of peoples. Instead of this *Stammbaum* or family tree approach he is contemplating something much closer to the wave theory for linguistic change, where innovations develop within one area, here Gaul and Britain, but do not extend to regions outside the locus of the wave (Iberia and Ireland).

This I find a very fruitful approach, and one which it is tempting to extend to the Celtic phenomenon as a whole. I would prefer to see the development of the Celtic languages, in the sense that they are Celtic as distinct from generalized Indo-European, as taking place essentially in those areas where their speech is later attested. That implies an Indo-European-speaking population in France and in Britain and in Ireland, and probably in much of Iberia also, by before 4000 BC. Linguistic development would, of course, continue after that time. Some of the changes would be peculiar to only parts of the entire territory: that is the phenomenon of linguistic divergence which would result in the separation between the Goidelic and Brithonic languages, but other changes would take place in the territory as a whole.

It is helpful to think of these changes in terms of Schmidt's wave model. In some cases the wave would extend to the most distant Celtic-speaking regions, so that the Celtic languages would be evolving together. If the wave did not extend further, that would imply a process of linguistic differentiation for Celtic as a whole, serving to distinguish the Celtic languages from their neighbours, i.e. the Italic and Germanic languages. But it is not always necessary to think of a wave starting from a very specific centre. It is permissible to refer again here to the concept of peer-polity interaction in archaeology, and to the existence of long-distance trading networks which effectively established contacts over considerable areas. Developments could thus take place in step, so to speak, without our having to think of any one local region as a prime innovating centre. Just as in archaeology we have come to reject both dominance models and models of complete independence in favour of interaction models, so in historical linguistics we may perhaps think of a whole language area, like the one where early Celtic was originally spoken, moving in some senses together. So that while there would, all the time, be processes at work serving to separate out the individual dialects, yet simultaneously there would be others keeping them to some extent together, while nonetheless distinguishing them progressively from languages and dialects in other language groups, such as Italic or Germanic.

'Cumulative Celticity'

Here we can take up once again Christopher Hawkes's evocative term 'cumulative Celticity', and use it in a more mutual and collective sense: 'cumulative mutual Celticity'. Instead of always thinking of England as the recipient of these accumulating Celtic qualities, we would think rather of England and continental Europe as starting on a more equal footing, and developing together that cumulative mutual Celticity which results in the position which we see at the time of Christ. It is perhaps not necessary to see one region as always the donor and the other the recipient. In this perspective there need be no one, localized Celtic 'homeland'. The homeland of the Celts would in fact be constituted by the full extent of the area where Celtic languages came to be spoken (always excluding such later offshoots as Galatia and perhaps Italy, if it is clear that Celtic speech there really was the result of demonstrable later migrations).

This view of the linguistic development of the Celtic and Germanic languages has been put forward by the Spanish linguist, Antonio Tovar. (Although it should be noted that he accepts the conventional chronological picture, and hence the arrival of the first Indo-European speakers in Europe in the later third millennium BC.) Tovar[64] discusses at some length the studies made by H. Krahe of the river names of central and western Europe, many of which have forms which can be interpreted as reflecting an early and undifferentiated form of Indo-European, at a time well prior to the formation of the individual Celtic languages. As Krahe[65] put it in 1951:

> Non-Indo-German elements are not observable in the whole extensive area north of the well-defined line extending east and west from the Alps. That indicates that all the lands of Europe north of the Alps were an Indo-German territory from the earliest times.

Krahe envisaged an early division of Indo-European into Hittite, Greek and Aryan, while in the central and western areas the individual languages which we later recognize had not yet separated but are represented rather in these undifferentiated place- and river-names. The picture as Tovar develops it thus rules out the suggestion of any new migrations to account for the western Indo-European languages (notably Celtic and Germanic):[66]

> It is in no way adventurous to think that Germanic and Celtic in their final forms were fashioned in the western territories of Europe following its domination by the Indo-German tribes.

He argues, in the developmental process, for a combination of the *Stammbaum* (family tree) and wave theories. At an early stage the oldest Indo-European languages had separated, like the branches of a tree, while those languages which are recognized later were formed by waves spreading out from secondary centres. This is, of course, very much the picture which we have been developing here, with the very early separation of the ancestors of Hittite and Greek, and then a later process of differentiation, in Europe, for the European languages.

The wave model process is further discussed in terms which harmonize very well with the archaeological peer-polity interaction model, which was mentioned earlier. Tovar thinks in terms of significant centres for the formation of individual languages where an innovation package (*Neuerungsbündel*) sets in train a process of linguistic development. Between such centres would be more conservative regions enjoying a peaceful linguistic life (*ruhiges Sprachleben*). He makes the specific point that extralinguistic factors were amongst those which would explain the nature and behaviour of these centres[67] – factors including war, religion and economy. My own mental picture of the process of linguistic development – or 'crystallization', to use another of Tovar's metaphors – is very close to that. One can imagine regions in which the interaction networks were particularly intense and effective, separated from other such regions by areas less intensively networked. In favourable circumstances these intensive contacts could lead to dialect formation, and the effective separation between regions could result in linguistic differentiation. Rather than thinking of a wave emanating from a single centrally-placed location, I prefer to imagine an area within which the network linkages are particularly intense and effective. Such a reformulation of Schmidt's wave model perhaps does no more than modify somewhat his original ideas.

This approach has been developed in greatest detail by Tovar in relation to the late differentiation of the Germanic languages;[68] and he is able to point to analogous processes at work in the formation of the High German (*Hochdeutsch*) and Castilian languages during the middle ages.

This processual approach seems a very suitable one to apply to the development of the Celtic languages. It gives a more coherent account of the process of largely *in situ* development from the common, early western, Indo-European base postulated by Krahe. Indeed it seems quite appropriately denominated by the term of cumulative collective Celticity,[69] adapted from Christopher Hawkes.

It is only when it comes to chronology that there are severe differences. They arise, of course, because Tovar is following the traditional archaeological view, and is thus led to accept what appears in the perspective presented here as a very low chronology. Against this view, however, can be set the conclusions of Wolfgang Meid,[70] who is otherwise quoted by Tovar with approval. He distinguishes a Late Period of Indo-European development, when individual languages can first be recognized. The earliest of these is Hittite, and its emergence around 2000 BC is a significant date, which allows him to place the Late Indo-European period in the third and second millennia BC. The Middle Period is set in the fourth and possibly the fifth millennia BC, while the previous Early Indo-European period lies in that long preceding period which is 'lost in the mists of linguistic origins' (*im Nebelland der Glottogonie*).[71] Tovar and Meid consider that the undifferentiated Indo-European of central and western Europe belongs in that Late Period. Such a view corresponds very well with the one put forward here, and Meid's chronology would not contradict an ultimately Anatolian origin somewhere before 6000 BC.

The findings of a number of very eminent linguists can thus be made to harmonize quite effectively with the archaeological views propounded here – although it does not follow that those linguists themselves would accept them.

So who were the Celts?

In the more precise sense advocated here and by most linguists the term 'Celt' is applied to those speaking a Celtic language. The Celtic languages are seen to emerge, by a process of differentiation or crystallization, from an undifferentiated early Indo-European language which was spoken in Europe north and west of the Alps, and may still be preserved in certain river names. Insular and Continental Celtic will have developed in the areas where they were spoken in the first century BC, and indeed if they are still spoken, where they have subsequently survived, (although Scottish Gaelic and Breton may have moved to their present areas in around the fifth century AD by a process of élite dominance). The earliest Indo-European speakers will have reached these areas by 4000 BC, although the differentiation into individual languages may have taken place very much later. But in a very real sense, the undertaking of becoming Celtic began then, and continued through the workings of the process of cumulative Celticity. The Celtic languages may have reached Italy rather later, although there is no clear reason why the Lepontic language should not have taken part in this formation process. Later adventures, such as the sack of Rome, the attack on Delphi and the supposed movement into Galatia in Anatolia were not part of this process. Some of them may be seen as consequences of the system collapse at the end of the brief empire of Alexander the Great.

In the broader sense, however, we are entitled to apply the term Celtic to the customs, material culture and the art of these Celtic-speaking communities. It is perfectly appropriate to contrast the order and discipline of classical art, for instance, with the linear movement and the imagination of La Tène art. Celtic art clearly ranks as one of the major art styles of the ancient world. The origins of that art and culture are to be found in the same lands and therefore among people speaking Celtic languages, as we have defined them.

What is not admissible, however, is to restrict Celtic origins in any artificial narrow way to a specific area localized north of the Alps, as some have done. That is the area, certainly, where aristocratic chieftains of the iron age are first seen, and where La Tène art developed, but it has no specially privileged claim to be the unique and original homeland of the Celts.

Seventy years ago, the founder of the periodical *Études Celtiques*, Joseph Vendryes,[1] published an article entitled 'Vocabulary equivalences between Indo-Iranian and Celtic', in which he suggested the existence in these early languages of certain very similar terms relating amongst other things to ritual and religion and hence to religious traditions common to the two areas and languages. Following this evidence, it has been suggested that the brahmans (the priests mentioned in the Vedic Sanskrit texts of India), the Magi of the early Iranian *Avesta*, the *flamines* and pontifs of the Roman religion, and the druids of the early Celts played closely analogous roles in their different communities, and that these analogies were due to their common origin in still earlier Indo-European institutions. These are exciting proposals, and they were taken up with enthusiasm by many scholars. Comparable suggestions have been made about the early Irish and Indian law books:[2] they consisted of canonical texts, invested with a sacred origin, and interpreted exclusively by a privileged caste. There were law schools in both countries and the relations between pupil and teacher were similar, with eventual rights of succession.

Subsequently many similar comparisons have been made in the fields of social organization and mythology, as well as law and religion, where similarities in the forms of belief or behaviour in different regions can plausibly be used to suggest a common origin for each. In many cases it has been proposed that these similarities exist because of a shared background which is not simply linguistic, in the common Indo-European ancestral language, but also cultural. The assumption is often made that these similarities are to be traced back to those early Indo-European speaking communities which are responsible for the common linguistic heritage.

This seemed very plausible when the historical reality underlying that common linguistic heritage was understood to be the relatively recent spread across Europe and parts of western Asia of well-organized tribesmen speaking an early Indo-European language. It seemed, at least at first sight, likely that this 'spread' was responsible not only for the modern distribution of the Indo-European languages, but also for a whole series of institutions, customs, beliefs and myths which could be seen as part of the common Indo-European heritage.

Today, however, there are serious difficulties to holding such a view. For while the notion of the spread of farming, and with it of Indo-European speech, may adequately explain the linguistic communality, it will certainly not do for some of these supposedly shared social institutions. In 6000 BC these were very simple farming communities and we cannot assume that they already had the sort of specialized and differentiated social structure which we associate with the brahmans and druids, *flamines* and pontifs of very much later ages. The time has come to ask whether some of these institutional similarities may not be due to coincidences of various kinds, or to similarities in development rather than to a common origin in some supposedly proto-Indo-European social structure. To say this, however, has potentially devastating consequences for a major field of scholarship which has in recent years won very widespread acceptance.

For most of the past fifty years, this particular field of study was dominated by the distinguished French student of early Indo-European culture, Georges Dumézil. In his early work, he compared the mythologies of Vedic India, early Rome and other Indo-European cultures, discussing the role of the Vedic brahman and the Latin *flamen*,[3] following the lead which Vendryes and others had given. After 1938 he moved beyond this direct comparative mythology, and increasingly worked in terms of analogous structures to be perceived within the myths and the institutions of the lands in question, developing his notion of any underlying 'tripartite ideology', in many Indo-European thought structures.[4]

This view has been documented in an impressive and very copious series of works, ranging far over the structure and mythology of most Indo-European societies. It is difficult to summarize[5] the main points concisely, but they can be most effectively approached by beginning with the ancient Indo-European speaking communities of northern India.

Classical Indian social organization was based upon a stratified system, consisting of four main castes: the *brahmans* or priests, the *ksatriyas* or warriors, the *vaisyas* or cultivators, and the low-grade *sudras*, who served the others. Dumézil deals primarily with the first three, the fourth being of very low rank. If one analyses the ancient Sanskrit religious literature, according to Dumézil, one can see the earliest Indian pantheon reflecting this caste organization. It is possible to discern three hierarchically ranked, functionally differentiated strata of gods. The highest of these contains the joint sovereign deities, Mitra and Varuna, whom Dumézil considers as collective representatives of the brahman caste, and embodying 'the first function', namely sovereignty and religious office. At the next level is Indra, the war god, embodying 'the second function', that of the warrior, as seen in the *ksatriya* caste. At the lowest level are several deities, including the Asvins and the goddess Sarasavati. These deities represent the 'third function', that of the food-producing class, the *vaisyas*, with which are associated various other attributes, including fertility and health.

The interest of this tripartite functional scheme is that it can, supposedly, be shown to underlie the structure of other early Indo-European societies. Thus in early Rome Dumézil sees an expression of the tripartite system in the so-called archaic triad of divinities, Jupiter (sovereign deity), Mars (god of war) and Quirinus (patron of production). Similar classifications have been applied to Celtic society (where Caesar[6] had spoken of druids, knights and common people) and later to Germanic society also. It is, of course, impossible to convey in so bald a statement the wide range of erudition which Dumézil brings to bear, and the great wealth of sources which he cites.

For our present interest, however, there is a very real difficulty. The societies described in this tripartite functional scheme are hierarchically ordered. In the vocabulary of anthropology[7] these are stratified societies; that is to say they show one of the principal attributes of what are termed state societies. Of course ancient Greece and Rome were indeed state societies at the times in question, and so was India by the time the caste system was fully formed, although the social organization at the earlier time when the *Rigveda* was composed is open to discussion. Early Celtic societies at the time of Caesar may generally be regarded as chiefdoms, in the terminology of the anthropologist, reflecting pronounced social ranking, but in general lacking the central institutions which are characteristic of state societies. It has been persuasively argued that state societies first emerged in Gaul during the first century BC and at that time or later in most other parts of the Celtic world.[8] Whether the communities represented in the early Irish epics should be considered developed chiefdom societies or state societies would be a matter for discussion.

The real difficulty lies in the previous stages of this social development. For even if the distribution of the Indo-European languages were due to a dispersal of peoples as late as the third millennium BC, there seems no way in the light of what we know of their archaeology, that these peoples could already have possessed such complex institutions. Even if we follow this relatively low chronology, and think in terms of the Kurgan cultures as the point of origin, as has been widely suggested, these were certainly not state societies, and there is very little evidence in their material culture for the prominent ranking of individuals which is characteristic of chiefdoms. This difficulty is of course much compounded if one follows the earlier chronology proposed here. If we are thinking in terms of the first farmers as the earliest Indo-European speakers of Europe, in the sixth and fifth millennia BC, we are speaking of what are generally regarded as egalitarian peasants. Their societies, as noted above, probably embodied no hierarchical ordering whatever: certainly their material culture does not reflect it. This does not mean that they were without some social organization, and no doubt individual communities often did have effective leaders, but there is no reason to suggest the existence in them of hereditary chieftains, and certainly none to warrant a specialized functional division of the population into warriors, priests and common people. These terms seem a complete anachronism.

This is a difficulty which Dumézil never seems to have confronted, although it undoubtedly represents one of the most telling arguments against his entire system. He is not too specific about the practical meaning of these divisions:[9]

> (This structure) . . . naturally cannot teach us very much about the concrete form – or the different forms – in which this conception is achieved.

But he does make clear in several places that some underlying historical reality is posited:[10]

> The most ancient Romans, the Umbrians, had brought with them to Italy the same conception which the Indo-Iranians also knew, and on which the Indians in particular had founded their social order.

There is thus no doubt that he is thinking in this passage of the first Indo-Europeans to reach Italy, who, on the model proposed here, were some of the first farmers at a date before 5000 BC. Even on the Kurgan invasion theory, as propounded by Marija Gimbutas, we are dealing with a date well in advance of 2000 BC, and consequently with a society, in terms of what we know of early bronze age Italy, reflecting at most a modest chiefdom organization.

These comments are not mere pedantry. They bring into question one of the most essential foundations of the whole edifice of Dumézilien scholarship: its historical reality. What we see of analogous social institutions and similarly stratified societies in India, Rome and Gaul in the first century BC, or a little earlier, was simply not common to these societies or to their predecessors in 2000 BC, let alone in 4000 BC.

It is indeed curious that Dumézil never seems to have grasped this fundamental problem. For if the social institutions of Indo-European-speaking groups as far removed in space as the Celts and the Indians appear to have common forms traceable back to a common ancestor, it is obviously necessary to have some notion of what that ancestral society was, when it flourished and where it was located. This is a historical reality which Dumézil never quite seems to offer. The proto-Indo-Europeans are left as a very nebulous entity indeed. Now the critic may well feel that there is a good reason for this – that there never was an early proto-Indo-European society sharing these various social forms, and with those elements of shared mythology which Dumézil and his followers see as proto-Indo-European. And even if the protagonists of the 'shared institutions' view of early Indo-European society can with justice reply that they are not themselves archaeologists and cannot be expected to provide a satisfactory answer, they should at least contemplate the possibility that there may be no satisfactory answer, and that this concept of a shared proto-Indo-European mythology may itself be a construct of very recent formation.

To adopt this solution here is not necessarily, however, to deny that interesting similarities existed between many of the societies in question at the time when they were first well documented. In addition to Vendryes and to Dumézil himself, Emile Benveniste[11] has written a very thorough study, indicating a number of common institutions. However if we take a processual, anthropological viewpoint, it is not in the least surprising that societies on the brink of literacy in different parts of the world should show some general similarities of this kind. The early Indian society portrayed in the Vedic hymns, or Homeric Greece, or Celtic Ireland as depicted in the earliest writings, and the northern Europe of the Norse sagas can all, in a certain sense, be characterized as 'heroic societies' – but that does not necessarily mean that the 'heroic' features seen within them had common origins. These were all chiefdom societies (to use a term recently favoured by anthropologists). In many areas of the world, as social organization develops, we see emerging governmental institutions, associated with craft specialization. Religious roles likewise become more specialized, and are often linked with governmental ones. Polynesian society, for instance, as first depicted by Captain Cook, and now much better understood by contemporary anthropologists,[12] shows many of the features described; this is certainly so for its social reality, if not necessarily for its religious structure. Moreover, in many of the countries in question, archaeology today actually allows us to follow the development of social complexity. This is particularly clear in north-west Europe, where we can trace the early origins of ranked societies among the neolithic monument builders[13] (including the builders of Stonehenge), and further developments are documented in the wealthy burials of the bronze age. There is a further striking development in the Hallstatt and La Tène iron ages of central Europe – here one might indeed begin to speak of warriors, and perhaps priests. Then, in the first century BC, as Carole Crumley and Daphne Nash[14] have shown, we have state societies which no doubt possessed some degree of social stratification. Similar comments may be made for mainland Italy, where prominently ranked society is first seen in the first millennium BC. So too, for India.

The solution here is to recognize that there are indeed structural similarities between these societies, but to question whether very many of these are the result of their common proto-Indo-European heritage. These were barbarian (i.e. non-urban), heroic societies. What we know of them has come to us in the main from epic poetry, whether the *Rigveda*, Homer or the Irish epics, in which warfare is glorified and the 'second function' is given free reign. We could make similar remarks if we were to compare them with chiefdom societies in Mesoamerica at the appropriate time.

There are further problems, however, for it is not clear how many of the apparent equivalences in the various myths should indeed be regarded as equivalent at all. As Dumézil himself has stressed, an essential feature of his method (and in this it resembles all structuralist methods) is not to compare A in one place directly with A' in another. That would be a prosaic and atomistic approach. It is rather the structural relationship between A, B and C in the first context which has to be compared with the relationship between A', B' and C' in the second. In such cases, as many critics of structuralist method have pointed out, the basis for the claim of equivalence is very difficult to verify. As Ernest Gellner[15] has put it, in relation to the binary opposites favoured by the followers of Lévi-Strauss:

> The structuralists seem to be far too willing simply to trust their intuitions in this matter and to expect their readers to extend this trust to them. Polar extremities no doubt abound in many texts, but has anyone ever put it to the test by locking diverse structuralists in insulated cubicles with the same text, and seeing whether they all emerge with the same binary opposites at the end?

A related point has recently been made, in relation especially to interpretations of the Germanic myths, by R. I. Page[16] in his paper 'Dumézil revisited'. He writes, some scholars 'have wondered – in considering his Norse work, at any rate – whether he builds upon facts or opinions'.

The whole tripartite system, which Dumézil claims to be not only common to Indo-European groups, but also effectively exclusive to them, was subjected to a critical, indeed satirical review by John Brough.[17] He adopted the ingenious, *reductio ad absurdum* approach of showing how a number of Old Testament texts seem to be open to interpretation in precisely the same tripartite terms which Dumézil claims are specifically (and exclusively) Indo-European, yet obviously the writers of the Old Testament were writing in a Semitic not an Indo-European tradition. It is only fair to say that Dumézil replied in detail to this criticism, indicating shortcomings in Brough's analysis, and suggesting that a number of the elements which he discerned might indeed have been borrowed, through contact, from Indo-European traditions.

Rather curiously, a somewhat similar and disquieting case has been used in an analogous way, but with very different intentions, by one of Dumézil's own pupils and most ardent supporters, Atsuhito Yoshida.[18] He has considered the early mythology of his native Japan with a Dumézilien eye and arrived at what seems at first a conclusion as bizarre as that reached by John Brough for the Old Testament:

> Japanese mythology is articulated, in effect, as much in its entirety as in its details, following the framework offered by the ideology of the three functions of the Indo-Europeans. Moreover it contains a great number of themes whose origins undoubtedly go back to Indo-European sources.

He has suggested that the historical explanation for these supposed Indo-European elements in early Japanese mythology is contact between (Indo-European) Scythian nomads and the (non-Indo-European) inhabitants of Korea, whence they would have been transmitted to Japan at the time of early state formation in the sixth century AD. This is, as so often, a matter where a non-specialist is not in a position to assess the evidence properly, but the story seems inherently implausible. It is pertinent to note that the notion of Korean immigrants playing a decisive role in the formation of the early Japanese state has recently been questioned by qualified experts.[19] One is therefore left with the uneasy suspicion that the tripartite aspect of Japanese mythology is as fortuitous as that deliberately and frivolously conjured up for the Semitic by Brough, and totally unconnected with Indo-European systems. However this time the claim has come from an authorized analyst, working within the Dumézilien canon, and cannot be rejected as a frivolous exercise, as was Brough's example. It is difficult here to escape the view that some of the claims of the Dumézil school have been overstated. In these circumstances we are not obliged to consider incompatibilities between it and the view of Indo-European origins advanced here as a decisive refutation of the latter.

These remarks are not intended as adverse reflection upon the enormous contributions which Dumézil made to the wider study of mythology. Indeed it is specifically through a broadly structuralist approach that he has been able to examine more effectively than hitherto the relationships embodied within the various myths. But it should be noted that the other great French scholar and student of myth, Claude Lévi-Strauss, has generally attributed structural homologies of the kind that we have been discussing to more general factors, and not to a specific, historical communality of origin. It may be, then, that they should not be allowed to weigh too heavily within the field of historical linguistics.

Very much the same point has been made in answer to those who have endeavoured to recognize a characteristically Indo-European system of kinship.[20] The British social anthropologist, Jack Goody,[21] has specifically taken issue with the frequent claim that early Indo-European society was of a 'patriarchal' character, a claim based principally on the existence of common kin terms in the various languages. It may be also that the arguments which have been made in favour of close resemblances between the early legal systems of Ireland and India[22] could be clarified by an analogous analysis. Some of the features in question may be common to many early legal systems which had only recently come to rely upon a written law code. This again is a specialist field where the amateur cannot properly comment, but it would be interesting to see the matter examined in this wider comparative light.

It is when we come to specific items of vocabulary that the shared Indo-European elements are less easily dismissed. While several of the relationships and similarities indicated by Dumézil and his followers may be fortuitous, and others the result of parallel developmental processes, and others again perhaps very general structural similarities of the kind discussed by Lévi-Strauss on a global level, this can hardly be so when the word in question evidently has a common, proto-Indo-European origin. Benveniste,[23] for instance, has discussed in considerable detail the well-known relationship between the Latin word *rex* (king) along with the Irish *ri* on the one hand and the Sanskrit root *raj-*, ancestral to the modern Indian *raja*, on the other. Of course it must be admitted that there are some linguistic resemblances between unrelated tongues that occur by chance; the Persian word *bad*, having the same meaning as the English word, is apparently not related to it: this is a case of accidental homonymy. But such is emphatically not the case for this instance or for the others cited by Benveniste. The problem here, however, is not with the word itself, since we expect plenty of words with common roots among the Indo-European languages. The difficulty is rather with the concept, the meaning. For king, in the sense of head of state, is not a term to be expected among the egalitarian communities from which both the Irish and Vedic Indian societies (as well as the Roman) evolved.

There is, however, nothing to exclude the possibility that the common source word in Proto-Indo-European meant 'leader', or 'prominent man', without in any way implying the institution of kingship or even of chieftainship of a formal, hereditary kind. As social complexity and eventually a stratified society developed, so the term for the most prominent man may have been, in one or two instances, retained and upgraded, although not, we should note, in the majority of the later Indo-European languages. In this way, to find the same word in one or two languages designating this rather advanced social concept need not cause surprise.

Comparable arguments may be applied to the occurrence of related words for certain deities: for Zeus, the name of the Greek god, for the Vedic, Dyau, and for the Latin, Jupiter. The common root word may have been an early divine term of some kind: its existence does not imply an equivalence between the pantheons of the areas at the time in question, or even the existence in them of a formal pantheon at all. As Dumézil himself[24] puts it:

The most incontestable equation has shown itself to be deceptive:

in the Vedic Dyau, the 'sky' is quite differently conceived than in the Greek Zeus or the Roman Jupiter, and the comparison teaches us almost nothing.

It is difficult, therefore, to learn a great deal through the methods of vocabulary analysis about the social institutions of those groups speaking an early form of Indo-European before this differentiated into different language families. Our problem is not simply one of vocabulary change, it is also one of changes of meaning. Yet it must be admitted that looking through the pages of Benveniste's major work one does indeed find a rich vocabulary of words which undoubtedly have common roots.

The interesting possibility has also been raised[25] that early metrical forms of verse seen in archaic Irish and in Vedic Sanskrit, as well as in Homeric Greek, appear to be related. That is an attractive suggestion, although one which it may prove difficult to evaluate rigorously. It is inherently likely that our first farmers will have had an oral literature, perhaps including lyric verse, as do many peasants in different parts of the world. It is therefore possible that some specific metrical forms could have been preserved over the millennia. But it is still a remarkable similarity.

In each of these cases, however, it is difficult to avoid the conclusion that the specialist in the field in question has been profoundly influenced by the prevailing historical consensus. The notion of a warlike, early Indo-European society, propagated by nomadic horsemen in the course of their wanderings has of course been a very attractive one. And coupled as it was with the substantial body of archaeological data set out by Childe and later by Gimbutas, it appeared to offer an authoritative historical framework within which specialists in kinship, in law, in social institutions and so forth could operate. This was all perfectly legitimate, for there is no doubt that the observations in these various special fields were indeed perfectly compatible with that historical explanation for the Indo-European phenomenon which set the homeland of the early Indo-Europeans in the steppes of western Russia somewhere just prior to the beginning of the bronze age.

Such compatibility between the observations in these different fields of scholarship and the traditional view of early Indo-European origins should not be too readily cited, however, in support of that traditional view. For, as I have sought to show, if a different explanation be offered for the distribution of the Indo-European languages, and one which offers a much greater time depth, very few serious difficulties are presented by these important adjacent fields of scholarship. The compatibilities can quite readily be adjusted. Most of the apparent difficulties are in fact a product of the acceptance of the traditional historical view, and suitable adjustments can be made if that is rejected and replaced by the alternative offered here.

Certainly a number of the arguments offered by Dumézil and his colleagues do appear very difficult to reconcile with the chronology. It is necessary then to suggest, as I have indicated above, that many of the similarities or apparent similarities recognized by Dumézil are not in fact to be explained in terms of a common origin in some proto-Indo-European cultural milieu. That, then, is the conclusion which I offer here. It seems to me that Dumézil, by avoiding the issue of the concrete historical reality lying behind the various similarities between cultural forms which he seeks to recognize, has allowed himself a much freer hand and perhaps a less disciplined methodology than might have been prudent. As a result, many of his interpretations will have to be called into question, and perhaps some more cautious explanations offered for some of the similarities which are recognized among the myths and the social institutions of different societies where Indo-European languages were spoken.

There is also some more positive work of interpretation to be undertaken. For while my view does not seem compatible with a common Indo-European background of priest, kings and warriors, the question does still remain as to what precisely the shared cultural background might be. If we take the view that in many areas the spread of Indo-European languages was indeed due to the demographic processes associated with the development of agriculture, it is certainly pertinent to ask what common cultural elements these early farmers brought with them in addition to their language. There may well have been some common institutions, and a shared belief system, although it was a belief system of peasant farmers, not of warlike nomads with a highly ranked social structure. I do not doubt that a sensitive analysis and interpretation of the shared early vocabulary, insofar as it can be constructed, of very much the kind undertaken by Benveniste, can answer some of the relevant questions.

We can see now, however, that such a work of interpretation will need to make rather fewer prior assumptions about the general nature of that society. And it will certainly need to attempt a reconstruction which is compatible with the world of early peasant farmers. That seems a major new task for Indo-European scholarship, and a not unworthy one, if we are to seek some clearer picture of our common Indo-European origins. But it is a task where greater methodological awareness, and perhaps greater caution will need to be exercised.

11. Archaeology and Indo-European Origins: An Assessment

No other article I have ever written in my life was so difficult for me as this one. Here I argue with famous and respected scientists with numerous high merits in linguistics. This time, too, they have accomplished an enormous task, working sometimes in absolutely untouched areas of science. Why is it that the results of their efforts have to be so severely criticised? Obviously, when dealing with so important and incredibly difficult problems as this one, a linguist should exercise even more rigour than usual, and a historian should abstain from speculations and try to represent real people in concrete historical conditions. Then all impossible solutions will disappear, and the only possible one will emerge.

I. M. Diakonov, 1984, 75

The diffidence expressed by the distinguished Soviet academic in the above passage is certainly appropriate in the field which he, and we, are considering. For these are questions which have been much discussed in the past by generations of leading scholars, and the position presented here disagrees with most of them. One should not underestimate, then, the controversial nature of the views which I have presented, nor the difficulties which they may encounter in their more detailed application. The subject matter is vast, embracing the full sweep of the languages today classified as Indo-European, as well as the complex prehistoric archaeology of much of the Old World, from western Europe through to Anatolia, the Levant, central Asia, the Indian sub-continent and indeed, in the deserts of Sinkiang, to what is today part of the People's Republic of China. That someone who can make no claim to be a linguist should dabble in such matters certainly smacks of temerity. And when the inevitable consequences of the views advanced are to call into question several large, and now quite well-developed, fields of scholarship, the enterprise may even seem not a little foolhardy.

We have seen in earlier chapters how the conventional view has been built up in a system of logic where the historical linguists generally accept some of the premises offered by the prehistoric archaeologists, and the archaeologists accept those of the linguists. Amongst those premises are several crucial ones which have rarely been called into question, and it is there that the fatal flaw in the logic of the entire inferential edifice may lie. No one person can today be a specialist in all the fields which are directly relevant to a serious study of these questions. Yet the results are of fundamental importance to a whole series of such fields of study. If the views presented here, and the arguments which sustain them, carry some weight, then their consequences are of urgent relevance for all those areas of inquiry. They certainly have a significant bearing on the whole way we think about European and Indian societal origins. In a sense the implications of the approach go even deeper: they bear on the way in which we consider the relations between archaeology and language anywhere. So in conclusion I shall consider some of the implications which arise from the view advocated which bear more widely on language groups quite unrelated to the Indo-European, and which are thus in a sense applicable on a world-wide basis.

In previous chapters a fresh approach to the study of early language origins was advocated which would at the same time consider anew the processes by which languages develop and change, with due respect for the recent advances in sociolinguistics, and at the same time take a processual approach to the prehistoric archaeology. It was argued that while we cannot expect to find direct evidence in the archaeological record for a specific prehistoric language or language group, we can indeed study processes of demographic and social change. It is these processes of change which we may seek, however hypothetically, to correlate with language change in those areas.

Whatever the limitations of the specific suggestions for the Indo-European languages which then followed, I would certainly argue that the approach advocated offers in effect the only valid way to go about studying early language origins. So that while critics may quite reasonably quarrel with the proposals set out in Chapter 7, I should be surprised if they did not find those of Chapter 6 reasonably acceptable.

In proposing a specific solution I found it difficult to accept the arguments put forward for profound population and language changes across the whole of Europe at the beginning of the bronze age, somewhere in the third millennium BC. (The arguments, derived from 'linguistic palaeontology', which supposedly supported such changes were criticized in Chapters 2 and 4.) The main objection to this solution was archaeological: that there does not seem to be any sufficiently profound and widespread shift in the archaeological record at that time to justify such a conclusion. If the evidence of the Beaker phenomenon and of Corded Ware were accepted, as it was until recently, as indicating widespread migrations of people, then the case might still be tenable. But archaeologists today, as we have seen, are less and less inclined to make such an interpretation.

In surveying European prehistory I do not believe that we can see any one process, nor any series of processes at once sufficiently profound in social and demographic consequences and so widespread geographically as to suggest a viable background for such radical linguistic changes, until we go right back to the time of the spread of farming. Of course there remain other possibilities, even if that point is accepted. It would still be logically possible for the changes in question to have occurred *before* the spread of farming, a possibility which takes the argument back to the palaeolithic era. And of course it is possible to argue, as some have done, that an explanation in terms of the *spread* of some early Indo-European language or languages is not the right approach. Some different, in some senses more static, model could be proposed.

The language-farming theory carried with it the hypothesis that farming came to Europe (we shall refer again to Iran and India later) not simply through the acquisition by the pre-existing mesolithic population of the various areas of the necessary plant and animal species, but rather through successive displacements, over the generations, of peasant farmers. No individual needs to have moved more than a few kilometres in the search for new farmland, yet the gradual, cumulative effect of such displacements, as Ammerman and Cavalli-Sforza showed in their elegant wave of advance model, is the spread of a new population whose descent can in the main be traced back through the successive farming gener-

ations to the original early farming areas and their population at the
time.

This argument, stated so baldly, has certainly the merits of
simplicity, but it should be recognized for what it is – a 'homeland'
model. The critic may well say that we have done little more than
resuscitate an *Urvolk*, an original group of proto-Indo-European
speakers, in an *Urheimat*, a homeland, in a rather unexpected place.
To some extent such an observation is not unreasonable: I have
indeed argued that before about 6000 BC there were, in the eastern
part of Anatolia, and perhaps in some adjacent lands to the east and
south-east, and probably nowhere else, people speaking languages
ancestral to all the Indo-European languages of today. So that is
indeed a kind of 'homeland' model, but it is certainly not a
migrationist model of the old-fashioned and traditional kind. It
does not assume a sudden and unexplained eruption from some
rather ill-defined nuclear area, linked perhaps in some way to
warlike nomad pastoralists. On the contrary, it links the spread of
early Indo-European languages to a well-defined demographic
process itself closely correlated with the adoption of a farming
economy. The development of nomad pastoralism is indeed relevant, but it is argued that this may have happened rather later, first
on the western part of the Russian steppes, relying on domestic
animals previously used in the settled farming communities of that
area. To the extent that one can speak of a directional process here,
nomad pastoralism seems to have spread from eastern Europe
eastwards rather than the converse. In any case the subsequent
adoption of a nomad pastoralist economy in parts of eastern Europe
west of the Russian steppes was not a process which radically
affected Europe as a whole.

This hypothesis, as I have outlined it, is clearly vulnerable in at
least one important respect; for it is far from clear that, in western
Europe at any rate, the spread of farming economy was indeed
accompanied by the movement, even over short distances of
peasant farmers. In south-eastern Europe, as we have seen, such an
argument can much more readily be accepted: most students of the
early neolithic period in Greece agree that the new cereal crops, as
well as the domesticated sheep, goat and probably cattle were
imports to the area from Anatolia. At the moment it is perfectly

plausible to see the phenomenon of village life there, and indeed the villagers themselves, as something which came across the Aegean. That is to say that we are indeed speaking of the movements of small groups of farmers in their boats, with their plants and animals. The wave of advance model seems appropriate also for the transmission to the Balkans, and particularly so for the spread of the earliest farmers of the Danube with their Bandkeramik pottery up to the North Sea and almost to the English Channel.[1] It is likely that the first farmers to reach England came across the channel in small boats, just as their remote ancestors had crossed the Aegean some two thousand years earlier. We should nonetheless note here that an alternative case can be made, albeit resting so far on very scant evidence, that south-east Europe was itself part of the nuclear zone in which the wild prototypes of the essential domesticates could be found, and where the initial domestication process took place.[2]

In the west Mediterranean, however, it is much easier to question the wave of advance model and to stress the resilience of the pre-existing mesolithic populations, and the very long time which the process of 'acculturation' – i.e. the adoption of a farming economy – took. Indeed most of the best qualified recent writers stress these features,[3] and prefer to think in terms of largely indigenous processes. As Whittle[4] writes:

> The gradual nature of change in most of the western Mediterranean remains at present the most striking feature of these two millennia (of early farming) and the contrast with other parts of Europe is notable. Depending of course on one's view of the origins of the south-east Italian communities, all the observed changes can be seen in the context of local rather than external events.

Certainly it can be conceded that the process was a complex one, and that the adoption or development of farming did not occur in any steady or smooth way as the result of a uniform spread from the south-east. The wave of advance model was never intended to offer a detailed description of the process as it occurred in local regions, but rather to offer an understanding of the general underlying mechanism. It should be noted that those pre-existing mesolithic communities which adopted a farming economy, speaking presumably some non-Indo-European language, would themselves be expected to undergo, other things being equal, the same process of population increase as other peasant farmers occupying hitherto uncultivated lands. The model of partial acculturation would thus predict the presence of large pockets of other local languages remaining among those Indo-European languages whose presence was ultimately due to the spread of the farmers themselves.

The early reality in the west may well have been some such mosaic, where due to regional differences some areas adopted farming rapidly as a result of a 'spread' of the economy, and others developed more gradually, retaining a human population not significantly augmented by incomers. The most convenient explanation for the presence in central Italy of an important non-Indo-European language, Etruscan, comes from adopting this view. The same is true for Basque, and for those other early, non-Indo-European languages of Iberia of which we have a glimpse from the fragmentary inscriptions of the last few centuries BC.

Indeed it is important to realize that the picture as we have it today is a palimpsest, whose foundations may have been established in the early farming period, but whose detail is the product of many processes over subsequent millennia. These processes will inevitably have involved the extinction of several dialects and languages without leaving any significant record for us. There must have been Indo-European languages which did not survive, and there must also have been languages associated with pre-existing populations (and hence on my hypothesis, non-Indo-European) which survived for centuries and millennia before becoming extinct as the result of other social, demographic and linguistic processes. Basque and Etruscan are only, as it were, the tips of icebergs protruding into our present knowledge: many other non-Indo-European languages will have survived through several subsequent millennia, but for us they are nonetheless now lost beneath the waters of time.

The picture outlined here is thus not necessarily incompatible with the more sophisticated view of the origins of European farming adopted by many recent writers, and it is certainly consonant with a recognition of the regional diversity involved, and of the complexity of the processes. But it is difficult to see how it could be reconciled with the argument that the development of farming in

the west Mediterranean was entirely the result of indigenous processes, or with the adoption by local populations of a farming
economy without a significant proportion of incomers at that time.
In terms of the general picture proposed here, that would have
resulted in a later neolithic situation around 4000 BC where populations in south-east, eastern and central Europe would have spoken
a number of Indo-European languages (albeit with local compli-
cations), and with populations in the west Mediterranean and
Atlantic Europe speaking non-Indo-European languages derived
from their mesolithic forebears. By stressing the complexity of
the situation I am not seeking to confuse the issue. My theory of
Indo-European origins probably is in fact incompatible with the
view on local neolithic origins for the west Mediterranean held by
such well-informed writers as Barker and Lewthwaite,[5] and it is
well to admit it.

The hypothesis that early Indo-European languages were spoken
as early as the seventh millennium BC in eastern Anatolia certainly
also gains considerably in plausibility in the light of recent work by
the Soviet authors Gamkrelidze and Ivanov. Their study is of vastly
greater scope than my own, proposing radically new linguistic
theories both on the evolution of the consonants in the Indo-
European languages and a revised grammatical structure. Various
arguments lead them to place in eastern Anatolia the original area
where a proto-Indo-European language was spoken – that is to say
in precisely the same area to which very different arguments have
led me: 'the original territory of the original Indo-European homeland coincided with a region contained within eastern Anatolia, the
southern Caucasus and northern Mesopotamia in the fourth-fifth
millennia BCE'.[6] It should be noted that the date which they
propose is earlier than most scholars would suggest, although later
than my own. Their arguments are primarily linguistic, depending
among others on various Semitic loan-words which are shared by
many Indo-European languages and which can be used to support
some geographical proximity at an early stage. It is therefore
encouraging that archaeological arguments, which are quite independent of their linguistic ones, have led me to very much the same
conclusion.

It should be noted at once, however, that their solution differs
fundamentally from mine in one very major respect. For while they

too see the Hittite language evolving locally, and the location of Greek in Greece as a result of westward movement from Anatolia, they make the other Indo-European languages of Europe reach their destination by a complex series of migrations which lead them first (by a route extending far to the east) to that area north of the Black Sea where so many earlier writers have set their origins:[7] 'The region north of the Black Sea region and the Volga steppes may be considered the basic common (although secondary) homeland for the "Ancient European" languages.' This position runs, of course, against all the archaeological counter-arguments set out earlier, and cannot be accepted here. But the great encouragement which I draw from their work is that the linguistic situation is evidently of sufficient fluidity to allow such eminent authorities to propose a nuclear area in eastern Anatolia, at a much earlier date than has been conventionally accepted. Their work has certainly been well received by some western scholars.[8]

At the same time, they have been criticized quite severely by the Soviet scholar, I. Diakonov,[9] on very much the same grounds (among other more technical and linguistic ones) which I would myself choose:

> Essential questions should be asked: who migrated? Why? How many of them were there? Was it actually a migration of people, or rather the transfer of a language from one population to another? These are difficult questions, but they should at least be asked when we try to solve such a complicated historical problem as that of the spreading of the Indo-European languages all over Eurasia.

What Diakonov is here advocating is precisely the central thrust of this book: that it is necessary to take a processual approach which can give some meaning in human terms (and in archaeological terms) to the realities underlying such linguistic changes. All of this emboldens me to feel that the language-farming thesis advanced here remains a distinctly tenable one, at least for Europe.

There can be no doubt, however, that the work by these Soviet scholars represents a significant re-opening of the Indo-European question from a linguistic standpoint[10]. That I think is very necessary if further progress is to be made.

As far as the Indo-Iranian languages are concerned, along with Tocharian, the situation is certainly more complicated, and there can be no doubt that the development of a nomad pastoral economy was a significant factor, at least for central Asia. As we have seen that economic adaptation seems to have been evolved at the western end of the Russian steppe lands, and to have spread eastwards. Such a view is quite different from the traditional Childe-Gimbutas thesis. Whether the first Indo-European languages spoken in the northern Indian sub-continent came there as a result of a wave of advance farming spread, as early as the sixth millennium BC, seems at present very uncertain. It would seem that the later spread of a nomad pastoralist economy in the third millennium BC, and later, of a more highly-ranked social organization based upon horse riding must also be part of the picture, but it is perfectly possible that the languages used in the Indus Valley civilization as early as 3000 BC were already Indo-European.

It is also interesting to note how a similar language-farming explanation is certainly valid for much more recent times. In north America the first European immigrants brought with them very much the same farming economy, based upon cereal crops, sheep and cattle, which originated in the Near East some ten millennia earlier. Again there was a wave of advance, from east to west, although naturally a whole series of local factors made the detailed local histories very different. Closely similar observations can be made for Australia, New Zealand and much of South America. In each case the Indo-European languages in question became dominant through the working of demographic processes associated with the spread of the new farming pattern.

Of course in these lands there were other differences such as technology, and the incoming immigrants did have a highly ranked society, so that the factor of élite dominance is also a very important one. It would be completely misleading to equate the position in prehistoric Europe with the European expansion of imperial and colonialist times. Nor am I seeking to argue some mystical association between wheat and barley and the Indo-European languages. Wheat and barley came to be just as firmly associated with the Semitic languages in Mesopotamia and the Levant. My point is simply that language spread often is indeed associated with intelligible social, demographic and economic processes which the archaeologist can well aspire to study and understand: that is the nub. The finer details of the solution proposed remain to be investigated and may well be modified through further work. It is this central principle which is the more important.

If the central arguments set out in previous chapters be accepted, whatever the view taken over various details which no doubt remain uncertain, the consequences for our understanding of the early development of the areas and languages concerned are profound; for this is not simply an intriguing philological question of interest to specialist prehistorians, it also impinges upon all those areas of study where the early histories of peoples and of nations are considered to be of significance.

We are faced, then, with a vastly greater time depth, where the Indo-European antecedents of the modern European world are to be traced back six or seven thousand years, all of it on European soil. My theory does indeed argue for ultimately Anatolian origins, and it is indeed to these common origins that the shared linguistic unity of the Indo-European languages is largely to be ascribed; but they are remote origins, these common elements of linguistic parentage. Many of the other points of similarity are not so much due to that common source, but to a shared 'life history' as it were. The path of development from early farming to metal-using through to iron age society has in several ways been a similar one in different parts of Europe. This I think is in large measure due to shared environmental conditions, and to shared experiences over millennia of history: there is nothing particularly 'Indo-European' about most of it.

It is an important feature, almost a paradoxical feature in some ways, that this long consideration of the origins of the Indo-European languages should serve in some senses to de-emphasize the significance of our shared Indo-European heritage. This heritage is indeed there in the common linguistic structures and elements of vocabulary which are shared by the Indo-European languages of today and by their ancestors, right back to that original and hypothetical group of proto-Indo-European dialects some eight or nine thousand years ago. However it should be observed at once that if an early Indo-European language came to be spoken in many

of the lands now under consideration as early as the initial development of a farming economy, and if that was the decisive process
leading to our shared Indo-European heritage, then that community or communality was culturally rather simple, although no
doubt linguistically very rich. We are talking here of simple peasant
farmers, with a restricted range of domestic plants and animals and
a limited range of crafts. These may generally have included
weaving and pottery-making and other farming skills, but theirs
were egalitarian societies. To call them 'tribal', at any rate at the
outset, might be to overstate the case, since different communities
were probably not strongly linked by social ties in the early days.
On the contrary, they can probably be more satisfactorily described
as 'segmentary societies', laying stress on the almost autonomous
nature of individual village or neighbourhood communities.
Naturally there were links and marriage exchanges between these,
but in the early days at least it may be wrong to think of much
larger regional associations such as one might term 'tribes'.

It is implicit in this view that more sophisticated social organization, with the development of ranked society and eventually of
'chiefdoms', only emerged later in some areas. The hierarchical
tendencies which we discern in many of the areas in question in
early historical times – the warlike chiefs, the warrior aristocracy –
cannot possibly have been part of that original, shared Indo-
European heritage which we can associate with those first farmers
and with their egalitarian societies. This would seem an inescapable
consequence of the view advanced here. But it is in some ways a
revolutionary one, for a whole discipline of scholarship has
emerged in recent decades which concerns itself with early Indo-
European society and which has reached diametrically opposite
conclusions. Its weakness, as I see it, is that it has rarely considered
the fundamental historical question as to what the concrete historical reality was behind the supposed communal features of the
Indo-Europeans.

Three issues now remain that we should look at: language
origins, language dispersals, and the relationship between archaeology and linguistic studies. It is possible here only to touch upon
these in summing up, but I should like to do so in order to indicate
areas where more work needs to be done.

Archaeology and Language Origins

The problem of the origins of language is as old as scholarship itself, and our own more specific problem of linguistic diversity is of course inseparable from it. Unfortunately the physical, that is to say anatomical, aspects of language production give us little clear-cut information. It is arguable that all the known hominids from the time of *Australopithecus*, some three million years ago, have been endowed with sufficient in the way of vocal chords to make the production of some form of spoken language, in the human sense, a possibility:[11] the question is, rather, a neurophysiological one.

The problem of language today is thus seen less as involving simple physical questions than as raising more crucial issues of symboling ability.[12] It is argued that language is not only a means of communication, but a device which allows the handling by the individual of symbolic concepts and as such it is indispensable to structured thought. If this viewpoint be followed, it is at least arguable that the development of the relevant abilities of reasoning, of conceptualizing, should be reflected in human behaviour patterns. It is of course possible to study these through the material remains. Such is the perspective now widely accepted. Quite naturally it places much emphasis upon the symbolic aspects of material culture, and not least upon such early depictions as are seen in upper palaeolithic cave art; both the paintings and the small portable objects.[13]

Many contemporary writers would be inclined to equate the development of language-as-we-know-it with the emergence of fully modern man in the physical sense, that is to say of *Homo sapiens sapiens* some 40,000 years ago. The equation here is based on the current view that the emergence of the physical characteristics of *Homo sapiens sapiens* was approximately contemporary with the development of the whole new range of behaviours which we see in the upper palaeolithic period. In western Europe it has generally been held that *Homo sapiens sapiens* in the physical sense can be equated with the material culture of the Aurignacian (Perigordian I) phase, and further east with the Gravettian. The earlier and less varied Mousterian material culture can be equated with modern man's predecessor in Europe and elsewhere: neanderthal man,

Homo sapiens neanderthalensis. One very interesting aspect of current research is the investigation of the validity of this correlation, which in some respects has been called into question. Moreover there is now growing evidence for the very much earlier emergence in southern Africa, perhaps as far back as 90,000 years ago, of anatomically modern humans, accompanied by some change in their behaviour patterns as reflected in the tool industries. These behaviour patterns are to be contrasted with those of earlier hominids, which have recently been reassessed and judged by some to have been much simpler than had earlier been thought.

Such questions are being intensively researched at present, and to draw any firm conclusion would be premature, but it certainly now looks very possible that the development of human language as a powerful vehicle for symbolic and conceptual ability is to be associated with the emergence of *Homo sapiens sapiens*. On that view, earlier hominids would have had very restricted linguistic abilities indeed.

Such conclusions would have immediate implications for historical linguistics. For they would set a rather well defined time frame within which the subject could operate. We could expect a process of differentiation of different 'languages', in the modern sense, to be underway from around 40,000 years ago in all areas with a human population.

There is no doubt that the historical reconstruction of the global dispersal of *Homo sapiens sapiens* can be undertaken by archaeological means. Indeed the task is very much simpler if the physical anthropology (i.e. the physical form, including the skeletal remains) may be equated with the well-defined material culture of the upper palaeolithic. Whether fully modern man emerged first in Africa, and dispersed from there around 40,000 years ago is still a matter for debate, but it is a debate which further research will resolve. Already, I think, we can assume that this is the time frame within which historical linguistics may operate.

A logical distinction must of course be drawn between the problem of the origins of human linguistic ability in a general sense, and that of the origins of individual languages or linguistic groups in all their rich diversity, but at the same time the two are inseparably linked. It is generally agreed that humans today carry with them at birth an innate linguistic ability which ensures that, during their early development, they come to speak at least one language, normally the language spoken around them in their early years. The precise form of specific words used to designate individual concepts is in most cases arbitrary. Given therefore a tendency of linguistic drift, in which the forms of the language between groups not in direct contact gradually diverge, the emergence of linguistic diversity would seem inevitable. We must therefore expect that linguistic diversity would have emerged almost as early as the full development of human speech ability.

The question then arises as to how far back in time we may be able to trace the different language groupings in the modern world which we have been discussing. Rather than seeking the origins of the Indo-European language group in the demographic processes associated with the development of farming around 8000 BC, should we instead set them very much earlier and link them rather with the spread of *Homo sapiens sapiens*? Certainly this is a position which has been adopted by some archaeologists in the past, and it cannot be rejected immediately on *a priori* grounds.

Such a view would, of course, run counter to the conclusions which have been drawn from the procedures of glottochronology. In Chapter 5 it was concluded that while lexicostatistics can be of real value in offering some quantitative measure of similarities and differences between languages, or at least between language vocabularies, the assumptions about constant rates of change which underlie glottochronology seem very doubtful. So I felt able to argue that to situate the time of differentiation between some of the early Indo-European dialects as much as 10,000 years ago, instead of 5,000 years ago, need not run counter to lexicostatistical considerations, but it may be that to place these events as far back as 40,000 years ago would create difficulties.[14]

On the other hand we might not be obliged to go as far back as this. The separation between the major language groups of the world might well date from that early time, while the differentiation within them could have taken place much later, during the course of the upper palaeolithic period and of course in more recent times as well. At the moment these are relatively new ideas, within the context of recent developments in palaeolithic studies (although, as we have seen, some of them have been anticipated by earlier writers). At the moment it may be sufficient to be aware of a whole, vast field of research centred upon a coherent time frame within which it may be possible one day to fit the entire picture of language differentiation on a global level. Such a project, as we have stressed, would address the underlying social, economic and demographic processes at work, and in doing so might be able to bring the available archaeological evidence to bear in concrete fashion.

Archaeology and Language Dispersals: in particular the Polynesian and Bantu Languages

The problem of the Indo–European languages, and the solution to it which is offered here, offers so many analogies to one or perhaps two comparable problems which present themselves elsewhere on the globe, that a brief discussion may be worthwhile. In the Polynesian case the outline solution generally accepted seems so well grounded that the comparison is likely to be more useful to Indo-European than to Polynesian studies. In the Bantu case, however, the whole issue remains controversial, and the juxtaposition of the Indo-European and Bantu questions may be mutually informative.

Polynesian

The community among the Polynesian languages has been recognized since the time of Captain Cook. Indeed the similarity in relationships between even the least similar of them may be compared with those operating within one of the Indo-European subgroups (such as the Romance languages): they are all much closer to each other than is, for instance, Hindi in relation to Greek. The Polynesian languages indeed form part of a much larger classificatory grouping, that of the Austronesian languages, of which there are about eight hundred, spoken in Indonesia, the Philippines, Micronesia, Polynesia and beyond.[15] On the other hand the languages of Australia, of much of New Guinea and of much of the Solomon Islands are unrelated to the Austronesian languages. These relationships are summarized in the family tree, Fig. 11.2.

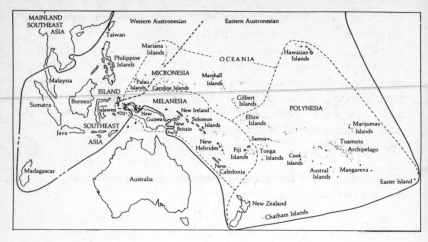

FIG. 11.1 Map of the Pacific showing the major Austronesian linguistic divisions (*after Jennings*).

Although the languages of Polynesia form a rather minor branch of the larger Austronesian family, their island distribution in the central and eastern Pacific makes study particularly informative. In particular, the progress of Pacific archaeology has now managed to establish the initial date of colonization of most of these islands.[16] The material culture and the economy of these initial settlers can be investigated. In most cases it is clear that the initial population of the island in question formed the ancestors of the modern inhabitants, and the historical reconstruction now looks increasingly uncontroversial – which is not to say that it has been without controversy in the past.

It is now clear that the first settlers in western Polynesia arrived in Tonga about 1300 BC. The associated material assemblage is known as the Lapita culture, which is seen further west earlier, for instance in Fiji. The whole of western Polynesia was colonized by the beginning of the modern era (i.e. before AD 1), and the island economy was that of horticulturalists, who used some at least of the crops already available in the islands of south-east Asia by 3000 BC (including cultivated taro, yams, breadfruit and coconut), as well as pigs and dogs. The material culture included pottery and stone tools

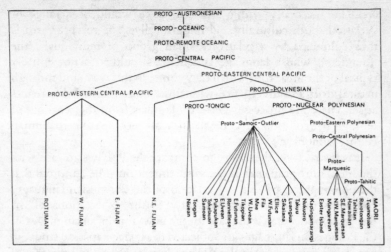

FIG. 11.2 Family tree diagram for the Fijian and Polynesian languages (*after Bellwood*).

and (of crucial importance for the dispersal itself) outrigger canoes with sails.

The early settlement of eastern Polynesia was initiated between AD 300 and 700 in the Marquesas Islands, Tahiti, Hawaii and Easter Island. New Zealand was reached by AD 1100.

This was a process of initial colonization, in areas previously without human population. In this respect it certainly differed markedly from the demographic processes at work in Europe at the time of the development there of early farming. But at the same time we should recognize that this process was indeed also one where the rapid diffusion of language, and the differentiation into a number of local languages, was associated with the spread of a farming (or horticultural) economy, and thus of specific plant and animal domesticates.

In particular it is informative to compare the process of linguistic differentiation with that which may have operated in Europe. In Polynesia, as in all such dispersals, the 'founder effect' is in evidence.[17] There the offshoot from a donor area (if we imagine the process operating in a chain-like sequence with each link in the chain acting as a 'donor' for the next) is not entirely typical of that area. For naturally within any area there would be a range of variation, both culturally and linguistically. The receptor area is thus colonized by a relatively small group of individuals (the 'founders') whose language and material culture is not entirely typical of the area from which they come. In this way, and through natural drift and divergence with time, quite marked differences arise. These are processes perfectly familiar from the working of biological evolution in general: they are not specific to human culture alone.

It is instructive, therefore, to compare the Polynesian case with the Indo-European, but at the same time it must be admitted that the geographical pattern of variation of the Polynesian languages conforms much more conveniently to the expectations of the dispersal model than is the case for the Indo-European languages. If the Polynesian languages are subjected to a lexicostatistical study, in general the pattern of similarities between languages follows that of

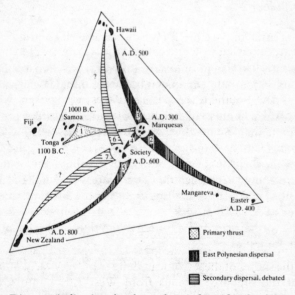

FIG. 11.3 Diagram indicating the chronology of Pacific island discovery by founding populations, based on archaeological interpretations and radiocarbon dates. Tonga is believed to have been colonized from Fiji around 1200 BC (*after Jennings*).

the dispersal path, so that the languages which are the most similar are those which diverged most recently from a common ancestor, in a way predictable from the reconstructed path of dispersal. As we have seen, for the Indo-European languages no such absolutely clear-cut pattern emerges, whereby the assumed path and the historical sequence of dispersal might allow the prediction of lexicostatistical similarity.

On the other hand, if one looks at the picture *within* a particular sub-group of the Indo-European languages, such as the Germanic languages, a more intelligible pattern of relationships of similarity does sometimes emerge. It is when the languages are much less similar to each other, no doubt because they are further removed historically, that difficulties arise, and this is to some extent true in the Austronesian case also. But the comparison is certainly informative, precisely because in Polynesia the archaeological and the linguistic evidence agree so very well.

Bantu

The case of the Bantu languages of Africa is a very different one, for neither the linguistic nor the archaeological picture is very clear-cut as yet. What is abundantly clear, however, is that, over a vast area of central and southern Africa, languages are spoken which are classified by linguists as belonging to a single language family.[18] Just as in the case of the Indo-European languages, it is widely assumed that the modern distribution is the result of a dispersal process, for which a primary area of origin should be sought, but it should be noted that, as in the Indo-European case, this assumption need not go unquestioned. Instead, Lwanga-Lunyiigo has suggested:[19]

> The Bantu-speaking Negroes occupied a broad swathe of territory running from the great-lakes region of Eastern Africa to the shores of the Atlantic in Zaire from very early times and that the supposed exodus from West Africa into Central, Eastern and Southern Africa did not take place.

To the extent that he is arguing against a homeland/dispersion model, and in favour of a very much larger initial area in which a

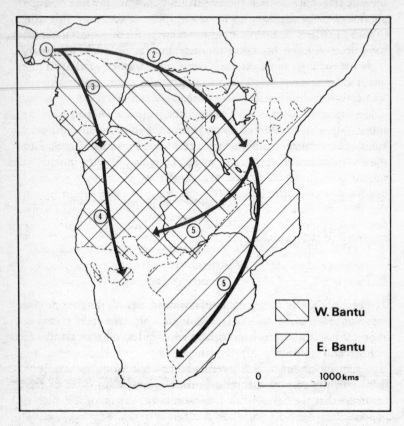

FIG. 11.4 The dispersal of the Bantu languages of Africa (*prepared and drawn by C. Scarre*).

1 Home area of the early Bantoid languages: the locus of early iron-working in Africa.

2 The spread of iron-working to the inter-lacustrine area: the early formation of the East Bantu languages.

3 The spread of early farming and iron-working to the Congo and beyond: the West Bantu languages.

4 and 5 The further spread of iron-working and of cattle pastoralism and of the East Bantu languages.

degree of linguistic unity emerged, his position may be compared with that of Trubetskoy for Indo-European studies.

Once again, linguists disagree about the interpretation of the linguistic evidence pointing towards a supposed homeland, with Greenberg[20] seeing the original focal area as lying close to the region with the greatest modern linguistic diversity, while Guthrie[21] seeks the *Urheimat* in the area where the modern languages show a high proportion of words with common Bantu roots. Once again it is possible to suggest that many arguments develop in a circular path, with the archaeologists quoting the authority of the linguists for some of their assumptions, and vice versa. In the words of Vansina:[22]

> La prépondérance de la linguistique a conduit à des situations surprenantes: les archéologues utilisent les conclusions des linguistes pour asseoir leurs inférences sur la culture materielle, et les linguistes partent des conclusions des archéologues pour attester l'existence de locuteurs d'une quelconque sous-famille ou rameau bantu dans un secteur géographique.

Here too there has been a tendency to equate languages with specific aspects of material culture, in this case iron working. Sometimes the alleged warlike propensities of the Bantu are adduced in support.

Recently however, as Oliver and then Phillipson[23] have pointed out, there have been efforts to link the initial expansion of early Bantu languages from the north-western part of their present distribution with the inception there of agriculture and of the early use of domestic goats. In a subsequent phase during the early first millennium BC new cereal crops (including sorghum) came to be cultivated in the eastern part of the zone now occupied by Bantu-speaking groups, and the herding of domesticated sheep (and cattle in some cases) was developed, along with iron metallurgy.

These arguments have not yet been fully elaborated in demographic terms, but they do have the merit (advocated in Chapter 6), that a coherent processual reason should be given for the social or demographic forces postulated as underlying language change. Here, as in the Indo-European case, the expansion of a language group is linked to the expansion of a farming economy at the expense of a hunter-gatherer population. Before the development of these more recent theories it was certainly possible to object that no coherent reason was given for the supposed migrations of these various Bantu-speaking tribes, other than a supposed warlike character and the possession of iron tools and weapons. Now that the underlying dynamic of the supposed expansion is considered, the case becomes very much more plausible.

Of course I am not in a position to assess the merits of the archaeological evidence offered in favour of these various hypotheses, and still less the linguistic arguments, but I do feel that the discussion here of our Indo-European problems does have a certain general relevance for Bantu studies. It sets a high priority on the investigation of the demographic processes at work, and therefore on the reconstruction of the subsistence economies of the different areas under consideration. It is clear that the élite dominance model is as inappropriate to the early Bantu groups as it is to the early Indo-Europeans of the fourth millennium BC. In the Polynesian case one was faced with an instance of initial colonization, but here, when dealing with language replacement, some version of the subsistence/demography approach should be sought. It is clear, then, that there may be some real similarities between the two problems and in particular between the approaches of linguists and archaeologists towards their solution. Scholars in each geographical area may perhaps have something to learn from the mistakes and the advances made by workers in the other.

The Relationship between Archaeology and Linguistic Studies

The study of linguistics has undergone a revolution over the past generation, and we are all learning to think much more deeply about the extraordinary and unique linguistic facility which increasingly seems inseparable from the human ability to use symbols and concepts, and is thus in a sense the prime distinguishing mark of humankind.

Archaeology too has had its significant advances, and the great project of prehistoric archaeology of enabling us to understand more effectively the emergence and subsequent paths of development of the human species is so well advanced that some at least of the landmarks along those paths are becoming reasonably clear.

The underlying lesson of this book, as I have increasingly come to grasp in writing it, is that these two disciplines have not yet interacted very significantly one with another. Although my prime concern has been with a single language group, albeit a major one, the issues confronted in discussing it have been very much the same as those which have to be addressed in discussing any other language group. The Indo-European languages have an outstanding advantage, which they share with the Semitic languages, with Chinese and with perhaps one or two other groups, that through the early evolution of writing among some of their speakers, we have a considerable time depth to work with. But despite this advantage, it is difficult to avoid the conclusion that there is something profoundly unsatisfactory about most, perhaps all, prevailing views of their early development.

I have tried to show, in this specific Indo-European case, that there has hitherto been no valid methodology for matching the evidence obtained from the study of the languages themselves, that is to say from historical linguistics, with the material evidence of archaeology. This has meant that the accounts seeking to use both classes of evidence have had little or no concrete reality. In making that assertion I am certainly not claiming some primacy in this field of archaeological evidence and reasoning over linguistic inferences. On the contrary, the primary difficulty in the entire enterprise is that the archaeological evidence from an early (and non-literate) period can tell us nothing directly about the languages which were spoken. At least the archaeological remains, the material culture, can be set firmly within a chronological framework. We can tell *when* these things were made and buried. The discipline of historical linguistics suffers from the disadvantage that, even when it is possible with reasonable plausibility to construct an early language form from more recent evidence, there is no way of setting that firmly within a chronological framework. The claims for glotto-chronology as offering a firm absolute chronology can be roundly dismissed (which is not, however, to deny that lexicostatistics, and other quantitative approaches, do shed light upon linguistic relationships; but they cannot *date* them).

The temptation is there, in consequence, for the historical linguist to work in some notional world following a linguistically
determined time scale, and not to ask with any great force or clarity
precisely what the arguments about movements, influences and
environmental changes would mean in real terms, out there in the
physical world of material objects, where a firm time scale in
calendar years operates. It is this willingness to operate in a closed
and rather cosy mythological world which I have criticized in the
work of Dumézil and his followers. They operate in a golden land
of proto-Indo-European society and belief which is rooted neither
in time nor in space. It is rather like the Dream Time of the
Australian aborigines or the Camelot of Arthurian fable: so much
so, indeed, that it seems almost churlish to ask such prosaic
questions as 'when?' or 'where?'.

But 'when?' and 'where?' are precisely the questions which
archaeologists in their prosaic way like to ask, and are equipped to
answer. The real problem is to bring these two worlds of argument,
these two fields of discourse, into some sort of constructive relationship. I have tried to indicate that a methodology for doing so
can be developed. The task is to be undertaken by understanding
better the relationships between the *processes* of *change*: on the one
hand the linguistic process, on the other hand those which leave
material traces in the archaeological record. The mediating phenomena appear to be largely social and demographic. Linguistic
change does not take place in a vacuum, irrespective of other
features of society: that is one of the emerging lessons of sociolinguistics. And those factors in society which correlate with or
promote linguistic change are at the same time influential in the
material sphere and find traces in the archaeological record. This is
the nexus which requires further investigation, and where I feel
optimistic that progress can be made.

The sceptic, of course, may be cautious about the feasibility of
such a project. I myself am optimistic that our two disciplines are on
the threshold of a significant advance. It is likely that over the next
decade or two we shall come to understand very much better the
details of the when and the where of the emergence of our own
species, *Homo sapiens sapiens*. It is also likely, I think, that further
research in developing fields such as semiotics will lead us to

understand rather more adequately the relationships between linguistic (and conceptual) ability and other aspects of human behaviour. If this advance comes about, it may well be possible, through the analysis of human actions, as reflected in the material and artefactual remains of the palaeolithic period, to be more precise about the time when the linguistic and conceptual abilities of fully modern man made their appearance.

When this day comes, we shall be in possession of a new time frame within which to set the whole story of the evolution and development of human linguistic diversity. At the moment it looks as if the relevant time, for most of the world at any rate, may be some 40,000 years ago. Within that time frame we would have to set not only the evolution of the Indo-European languages, but also all those relationships between that broad linguistic group and other major language groups (these are relationships which I have not discussed here, mainly because I am very unsure of the methodology which at present can serve to underlie such discussions.) It may then be possible to achieve a much more rewarding rapprochement between prehistoric archaeology and historical linguistics than has hitherto been feasible. Instead of such a rapprochement, based on a coherent methodology and open to sceptical assessment, we have hitherto been working rather naïvely, building on each other's myths. In the Indo-European field, linguists have been willing to follow the archaeological orthodoxy of nearly a century ago, while archaeologists have taken the conclusions of the historical linguists at their face value, failing to realize that they were themselves based upon archaeological assumptions which had not been questioned, yet which were not in some cases justifiable.

There will of course be those who question whether all of this matters in the least. Why should we care 'What song the sirens sang'? Or as Horace Walpole once succinctly said: 'I have no curiosity to know how awkward and clumsy men have been in the dawn of arts or in their decay.' But many of us today take a different view. We see in large measure that our identity, or at least our sense of it, lies with our own pasts. We are what we have become. To understand this, and these processes, we need also to know, or at any rate to begin to understand, what we *were* and where we have come from.

The habitual way of thinking about human groups, of assuming that it is automatically sound to distinguish them into separate 'peoples' is very much a legacy of the nineteenth century. In some measure it derives from the classical historians and geographers, who tended to assume that their own concepts of ethnicity or nationhood could readily be projected upon those other, sometimes remote, lands which they were describing. In the nineteenth century, and earlier, European travellers had in many ways much the same outlook about 'out there', the world beyond, as did the classical geographers. Beyond the civilized world were strange lands peopled by barbarian tribes, uncouth of speech, whom it was necessary to classify, to name, to divide into groups in order that they might in a certain sense be categorized and hence managed, or indeed governed.

Now, as I have tried to show, we can attempt to rethink these issues, with less emphasis on specific ethnic groups and their supposed migrations, and rather more upon the underlying economic and social processes at work. We can ask, as I have tried to do, precisely what are the mechanisms of language change: with what social realities do they correspond, and how do we expect to find these social realities reflected in the archaeological record? Applied to the Indo-European problem, these ideas have led me to suggest that the conventional view of Indo-European origins is not a sound one. Instead we can discern one crucially important episode in the prehistory of Europe and the Near East which transformed the way of life of the populations of the time: the inception of farming. The archaeological evidence for the development of farming is sufficient for a clear outline to be given, and the dispersal of the basic crop plants, wheat and barley, from Anatolia to Greece and so through Europe as far as Britain and Ireland can now be documented. Such profound economic and demographic changes must have had significant implications for the languages spoken within the areas in question. It seems likely then that the first Indo-European languages came to Europe from Anatolia around 6000 BC, together with the first domesticated plants and animals, and that they were in fact spoken by the first farmers of Europe. That, I suggest, is the key to the solution of the Indo-European problem.

Such a view has many consequences for the understanding of the history of the Indo-European languages: some of them have been indicated above. Others will need to be examined by historical linguists and by archaeologists, or indeed by both. For too long archaeologists and linguists have been content to take on trust each others' view of the past. The task now is to develop the methodologies necessary to reconcile those different views; to unearth, to re-examine and then to reformulate some of the preconceptions which have made them, in the last analysis, incompatible.

Notes

Preface: What Song the Sirens Sang

1 Browne 1658, Chapter 5.
2 Shakespeare, *Hamlet*, Act 2, Scene 2.
3 Myres 1930; Childe 1950.
4 Childe 1926.
5 Kossinna 1902.
6 Myres 1930, 538.

1. *The Indo-European Problem*

1 Jones, Sir W. 1786, reprinted in Jones 1807, and in Lehmann 1967, 7–20.
2 For a convenient text of the *Avesta* in English, see Darmesteter 1884 and 1887, and Mills 1887.
3 The verb 'to bear, to carry', see Childe 1926, 14; Bodmer and Hogben 1943, 189.
4 Young 1813.
5 For an English translation of the *Hymns of the Rigveda* see Müller 1891 and Oldenberg 1897, also Griffith 1973.
6 Schlegel 1849.
7 Bopp 1816.
8 Darwin 1859.
9 *The Book of Genesis* gives a clear account in Chapter 9:

> 9.18 And the sons of Noah, that went forth of the ark, were Shem, and Ham, and Japheth: and Ham is the father of Canaan.
> 9.19 These are the three sons of Noah: and of them was the whole earth overspread.

The account continues in Chapter 10, where the descendants of Japheth are first listed, with the conclusion:

> 10.5 By these were the isles of the Gentiles divided in their lands; every one after his tongue, after their families, in their nations.

The descendants of Ham and Shem are then similarly listed. It is interesting that the immediately succeeding chapter gives an entirely different account of Glottogenesis, which clearly belongs to a different mythological tradition, although the two could no doubt be reconciled:

> 11.1 And the whole earth was of one language, and of one speech . . .
> 11.6 And the Lord said, Behold, the people is one, and they have all one

> language; and this they begin to do: and now nothing will be restrained from them, which they have imagined to do.
>
> 11.7 Go to, let us go down, and there confound their language, that they may not understand one another's speech.
>
> 11.8 So the Lord scattered them abroad from thence upon the face of all the earth: and they left off to build the city.
>
> 11.9 Therefore is the name of it called Babel; because the Lord did there confound the language of all the earth: and from thence did the Lord scatter them abroad upon the face of all the earth.

10 See Pictet 1877.
11 Schrader 1890: for a good survey of the early development of Indo-European studies, see Mallory 1973.
12 Kossinna 1902.
13 Childe 1915.
14 Childe 1925.
15 Childe 1926.
16 'The influence of Indo-Europeans in prehistoric Greece', see Green 1981, 18.
17 Childe 1926, 212.
18 Childe 1950.
19 Bosch-Gimpera 1960, 1961; Devoto 1962; Hencken 1955.
20 Gimbutas 1968, 1970, 1973a, 1973b, 1977, 1979, 1980.
21 Gimbutas 1970, 156.
22 Friedrich 1970b, 1; see Friedrich 1970a.

2. *Archaeology and the Indo-Europeans*

1 Vansina 1965.
2 Daniel 1962, 30–9.
3 Renfrew 1974b, 12.
4 Childe 1929, v–vi.
5 Childe 1956, 111–31.
6 MacKendrick 1962, 162–5.
7 Coldstream 1977.
8 Bloch 1960.
9 Malone and Stoddart 1985.
10 The early history of Celtic archaeology is well surveyed by De Navarro 1936.
11 Collis 1984.
12 For an excellent review, see Champion *et al.*, 1984.
13 Gamkrelidze and Ivanov 1983a and 1983b; also 1984b.
14 Sayce 1927, quoted by Mallory 1973, 45.
15 Dhar 1930.
16 Koppers 1934.
17 W. Schmidt 1949.
18 Diakonov 1984.

19 Kühn 1934.
20 Schwantes 1958.
21 Kossinna 1902.
22 Schrader 1890.
23 Childe 1926, 183–4 and 188.
24 Childe 1926, 196–8.
25 Sulimirski 1933.
26 Childe 1950.
27 Gimbutas 1960; 1968; 1970; 1973a; 1973b; 1979; 1980.
28 Gimbutas 1970, 184.
29 Gimbutas 1973b, 166.
30 Piggott 1965; but not in Piggott 1983.
31 Bosch-Gimpera 1960.
32 Devoto 1962.
33 Hencken 1955.

3. *Lost Languages and Forgotten Scripts*

 1 Demoule 1980.
 2 Müller 1891; Oldenberg 1897; Darmsteter 1887; 1894; Mills 1887.
 3 Herodotus Book I (Godley 1920, 1–272).
 4 Garcia Silva Figueroa, 1620, *De Rerum Persicarum Epistola*, Antwerp, quoted by Pope 1975, 85.
 5 For a general review of writing and decipherment, see Gelb 1963; Pope 1975.
 6 Pope 1975, 112.
 7 Goyvaerts 1975, 224. Other recognized languages of the modern Indian branch of the group include (Lockwood 1972, 192–252): Sindhi, Lahnda, Panjabi, Gujurati, Matchi, Rajasthani, Bhili, Khandeshi, Bihari, Oriya, Western Pahari, Kuamoni, Garhwali, Nepali, Assamese, Sinhalese and Maldivian.

   Other New Persian languages include Balochi, Tati, Talishi, Gilani, Mazandarani, Gorani, Zaza, Pashto, Yaghnobi, Mamjani, Yidgha, Parachi, Ormuri and Pamir.
 8 The story of the discovery of the Hittite civilization and language is well told by Ceram 1956; for Hittite archaeology, see Gurney, 1962.
 9 Gurney 1962, 6; Pope 1975, 141.
10 Hrozný 1915.
11 Hrozný 1917, quoted by Ceram 1975, 82.
12 The eight languages which occur (in some cases briefly) in the Boghazköy tablets are:

    1 Akkadian (a Semitic language).
    2 Cuneiform Hittite, also called Hittite or Nesite.
    3 Sumerian (non-Indo-European).
    4 Hurrian (non-Indo-European).
    5 Luwian. Note that hieroglyphic Hittite, found on seals and inscriptions but not on the tablets, records a dialect of Luwian.

6 Palaic (which, like Luwian, is an Anatolian (i.e. Indo-European) language, related to Hittite).

7 Proto-Hittite, also called Hattic or Hattian (non-Indo-European).

8 Indo-European terms, in a different language from the preceding, occur in a treatise on horsemanship, written in Hittite by Kikkuli, a Hurrian from the Land of Mitanni.

13 Crossland 1967, 9–16 with references; Gurney 1962, Chapter 6; for an unreferenced overview, Lockwood 1972, 259–74.

14 Kossinna 1902.

15 Forrer 1922.

16 Goyvaerts 1975, 222. There are several other Anatolian languages, the so-called 'new Anatolian languages', which were spoken in classical times, and of which we have a little knowledge (Lockwood 1972, 266). Among them are Carian and Lydian as well as a whole series of other languages which ultimately gave way to Greek. These include Bithynian, Cappadocian, Cataonian, Cilician, Isaurian, Lyaconian, Mariandynian, Mysian, Pamphylian, Paphlagonian, Pisidian, Phrygian and Pontic. Not much is known of any of them, although Bithynian and Phrygian are generally classed with Thracian (and sometimes with Armenian) to form the Thraco-Phrygian family. This will be mentioned later: Armenian, of course, is a living language.

17 Myres 1930.

18 Evans 1895; 1909; 1952; Pope 1975, Chapters 8 and 9; Hooker 1980, 7–18.

19 Chadwick 1961; Ventris and Chadwick 1973.

20 Chadwick 1961, 71.

21 Chadwick 1961, 135 and 147.

22 The story is well told by Hopkirk 1984.

23 Stein 1912.

24 Strabo, *Geography* 11.8.2 (Jones 1928, 261).

25 von le Coq 1928; Hopkirk 1984, Chapter 10.

26 Hoernle 1911; 1916.

27 Sieg and Siegling 1921; Sieg, Siegling and Schulze 1931.

28 Keith 1938; Bosch-Gimpera 1960, 46–8; Lockwood 1972, 253–8; Lane 1970.

29 Sinov 1963, 221.

30 Goyvaerts 1975, 222.

31 Among the major treatments of the early Italic languages are Pulgram 1958, 1978; Conway, Whatmough and Johnson 1933; Devoto 1974; Lejeune 1971; 1974. The linguistic scene in Italy, before the complete domination by Latin, was one of great variety, and is of much interest to the central questions of this book. Of the extinct mainland Italian languages in addition to Etruscan and Umbrian, Pulgram (1978) distinguishes:

Ligurian: known from scanty indications including a handful of glosses and a few local names: 'What little one knows of this dialect does not exclude its being Indo-European' (Pulgram 1978, 35).

Lepontic: known from a few inscriptions and 'fitting in perhaps between Keltic (Gallic) and Italic', it is classed by Lejeune (1971) as a Celtic language.

Raetic: relating to a group of tribes known to the Romans as Raeti. Their language was probably an Indo-European one.

Venetic: Indo-European language with Italic features (Lejeune 1974).

East Italic: the language of Picenum. None of the texts has yielded a translation, and Pulgram is uncertain as to whether or not it should be regarded as Indo-European.

Messapic: the early language of Calabria. Some ancient authors suggest that its speakers came first to Calabria from Illyria, but direct evidence for the Illyrian language is itself very scanty. As Pulgram comments (1978, 63): 'To connect Messapic with an unknown "Illyrian" seems a senseless enterprise.'

In addition, there is at least one language in Sicily:

Sicel (or Sicilian): for which three inscriptions are known, and about which much has been written, mainly juggling with ethnic names. Its status as an Indo-European language appears to be uncertain.

32 Devoto 1974.

33 Pallottino 1975; Devoto 1943, 1944, 1963.

34 Goyvaerts 1975, 223.

35 Goyvaerts 1975, 224 with modifications (including the omission of Greek, which is curiously listed as a Slav language).

36 For an excellent introduction to the Etruscan language, see Pallottino 1955, Chapters 10 to 12; Pallottino 1975. It should be noted that some scholars, including Mr John Ray, consider Etruscan to be an Indo-European language, probably an Anatolian language. This would harmonize with the theory of a migration from Lydia in western Anatolia.

37 Tovar 1970; 1977b; Stevenson 1983, 30–3; Collins 1986.

38 Lockwood 1972, 175–182. For the archaeological background, see Burney and Lang 1971, Chapter V.

39 Lockwood 1972, 172–5; Hencken 1955, 38.

40 Stevenson 1983, 44.

41 Hrozný 1931; Conteneau 1948; Kammenhuber 1961.

42 Lesny 1932; Gelb 1944; O'Callaghan 1948.

43 Names of Indo-European divinities in a Hittite-Mitanni treaty of the fourteenth century BC should also be noted: see Thieme 1960.

44 The further question of deeper underlying relationships between Hittite and the early languages of India has also been discussed: Sturtevant 1947, 1962; Bonfante 1946; Pisani 1949; Adrados 1982.

45 The diagram is based on the preceding discussion, synthesizing various tree models, including those of Stevenson (1983) and Goyvaerts (1975). It should be considered a convenient listing or taxonomy of the languages, not as a model for their origins.

4. *Homelands in Question*

1 Müller 1888.

2 Montagu 1964.

3 Lehmann 1973, 232.
4 Lehmann 1973, 233.
5 Fraser 1926, 266–7.
6 Goody 1959.
7 Lehmann 1973, 232.
8 Piggott 1950, 246.
9 Friedrich 1970a; 1970b.
10 Fraser 1926, 266–7.
11 Friedrich 1970b.
12 Childe 1926, 91–3.
13 Barth 1961, 9–10.
14 Pulgram 1958, 146–7.
15 van Wijngaarden-Bakker 1974; Champion *et al.* 1984, 207; Bökönyi 1979.
16 Sangmeister 1963.
17 Clark 1966.
18 Shennan 1977.
19 Renfrew 1974, 74.
20 Shennan 1982, 159; Shennan 1986.
21 Burgess and Shennan 1976.
22 Whittle 1981, 335.
23 Gallay 1981.
24 Shennan 1986.
25 Neustupný 1969.
26 Haüsler 1981.
27 Tilley 1984, 121 and 142.
28 Menk 1980, 361.
29 Gimbutas 1970.
30 Sherratt 1981.
31 Goodenough 1970, 258 and 262; see also Anthony 1986. That there was some westward transmission of the Pontic form of Kurgan burial does seem documented by the Hungarian evidence (Ecsedy 1979).

5. *Language and Language Change*

1 Among useful introductory works on linguistics and historical linguistics, see Lehmann 1973; Bynon 1977; Stevenson 1983; Lyons 1981. Among earlier and still useful classic works: de Saussure 1959; Meillet 1934; Bloomfield 1935; Meillet 1970.
2 Lehmann 1973, 8.
3 Schleicher 1863.
4 Lehmann 1973, 7–8.
5 Bloomfield 1935, 310.
6 Bloomfield 1935, 311.
7 Bynon 1977, 218.
8 J. Schmidt 1872.

9 Bloomfield 1935, 316.

10 Lehmann 1973, 27.

11 Kilian 1983, 13.

12 Trubetskoy 1939 in Scherer 1968, 215.

13 Trubetskoy 1939 in Scherer 1968, 216.

14 For area linguistics, see Masica 1976; Emeneau 1980.

15 Bloomfield 1935, 317.

16 Lehmann 1973, 57.

17 K. H. Schmidt (1977, 5) in a discussion of linguistic comparison and typology, usefully quoted Roman Jakobson: 'on the "three" cardinal methods of language classification': 'The genetic method operates with kinship, the areal with affinity and the typological with isomorphism.' It should be remembered that classification is never a natural undertaking, but carries a range of assumptions with it which in each case have a major role in governing the outcome.

18 Bynon 1977, 198–215; Labov 1966; Goyvaerts 1975, 156–83.

19 Bloomfield 1935, 464 (Mr John Ray kindly points out that Egyptian demotic is an exception to this rule, having very few Greek loan-words.)

20 Narroll 1964; Barth 1969; Dragadze 1980.

21 Swadesh 1972; Lees 1953; Rea 1973; Swadesh 1960.

22 Quoted from Bynon 1977, 268.

23 Lees 1953.

24 The formula proposed is $t = \log c / 2 \log r$, where c is the percentage of cognates (in the list of 100 words) and r is the constant, the assumed percentage of cognates retained after a millennium of separation.

25 Rea 1973; Tischler 1973; Bird 1982; Robin 1973.

26 Kruskal, Dyen and Black 1971; Dobson 1981; Cavalli-Sforza and Feldman 1981, 27–9.

27 Sokal and Sneath 1973.

6. *Language, Population and Social Organization*

1 For a general discussion of the use of models in archaeology, see Clarke 1972.

2 Bynon 1977, 256–61; Hymes 1971; Taylor 1956; Hall 1958.

3 Clark 1966.

4 Shennan 1986; Burgess 1980.

5 Ammerman and Cavalli-Sforza 1984, 63; Hassan 1981.

6 Hassan 1981.

7 Phillipson 1977, Chapter VIII; Guthrie 1970; Mann 1970; Ehret and Posnansky 1982.

8 Ammerman and Cavalli-Sforza 1973; 1979; 1984.

9 Ammerman and Cavalli-Sforza 1973, 344.

10 Alexander 1977; 1978.

11 Fried 1967.

12 Service 1962.

13 Renfrew 1979.

14 Renfrew 1978, Fig. 4.
15 Krader 1955, 1959; Barth 1961; Khazanov 1984, 52, 57, 63 and 80.
16 Diakonov 1984, 62.
17 White 1980, 42; also Littauer 1981. For a recent model relating to horse riding see Anthony 1986.
18 Goody 1971, 46.
19 Champion 1980, 42.
20 Childe 1958, 70.
21 Childe 1936; 1942.
22 Lattimore 1937; 1940; Watson 1971.
23 Binford 1968.
24 Roux 1966, 135–48.

7. Early Language Dispersals in Europe

1 J. M. Renfrew 1973.
2 Hansen and Renfrew 1978.
3 Theochares 1973.
4 Ammerman and Cavalli-Sforza 1973, 350–1.
5 Barker 1985; Ammerman and Cavalli-Sforza 1984.
6 Ammerman and Cavalli-Sforza 1973; 1979; 1984.
7 Bodmer and Hogben 1943, 309–42.
8 Tringham 1971, 68.
9 Péquart et al., 1937; Péquart 1954; Roche 1965; see also for Ireland Burenhult 1980, 113 and Burenhult 1984, 138–9.
10 Srejović 1972.
11 Higgs and Jarman 1969.
12 Barker 1985, 252.
13 Rodden 1965.
14 Nandris 1970.
15 Sherratt 1982.
16 Piggott 1965, 59; see also Clark 1965.
17 Phillips 1975.
18 Higgs 1972; 1975; Dennell 1983; Barker 1985.
19 Geddes 1985, 28; also Geddes 1980. (I am indebted to Mr Sebastian Payne for these references.)
20 Barker 1985, 251.
21 Dennell 1983, 156–7.
22 Ammerman and Cavalli-Sforza 1984, 99–100.
23 For Ireland, see Woodman 1976, 303: 'In summary, the scant evidence available points to this change in the way of life being caused by the arrival of people rather than just ideas.'
24 See Jackson 1955.
25 For instance, among the early languages of Italy and Sicily, quite apart from Etruscan, it is far from certain that Ligurian, Sicel or East Italic (of Picenum) were Indo-European (Pulgram 1978).

26 Krahe 1954; 1957.

27 Krahe 1957, 454.

28 Georgiev 1961; 1973.

29 Bosch-Gimpera 1960; 1961., J. Neustupný (1976, 14) proposed a correlation between the spread of farming and the Indo-European languages of Europe.

30 Wertime 1964.

31 Swadesh 1960, 345.

32 Aspinall, Feather and Renfrew 1972.

33 Mellaart 1967.

34 Mellaart 1962; 1964; 1981.

35 Zohary 1969.

36 Mellaart 1975.

37 Masson and Sarianidi 1972.

38 The similarities between this view and those recently propounded by Gamkrelidze and Ivanov (1983a; 1983b; 1984) are further discussed in Chapter 11.

39 Childe 1915.

40 Chadwick 1973, 255.

41 Myres 1930, 538; for a recent contrary view see Sakellariou 1980.

8. *The Early Indo-Iranian Languages*

1 Emeneau 1966, 123 and 127.

2 Griffith 1973, 90–1.

3 In his chapter 'Dasa and Dasyu in the Rigveda-Samhita', Chattopadyaya (1976, 206–14) suggests that these terms refer to supernatural beings, specifically demons. This plausible reading underlines the weakness of the argument of those who would identify them as pre-Vedic inhabitants of the area, possibly speaking a Dravidian language. Whether human or demonic, they do not add to our understanding of the origin of the Aryas, whose supposedly immigrant status rests entirely upon a linguistic assumption.

4 Marshall 1924.

5 Parpola 1971; Koskenniemi *et al.*, 1973.

6 Alekseev *et al.*, 1969; Zide and Zvelebil 1976.

7 Rao 1973; 1982.

8 Wheeler 1947, 78–82.

9 Griffith 1973, 65.

10 Jarrige 1985.

11 Allchin 1982.

12 Allchin and Allchin 1982, 182, Fig. 7.11; Agrawal 1982, 165.

13 Allchin and Allchin 1982, 213, Fig. 8.18; Marshall 1931, 58.

14 Agrawal 1982, 154: Allchin and Allchin 1982, 211, Fig. 8.16.

15 Thapar 1973.

16 Allchin and Allchin 1982, 303.

17 Masson 1981.

18 Masson and Sarianidi 1972, 45.

19 Bird 1982.

20 Jarrige 1980.

21 For example Hymn CLXII, 17: 'If one, when seated, with excessive urging, hath with his heel or whip distressed thee . . .' (Griffith 1973, 108).

22 In the Homeric Hymns (Evelyn White 1914, 286–463) there are very few indications of urban life, although Athena (Hymns XI and XXVIII) bears the epithet 'guardian of the city' ('*erusíptolin*).

23 Sankalia 1973.

24 Khazanov 1984, 98; Briant 1982; also Anthony 1986.

25 Piggott 1983, 57, 63 and 103; Wiesner 1939.

26 Piggott 1983, 29.

27 Allchin and Allchin 1982, 190, Fig. 7.17.

28 Marinatos and Hirmer 1960, pl. 146 and 147; for Mesopotamia see Littauer and Crouwel 1979.

29 Hittite war chariots are shown on Egyptian reliefs: e.g. Akurgal 1962, pl. 3; Meyer 1914, 13, Fig. 4; and in Hittite reliefs of the late period: e.g. Akurgal 1962, pl. 105; Meyer 1914, pl. VI–VIII.

30 Childe 1958b, 727, Fig. 527; there are earlier chariot scenes from the reign of Amenophis IV, c. 1450 BC.

31 Potratz 1939; Briant 1982. The only representation of a horse-rider from Mycenaean Greece is a small terracotta figurine from the Late Helladic IIIB period (Hood 1953).

32 e.g. Meyer 1914, 60, Fig. 48. Textual evidence from Mesopotamia suggests that riding was known in the early second millennium BC (Littauer and Crouwel 1979, 67).

33 Wiesner 1939, pl. III.5. See also the wooden model, without good provenance, in the Metropolitan Museum, New York (Zeuner 1963, 320, Fig. 12.12) for which a date as early as c. 1580 BC has been suggested.

34 Potratz 1966; although Littauer and Crouwel (1979, 61) indicate the early occurrence of rigid cheekpieces with soft mouthpieces north of the Caucasus.

35 Piggott 1983, 87–90; Lichardus 1980. Even if these were indeed used as bits, they may have been used with chariots rather than for riding; see also Anthony 1986.

36 White 1962; Littauer 1981.

37 Bökönyi 1978.

38 Masson and Sarianidi 1972, 120; for the camel see Bulliet 1975.

39 Childe 1958b, 718, Fig. 517; Littauer and Crouwel 1979, 25.

40 Childe 1957, 149–58; Gimbutas 1970.

41 Hančar 1956; Bökönyi 1974, 238, where a context in the Tripolye B culture is proposed; also Bökönyi 1978. A site with notably early finds of domesticated horse bones is Dereivka, of the Srednij Stog culture (Telegin 1986). As Merpert (1977, 377) writes:

    'I never believed that it was a migration from the Volga that created the Srednij Stog culture, and I would regard such an assertion as wrong. The basic correlation of the Srednij Stog culture is with the Neolithic of the Dnieper . . .'

See also Anthony 1986.

42 Masson and Sarianidi 1972, 153.
43 Lockwood 1972, 233; Talbot Rice 1957, 39.
44 Sinov 1963.
45 Lockwood 1972, 246.
46 Jarrige 1980.
47 Henning 1978.
48 Henning 1978, 219.
49 Shaffer 1984.
50 Allchin and Allchin 1982; Agrawal 1982; Possehl 1982.

9. Who were the Celts?

1 Strabo IV. iv. 2, quoted from Tierney 1960, 267.
2 Diodorus Siculus V.31, quoted from Tierney 1960, 251.
3 Dragadze 1980; Bromley 1974; Gellner 1980, xi.
4 Hubert 1934a, frontispiece; Moreau 1958, pl. I.
5 Powell 1958, 13.
6 Childe 1929, v–vi.
7 Narroll 1964; Barth 1969.
8 By Bromley and Kozlov, quoted by Dragadze 1980, 162.
9 Goody 1967.
10 Tierney 1960.
11 Tierney 1960, 198–9.
12 Tierney 1960, 199–200.
13 See Tierney 1960, 190.
14 Powell 1958, 17.
15 Hubert 1934a, 24.
16 Caesar, De Bello Gallico I, 1 (quoted from Edwards 1963, 3). Hubert (1934a, 22) plays down the importance of the distinction between Celtae and Galli made by Caesar: 'At the very most the passage might mean that Caesar considered that there were two different pronunciations of the same word.'
17 Diodorus Siculus V.21 (quoted from Oldfather 1939, 155).
18 Diodorus Siculus V.24 (Oldfather 1939, 163).
19 Diodorus Siculus V.32 (Oldfather 1939, 181).
20 Diodorus Siculus V.33 (Oldfather 1939, 185).
21 Strabo 4.1.14 (quoted from Jones 1923, 211).
22 Strabo 4.5.2 (quoted from Jones 1923, 255).
23 Caesar, De Bello Gallico V.12 (quoted from Edwards 1963, 249).
24 Ross 1974, 33.
25 Greene 1964, 14.
26 Dillon, in a lecture 'The Coming of the Celts', quoted Evans 1977, 67.
27 For convenient short summaries of knowledge concerning the Celtic languages

see Greene 1964; Dillon and Chadwick 1972, Chapters 1 and 9; and Greene 1977; for Continental Celtic I have followed Evans 1979, Tovar 1977c, and Schmidt 1979.

28 Jackson 1955, 151 and 152.
29 Dillon and Chadwick 1972, 199.
30 Watkins 1963; 1970.
31 Quoted from Dillon and Chadwick 1972, 220.
32 Quoted from Dillon and Chadwick 1972, 208.
33 Quoted from Evans 1977, 66.
34 Whatmough 1970.
35 Lejeune 1971.
36 Tovar 1949; 1977b, 1977c.
37 Powell 1958, pl. 76.
38 Fleuriot 1975 and further references in de Hoz 1982.
39 Untermann 1963; de Hoz 1982.
40 Tovar 1970.
41 See Filip 1977.
42 Szabo 1971.
43 Stahelin 1907.
44 Greene 1964, 14.
45 Powell 1958; Filip 1977.
46 For recent discussions of early Celtic art, see Hawkes 1976; Frey 1976; Schwappach 1976. All make considerable use of Jacobsthal 1944.
47 Filip 1977, pl. 24 and 25; T. Taylor (pers. comm.).
48 Piggott 1968, 25.
49 Merriman (in press).
50 Wells 1980, *passim*.
51 Hawkes 1976; Champion and Champion, 1986.
52 Renfrew and Cherry 1986.
53 Hawkes 1973; 1976.
54 Bosch-Gimpera 1940.
55 Arribas 1964.
56 Schmidt 1979, 190–1 (omitting references).
57 Kimmig 1962.
58 Dillon and Chadwick 1972, 2–3.
59 Clark 1966.
60 Hodson 1964.
61 Hawkes 1973.
62 Livy, Book V. xxiii.
63 Dillon and Chadwick 1972, 205.
64 Tovar 1977a.
65 Krahe 1957.
66 Tovar 1977c, 49.
67 Tovar 1977a, 29.
68 Tovar 1975.

69 Hawkes 1973.
70 Meid 1975.
71 Meid 1975, 209.

10. *Indo-European Mythologies*

1 Vendryes 1918.
2 Dillon and Chadwick 1972, 11 and 88; Binchy 1943; Benveniste 1969a, Chapter 3 and 1969b, Chapter 3.
3 Dumézil 1935.
4 Dumézil 1958.
5 A convenient summary is found in Littleton 1973, on which this synopsis is based and also in Rivière 1973. See also Bonnet 1981 for discussions (entirely favourable) of the work of Dumézil.
6 Caesar, *De Bello Gallico* VI.13: *druides, equites* and *plebs*.
7 See for instance Service 1962; Fried 1967; Renfrew 1982.
8 Crumley 1974; Nash 1978; Frankenstein and Rowlands 1978.
9 Dumézil 1958, 18.
10 Dumézil 1968, 15.
11 Benveniste 1969a and b.
12 Sahlins 1958; Oliver 1974.
13 Renfrew 1984, Chapters 6 to 8; Bradley 1984.
14 Crumley 1974; Nash 1978.
15 Gellner 1982, 122.
16 Page 1979, 68.
17 Brough 1959.
18 Yoshida 1981, 321.
19 Barnes 1986.
20 Benveniste 1979a; Friedrich 1966.
21 Goody 1959.
22 Binchy 1943; Binchy 1970; Watkins 1970.
23 Benveniste 1979b, Chapter 1.
24 Dumézil 1968, 11.
25 Watkins 1963, 194; Kurlowicz 1970.

11. *Archaeology and Indo-European Origins*

1 Tringham 1971, 68–70; Champion *et al.*, 1984, 100 and 120; Whittle 1985, 65.
2 Dennell 1983, 63.
3 Barker 1985, 71 and 252–3; Mathers 1984.
4 Whittle 1985, 112.
5 Barker 1985; Lewthwaite 1981.
6 Gamkrelidze and Ivanov 1983b; see Diakonov 1984, 54.
7 Gamkrelidze and Ivanov 1983b, 75.
8 Review of Gamkrelidze and Ivanov 1984b by Greppin (1986).
9 Diakonov 1984, 53.

10 The differences between the positions of Gamkrelidze and Ivanov on the one hand and Diakonov on the other are well brought out by comparing the maps which they prepared to illustrate their historical interpretations. In their *magnum opus*, Gamkrelidze and Ivanov (1984b, 956) show the Hittite, Hattic, Palaic and Luwian languages as at home in Anatolia, locating the language of the Mitanni to the east, and with a proto- or pre-Greek language in western Anatolia. Further to the east are the Iranian languages. To bring these various languages to the areas where their modern successors are spoken requires only a series of small displacements. But the ancestors of the dialects of Ancient Europe are obliged to undertake a vast migration, indicated by a sweeping arrow, which takes them to the *east* of the Caspian Sea, past the Aral Sea and so west across the Volga to the Dnieper where they at last reach that 'secondary centre' from which they are considered to have later dispersed, very much in accordance with the traditional view criticized in this book.

Diakonov (1984, 76 and 77), in two maps of his own, offers his alternative hypothesis. He places in the Balkans, within a circle extending from the Aegean to the Carpathians (and thus including much of north Greece, Serbia, Bulgaria and Romania) what he terms the 'centre of the common-Indo-European area in the fifth millennium BCE and its expansion'. His second map shows 'the migration of the speakers of definite proto-languages since the third millennium BCE'. Here the European languages follow paths leading to their present locations, while the proto-Indo-Iranian language enters the Russian steppes *from west to east* across the River Dnieper. Despite his sound processual perspective, Diakonov does not, to my way of thinking, clarify why the Balkans should in this way be a centre for outward movements which include a displacement of population to the south (to Greece) and to the south-east (to Anatolia) for the Hitto-Luwian dialects. Where I am in wholehearted agreement with him is in his view of the colonization of the Russian steppes from the west, in a process involving the development of nomad pastoralism.

My own hypothesis, although formulated before the publication of the work of Gamkrelidze and Ivanov, and the comments of Diakonov upon it, does in fact show features of both models. It is in agreement with the early date and east Anatolian nuclear area of the former authors, and of their proposed population displacement to Greece. It postulates the further transmission of the early Indo-European dialects from Greece to south-eastern Europe along with the spread of farming, and from there it has much in common with the solution proposed by Diakonov. Of course the underlying socio-economic process is a different one and, I would argue, is more clear.

In making these comments, however, I am referring essentially to the archaeological evidence. These three Soviet authors deploy a series of linguistic arguments which I do not feel capable of assessing. What is at this point encouraging is the degree of convergence between the three positions.

11 Passingham 1981. The converse, however, is argued for Neanderthal man by Lubermann and Crelin 1971.

12 Parker and Gibson 1979; Brown 1981. For early brain size and form see Falk 1983; Holloway 1983; Isaac 1976; Tobias 1981.
13 Marshack 1976.
14 See Mallory 1976.
15 Blust 1976.
16 Bellwood 1978.
17 Clark and Terrell 1978.
18 Phillipson 1976; 1977; 1985; Ehret and Posnansky 1982.
19 Lwanga-Lunyiigo 1976, 282.
20 Greenberg 1972.
21 Guthrie 1962; 1970.
22 Vansina 1984, 131, quoted by Holl 1985, 146.
23 Oliver 1966; 1979; Phillipson 1976.

Bibliography

Adrados F. R., 1982, 'The archaic structure of Hittite: the crux of the problem', *Journal of Indo-European Studies* 10, 1–35.

Agrawal D. P., 1982, *The Archaeology of India*, London, Curzon.

Akurgal E., 1962, *The Art of the Hittites*, London, Thames & Hudson.

Alekseev G. V., Knorozov Y. V., Kondratov A. M. and Volchov B. Y., 1969, *Soviet Studies on Harappan Script*, Coconut Grove, Florida, Field Research Projects, Occasional Paper no. 6.

Alexander J. A., 1977, 'The frontier concept in prehistory: the end of the moving frontier', in J. V. Megaw (ed.), *Hunters, Gatherers and Farmers beyond Europe*, Leicester University Press, 25–40.

Alexander J. A., 1978, 'Frontier theory and the beginnings of farming in Europe', in D. Green, C. Haselgrove and M. Spriggs (eds), *Social Organisation and Settlement*, B.A.R. International Series 47 (i), Oxford, British Archaeological Reports, 13–30.

Allchin B. and Allchin R., 1982, *The Rise of Civilisation in India and Pakistan*, Cambridge, Cambridge University Press.

Allchin F. R., 1982, 'The legacy of the Indus civilisation', in G. L. Possehl (ed.), *Harappan Civilisation, a Contemporary Perspective*, Warminster, Aris & Phillips, 325–34.

Altmann G., 1973, *Allgemeine Sprachtypologie*, München, Uni-Taschenbücher.

Ammerman A. J. and Cavalli-Sforza L. L., 1973, 'A population model for the diffusion of early farming in Europe', in C. Renfrew (ed.), *The Explanation of Culture Change, Models in Prehistory*, London, Duckworth, 343–58.

Ammerman A. J. and Cavalli-Sforza L. L., 1979, 'The wave of advance model for the spread of agriculture in Europe', in C. Renfrew and K. L. Cooke (eds), *Transformations, Mathematical Approaches to Culture Change*, New York, Academic Press, 275–94.

Ammerman A. J. and Cavalli-Sforza L. L., 1984, *The Neolithic*

Transition and the Genetics of Populations in Europe, Princeton, Princeton University Press.

Anthony D. W., 1986, 'The "Kurgan culture", Indo-European origins and the domestication of the horse: a reconsideration', *Current Anthropology* 27, 291–314.

Ardener E., 1972, 'Language, ethnicity and population', *Journal of the Anthropological Society of Oxford* 3, 125–32.

Arribas A., 1964, *The Iberians*, London, Thames & Hudson.

Aspinall A., Feather S. W. and Renfrew C., 1972, 'Neutron activation analysis of Aegean obsidians', *Nature* 237, 333–4.

Barker G., 1985, *Prehistoric Farming in Europe*, Cambridge, Cambridge University Press.

Barnes G. L., 1986, '*Jiehao, Tonghao*: peer relations in East Asia', in C. Renfrew and J. F. Cherry (eds), *Peer-Polity Interaction and Sociopolitical Change*, Cambridge, Cambridge University Press.

Barth F., 1961, *Nomads of South Persia*, Oslo, Oslo University Press.

Barth F. (ed.), 1969, *Ethnic Groups and Boundaries*, Oslo, Oslo University Press.

Bellwood P., 1978, *The Polynesians*, London, Thames & Hudson.

Benveniste E., 1969a, *Le vocabulaire des institutions indo-européennes, I, économie, parenté, société*, Paris, Éditions de Minuit.

Benveniste E., 1969b, *Le vocabulaire des institutions indo-européennes, II, pouvoir, droit, religion*, Paris, Éditions de Minuit.

Binchy D. A., 1943, 'The linguistic and historical value of the Old Irish law tracts', *Proceedings of the British Academy* 29, 195–228.

Binchy D. A., 1970, 'Celtic suretyship, a fossilized Indo-European institution?', in G. Cardona, H. M. Hoenigswald and A. Senn (eds), *Indo-European and Indo-Europeans*, Philadelphia, University of Pennsylvania Press, 355–68.

Binford L. R., 1968, 'Post-Pleistocene adaptations', in L. R. and S. R. Binford (eds), *New Perspectives in Archaeology*, Chicago, Aldine, 313–41.

Bird N., 1982, *The Distribution of Indo-European Root Morphemes*, Wiesbaden, Ottoa Harrassowitz.

Bloch R., 1960, *The Origins of Rome*, London, Thames & Hudson.

Bloomfield L., 1935, *Language*, London, Allen & Unwin.

Blust R., 1976, 'Austronesian culture history: some linguistic inferences and their relations to the archaeological record', *World Archaeology* 8, 19–43.

Bodmer F. and Hogben L., 1943, *The Loom of Language, a Guide to Foreign Languages for the Home Student*, London, Allen & Unwin.

Bökönyi S., 1974, *History of Domestic Mammals in Central and Eastern Europe*, Budapest, Akademiai Kiado.

Bökönyi S., 1978, 'The earliest wave of domestic horses in East Europe', *Journal of Indo-European Studies* 6, 1–16.

Bökönyi S., 1979, 'Copper age vertebrate fauna from Ketegyhaza', in I. Ecsedy (ed.), *The People of the Pit-Grave Kurgans in Eastern Hungary*, Budapest, Akademiai Kiado, 101–18.

Bonfante G., 1946, 'Indo-Hittite and areal linguistics', *American Journal of Philology* 67, 289–310.

Bonnet J., et al., 1981, *Pour un Temps: Georges Dumézil*, Paris, Centre Pompidou.

Bopp F., 1816, *Über das Conjugationssystem der Sanskritsprache in Vergleichung mit jenem der griechischen, lateinischen, persischen und germanischen Sprache*, Frankfurt am Main, Andreä.

Bopp F., 1839, *Die Celtischen Sprachen in ihrem Verhältnisse zum Sanskrit, Zend, Griechischen, Lateinischen, Germanischen, Litauischen und Slawischen*, Berlin.

Bosch-Gimpera P., 1940, 'Two Celtic waves in Spain', *Proceedings of the British Academy* 26, 29–148.

Bosch-Gimpera P., 1960, *El Problema Indoeuropeo*, Mexico, Direccion General de Publicaciones.

Bosch-Gimpera P., 1961, *Les Indo-Européens*, Paris, Payot.

Bradley R., 1984, *The Social Foundations of Prehistoric Britain*, Harlow, Longman.

Briant P., 1982, *État et pasteurs au Moyen-Orient ancient*, Cambridge, Cambridge University Press.

Bromley Y. (ed.), 1974, *Soviet Ethnology and Anthropology Today*, The Hague, Mouton.

Brough J., 1959, 'The tripartite ideology of the Indo-Europeans, an experiment in method', *Bulletin of the School of Oriental and African Research* 22, 69–85.

Brown R. W., 1981, 'Symbolic and syntactic capacities', *Philo-*

sophical Transactions of the Royal Society of London, Series B 292,
197–204.

Browne T., 1658, *Hydriotaphia, Urne Buriall*, London.

Buchvaldek M., 1980, 'Corded ware pottery complex in Central
Europe', *Journal of Indo-European Studies* 8, 361–92.

Bulliet R. W., 1975, *The Camel and the Wheel*, Cambridge, Mass.,
Harvard University Press.

Burenhult G., 1980, *The Archaeological Excavations at Carrowmore,
Co. Sligo, Ireland, Excavations Seasons 1977–9*, Stockholm, Verlag
G. Burenhult.

Burenhult G., 1984, *The Archaeology of Carrowmore*, Stockholm,
Verlag G. Burenhult.

Burgess C. B., 1980, *The Age of Stonehenge*, London, Dent.

Burgess C. and Shennan S., 1976, 'The beaker phenomenon, some
suggestions', in C. Burgess and R. Miket (eds.), *Settlement and
Economy in the Third and Second Millennia B.C.* (B.A.R. 33),
Oxford, British Archaeological Reports, 309–26.

Burney C. and Lang D. M., 1971, *The Peoples of the Hills, Ancient
Ararat and the Caucasus*, London, Weidenfeld & Nicolson.

Bynon T., 1977, *Historical Linguistics*, Cambridge University Press.

Caskey J. L., 1960, 'The Early Helladic period in the Argolid',
Hesperia 29, 285–303.

Cavalli-Sforza L. L. and Feldman M. W., 1981, *Cultural Transmission and Evolution: a Quantitative Approach*, Princeton, Princeton
University Press.

Ceram C. W., 1956, *Narrow Pass, Black Mountain*, London, Gol-
lancz.

Chadwick J., 1961, *The Decipherment of Linear B*, Harmondsworth,
Penguin.

Chadwick J., 1963, 'The prehistory of the Greek language', *Cambridge Ancient History* II, Ch. XXXIX, Cambridge, Cambridge
University Press.

Chadwick J., 1973, Discussion of V. I. Georgiev, 'The arrival of the
Greeks, linguistic evidence', in R. A. Crossland and A. Birchall
(eds), *Bronze Age Migrations in the Aegean*, London, Duckworth,
254–5.

Champion T. C., 1980, 'Mass migration in later prehistoric Europe', in P. Sörbom (ed.), *Transport Technology and Social Change*, Stockholm, 33–42.

Champion T. and Champion S., 1986, 'Peer-polity interaction in the European iron age', in C. Renfrew and J. F. Cherry (eds), *Peer-Polity Interaction and Sociopolitical Change*, Cambridge, Cambridge University Press 59–68.

Champion T., Gamble C., Shennan S., and Whittle A., 1984, *Prehistoric Europe*, London, Academic Press.

Chattopadhyaya K., 1976, *Studies in Vedic and Indo-Iranian Religion and Culture* I, Varanasi, Varanasi Mudran Sansthan.

Childe V. G., 1915, 'On the date and origin of Minyan ware', *Journal of Hellenic Studies* 35, 196–207.

Childe V. G., 1926, *The Aryans, a Study of Indo-European Origins*, London, Kegan Paul, Trench & Trubner.

Childe V. G., 1929, *The Danube in Prehistory*, Oxford, Clarendon.

Childe V. G., 1936, *Man Makes Himself*, London, Watts.

Childe V. G., 1942, *What Happened in History*, Harmondsworth, Penguin.

Childe V. G., 1950, *Prehistoric Migrations in Europe*, Oslo, Aschehoug.

Childe V. G., 1956, *Piecing Together the Past*, London, Routledge & Kegan Paul.

Childe V. G., 1957, *The Dawn of European Civilization* (6th edition), London, Routledge & Kegan Paul.

Childe V. G., 1958a, 'Retrospect', *Antiquity* 32, 69–74.

Childe V. G., 1958b, 'Wheeled Vehicles', Ch. 27 in C. Singer, E. J. Holmyard and A. R. Hall (eds), *A History of Technology* I, Oxford, Clarendon, 716–29.

Clark J. G. D., 1966, 'The invasion hypothesis in British Prehistory', *Antiquity* 40, 172–89.

Clark J. G. D., 1965, 'Radiocarbon dating and the expansion of farming from the Near East over Europe', *Proceedings of the Prehistoric Society* 21, 58–73.

Clark J. T. and Terrell J., 1978, 'Archaeology in Oceania', *Annual Review of Anthropology* 7, 293–319.

Clark R., 1979, 'Language', in J. D. Jennings (ed.), *The Prehistory of*

Polynesia, Cambridge, Mass., Harvard University Press, 249–70.

Clarke D. L. (ed.), 1972, *Models in Archaeology*, London, Methuen.

Coldstream J. N., 1977, *Geometric Greece*, London, Methuen.

Collins R., 1986, *The Basques*, Oxford, Blackwell.

Collis J., 1984, *The European Iron Age*, London, Batsford.

Conteneau G., 1948, *La Civilisation des Hittites et des Hurrites du Mitanni*, Paris, Payot.

Conway R. S., Whatmough J., and Johnson S. E., 1933, *The Prae-Italic Dialects of Italy*, published for the British Academy by Oxford University Press.

Crossland R. A., 1967, 'Immigrants from the north', *Cambridge Ancient History* I, Ch. XXVII, Cambridge, Cambridge University Press.

Crumley C. L., 1974, *Celtic Social Structure: the Generation of Archaeologically Testable Hypotheses from Literary Evidence* (Anthropological Papers, Museum of Anthropology, University of Michigan 54), Ann Arbor, University of Michigan.

Daniel G. E., 1954, 'Who are the Welsh?' (Sir John Rhŷs Memorial Lecture), *Proceedings of the British Academy* 40, 145–67.

Daniel G. E., 1962, *The Idea of Prehistory*, London, Watts.

Darmesteter J., 1884, *The Zend-Avesta Part II, The Sirozahs, Yasts and Nyayis*, Oxford, Oxford University Press.

Darmesteter J., 1887, *The Zend-Avesta Part I, The Vendidad*, Oxford, Oxford University Press.

Darwin C., 1859, *The Origin of Species by Means of Natural Selection*, London, Murray.

De Navarro J. M., 1936, 'A survey of research on an early phase of Celtic culture', *Proceedings of the British Academy* 22, 3–47.

Demoule J.-P., 1980, 'Les Indo-européens ont-ils existé?' *L'histoire* 28, 109–120.

Dennell R., 1983, *European Economic Prehistory, a New Approach*, London, Academic Press.

Devoto G., 1943, 'Pelasgo e peri-indeuropeo', *Studi Etruschi* 17, 359–67.

Devoto G., 1944, 'Etrusco e peri-indeuropeo', *Studi Etruschi* 18, 184–97.

Devoto G., 1962, *Origini indeuropeo*, Florence, Instituto Italiano di Preistoria e Protoistoria Italiana.

Devoto G., 1963, 'Etrusco e peri-indeuropeo II', *Studi Etruschi* 31, 93–8.

Devoto G., 1974, *Le Tavole di Gubbio*, Florence, Sansoni.

Dhar L., 1930, *The Home of the Aryas*, Delhi, Imperial Book Depot Press.

Diakonov I. M., 1984, 'On the original home of the speakers of Indo-European', *Soviet Anthropology and Archaeology* 23, 2, 5–87. (Translated from *Vestnik drevnei istorii* 1982,3, 3–30 and 1982, 4, 11–25).

Dillon M. and Chadwick N., 1972, *The Celtic Realms* (2nd edn), London, Weidenfeld & Nicolson.

Dobson A. J., 1978, 'Evolution times of languages', *Journal of the American Statistical Association* 73, 58–64.

Dolukhanov P., 1979, *Ecology and Economy in Neolithic Eastern Europe*, London, Duckworth.

Dragadze T., 1980, 'The place of "ethnos" theory in Soviet anthropology', in E. Gellner (ed.), *Soviet and Western Anthropology*, London, Duckworth, 161–70.

Dumézil G., 1935, *Flamen-Brahman* (Annales du Musée Guimet, Bibliothèque de Vulgarisation 51), Paris.

Dumézil G., 1958, *L'idéologie tripartie des Indo-Européens*, Bruxelles, Berchem Latomus.

Dumézil G., 1968, *Mythe et Épopée I, L'idéologie des trois fonctions dans les épopées des peuples indo-européens*, (4th edn), Gallimard.

Dyen I., 1970, 'Background "noise" or "evidence" in comparative linguistics: the case of the Austronesian-Indo-European hypothesis', in G. Cardona, H. M. Hoenigswald and A. Senn (eds), *Indo-European and Indo-Europeans*, Philadelphia, University of Pennsylvania Press, 431–40.

Ecsedy I., 1979, *The People of the Pit-Grave Kurgans in Eastern Hungary* (Fontes Archaeologici Hungariae), Budapest, Akademiai Kiado.

Edwards H. J., 1963, *Caesar, the Gallic War*, (Loeb Classical Library), London, Heinemann.

Ehret C., 1976, 'Linguistic evidence and its correlation with archaeology', *World Archaeology* 8, 5–19.

Ehret C. and Posnansky M. (eds), 1982, *The Archaeological and Linguistic Reconstruction of African History*, Berkeley, University of California Press.

Emmeneau M. B., 1966, 'The dialects of old Indo-Aryan', in H. Birnbaum and J. Puhvel (eds), *Ancient Indo-European Dialects*, Berkeley, University of California Press, 123–38.

Emmeneau M. B., 1980, *Language and Linguistic Area*, Stanford, Stanford University Press.

Evans A. J., 1895, 'Primitive pictographs and a prae-Phoenician script from Crete and the Peloponnese', *Journal of Hellenic Studies* 14, 270–372.

Evans A. J., 1909, *Scripta Minoa* I, Oxford, Clarendon Press.

Evans A. J., 1952, *Scripta Minoa* II (edited by J. L. Myres), Oxford, Oxford University Press.

Evans D. E., 1977, 'The contribution of (non-Celtiberian) Continental Celtic to the reconstruction of the Celtic "Grundsprache"', in K. H. Schmidt (ed.), *Indogermanisch und Keltisch*, Wiesbaden, Ludwig Reichert, 66–88.

Evans D. E., 1979, 'The labyrinth of Continental Celtic', *Proceedings of the British Academy* 65, 497–538.

Evelyn-White H. G., 1914, *Hesiod, the Homeric Hymns and Homerica* (Loeb Classical Library), London, Heinemann.

Falk D., 1983, 'Cerebral cortices of East African early hominids', *Science* 221, 1072–74.

Filip J., 1977, *Celtic Civilisation and its Heritage*, Wellingborough, Collett's.

Fleuriot L., 1975, 'L'inscription celtibère de Botorrita', *Études Celtiques* 14, 405–42.

Forrer E., 1922, 'Die Inschriften und Sprachen des Hatti Reiches', *Zeitschrift der deutschen morgenlandischen Gesellschaft* 76, 174–269.

Frankenstein S. and Rowlands M. J., 1978, 'The internal structure and regional context of Early Iron Age society in south-western German', *Bulletin of the Institute of Archaeology* 15, 73–112.

Fraser J., 1926, 'Linguistic evidence and archaeological and ethnological facts', *Proceedings of the British Academy* 12, 257–72.

Frey O.-H., 1976, 'Du premier style du Style de Waldalgesheim', in P.-M. Duval and C. Hawkes (eds), *Celtic Art in Ancient Europe*, London, Seminar Press, 141–56.

Fried M. H., 1967, *The Evolution of Political Society*, New York, Random House.

Friedrich P., 1966, 'Proto-Indo-European kinship', *Ethnology* 5, 1–36.

Friedrich P., 1970a, 'Proto-Indo-European trees', in G. Cardona, H. M. Hoenigswald and A. Senn (eds), *Indo-European and Indo-Europeans*, Philadelphia, University of Pennsylvania Press, 11–34.

Friedrich P., 1970b, *Proto-Indo-European Trees*, Chicago, Chicago University Press.

Gallay A., 1981, 'The western Alps from 2500 to 1500 bc (3400 to 2500 BC), traditions and cultural changes', *Journal of Indo-European Studies* 9, 33–55.

Gamkrelidze T. V. and Ivanov V. V., 1983a, 'The ancient Near East and the Indo-European problem', *Soviet Studies in History* 22, 1–2; 3–52 (translated from *Vestnik drevnei istorii* 1980,3, 3–27).

Gamkrelidze T. V. and Ivanov V. V., 1983b, 'The migration of tribes speaking the Indo-European dialects from their original homeland in the Near East to their historical habitations in Eurasia', *Soviet Studies in History* 22, 1–2; 53–95 (translated from *Vestnik drevnei istorii* 1981, 2, 11–33).

Gamkrelidze T. V. and Ivanov V. V., 1984a, 'The problem of the original homeland of the speakers of related dialects and on the methods of its determination', *Vestnik drevnei istorii* 1984,2, 107–22.

Gamkrelidze T. V. and Ivanov V. V., 1984b, *Indoevropeiskii Yazik i Indoevropeitsyi*, Tbilisi, Publishing House of the Tbilisi State University.

Geddes D., 1980, 'De la chasse au troupeau en Mediterranée occidentale: les débuts de l'élevage dans le bassin de l'Aude', *Archives d'Écologie Préhistorique* (Toulouse) 5.

Geddes D., 1985, 'Mesolithic domestic sheep in west Mediterranean Europe', *Journal of Archaeological Science* 12, 25–48.

Gelb I. J., 1944, *Hurrians and Subarians* (Studies in Ancient Oriental Civilisation 22), Chicago, Oriental Institute.

Gelb I. J., 1963, *A Study of Writing*, Chicago, University of Chicago Press, 2nd edition.

Gellner E., 1980, Preface, in E. Gellner (ed.), *Soviet and Western Anthropology*, London, Duckworth, ix–xvii.

Gellner E., 1982, 'What is structuralisme?', in C. Renfrew, M. Rowlands and B. A. Segraves (eds), *Theory and Explanation in Archaeology*, New York, Academic Press, 97–124.

Georgiev V. I., 1961, *La Toponymie Ancienne de la Péninsule Balkanique et la Thèse Mediterranéenne*, Académie bulgare des sciences, Sofia.

Georgiev V. I., 1973, 'The arrival of the Greeks in Greece: the linguistic evidence', in R. A. Crossland and A. Birchall (eds), *Bronze Age Migrations in the Aegean*, London, Duckworth, 243–54.

Gimbutas M., 1960, 'Culture change in Europe at the start of the second millennium B.C.', in A.F.C. Wallace (ed.), *Men and Cultures: Selected Papers of the Fifth International Congress of Anthropological and Ethnological Sciences, Philadelphia, 1956*, Philadelphia, University of Pennsylvania Press, 540–52.

Gimbutas M., 1963, 'The Indo-Europeans, archaeological problems', *American Anthropologist* 65, 815–36.

Gimbutas M., 1968, 'Die Indoeuropäer: archäologische Probleme', in A. Scherer (ed.), *Die Urheimat der Indogermanen*, Darmstadt, Wissenschaftliche Buchgesellschaft, 538–71.

Gimbutas M., 1970, 'Proto-Indo-European culture: the Kurgan culture during the 5th to the 3rd millennia B.C.', in G. Cardona, H. M. Koenigswald and A. Senn (eds), *Indo-European and Indo-Europeans*, Philadelphia, University of Pennsylvania Press, 155–98.

Gimbutas M., 1973a, 'Old Europe c. 7000–3500 B.C., the earliest European cultures before the infiltration of the Indo-European peoples', *Journal of Indo-European Studies* 1, 1–20.

Gimbutas M., 1973b, 'The beginning of the bronze age in Europe and the Indo-Europeans 3500–2500 B.C.', *Journal of Indo-European Studies* 1, 163–214.

Gimbutas M., 1977, 'The first wave of Eurasian steppe pastoralists into Copper Age Europe', *Journal of Indo-European Studies* 5, 277–338.

Gimbutas M., 1979, 'The three waves of the Kurgan people into Old Europe', *Archives suisses d'anthropologie générale* 43, 113–17.

Gimbutas M., 1980, 'The Kurgan wave migration (c. 3400–3200 B.C.) into Europe and the following transformation of culture', *Journal of Near Eastern Studies* 8, 273–315.

Godley A. D., 1920, *Herodotus* I (Loeb Classical Library), London, Heinemann.

Goodenough W., 1970, 'The evolution of pastoralism and Indo-European origins', in G. Cardona, H. M. Hoenigswald and A. Senn (eds), *Indo-European and Indo-Europeans*, Philadelphia, University of Pennsylvania Press, 253–66.

Goody J., 1959, 'Indo-European Society', *Past and Present* 16, 88–92.

Goody J., 1967, *The Social Organisation of the LoWiili*, Oxford, Oxford University Press.

Goody J., 1971, *Technology, Tradition and the State in Africa*, Oxford, Oxford University Press.

Goyvaerts D. L., 1975, *Present-Day Historical and Comparative Linguistics*, Ghent, Story-Scientia.

Green S., 1981, *Prehistorian, a Biography of V. Gordon Childe*, Bradford-on-Avon, Moonraker Press.

Greenberg J., 1972, 'Linguistic evidence concerning Bantu origins', *Journal of African History* 13, 189–216.

Greene D., 1964, 'The Celtic languages', in J. Raftery (ed.), *The Celts*, Cork, Mercier Press, 9–22.

Greene D., 1977, 'Archaic Irish', in K. H. Schmidt (ed.), *Indogermanisch und Keltisch*, Wiesbaden, Ludwig Reichert, 11–33.

Greppin J. A. C., 1986, 'Language on the move', *Times Literary Supplement*, 14 March 1986, 278 (Review of Gamkrelidze and Ivanov 1984b).

Griffith R. T. H., 1973, *The Hymns of the Rigveda*, Delhi, Motilal Banarsidass (Revised edn, 1st edn 1889).

Gurney O., 1962, *The Hittites*, Harmondsworth, Penguin.

Guthrie M., 1962, 'Some developments in the prehistory of the Bantu languages', *Journal of African History* 3, 273–82.

Guthrie M., 1970, 'Contributions from comparative Bantu studies to the prehistory of Africa', in D. Dalby (ed.), *Language and History in Africa*, London, Frank Cass, 20–33.

Hachmann R., 1971, *The Germanic Peoples*, London, Barrie & Jenkins.

Hall R. A., 1958, 'Creolized languages and "genetic relationships"', *Word* 14, 367–73.

Hančar F., 1956, *Das Pferd in prähistorischen und frühe historischen Zeit*, Wien, Herold.

Hansen J. and Renfrew J. M., 1978, 'Palaeolithic-neolithic seed remains at Franchthi Cave, Greece', *Nature* 271, 349–52.

Harrison R., 1974, 'Origins of the Bell Beaker culture', *Antiquity* 48, 99–109.

Hassan F., 1981, *Demographic Archaeology*, New York, Academic Press.

Haüsler A., 1981, 'Zu den Beziehungen zwischen dem nordpontischen Gebiet südost – und Mitteleuropas im Neolithikum und in den frühen Bronzezeit und ihre Bedeutung für den indo-europäische Problem', *Prezgled Archeologiczny* 29, 101–49.

Hawkes C. F. C., 1973, 'Cumulative Celticity in pre-Roman Britain', *Études Celtiques* 13, 2, 607–28.

Hawkes C., 1976, 'Celts and cultures: wealth, power and art', in P.-M. Duval and C. Hawkes (eds), *Celtic Art in Ancient Europe*, London, Seminar Press, 1–21.

Hencken H., 1955, *Indo-European Languages and Archaeology*, (American Anthropologist Memoir 84), New York, American Anthropological Association.

Henning W. B., 1978, 'The first Indo-Europeans in history', in G. L. Ulmen (ed.), *Society and History, Essays in Honour of Karl August Wittfogel*, The Hague, Mouton, 215–30.

Higgs E. S. (ed.), 1972, *Papers in Economic Prehistory*, Cambridge, Cambridge University Press.

Higgs E. S. (ed.), 1975, *Palaeoeconomy*, Cambridge, Cambridge University Press.

Higgs E. S. and Jarman M. R., 1969, 'The origins of agriculture: a reconsideration', *Antiquity* 43, 31–41.

Hodson F. R., 1964, 'Cultural groupings within the British pre-Roman iron age', *Proceedings of the Prehistoric Society* 30, 99–110.

Hoernle A. F. R., 1911, 'The "unknown languages" of Eastern Turkestan II', *Journal of the Royal Asiatic Society* 1911, 447–77.

Hoernle A. F. R., 1916, *Manuscript Remains of Buddhist Literature Found in Turkestan*, Oxford, Clarendon.

Holl A., 1985, Review of D. W. Phillipson, *African Archaeology*, in *L'Ethnographie* 1985, 141–8.

Holloway R. L., 1983, 'Cerebral brain endocast pattern of *Australopithecus afarensis* hominid', *Nature* 303, 420–22.

Hood M. S. F., 1953, 'A Mycenaean cavalryman', *Annual of the British School of Archaeology at Athens* 48, 84–93.

Hooker J. T., 1980, *Linear B: an Introduction*, Bristol, Bristol Classical Press.

Hopkirk P., 1984, *Foreign Devils on the Silk Road*, Oxford, Oxford University Press.

Howells W., 1973, *The Pacific Islanders*, London, Weidenfeld & Nicolson.

Hoz J. de, 1982, 'Cronica de linguistica y epigrafia de la Penisula Iberica', 1981, *Zephyrus* 34–5, 295–311.

Hrozný B., 1915, 'Die Lösung des hethitischen Problems', *Mitteilungen der deutschen Orientgesellschaft* 56, 17–50.

Hrozný B., 1917, *Die Sprache der Hethiter, ihr Bau und ihre Zugehörigkeit zum indogermanischen Sprachstamm*, Leipzig.

Hrozný B., 1931, 'L'entrainement des chevaux chez les anciens indo-européens d'après un texte Mitannien-Hittite provenant du 14me siècle avant J.C.', *Archiv Orientalni* 3, 431–61.

Hubert H., 1934a, *The Rise of the Celts*, London, Kegan Paul, Trench & Trubner.

Hubert H., 1934b, *The Greatness and Decline of the Celts*, London, Kegan Paul, Trench & Trubner.

Hymes D. (ed.), 1971, *Pidginisation and Creolisation of Languages*, Cambridge, Cambridge University Press.

Isaac G. L., 1976, 'Stages of cultural elaboration in the Pleistocene: possible indicators of the development of language capabilities', in S. R. Harmad, H. D. Stentis and J. Lancaster (eds), *Origins and Evolution of Language and Speech*, (Annual of the New York Academy of Sciences 280), Lancaster N. Y., 275–88.

Jackson K. H., 1955, 'The Pictish language', in F. T. Wainwright (ed.), *The Problem of the Picts*, Edinburgh, Nelson, 129–66.

Jacobsthal P., 1944, *Early Celtic Art*, Oxford, Clarendon.

Jarrige J.-F., 1980, 'The antecedents of civilisation in the Indus valley', *Scientific American* 243 no. 2, 122–33.

Jarrige, J.-F., 1985, 'Continuity and change in the north Kachi Plain (Baluchistan, Pakistan) at the beginning of the second millennium B.C.' (Unpublished paper delivered in Cambridge on 24th April 1985.)

Jennings J. D. (ed.), 1979, *The Prehistory of Polynesia*, Cambridge, Mass., Harvard University Press.

Jones H. L., 1923, *The Geography of Strabo* II (Loeb Classical Library), London, Heinemann.

Jones H. L., 1928, *The Geography of Strabo* V, (Loeb Classical Library), London, Heinemann.

Jones Sir W., 1786, Third anniversary discourse: 'On the Hindus', reprinted in *The Collected Works of Sir William Jones* III, 1807, London, John Stockdale, 23–46.

Keith A. B., 1938, 'The relation of Hittite, Tocharian and Indo-European', *Indian Historical Quarterly* 14, 201–33.

Khazanov A. M., 1984, *Nomads and the Outside World*, Cambridge, Cambridge University Press.

Kilian L., 1983, *Zum Ursprung der Indogermanen*, Bonn, Habelt.

Kimmig W., 1962, 'Die Herkunft der Kelten als historisch-archäologisches Problem', in M. Renard (ed.), *Hommages à Albert Grenier* II, Bruxelles, Latomus, 884–99.

Kohl P. L. (ed.), 1981, *The Bronze Age Civilisations of Central Asia, Recent Soviet Discoveries*, Armonk, N.Y., M. E. Sharpe.

Koppers W., 1934, 'Die Indogermanenfrage im Licht der vergleichenden Völkerkunde', *Congrès International des Sciences Anthropologiques et Ethnologiques*, London, Royal Anthropological Institute, 185–7.

Koskenniemi S., Parpola A. and Parpola S., 1973, *Materials for the Study of the Indus Script I, A Concordance of Indus Inscriptions*, Helsinki, Suomalainen Tiedrakatemia.

Kossinna G., 1902, 'Die indogermanische Frage archäologisch beantwortet', *Zeitschrift fur Ethnologie* 34, 161–222 (reprinted in A. Scherer, 1968, *Die Urheimat der Indogermanen*, Darmstadt, Wissenschaftliche Buchgesellschaft 25–109).

Krader L., 1955, 'Ecology of central Asian pastoralism', *South Western Journal of Anthropology* 4, 301–26.

Krader L., 1959, 'The ecology of nomad pastoralism', *International Social Science Journal* 1959, 499–510.

Krahe H., 1954, *Sprache und Vorzeit*, Heidelberg, Quelle & Meyer.

Krahe H., 1957, 'Indogermanisch und Alteuropäisch', *Saeculum* 8, 1, 1–16 (reprinted in A. Scherer (ed.), 1968, *Die Urheimat der Indogermanen*, Darmstadt, Wissenschaftliche Buchgesellschaft, 426–54).

Kruskal J. B., Dyen I. and Black P., 1971, 'The vocabulary method of reconstructing language trees: innovations and large-scale applications', in F. R. Hodson, D. G. Kendall and P. Tautu (eds), *Mathematics in the Archaeological and Historical Sciences*, Edinburgh, Edinburgh University Press, 361–80.

Kühn H., 1934, 'Herkunft und Heimat der Indogermanen', in *Proceedings of the First International Congress of Prehistoric and Protohistoric Sciences (London 1932)*, Oxford, Oxford University Press, 237–42.

Kurlowicz J., 1970, 'The quantitative meter of Indo-European', in G. Cardona, H. M. Hoenigswald and A. Senn (eds), *Indo-European and Indo-Europeans*, Philadelphia, University of Pennsylvania Press, 421–30.

Labov W., 1966, *The Social Stratification of English in New York City*, Washington D.C., Center for Applied Linguistics.

Lane G. S., 1970, 'Tocharian: Indo-European and non-Indo-European relationships', in G. Cardona, H. M. Hoenigswald and A. Senn (eds), *Indo-European and Indo-Europeans*, Philadelphia, University of Pennsylvania Press, 73–88.

Lattimore O., 1937, 'Origins of the Great Wall of China, a frontier concept in theory and practice', *Geographical Review* 27, 529.

Lattimore O., 1940, *Inner Asian Frontiers of China*, Oxford, Oxford University Press.

Le Coq A. von, 1928, *Buried Treasures of Chinese Turkestan*, London, Allen & Unwin.

Lees R. B., 1953, 'The basis of glottochronology', *Language* 29, 113–25.

Lehmann W. P., 1967, *A Reader in Nineteenth Century Historical Indo-European Linguistics*, Bloomington, Indiana University Press.

Lehmann W. P., 1973, *Historical Linguistics, an Introduction*, New York, Holt, Rinehart & Winston.

Lejeune M., 1971, *Lepontica*, Paris, Société d'édition 'Les Belles Lettres'.

Lejeune M., 1974, *Manuel de la langue vénète*, Heidelberg, Carl Winter, Universitätsverlag.

Lesny V., 1932, 'The language of the Mitanni chieftains – a third branch of the Arya group', *Archiv Orientalni* 4, 257–60.

Lewthwaite J., 1981, 'Ambiguous first impressions: a survey of recent work on the early neolithic of the West Mediterranean', *Journal of Mediterranean Anthropological Archaeology* 1, 292–307.

Lichardus J., 1980, 'Zur Funktion der Geweihspitzen des Typus Ostdorf', *Germania* 58, 1–24.

Liebermann P. and Crelin E. S., 1971, 'On the speech of Neanderthal man', *Linguistic Inquiry* 11, 203–22.

Littauer M. A., 1981, 'Early stirrups', *Antiquity* 55, 99–105.

Littauer M. A. and Crouwel J. H., 1979, *Wheeled Vehicles and Ridden Animals in the Ancient Near East*, Leiden, Brill.

Littleton C. S., 1973, *The New Comparative Mythology*, Berkeley, University of California Press.

Lockwood W. B., 1972, *A Panorama of Indo-European Languages*, London, Hutchinson.

Lwanga-Lunyiigo S., 1976, 'The Bantu problem reconsidered', *Current Anthropology* 17, 282–5.

Lyons J., 1981, *Language and Linguistics*, Cambridge, Cambridge University Press.

MacKendrick P., 1962, *The Greek Stones Speak*, London, Methuen.

Mallory J., 1973, 'A short history of the Indo-European problem', *Journal of Indo-European Studies* 1, 21–65.

Mallory J. P., 1976, 'Time perspective and proto-Indo-European culture', *World Archaeology* 8, 44–56.

Malone C. and Stoddart S. (eds), 1985, *Pattern in Protohistory: Papers in Italian Archaeology IV*, (BAR International Series 245), Oxford, British Archaeological Reports.

Mann W. M., 1970, 'Internal relationships of the Bantu languages: prospects for topological research', in D. Dalby (ed.), *Language and History in Africa*, London, Frank Cass, 133–45.

Marinatos S. and Hirmer M., 1960, *Crete and Mycenae*, London, Thames & Hudson.

Marshack A., 1976, 'Some implications of the paleolithic symbolic evidence for the origin of language', *Current Anthropology* 17, 274–82.

Marshall Sir J., 1924, 'First light on a long forgotten civilisation', *Illustrated London News*, 20 Sept. 1924, 528–32.

Marshall Sir J., 1931, *Mohenjo-Daro and the Indus Civilisation* I, London, Probsthain.

Masica C., 1976, *Defining a Linguistic Area: South Asia*, Chicago, Chicago University Press.

Masson V. M., 1981, 'Seals of a Proto-Indian type from Altyndepe', in P. L. Kohl (ed.), *The Bronze Age Civilisation of Central Asia, Recent Soviet Discoveries*, Armonk, N.Y., M. E. Sharpe, 149–64.

Masson V. M. and Sarianidi V. I., 1972, *Central Asia, Turkmenia before the Achaemenids*, London, Thames & Hudson.

Mathers C., 1984, 'Beyond the grave: the context and wider implications of mortuary practices in south-eastern Spain', in

T. F. C. Blagg, R. F. J. Jones and S. J. Keay (eds), *Papers in Iberian Archaeology* (B. A. R. International Series 193), Oxford, British Archaeological Reports, 13–46.

Meid W., 1975, 'Probleme der räumlichen und zeitlichen Gliederung des Indogermanischen', in H. Rix (ed.), *Flexion und Wortbildung*, Wiesbaden, Ludwig Reichert. 204–18.

Meillet A., 1934, *Introduction à l'étude comparative des langues Indo-Européennes*, Paris, Hachette.

Meillet A., 1970, *The Comparative Method in Historical Linguistics*, Paris, Champion.

Mellaart J., 1960, 'Anatolia and the Balkans', *Antiquity* 24, 270–8.

Mellaart J., 1962, 'Anatolia c. 4000–2300 B.C.', *Cambridge Ancient History* I, Ch. 18, Cambridge, Cambridge University Press.

Mellaart J., 1964, Anatolia c. 2300–1750 B.C., *Cambridge Ancient History* I, Ch. 24, Cambridge, Cambridge University Press.

Mellaart J., 1967, *Catal Hüyük, a Neolithic Town in Anatolia*, London, Thames & Hudson.

Mellaart J., 1975, *The Neolithic of the Near East*, London, Thames & Hudson.

Mellaart J., 1981, 'Anatolia and the Indo-Europeans', *Journal of Indo-European Studies* 9, 135–49.

Menk R., 1980, 'A synopsis of the physical anthropology of the Corded Ware complex on the background of the expansion of the Kurgan cultures', *Journal of Indo-European Studies* 8, 361–92.

Merpert N. J., 1977, Comments on 'The chronology of the Early Kurgan tradition', *Journal of Indo-European Studies* 5, 373–8.

Merriman N., 1987, 'Value and motivation in prehistory: the evidence for "Celtic spirit"', in I. Hodder (ed.), *The Archaeology of Contextual Meanings*, Cambridge, Cambridge University Press, 111–6.

Meyer E., 1914, *Reich und Kultur der Chetiter*, Berlin, Verlag Karl Curtius.

Mills L. H., 1887, *The Zend-Avesta, Part III, The Yasna, Visparad, Afrinagan, Gahs, and Miscellaneous Fragments*, Oxford, Oxford University Press.

Montagu M. F. A., 1964, *The Concept of Race*, New York, Free Press.

Moreau J., 1958, *Die Welt der Kelten*, Stuttgart, Gustav Kilpper.

Müller F. M., 1888, *Biographies of Words and the Home of the Aryas*, London, Longmans Green.

Müller F. M., 1891, *Vedic Hymns, Part I, Hymns to the Maruts, Rudra, Vayu and Vata*, Oxford, Oxford University Press.

Myres J. L., 1930, *Who were the Greeks?* Berkeley, University of California Press.

Nandris J., 1970, 'Groundwater as a factor in the First Temperate Neolithic settlement of the Koros region', *Zbornik Narodnog Muzeja (Beograd)* 6, 59–73.

Narroll R., 1964, 'On ethnic unit classification', *Current Anthropology* 5, 283–312.

Nash D., 1978, *Settlement and Coinage in Central Gaul, c. 200–50 B.C.* (BAR Supplementary Series 39), Oxford, British Archaeological Reports.

Neustupný E., 1969, 'Economy of the corded ware cultures', *Archeologicke Rozhledy* 21, 1, 43–68.

Neustupný J., 1976, 'Archaeological comments to the Indo-European problem', *Origini* 10, 7–18.

O'Callaghan R. T., 1948, *Aram Naharaim: A Contribution to the History of Upper Mesopotamia in the Second Millennium B.C.* (Analecta Orientalia 26), Rome, Pontificium Institutum Biblicum.

Oldenberg H., 1897, *Vedic Hymns, Part II, Hymns to Agni (Mandalas I to V)*, Oxford, Oxford University Press.

Oldfather C. H., 1939, *Diodorus of Sicily*, III (Loeb Classical Library), London, Heinemann.

Oliver D., 1974, *Ancient Tahitian Society*, Honolulu, University Press of Hawaii.

Oliver R., 1966, 'The problem of the Bantu expansion', *Journal of African History* 7, 361–76.

Oliver R., 1979, 'Cameroun – the Bantu cradleland?', *Sprache und Geschichte in Afrika* 1, 7–20.

Page R. I., 1979, 'Dumézil revisited', *Saga-Book* 20 (Viking Society for Northern Research), 49–69.

Pallottino M., 1955, *The Etruscans*, Harmondsworth, Penguin.

Pallottino M., 1975, *The Etruscans*, London, Allen Lane.

Parker S. T. and Gibson K. R., 1979, 'A developmental model for the evolution of language and intelligence in early hominids', *The Behavioral and Brain Sciences*, 2, 337–408.

Parpola A., 1971, 'Computer techniques in the study of the Indus script', *Kadmos* 10, 10–15.

Passingham R. E., 1981, 'Broca's area and the origins of human vocal skill', *Philosophical Transactions of the Royal Society of London, Series B* 292, 167–75.

Péquart M. L. N., Péquart S. J., Boule M. and Vallois H. V., 1937, *Téviec – station-nécropole mésolithique du Morbihan* (Archives de l'Institut de Paléontologie Humaine, Mémoires 18).

Péquart M. and Péquart St-J., 1954, *Hoëdic, deuxième station-necropole du mésolithique cotier Armoricain*, Anvers, De Sikkel.

Phillips P., 1975, *Early Farmers of West Mediterranean Europe*, London, Hutchinson.

Phillipson D. W., 1976, 'Archaeology and Bantu linguistics', *World Archaeology* 8, 65–82.

Phillipson D. W., 1977a, 'The spread of the Bantu languages', *Scientific American* 236 no. 4, 106–14.

Phillipson D. W., 1977b, *The Later Prehistory of Eastern and Southern Africa*, London, Heinemann.

Phillipson, D. W., 1985, 'An archaeological reconsideration of Bantu expansion', MUNTU 2, 69–84.

Pictet A., 1877, *Les origines indo-européens*, Paris, Sandoz et Fischbacker.

Piggott S., 1950, *Ancient India*, Harmondsworth, Penguin.

Piggott S., 1965, *Ancient Europe*, Edinburgh, Edinburgh University Press.

Piggott S., 1968, *The Druids*, London, Thames & Hudson.

Piggott S., 1983, *The Earliest Wheeled Transport from the Atlantic Coast to the Caspian Sea*, London, Thames & Hudson.

Pisani V., 1949, La question indo-hittite et le concept de la parenté linguistique, *Archiv Orientalni* 17,2, 251–64.

Polomé E. C., 1984, Introduction to Diakanov 1984, 3–4.

Pope M., 1975, *Decipherment*, London, Thames & Hudson.

Possehl G., (ed.), 1982, *Harappan Civilisation, a Contemporary Perspective*, Warminster, Aris & Phillips.

Potratz H. A., 1939, *Das Pferd in der Frühzeit*, Rostock.

Potratz J. A. H., 1966, *Die Pferdetrensen des alten Orient* (Analecta Orientalia 41), Rome, Pontificium Institutum Biblicum.

Powell T. G. E., 1958, *The Celts*, London, Thames & Hudson.

Pulgram E., 1958, *The Tongues of Italy*, Cambridge, Mass., Harvard University Press.

Pulgram E., 1978, *Italic, Latin, Italian*, Heidelberg, Winter.

Rao S. R., 1973, 'The Indus script, methodology and language', in Agrawal D. F. and Ghosh A. (eds), *Radiocarbon and Indian Archaeology*, Bombay, Tahta Institute, 323–40.

Rao S. R., 1982, *The Decipherment of the Indus Script*, Bombay, Asia Publishing House.

Rea J. A., 1973, 'The Romance data of the pilot studies for glottochronology', in T. S. Sebeok (ed.), *Current Trends in Linguistics II: Diachronic and Typological Linguistics*, The Hague, Mouton, 355–68.

Renfrew C., 1964, 'Crete and the Cyclades before Rhadamanthus', *Kretika Chronika* 18, 107–41.

Renfrew C., 1973, 'Problems in the general correlation of archaeological and linguistic strata in prehistoric Greece: the model of autochthonous origin', in R. A. Crossland and A. Birchall (eds), *Bronze Age Migrations in the Aegean*, London, Duckworth, 263–76.

Renfrew C., 1974a, 'Beyond subsistence and economy: the evolution of social organisation in prehistoric Europe', in C. B. Moore (ed.), *Reconstructing Complex Societies*, (Supplement to the *Bulletin of the American Schools of Oriental Research* 20), 69–96.

Renfrew C., 1974b, 'British prehistory, changing configurations', in C. Renfrew (ed.), *British Prehistory, a New Outline*, London, Duckworth.

Renfrew C., 1978, 'Dags att omvärdera folkvandringarna', *Forskning och Framsteg* 1978, 8, 24–30.

Renfrew C., 1979, 'Systems collapse as social transformation', in

C. Renfrew and K. L. Cooke (eds), *Transformations, Mathematical Approaches to Culture Change*, New York, Academic Press, 275–94.

Renfrew C., 1982, 'Socio-economic change in ranked societies', in C. Renfrew and S. Shennan (eds), *Ranking, Resource and Exchange*, Cambridge, Cambridge University Press, 1–8.

Renfrew C., 1984, *Approaches to Social Archaeology*, Edinburgh, Edinburgh University Press.

Renfrew C., 1985, 'Archaeology and the Indo-European languages – an unresolved problem', Paper delivered at the Fiftieth Anniversary Conference of the Prehistoric Society, Norwich, 30 March 1985.

Renfrew C., 1985, *The Archaeology of Cult: the Sanctuary at Phylakopi* (British School of Archaeology at Athens Supplementary Volume 18), London, Thames & Hudson.

Renfrew C., 1986, 'Peer-polity interaction and sociopolitical change', in C. Renfrew and J. F. Cherry (eds), *Peer-Polity Interaction and Sociopolitical Change*, Cambridge, Cambridge University Press.

Renfrew J. M., 1973, *Palaeoethnobotany*, London, Methuen.

Rivière J.-C., 1973, 'Pour une lecture de Dumézil', *Nouvelle École* 21–22, 14–79.

Rix H., 1954, 'Zur Verbreitung und Chronologie einiger keltischer Ortsnamtypen', in W. Kimmig (ed.), *Festschrift für Peter Goessler*, Stuttgart, Kohlhammer, 99–107.

Robertshaw P. T. and Collett D. P., 1983, 'The identification of pastoral peoples in the archaeological record: an example from East Africa', *World Archaeology* 15, 69–78.

Robin C., 1973, 'Lexicostatistics and the internal divisions of Semitic', in J. and Th. Bynon (eds), *Hamito-Semitica*, The Hague, Mouton.

Roche J., 1965, 'Observations sur la stratigraphie et la chronologie des amas coquilliers de Muge' (Portugal), *Bulletin de la Société Préhistorique Française* 62, 130–8.

Rodden R. J., 1965, 'Nea Nikomedeia, an early neolithic village in Greece', *Scientific American* 212 (4), 83–91.

Ross A., 1974, *Pagan Celtic Britain*, London, Cardinal.

Roux G., 1966, *Ancient Iraq*, Harmondsworth, Penguin.

Rutter J. B., 1979, *Ceramic change in the Aegean early bronze age*, (University of California at Los Angeles, Institute of Archaeology Occasional Paper 5), Los Angeles, University of California.

Sahlins M., 1958, *Social Stratification in Polynesia*, Seattle, University of Washington Press.

Sakellariou M., 1980, *Les Proto-Grecs*, Athens, Ekdotike Athenon.

Sangmeister E., 1963, 'La civilisation du Vase Campaniforme', in *Les Civilisations Atlantiques: Actes du Premier Congrès Atlantique, Brest 1961*.

Sankalia H. D., 1973, 'The "Cemetery H" culture', *Puratattva* 6, 12–19, reprinted in G. Possehl (ed.), 1979, *Ancient Cities of the Indus*, New Delhi, Vokas Publishing House, 322–7.

Saussure, F. de, 1959, *Course in General Linguistics* (ed. C. Bally and A. Sechehaye), New York, McGraw Hill.

Scherer A. (ed.), 1968, *Die Urheimat der Indogermanen*, Darmstadt, Wissenschaftliche Buchgesellschaft.

Schlegel F. von, 1849, *The aesthetic and miscellaneous works of Friedrich von Schlegel*, London, Bohn.

Schleicher A., 1863, *Die Darwinsche Theorie und die Sprachwissenschaft*, Weimar (French edition 1868, *La Theorie de Darwin et la Science du Langage* in *Receuil de Travaux Originaux ou Traduits relatifs a l'Histoire Littéraire* I, Paris, Franck).

Schmidt J., 1872, *Die Verwandtschaftsverhältnisse der indogermanischen Sprachen*, Weimar, Böhlau.

Schmidt K. H., 1977, *Der Sprachvergleich* (Innsbrücker Beitrage zur Sprachwissenschaft 17), Innsbrück, Institut für Sprachwissenschaft.

Schmidt K. H., 1979, 'On the Celtic languages of continental Europe', *Bulletin of the Board of Celtic Studies* 28, 189–205.

Schmidt W., 1949, 'Die Herkunft der Indogermanen und ihr erstes Auftreten in Europa', *Kosmos* 45, 116–18 and 159–60 (reprinted in A. Scherer (ed.), *Die Urheimat der Indogermanen*, Darmstadt, Wissenschaftliche Buchgesellschaft, 312–23).

Schrader O., 1890, *Prehistoric Antiquities of the Aryan Peoples*, New York, Scribner & Welford.

Schwantes G., 1958, *Die Indogermanen im Geschichte Schleswig Holsteins*, Neumünster, Karl Wacholtz Verlag.

Schwappach F., 1976, 'L'art ornamental du "premier style" celtique', in P.-M. Duval and C. Hawkes (eds), *Celtic Art in Ancient Europe*, London, Seminar Press, 61–109.

Service E. R., 1962, *Primitive Social Organisation*, New York, Random House.

Shaffer J. G., 1984, 'The Indo-Aryan invasions: cultural myth and archaeological reality', in J. R. Lukacs (ed.), *The People of South Asia, the Biological Anthropology of India, Pakistan and Nepal*, New York, Plenum Press, 77–90.

Shennan S. J., 1977, *Bell Beakers and their Context in Central Europe: a New Approach* (unpublished Ph.D. dissertation, University of Cambridge).

Shennan S. J., 1982, 'Ideology, change and the European early bronze age', in I. Hodder (ed.), *Symbolic and Structural Archaeology*, Cambridge, Cambridge University Press, 155–61.

Shennan S., 1986a, 'Interaction and change in third-millennium-BC western and central Europe', in C. Renfrew and J. F. Cherry (eds), *Peer Polity Interaction and Sociopolitical Change*, Cambridge, Cambridge University Press, 137–48.

Shennan S., 1986b, 'Central Europe in the third millennium B.C.: an evolutionary trajectory for the beginning of the European bronze age', *Journal of Anthropological Archaeology* 5, 115–46.

Sherratt A., 1981, 'Plough and pastoralism: aspects of the secondary products revolution', in I. Hodder, G. Isaac and N. Hammond (eds), *Pattern of the Past: Studies in Honour of David Clarke*, Cambridge, Cambridge University Press, 261–305.

Sherratt A., 1982, 'Mobile resources: settlement and exchange in early agricultural Europe', in C. Renfrew and S. Shennan (eds), *Ranking, Resource and Exchange*, Cambridge, Cambridge University Press, 13–26.

Sieg E. and Siegling W., 1921, *Tocharische Sprachreste*, Berlin, Gruyter.

Sieg E., Siegling W. and Schulze W., 1931, *Tocharische Grammatik*, Göttingen, Vanbenhoeck & Ruprecht.

Sinor D., 1963, *Introduction à l'Étude de l'Asie Centrale*, Wiesbaden, Harrasowitz.

Sokal R. R. and Sneath P. H. A., 1973, *Principles of Numerical Taxonomy*, San Francisco, Freeman.

Srejović D., 1972, *Europe's First Monumental Sculpture: New Discoveries at Lepenski Vir*, London, Thames & Hudson.

Stähelin F., 1907, *Geschichte der Kleinasiatischen Galater*, Leipzig, Teubner.

Stein Sir A., 1912, *Ruins of Desert Cathay*, London, Macmillan.

Stevenson V. (ed.), 1983, *Words, an Illustrated History of Western Languages*, London, Macdonald.

Sturtevant F. H., 1947, 'Hittite and areal linguistics', *Language* 23, 376–82.

Sturtevant F. H., 1962, 'The Indo-Hittite hypothesis', *Language* 38, 105–10.

Sulimirski T., 1933, 'Die schnurkeramische Kultur und das indoeuropäische Problem', *La Pologne au VIIe Congres des Sciences Historiques* I, Warsaw, 287–308 (reprinted in A. Scherer (ed.), *Die Urheimat der Indogermanen*, Darmstadt, Wissenschaftliche Buchgesellschaft, 117–40).

Swadesh M., 1960, 'Unas correlaciones de arquelogia y lingüistica', Appendix to P. Bosch-Gimpera, *El Problema Indoeuropeo*, Mexico, Direccion General de Publicaciones, 345–52.

Swadesh M., 1972, *The Origin and Diversification of Language* (ed. by J. Sherzer), London, Routledge.

Szabó M., 1971, *The Celtic Heritage in Hungary*, Budapest, Corvina.

Tablot Rice T., 1957, *The Scythians*, London, Thames & Hudson.

Taylor D., 1956, 'On the classification of creolized languages', *Word* 12, 407–14.

Telegin D. Y., 1986, *Dereivka: A Settlement and Cemetery of Copper Age Horse-Keepers on the Middle Dnieper*, (B. A. R. International Series 287), Oxford, British Archaeological Reports.

Thapar B. K., 1973, 'Synthesis of the multiple data as obtained from Kalibangan', in D. P. Agrawal and A. Ghosh (eds), *Radiocarbon and Indian Archaeology*, Bombay, Tata Institute, 264–71.

Theocharis D. (ed.), 1973, *Neolithic Greece*, Athens, National Bank of Greece.

Thieme P., 1960, 'The "Aryan" gods of the Mitanni treaties', *Journal of the American Oriental Society* 80, 301–17.

Tierney J. J., 1960, 'The Celtic Ethnography of Posidonius', *Proceedings of the Royal Irish Academy* 60, C, 189–275.

Tilley C., 1984, 'Ideology and power in the middle neolithic of southern Sweden', in D. Miller and C. Tilley (eds), *Ideology, Power and Prehistory*, Cambridge, Cambridge University Press, 111–46.

Tischler J., 1973, *Glottochronologie und Lexicostatik.* (Innsbrücker Beiträge zur Sprachwissenschaft 11), Innsbrück, Institut für Sprachwissenschaft.

Tobias P. V., 1981, 'From palaeo-anatomy to culture', in *Actas, X. Congreso, Union Internacional de Ciencias Prehistoricas y Protohistoricas, Mexico 1981*, Mexico City, UISPP, 120–48.

Tovar A., 1949, *Estudios sobre las primitivas lenguas hispanicas*, Buenos Aires, Coni.

Tovar A., 1970, 'Basque language and the Indo-European spread to the west', in G. Cardona, H. M. Hoenigswald and A. Senn (eds), *Indo-European and Indo-Europeans*, Philadelphia, University of Pennsylvania Press, 267–78.

Tovar A., 1975, 'Die späte Bildung des Germanischen', in H. Rix (ed.), *Flexion und Wortbildung*, Wiesbaden, Ludwig Reichert, 346–57.

Tovar A., 1977a, *Krahes alteuropäische Hydronymie und die westindogermanischen Sprachen* (Sitzungsberichte der Heidelberger Akademie der Wissenschaften, Philosophische-historische Klasse 1977, Abh.2), Heidelberg, Winter.

Tovar A., 1977b, *Einführung in die Sprachgeschichte der iberischen Halbinsel* (Tübinger Beiträge zur Linguistik 90), Tübingen, Gunter Narr.

Tovar A., 1977c, 'Indogermanisch, Keltisch, Keltiberisch', in K. H. Schmidt (ed.), *Indogermanisch und Keltiberisch*, Wiesbaden, Ludwig Reichert, 44–65.

Tringham R., 1971, *Hunters, Fishers and Farmers of Eastern Europe 6000–3000 B.C.*, London, Hutchinson.

Trubetzkoy N. S., 1939, 'Gedanken über das Indogermanenproblem', *Acta Linguistica* I, 81–9 (reprinted in A. Scherer (ed.), 1968, *Die Urheimat der Indogermanen*, Darmstadt, Wissenschaftliche Buchgesellschaft, 214–23).

Untermann J., 1963, 'Estudios sobre las areas lingüísticas pre-romanas de la peninsula iberica', *Archivos de Prehistoria Levantina* 10, 195–62.

Vansina J., 1965, *Oral Tradition*, London, Routledge.

Vansina J., 1984, Western Bantu expansion, *Journal of African History* 25, 129–45.

Vendryes J., 1918, 'Les correspondences de vocabulaire entre l'indo-iranien et l'italo-celtique', *Mémoires de la Société Linguistique de Paris* 20, 265–85.

Ventris M. G. F. and Chadwick J., 1973, *Documents in Mycenaean Greek*, Cambridge, Cambridge University Press (2nd edition).

Vouga P., 1923, *La Tène, Monographie de la station publiée au nom de la Commission de Fouilles de la Tène*, Leipzig, Hiersemann.

Watkins C., 1963, 'Indo-European metrics and archaic Irish verse', *Celtica* 6, 194–249.

Watkins C., 1970, 'Studies in Indo-European legal language, institutions and mythology', in G. Cardona, H. M. Hoenigswald and A. Senn (eds), *Indo-European and Indo-Europeans*, Philadelphia, University of Pennsylvania Press, 321–54.

Watson W., 1971, *Cultural Frontiers in Ancient East Asia*, Edinburgh, Edinburgh University Press.

Wells P., 1980, *Culture Contact and Culture Change: Early Iron Age Central Europe and the Mediterranean World*, Cambridge, Cambridge University Press.

Wertime T., 1964, 'Man's first encounters with metallurgy', *Science* 146, 1257–67.

Whatmough J., 1970, *The Dialects of Ancient Gaul*, Harvard, Harvard University Press.

Wheeler R. E. M., 1947, 'Harappan chronology and the Rigveda, *Ancient India* 3, 78–82 (reprinted in G. L. Possehl (ed.), *Ancient Cities of the Indus*, New Delhi, Vikas, 288–92).

White L., 1962, 'The origin and diffusion of the stirrup', in L. White, *Mediaeval Technology and Social Change*, Oxford, Clarendon, 14–28.

Whittle A., 1981, 'Later neolithic society in Britain, a realignment', in C. L. N. Ruggles and A. W. R. Whittle (eds), *Astronomy and Society in Britain during the period 4000–1500 B.C.* (B.A.R. 88), Oxford, British Archaeological Reports, 297–342.

Whittle A., 1985, *Neolithic Europe, a Survey*, Cambridge, Cambridge University Press.

Wiesner J., 1939, *Fahren und Reiten in Alteuropa und im Alten Orient* (Das Alte Orient 38, 2–4), Leipzig, J. C. Hinrechs.

Wijngaarden-Bakker L. H. van, 1974, 'The animal remains from the Beaker settlement at Newgrange, Co. Meath', first report, *Proceedings of the Royal Irish Academy* 74c, 313–83.

Woodman P. C., 1976, 'The Irish Mesolithic/Neolithic transition', in S. J. De Laet (ed.), *Acculturation and Continuity in Atlantic Europe* (Dissertationes Archaeologicae Gandenses 16), Brugge, Tempel, 296–307.

Yoshida A., 1977, 'Japanese mythology and the Indo-European trifunctional system', *Diogenes* 98, 93–116.

Yoshida A., 1981, 'Dumézil et les études comparatives des mythes japonais', in J. Bonnet el al., *Pour un Temps: Georges Dumézil*, Paris, Centre Pompidou, 319–24.

Young T., 1813, 'Mithradates, oder allgemeine Sprachenkunde', *The Quarterly Review* 10, 250–92.

Zeuner F. E., 1963, *A History of Domesticated Animals*, London, Hutchinson.

Zide A. R. K. and Zvelebil K. V. (eds), 1976, *The Soviet Decipherment of the Indus Valley Script*, The Hague, Mouton.

Zohary D., 1969, 'The progenitors of wheat and barley in relation to domestication and dispersal in the Old World', in P. J. Ucko and G. W. Dimbleby (eds), *The Domestication and Exploitation of Plants and Animals*, London, Duckworth, 47–66.

Index

acculturation, 147, 268
Agamemnon, 57
agriculture, *see* farming
Akhnaten (Amenophis IV), 49, 72
Akkadian, *see* Babylonian
Albanian language, 69
Alexander the Great, 43, 62, 183
Ali Kosh, 166, 173
Allchin, Bridget, 191
Allchin, Raymond, 190, 191
alphabetic scripts, 45, 65, 70, 71, 227
Altaic peoples, 35
Altyn-Tepe, 192
Amarna, 49, 198; archive/letters, 54, 72, 73
Amenophis III, 54, 72
Amenophis IV, *see* Akhnaton
Americas, and spread of European farming system, 130, 131, 152, 271
Ammerman, Albert, 126, 128, 158, 265
Anatolia/Anatolian languages, 205–8, 288; *see also* Hittite, Luwian, Lycian, Palaic, Hattic
Andronova culture, 203
Anglo-Saxon language, 136–7
Apennine bronze age, 26
Aquitani, in classical writers, 221, 223
Arabic language, 13, 174, 216
Aramaic language, 13
Argissa Maghoula, 147
Armenian language, 71–3
artefacts, as indicators of people, 3, 7, 15, 18, 23, 24, 30, 37, 75, 86, 120, 123, 139, 207, 215, 216
'Aryan', as used by Darius of cuneiform script for Old Persian, 45
Aryans, 15, 16, 38, 75, 182, 187–9; Aryan language, 247; *The Aryans*

(V. G. Childe), 4, 5, 16, 37, 38, 83, 140
Arzawa/'Arzawa language' (cuneiform Hittite), 49, 50
Ashoka, 178, 183
Assur, 56
Assyria, empire, 13, 47, 199; languages, 13, 45, 56
Aurignacian culture, 36
Australia, European settlers in, 151, 271
Australopithecus, 274
Austronesian languages, 277
Avebury, 89
Avesta, 10, 42, 44, 46, 47, 73, 193, 196, 209, 250
Aztecs, 136

Babylonian (Akkadian), 13, 45, 46, 49, 51, 54, 293
Baltic languages, 69
Baluchistan, 207
Bandkeramik pottery, 267
Banerji, R. D., 183
Bantu languages, 126, 277, 281, 283, 284
Barker, Graeme, 157, 269
Barth, Frederick, 84
Basque language/Basques, 70, 145, 151, 225, 232, 238, 268
Basseri, south Persian nomads, 84
battle axe, 32, 38, 40, 92
Battle Axe culture/people, *see* Corded Ware
Beaker (including Bell Beaker), élite, 91, 92; material culture, 33, 39, 86–93, 124, 236; people ('Beaker Folk'), 39, 87, 88, 93, 96, 124, 236, 243, 265
Behistun, inscriptions, 44, 45, 49

Benveniste, Emile, 255, 259, 260, 262
Bible, 68, 122, 257
Binford, Lewis, 143
Bird, Norman, 193
Blegen, Carl, 159
Bloomfield, Leonard, 103, 110, 112
Boghazköy, *see* Hattusas
Bökönyi, Sandor, 202
Bopp, Franz, 12
Bosch-Gimpera, Pedro, 17, 41, 165, 236
Brahma, 183
brahmans, 250, 251
Brahmi alphabets, 65
Braidwood, Robert, 173
Breton language, 164, 212, 228, 229, 249
Brithonic ('British'/P-Celtic) dialects, 213, 226–8, 244; *see also* Breton, Celtic languages, Cornish, Welsh
Brough, John, 257
Browne, Sir Thomas, 3

Caesar, descriptions of Celts and Gaul, 27, 28, 212, 219, 221, 222, 224, 244, 252
calque, 110
camels, for traction, 201
cart, *see* wheeled vehicles
caste, in India, 252
Castilian languages, 248
Çatal Hüyük, 153, 166, 171, 173
Catalan language, 67
cattle, for traction, 201
Caucasian languages, 203
Caucasus, area for development of pastoralism from farming, 201, 203
Cavalli-Sforza, Luigi, 126, 128, 158, 265
cavalry, heavy, *see* horse riding
cave art, 274
Çayönü, 166, 173
Celtae/Celti, *see* Celts

Celtiberians (and Hispano-Celtic language), 222, 223, 237, 244
'Celtic', alternative meanings of, 212, 214, 219, 220, 249
Celtic languages, 6, 10, 27, 28, 51, 160, 161, 211–4, 225, 226, 238, 240, 244–7, 249, 250; *see also* Breton, Cornish, Hispano-Celtic, Irish, Lepontic, Scots Gaelic; literature, 28
Celts, 3, 6, 26–8, 34, 211–4, 218–25, 234, 236–8, 240–6, 249, 250; art style, *see* La Tène art; described by classical writers, 20, 26, 27, 212, 214, 218–24, 234, 252
'centum' languages, 51, 66, 107; *see also* 'satem'/'centum' distinction
Chadwick, John, 60, 176, 177
Chadwick, N. K., 239
Champion, Timothy, 140
Champollion, Jean-François, 44
chariots, 12, 86, 138, 165, 180, 182, 187; horse-drawn, 39, 137, 182, 194, 195; war chariot, 28, 73, 182, 195, 198, 200; *see also* horses, wheeled vehicles
Châteauneuf-les-Martigues, 157
chiefdom societies, 89, 132, 163, 205, 253–5, 273
Childe, V. Gordon, 3–5, 16–8, 24, 30, 36–9, 41, 83, 88, 140, 141, 154, 165, 166, 175, 215, 216, 260, 271
China, 143
Cimbri, 219
Cimmerians, 163, 194, 204
Clark, Grahame, 88, 124, 241, 243
colonization (and language replacement), African, 126; European, 137; Iran, 130; New World, 130, 131; Norse, of Britain, 137; Polynesian, 2; waves of, 35; *see also* language replacement
comparative linguistics, 13, 77, 86, 99, 103, 109, 110; *see also* linguistic palaeontology
comparative philology, 6

Continental Celts, 226, 230, 239, 249;
see also Celts
copper metallurgy, 31, 166, 174
Corded Ware, material culture, 15, 17,
32, 37, 86, 87, 92, 93, 146, 174, 213,
265; people, 37–9, 87, 96, 200
Cornish language, 212, 228
creole (hybrid language), 123
Cretan hieroglyphic script, 59, 62
Criş culture, 155
Crumley, Carole, 255
Cucuteni culture, 97, 98, 156, 201, 202
'cultures', equated with artefact
groups, 7, 20, 24; *see also* pottery
'cumulative Celticity', 244, 246, 248,
249
cuneiform scripts, 43–5, 47; *see also*
Assyrian, Babylonian (Akkadian),
Elamite, Hittite, Hurrian

Dacian language, 69, 71, 160, 234
Dalriada, kingdom of, 164, 226
Danubian cultures, 41, 242; *see also*
Linear Pottery culture
Darius the Great, 43–6
Darwin, Charles, 13, 102
Dasya/Dasyu, 12, 182
della Valle, Pietro, 43
demic diffusion, 128
de Mortillet, Gabriel, 27
demography/subsistence, as model for
language replacement, 124
Demoule, Jean-Paul, 35, 42
Dennell, Robin, 157, 158
Dereivka, 95
Devoto, Giacomo, 17, 41
Dhar, Lachmi, 35
Diakonov, Igor, 138, 263, 270, 304
Dillon, Myles, 225, 228
Diodorus Siculus, 211, 219, 221, 222
Djeitun culture, 173, 192, 201
domestication, 153, 157, 266, 273, 279,
283
donor-recipient population systems,
143

Dorian Greeks, 57, 175
Dragadze, T., 216
Dravidian languages, 104, 185
druids, 250, 252
Dumézil, Georges, 7, 8, 251–9, 261,
286

Ebla, language of, 173
egalitarian societies, 253, 259, 273
Egyptian art, 198, 199;
hieroglyphic script, 44
Eisteddfod, 212
Elamite language, 45, 173
élite dominance, 95, 131, 136, 137,
139, 143, 152, 163–5, 174, 175, 196,
197, 200, 204, 205, 207–9, 226, 234,
249, 271
Emeneau, M. B., 178
Ephorus, 219
Estonia/Estonian language, 69, 70,
204
Escalente, Roberto, 167
ethnic groups/ethnicity, 2, 3, 7, 24,
113, 211, 214–8, 220–4, 288
ethnonym, 216, 221, 223
Etruscan language/people, 25, 26, 67,
70, 145, 151, 161, 234, 238, 268
'Etruscan' vases, *see* Greek pottery
Europe, earliest hominids in, 29; first
farmers, *see* farming
Evans, Sir Arthur, 58, 59, 61

farming, earliest in, Anatolia, 171,
203, 205; Balkans, 202; Bantu lands,
283; China, 173; Crete, 168; France,
242; Germany and Holland, 37, 242;
Greece, 150, 153, 161, 169, 242, 266;
Iberia, 242; India and Pakistan, 173,
189, 190, 197, 205, 209; Ireland, 242;
Orkney Islands, 242; Turkmenia,
192, 205; early European, 30, 125,
126, 146–8, 150, 152, 157, 158, 202,
238, 242, 265; language and, 15, 125,
126, 145, 202, 205, 238, 251, 253,

farming (cont.)
  260, 270; pastoral nomadism
  dependent on, 138, 142, 201
farming cultures, early European, *see*
  First Temperate Neolithic and
  Linear Pottery culture
fertile crescent, 173
Finnish language, 70
Finno-Ugrian languages, 69, 70, 204
First Temperate Neolithic, 153, 155,
  159; *see also* Criş, Karanovo, Körös,
  Starčevo
fishing, contribution to economy,
  201
flamines, 250
Franchthi cave, 147, 157, 168
Franks, Sir Augustus, 27
Fraser, J., 80, 82, 85
Friedrich, Paul, 18, 83
Funnel Beaker culture, *see*
  Trichterbecher culture

Gaelic languages/peoples, 164, 226,
  227; *see also* Irish, Manx, Scots
  Gaelic
Galatai/Galates, *see* Gauls
Galatia/Galatians, 232, 249
Gallay, Alain, 91
Galli, *see* Gauls
Gallo-Brittonic dialects, 227
Gamkrelidze, T. V., 35, 36, 269, 304
Gaul/Gauls, 211, 212, 218, 220–6, 230,
  231, 242, 253, 254
Geddes, David, 157
Gellner, Ernest, 256
Georgiev, Vladimir, 164
Germani/Germans, 219, 221, 222, 225,
  248, 252
Germanic languages, 10, 11, 51, 68,
  160, 212, 225, 245, 247, 248; *see also*
  German, Gothic, Norse
Gimbutas, Marija, 17, 18, 39, 41, 95,
  98, 146, 166, 176, 238, 254, 260, 271
glottochronology, 113, 114, 117, 123,
  165, 167, 168, 193, 276, 285

Goidelic (Q-Celtic) dialects, 213, 226,
  244; *see also* Celtic languages, Gaelic
  languages, Irish, Manx, Scots Gaelic
Gomez-Moreno, Manuel, 230
Goody, Jack, 80, 139, 217, 258
Goodenough, Ward, 97, 202
Gordon, Cyrus, 62
Gothic language, 10, 68
Greek language ('Ancient'/classical
  Greek), 10, 11, 50, 57, 62, 160,
  166–8, 176, 177, 228, 260, 270;
  modern, 62, 167, 177; Mycenaean,
  61, 166, 167, 172, 177, 246
Greek pottery, 24, 25, 196
Greece/Greeks, 24, 195, 216, 217, 224,
  252; alphabet, 45, 60, 70, 71; origins
  of, 1, 16; religion, 195; *see also*
  Mycenae, Mycenaean civilization
Greenberg, J., 283
Greene, David, 224
group-oriented chiefdoms, 89
Grünwedel, A., 65
Gubbio, bronze tablets of, 67
Gundestrup cauldron, 234
Guthrie, M., 283
Guti (Proto-Tocharian), 208, 209

Hallstatt culture/iron age, 27, 34, 213,
  234, 235, 239–41, 255
Hamitic languages, 13
Harappa, 183, 188, 189, 196, 207
Hattic language, 55, 56, 65, 172, 294
Hattusas (modern Boghazköy), 49, 54,
  55, 198; archive, 51, 55, 72, 73, 107
Haüsler, Alexander, 92
Hawkes, Christopher, 241, 246
Hebrew language, 13, 45, 46
Hellas/Hellenes, *see* Greece/Greeks
Hellenic languages, 62, 161; *see also*
  Greek language (including
  Mycenaean)
Hencken, Hugh, 17, 41
Henning, W. B., 208–9
Herodotus, 43, 70, 218, 220
Higgs, Eric, 153, 156

Hildebrand, B. E., 26
Hindu religion, 183, 190; see also Indus
    Valley civilization
historical linguistics, 6, 19, 78, 99, 106,
    113, 117, 238, 245, 263, 275, 285–9
Hittite languages, cuneiform Hittite,
    45, 47, 49, 50, 51, 55, 56, 65, 72, 73,
    107, 108, 172, 198, 207, 246, 248,
    270, 293; grammar, 50; hieroglyphic
    Hittite, 48, 51, 54, 55, 293;
    proto-Hittite, see Hattic;
    vocabulary, 50, 193
Hittites, empire/land ('land of Hatti'),
    35, 47–9, 51, 55, 198; people, 47, 49,
    55, 209; ruler, 49, 73, 198; see also
    Hattusas
Hodson, F. R., 241
homeland, of Proto-Indo-Europeans,
    see Proto-Indo-Europeans, Urheimat
Homer/Homeric writings, 21, 28, 57,
    122, 189, 195, 255, 256
Homo erectus, 29
homonymy, 259
Homo sapiens neanderthalensis, 29, 275
Homo sapiens sapiens, 1, 29, 30, 274,
    276, 286
horse, 12, 14, 35, 38, 82, 83, 95, 137,
    138, 163, 180–2, 194, 196, 202, 204,
    205, 208; bits, 138, 199; for traction,
    137, 138, 182, 194, 195, 198, 200,
    201, 203; pack animal, 138, 198, 200;
    riding, 39, 88, 133, 137–9, 165,
    193–5, 198–200, 208, 271;
    warhorse, 39, 163, 198, 200, 203,
    205; see also chariots, wheeled
    vehicles
horticulture, 278–9
Hrozný, Dr Bedřich, 50, 54
Hsiung-nu, 66
Hubert, Henry, 221, 301
Hungarian language/Hungary, 70,
    163, 204, 241
Huns, 66
Hurrian language, see Mitanni
hybrid language, see creole

hydronomy, see river names

Iberia/Iberian language, 70, 145, 161,
    220, 222, 223, 225, 226, 230, 232,
    233, 226, 228, 229, 268
Iberian neolithic, 159
Illyrian language, 69, 160; 232
Impressed Ware culture, 156, 159,
    242
India, 252, 254, 258, 259; religion,
    250–2
individualizing chiefdoms, 89
Indo-Aryans, 187, 191, 196; see also
    Indus valley civilization
Indo-European vocabulary, divinities,
    259, 260; kingship, 78, 80, 259; kin
    terms, 80; metals, 79, 165;
    subsistence, 78, 80; tree names, 81,
    82, 154
Indo-Germanic, 11, 246
Indo-Iranian languages, 47, 72, 73,
    108, 193, 195, 203, 207, 208, 250,
    271; see also Persian, Sanskrit
Indus Valley civilization, 183, 187,
    189–91, 195, 196, 201, 204, 207,
    271; decline, 183, 189, 205; script,
    183, 185, 190; settlement in
    Afghanistan, 193
Indus Valley language, as Dravidian,
    185, 192; as Indo-European, 185; as
    proto-Elamite, 185
Insular Celts, 226, 228, 249; see also
    Celts
Ionian Greeks, 57
Iranian languages, 204
Iranian plateau, 201, 203–5, 207
Irish, language/literature, 21, 28, 226,
    228, 243, 250, 253, 255, 256, 260;
    people: 221, 227, 258
iron metallurgy, 34, 229, 283
isoglosses, 105, 106
Italic languages, 161, 245; see also
    Latin, Oscan, Romance languages,
    Umbrian
'Italo-Celtic', 228

Italy, 230, 254
Ivanov, V. V., 35, 36, 268, 304

Jackson, K. H., 227
Jacobsthal, P., 235
Jakobson, Roman, 297
Japanese mythology, 257
Japhetic languages, 13
Jarmo, 173, 192
Jarrige, Jean-François, 190, 196
Jericho, 173
Jomon culture, 131
Jones, Sir William, 9–13, 183
Jupiter, 252

Kadesh, battle of, 48
Kalibangan, 191
Kanesh, see Kültepe
Karashahr, 66
Karanovo culture, 155, 159
Karatepe, 51
Karim Shahir, 173
Keith, A. B., 81
Keltika/Keltoi, see Celts
Kelteminar culture, 201
Kikkuli, treatise on chariotry by, 72, 198
Kimmig, Wolfgang, 239, 240, 243
Knossos, palace of, 59, 61, 147, 169; archive, 59, 60
Koppers, Wilhelm, 35
Korea, 257
Körös culture, 155, 159
Kossinna, Gustav, 4, 15, 17, 23, 36–9, 41, 94, 155, 165, 166
Koucha oasis, 66
Kouchean language, see Tocharian B
Krahe, Hans, 162, 164, 165, 246
Kühn, Herbert, 36, 165
Kültepe, site of Kanesh, 56
Kurgan culture, 39, 40, 97, 98, 145, 202, 238, 253; expansion, 39, 92, 254; kurgan burial mounds/ochre graves, 37, 38, 92, 95; language, 92; people, 40, 93, 95

language, changes in, continuous development, 121, 122, 247; convergence/divergence, 109, 122, 123, 150, 276, 280; differentiation, 247, 249, 277, 279; dispersal, 12, 277, 280, 281; initial colonization, 12, 123, 130, 279; replacement, 121, 123, 125, 126, 132, 200, 205, 235; see also colonization
Lapita culture, 278
La Tène culture/iron age, 27, 174, 213, 236, 239, 240, 241, 255; art style, 27, 28, 232–5, 237, 242, 249; site, 27
Latin language, 2, 10, 11, 50, 67, 163, 167, 228; common source of Romance languages, 67, 150, 226
Lehmann, Winfred, 78, 80, 111
Lepenski, Vir, 152
Lepontic languages, 230, 249
Lévi-Strauss, Claude, 256, 258, 259
Lewthwaite, J., 269
lexicostatistics, 118, 167, 168, 193, 276, 280, 285
Lhwyd, Edward, 212
Libyans, 219
Linear A script, 59, 61, 171
Linear B script, 59–61, 175, 176
Linear Pottery culture, 37, 156, 158, 159, 161, 242; see also Danubian cultures
linguistic palaeontology, 14, 17, 18, 37, 39, 78, 82, 86, 94, 98, 103, 109, 265; see also historical linguistics
Livy, 27, 241
loan-words, 78, 80, 91, 104, 109, 110, 112, 118, 145, 176, 191, 193, 269
LoWiili, 217
Lowland Maya civilization, collapse of, 135, 136; see also system collapse
Lusitanian language, 232
Luwian language, 51, 55, 172, 293
Lwanga-Lunyiigo, 281
Lycian language, 51

MacCana, Prionsias, 230
Magdalenian culture, 36
Magi, 250
Magyars, 70, 163
Maikop, 95
Manx language, 212, 226
Marnian culture, 214
Mars, 252
Marshall, Sir John, 183
Massalia (Marseilles), 34, 222–4, 234
Masson, V. M., 192, 203
Medes, 194, 204
megalithic tombs, 6, 31
Meid, Wolfgang, 238, 248
Mehrgarh, 190–3, 197, 207
Mellaart, James, 172
Melos, obsidian from, 154, 168
Menk, R., 93
Merpert, N. I., 300
Merriman, N., 234
Mesoamerica, 256
mesolithic populations, 267
Mikhailovka, 95
Minoan civilization, 33, 59, 61
Minoan Linear scripts, *see* Linear A, Linear B
Minyan ware, 16, 175
Mitanni, land of, 51, 72, 194; king/ruler of, 54, 72–4, 178, 193; language, Hurrian, 45, 51, 54, 55, 72, 73, 178, 194, 293; Indo-European elements in, 178, 294
Mohenjodaro, 183, 187–90
Mongols (in China), 143
mounted warrior, *see* horse riding
Müller, Max, 75
Mycenae, 57, 59
Mycenaean civilization, 26, 33, 57, 175, 195, 198; collapse of, 135, 176
Myres, Sir John, 6, 177

Nahuatl language, 136

Namazga, 201, 207
Nandris, John, 153
Nash, Daphne, 255
Natufian culture, 173; language, 174
Neanderthal man, *see Homo sapiens neanderthalensis*
Nea Nikomedeia, 147, 153
Nesa, Hittite city, 56
nesili/nasili, Hittite word for own language (cuneiform Hittite), 55
Nestor, palace of at Pylos, *see* Pylos
Neustupný, Evžen, 92
New Archaeology, 6
New Zealand, 152, 271, 279
nomad pastoralist groups, *see* pastoralism/pastoralists
Nordics, Aryans as, 16, 38
'nuclear zone' for domestication of plants and animals, 208, 267
numerical taxonomy, 118
Norse sagas, 255, 256

Ochre graves, *see* Kurgan
object-verb (OV) languages, 111
Ogam alphabet, 227–8
Old Iranian language, *see* Persian, Old
Old Persian language,*see* Persian, Old
Olympia, excavations at, 24
oral tradition, 21
Oscan language, 67
Ossetian language, 204

Page, R. I., 256
Palaic language, 51
Panini, 178
Parpola, A., 185
pastoralism/pastoralists (nomads), 15, 18, 23, 66, 84, 96–8, 137, 138, 142, 182, 194, 197–209, 260, 262, 266, 271; Indo-Europeans as pastoralists, 83, 84; Proto-Indo-Europeans as pastoralists, 15, 18, 79, 83, 84, 95, 197–209; *see also* chariot, horse, wheeled vehicles

Pausanias, 57

P-Celtic, *see* Brithonic dialects

peer-polity interaction, 90, 236, 245, 247

Pelliot, Paul, 65

Persepolis, palace of, 43

Persian, cuneiform, 44, 45, 47; empire, 43, 47, 218, 219; language, Old/Middle Persian, 10, 44–7, 73, 191, 192, 209; modern Persian, 46, 47

Persians, 204

Petrie, Sir Flinders, 14, 48, 49

Phoenician alphabet/language, 45, 51, 70, 237

Phrygian language, 71

physical anthropology, 275

Pictet, Adolphe, 14, 18

Pictish language/Picts, 161, 226–8, 238

Piggott, Stuart, 41, 81, 155, 234, 243

Pithecanthropus erectus, see Homo erectus

place names, 20, 112, 165, 176; *see also* river names

polity (political organization), 215

Polynesia, 2, 121, 122, 255, 277, 278–81

Posidonius, 219, 221, 224, 225

pottery, as indicator of a people, *see* artefacts

Powell, T. G. E., 220

pre-Indo-European languages, *see* place names, river names

processual approach/archaeology/ models, 5, 120, 141, 213, 238, 248, 264, 270, 286, 288

pronunciation, changes in, *see* sound-shift

Proto-Aryan culture, 37

Proto-Cucuteni culture, 159

Proto-Elamite language, 185, 191

Proto-Indo-European language, 14, 15, 18, 35, 77, 106, 108, 110, 111, 161; object-verb (OV) language, 111; tree names, 18, 81–3, 162;

vocabulary, 14, 17, 18, 75, 83, 269

Proto-Indo-Europeans, 7, 17, 19, 36, 39, 79, 83, 86, 94, 95, 107, 109, 261; homeland, 14, 18, 27, 75, 79, 81, 97, 266; *see also* pastoralism/pastoralists

protolexicon, 14, 77, 78, 79, 81, 85, 86, 103, 109, 110, 154, 165

Proto-Slavonic language, 110

Proto-Tripolye culture, 159

Proto-Tocharians (Guti), 208

Pulgram, Ernst, 85

Punjab, Aryan invasion of, 187, 188

Pylos, palace ('of Nestor'), 59, 60, 61; archive, 59

Pytheas, 219

Q-Celtic, *see* Goidelic dialects; *see also* Gaelic languages

Quirinus, 252

race, racial types (of physical anthropologists), 4, 76, 77, 88, 215; groups, 4; superiority, 4, 94; racialist thought, 16

ranked (stratified) social organization, 132, 252, 253, 255, 256, 262, 271, 273

Rawlinson, Henry, 44–6, 49

Ray, John, 295, 297

refugee phenomenon, 141

Renfrew, Jane, 146

river names, 20, 162, 246, 249; *see also* place names

Rigveda, 11, 42, 46, 47, 73, 178–82, 185–9, 191, 193–6, 252, 256; *see also* Sanskrit, Vedic

Rodden, Robert, 153

Romance languages, 67, 163, 212

Romans, alphabet, use of, 70; and Greeks, first literate European communities, 24; empire, 26, 136, 216, 226, 250, 252, 254; religion, 250, 252

Ross, Anne, 224

Saka, *see* Sythians
Sangmeister, Edward, 88
Sanskrit language, classical, 9–11, 65, 178, 179; common source of Indian languages, 47; Vedic, 11, 21, 47, 73, 122, 178, 179, 182, 190, 192, 209, 228, 250, 255, 260
Sarab, 192
Sardinian language, 67
Sargon of Agade, 143
Sarianidi, V. I., 192, 203
'satem'/'centum' distinction, 66, 107, 108
'satem' language group, 50, 66, 107, 207; *see also* 'satem'/'centum' distinction
Sayce, A. H., 35, 48, 49, 51
Schleicher, Augustus, 101
Schliemann, Heinrich, 57, 58
Schmidt, Karl Horst, 238, 239, 243, 244
Schmidt, Johannes, 105, 106, 245
Schmidt, Wilhelm, 35
Schrader, Otto, 15, 17, 18, 36, 37, 41, 83, 106, 238
Schwantes, Gustav, 36
Scots Gaelic, 226, 249; *see also* Gaelic languages
Scythians, 15, 20, 28, 163, 194, 199, 204, 219, 257
seafaring/ships, 137, 279
secondary products revolution, 96, 163
sedentary/mobile boundary shift, 142, 144
semantic drift, 102
semiotics, 286
Semitic languages, 13, 43, 45, 143, 144, 257, 269, 271
Shaffer, J. G., 209
shell middens, Brittany, 151; Portugal, 151
Shennan, Stephen, 88, 89, 93
Sherratt, Andrew, 96, 153
Silk Road, 64
Sitagroi, 176

Slavonic languages, 11, 69, 160, 164, 202, 207
social organization, effect on language, 132, 251
sociolinguistics, 99, 112, 117, 264, 286
sound change, *see* sound shift
sound shift, 11, 99, 100, 102, 110, 115
south Russian steppes, 15–7, 37, 38, 94–7, 199, 200, 201, 202, 205, 208
Srednij Stog II culture, 95
Starčevo culture, 155, 159
state society, 132, 133, 136, 252, 255, 257
Stein, Aurel, 64–6
steppe neolithic, 202
steppe pastoralists, *see* pastoralism/pastoralists
stirrup, 139, 163, 200, 204
stock breeding, 203
Stonehenge, 89, 255
Strabo, 27, 65, 219, 223
stratified social organization, *see* ranked social organization
structural linguistics, 119, 256, 258
Sulimirski, Tadeusz, 39
Sumerian language, 43, 51, 143, 173, 293
Suppiluliumas, Hittite ruler, 49
Swadesh, Morris, 114, 117, 167, 168
Swiss Romansch language, 67
syllabic scripts, 60
symbolic aspects of culture, 274
system collapse, 133, 135, 136, 176, 189, 232, 249

Taklamakan desert, 63
Tarim depression, 64, 65
Tartessian languages, 232
Tell Ramad, 173
Tepe Guran, 192
Tepe Yayha, 185, 191
Teutones, 219
Thracian, language, 69, 71, 160, 176; people, 28, 176, 232, 234
Thraco-Phrygian languages, 71

Three Age system, 22
Thucydides, 175
Thutmosis III, 48
Tierney, J. J., 218
Tilley, Christopher, 92, 93
Timber-Grave culture, 203
Tocharian languages (Tocharian
   A/Turfanian; Tocharian
   B/Kouchean), 63, 65–7, 107, 178,
   193, 204, 271
'Tocharoi', tribe, 65, 194
Togolok Tepe, 173
Tonga, 216, 278
Tovar, Antonio, 230, 238, 246, 248
tree names, see Indo-European, Proto-
   Indo-European
Treveri, 233
Trichterbecher (TRB) culture, 92, 156,
   159
Tringham, Ruth, 150
Tripolye culture, 97, 98, 156, 201, 202
Troy, 38, 57
Trubetskoy, N. S., 35, 42, 108, 109,
   118, 145, 283
Tumulus culture, 239–40
Tun-huang, 64, 66
Turfan oasis, 65, 66, 204
Turfanian language, see Tocharian A
Turkish language, 204
Turkmenia, 201, 203, 205, 207, 210

Ukraine, see south Russian steppes
Umbrian language, 67, 254
Ur, 201
Ural-Altaic languages, 204
Uralic languages, 70
Urartu, civilization, 72; language, 72
Urheimat, 14, 18, 35, 77; see also Proto-
   Indo-Europeans
Urnfield culture/complex/groups, 34,
   39, 94, 146, 174, 213, 235, 239, 240
Ursprache, 14, 77, 86
Urvolk, 77, 84, 86, 266

Ussher, Archbishop, 13

Vansina, J., 283
Vedic Sanskrit, see Sanskrit, Vedic
Vendryes, Joseph, 250, 255
Venetic language, 67
Ventris, Michael, 60, 61, 176
verb-object (VO) languages, 111
Vertesszöllös, 29
von le Coq, A., 65
von Schlegel, Friedrich, 12
Vučedol culture, 39

wagon, see wheeled vehicles
wave hypothesis (of language change),
   105, 145, 195, 209, 245, 247
wave model, see wave hypothesis
wave of advance model, 126, 128, 129,
   131, 137, 150, 152, 154, 158, 173,
   190, 193, 202, 207, 208, 209, 265,
   267, 271
Welsh language, 212, 228, 229
Wessex culture, 243
Whatmough, Joshua, 230
wheeled vehicles, 38, 86, 138, 198,
   201; see also chariot
Wheeler, Sir Mortimer, 187, 188, 190
White, Lynn, 139
Whittle, Alasdair, 90, 267
Winckler, Hugo, 49
Woodman, P. C., 298
writing, 1, 2, 20, 21, 285; see also
   alphabet

Xerxes, 43

Yamno (Pit Grave) culture, 202
Yangshao culture, 201
Yoshida, Atsuhito, 257
Young, Thomas, 11
Yü-chi, 66

Zoroastrian religion, 44

FOR THE BEST IN PAPERBACKS, LOOK FOR THE 🐧

In every corner of the world, on every subject under the sun, Penguin represents quality and variety – the very best in publishing today.

For complete information about books available from Penguin – including Pelicans, Puffins, Peregrines and Penguin Classics – and how to order them, write to us at the appropriate address below. Please note that for copyright reasons the selection of books varies from country to country.

In the United Kingdom: Please write to *Dept E.P., Penguin Books Ltd, Harmondsworth, Middlesex, UB7 0DA*

If you have any difficulty in obtaining a title, please send your order with the correct money, plus ten per cent for postage and packaging, to *PO Box No 11, West Drayton, Middlesex*

In the United States: Please write to *Dept BA, Penguin, 299 Murray Hill Parkway, East Rutherford, New Jersey 07073*

In Canada: Please write to *Penguin Books Canada Ltd, 2801 John Street, Markham, Ontario L3R 1B4*

In Australia: Please write to the *Marketing Department, Penguin Books Australia Ltd, P.O. Box 257, Ringwood, Victoria 3134*

In New Zealand: Please write to the *Marketing Department, Penguin Books (NZ) Ltd, Private Bag, Takapuna, Auckland 9*

In India: Please write to *Penguin Overseas Ltd, 706 Eros Apartments, 56 Nehru Place, New Delhi, 110019*

In Holland: Please write to *Penguin Books Nederland B.V., Postbus 195, NL–1380AD Weesp, Netherlands*

In Germany: Please write to *Penguin Books Ltd, Friedrichstrasse 10–12, D–6000 Frankfurt Main 1, Federal Republic of Germany*

In Spain: Please write to *Longman Penguin España, Calle San Nicolas 15, E–28013 Madrid, Spain*

In France: Please write to *Penguin Books Ltd, 39 Rue de Montmorency, F–75003, Paris, France*

In Japan: Please write to *Longman Penguin Japan Co Ltd, Yamaguchi Building, 2–12–9 Kanda Jimbocho, Chiyoda-Ku, Tokyo 101, Japan*

BY THE SAME AUTHOR

Before Civilization

'I have little doubt that this is one of the most important archaeological books for a very long time. The clarity of the style and the evident enthusiasm in every paragraph makes it a joy to read' – Barry Cunliffe in the *New Scientist*

The refinement of radiocarbon dating using the information from tree-ring counts has raised serious doubts about the accepted theoretical framework of European prehistory. Monuments in Central and Western Europe have proved to be considerably older than their supposed Near-Eastern forerunners, and the record must be almost completely rewritten in the light of these new dates.

Before Civilization is a preliminary attempt to do this with the help of analogies from more recent and well-documented primitive societies. The more glaring inconsistencies in the old theory are re-examined and Professor Renfrew shows convincingly how the baffling monuments of prehistoric Europe, like Stonehenge and the megalithic temples of ancient Malta, could have been built without recourse to help from the more civilized Near East.

'Here is pure stimulation from beginning to end ... this is a book which provokes thought, aids understanding, and above all is immensely enjoyable' – Anna Ritchie in the *Scotsman*

FOR THE BEST IN PAPERBACKS, LOOK FOR THE 🐧

A CHOICE OF PENGUINS AND PELICANS

The Second World War (6 volumes)   Winston S. Churchill

The definitive history of the cataclysm which swept the world for the second time in thirty years.

1917: The Russian Revolutions and the Origins of Present-Day Communism
Leonard Schapiro

A superb narrative history of one of the greatest episodes in modern history by one of our greatest historians.

Imperial Spain 1496–1716   J. H. Elliot

A brilliant modern study of the sudden rise of a barren and isolated country to be the greatest power on earth, and of its equally sudden decline. 'Outstandingly good' – *Daily Telegraph*

Joan of Arc: The Image of Female Heroism   Marina Warner

'A profound book, about human history in general and the place of women in it' – Christopher Hill

Man and the Natural World: Changing Attitudes in England 1500–1800
Keith Thomas

'A delight to read and a pleasure to own' – Auberon Waugh in the *Sunday Telegraph*

The Making of the English Working Class   E. P. Thompson

Probably the most imaginative – and the most famous – post-war work of English social history.

The Apartheid Handbook   Roger Omond

This book provides the essential hard information about how apartheid actually works from day to day and fills in the details behind the headlines.

The World Turned Upside Down   Christopher Hill

This classic study of radical ideas during the English Revolution 'will stand as a notable monument to . . . one of the finest historians of the present age' – *The Times Literary Supplement*

Islam in the World   Malise Ruthven

'His exposition of "the Qurenic world view" is the most convincing, and the most appealing, that I have read' – Edward Mortimer in *The Times*

The Knight, the Lady and the Priest   Georges Duby

'A very fine book' (Philippe Aries) that traces back to its medieval origin one of our most important institutions, marriage.

A Social History of England   New Edition   Asa Briggs

'A treasure house of scholarly knowledge . . . beautifully written and full of the author's love of his country, its people and its landscape' – John Keegan in the *Sunday Times*, Books of the Year

The Second World War   A J P Taylor

A brilliant and detailed illustrated history, enlivened by all Professor Taylor's customary iconoclasm and wit.

The Informed Heart   Bruno Bettelheim

Bettelheim draws on his experience in concentration camps to illuminate the dangers inherent in all mass societies in this profound and moving masterpiece.

God and the New Physics   Paul Davies

Can science, now come of age, offer a surer path to God than religion? This 'very interesting' (*New Scientist*) book suggests it can.

Modernism   Malcolm Bradbury and James McFarlane (eds.)

A brilliant collection of essays dealing with all aspects of literature and culture for the period 1890–1930 – from Apollinaire and Brecht to Yeats and Zola.

Rise to Globalism   Stephen E. Ambrose

A clear, up-to-date and well-researched history of American foreign policy since 1938, Volume 8 of the Pelican History of the United States.

The Waning of the Middle Ages   Johan Huizinga

A magnificent study of life, thought and art in 14th and 15th century France and the Netherlands, long established as a classic.

The Penguin Dictionary of Psychology   Arthur S. Reber

Over 17,000 terms from psychology, psychiatry and related fields are given clear, concise and modern definitions.

FOR THE BEST IN PAPERBACKS, LOOK FOR THE 🐧

PENGUIN DICTIONARIES

Archaeology

Architecture

Art and Artists

Biology

Botany

Building

Business

Commerce

Computers

Curious and Interesting
  Words

Curious and Interesting
  Numbers

Decorative Arts

Design and Designers

Economics

English and European
  History

English Idioms

Fairies

French

Geography

Geology

Historical Slang

Italian

Literary Terms

Microprocessors

Modern History 1789–1945

Modern Quotations

Physical Geography

Physics

Political Quotations

Proverbs

Psychology

Quotations

Religions

Rhyming Dictionary

Saints

Sociology

Telecommunications

The Theatre

Troublesome Words

Twentieth Century History